TENTH EDITION

Doll Values

ANTIQUE TO MODERN

Linda Edward

cb
COLLECTOR BOOKS
A Division of Schroeder Publishing Co., Inc.

On the front cover, Left 1st, 20" Bald head china, 1850s style. $2,800.00. Photo courtesy of Richard Withington, Inc. Left 2nd: 11" Littlest Angel, mint with hang tag. $225.00. Photo courtesy of McMasters Harris Auction Co. Left 3rd: 19" Bru Jne. $37,000.00. Photo courtesy of Richard Withington, Inc. Right: 16" Käthe Kruse model I doll with wide hips. $6,500.00. Photo courtesy of McMasters Harris Auction Co.

Back cover: 17" Poor Pitiful Pearl. $275.00. Photo courtesy of The Museum Doll Shop.

Cover design by Beth Summers
Book design by Lisa Henderson

COLLECTOR BOOKS
P.O. Box 3009
Paducah, Kentucky 42002-3009

www.collectorbooks.com

Copyright © 2009 Linda Edward

The current values in this book should be used only as a guide. They are not intended to set prices, which vary from one section of the country to another. Auction prices as well as dealer prices vary greatly and are affected by condition as well as demand. Neither the author nor the publisher assumes responsibility for any losses that might be incurred as a result of consulting this guide.

Searching for a Publisher?
We are always looking for people knowledgeable within their fields. If you feel that there is a real need for a book on your collectible subject and have a large comprehensive collection, contact Collector Books.

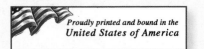

Proudly printed and bound in the
United States of America

ACKNOWLEDGMENTS

Thank you to the following collectors for sharing their dolls and those of their friends for this issue of *Doll Values*. Alderfer Auctions, Virginia Aris, Carole Barboza, Steve Carissimo, Ruth Cayton, LucyDiTerlizzi, Valerie Gomes, Talona Griffin, Jean Grout, Elaine Holda, Virginia Hyerdahl, William J. Janack Estate Appraisals & Auctioneers, Sidney W Jeffrey, Doris Lechler, McMasters-Harris Auctions, Ursula Mertz, Morris Museum, Glenda O'Connor, George & Cynthia Orgeron, Dominique Perrin, Louise Scala, Skinner Inc., Patricia Snyder, Nancy Stronczek, Turn of the Century Antiques, Patricia Vaillancourt, Suzanne Vlach, Helen Welsh, and Richard Withington Inc.

I would also like to thank every doll researcher and collector who has generously shared their dolls and knowledge through the many fine reference books, articles, seminars, special exhibits, and doll club programs. Without this constant exchange of information we would all be searching in the dark for answers.

Finally, I must like to thank my husband, Al Edward, for his encouragement, support, and belief in me and the work I pursue.

HOW TO USE THIS BOOK

This book is a tool for the collector, a place to start on a journey of study that can enrich a lifetime. The best piece of advice this collector ever received was "buy every doll reference book you can find." Each volume, be it old or new, contains some piece of information that will be of aid to the collector. Building a reference library of your own will pay you back many times over in the knowledge it will bring you, knowledge which will ultimately allow you to make better decisions when purchasing a doll for your own collection. In addition to building a reference library, I would also suggest that you take every opportunity to look at dolls wherever you go. Nothing beats first hand examination. Visit every doll museum and special display you can find, go to shows and really look at the dolls that interest you most. Join a doll club to learn more and share your discoveries with others. All of these experiences will put you in a better position to understand and evaluate a doll when you are considering a purchase.

The question of course is, how much is a doll worth? It is the question we contend with when buying our dolls, inheriting our dolls, insuring our dolls, and in deciding to sell our dolls. In the doll world there are basically two types of value: historic value and monetary value. Historic value speaks to how important an item is to us and to the world in general. Does an item teach us something about the past, is it significant to some particular event or person, does an item have special sentimental value to us personally? This type of value, although important, is not always reflected in an item's monetary value. Monetary value or market value relates to how much it would cost to go out and purchase any particular item at the present time. Market value is collector driven. Demand for particular items, combined with the current economic climate determine the market value of a doll. In other words, a perfectly wonderful example of any given doll will vary in market value during differing economic conditions. This makes certain times good "selling times" and other times good "buying times." This book can be a guide to helping the collector make wise decisions in regard to their collecting actions.

When evaluating any doll there are several questions to ask oneself. These relate to identification, quality, originality, condition, rarity and value. Each component is important to the overall picture of any doll. All dolls should be thoroughly examined before making a purchase.

Identification, what is this doll? A doll is classified by the material from which its head is made, therefore a doll with a composition head on a cloth body will be considered a composition doll or a doll with a papier-mâché head on a leather body will be considered a papier-mâché doll and so on. Look for and learn about maker's marks. These will be of invaluable aid in identifying the doll you are looking at. Many manufacturers marked their dolls on the back of the head or on the torso. An appendix of maker's initials and an appendix of known mold numbers are included in the back of this book to assist you.

Quality, as stated by Patsy Moyer in the first edition of this book "all dolls are not created equal." Any model of doll made by any particular manufacturer can range vastly in quality depending on the conditions on the day it was made. Remember these dolls were produced in factories which in many cases turned out thousands of dolls a year. How worn was mold when this doll was poured, what weather conditions affected the materials it was made from, how tired was the worker who cleaned or painted a particular doll that day? If you line up six AM 390s you will be looking at 6 different degrees of quality of finish. Therefore when preparing to make a purchase consider each example of doll carefully from a standpoint of quality. A sharply molded, evenly textured, well painted doll will always be of more value than an example of the same doll with blurry molding, uneven texture, or poor quality painting.

Originality is another important component of a doll evaluation. Does the doll have the correct eyes, wig, body type, clothing? Each of these parts adds value to the doll and dolls on incorrect bodies or with replaced clothing or wigs should not bring the same amount in the marketplace as examples in all original condition.

Condition, what is the overall condition of the doll? Check carefully to look for damage or repair to the doll. In most cases a damaged or repaired doll will not be worth as much as a perfect example.

Rarity, is perhaps one of the most important aspects of doll evaluation. How unusual is this doll? How many were made and survive? How difficult would it be to find another example of this doll today? Sometimes rarity can cause us to forgive problems of originality or condition that would in a more common doll deter us from adding a particular example to our collection.

Value takes into account all of the aforementioned qualifications we have discussed and combines them with somewhat more elusive components such as collector demand and trends. At various points in time collectors tend to favor certain dolls. A good example of this can be seen in the value of the Bye-lo baby. Every generation of collectors tends to start out collecting the dolls they had or wanted as children. In the 1950s and 1960s many adult collectors eagerly sought the Bye–lo baby from the 1920s and the dolls achieved comparatively high market price. In the past 20 years the value of the Bye-lo has changed very little compared to other antique dolls because collector demand for them has quieted down.

After evaluating each of the aforementioned aspects of any doll, this book will assist you in figuring out the current market value of the doll. Unless otherwise noted the values stated in this volume represent dolls in good overall condition with original or appropriate clothing. When looking at the values presented here gage the particular doll you are considering accordingly. Allow a lower value for dolls which do not meet the standard for the values listed here. This is especially important in judging vintage collectible or modern dolls. These must be in perfect and completely original condition with appropriate hang tags to attain the values listed in this guide. For example, an all original #3 Barbie in good condition will bring approximately ½ the price of the same doll mint-in-box.

This book is laid out in alphabetical order. You will notice that it is not divided into "antique" and "modern" sections as some other books are. The reason for this choice is threefold; firstly, the line between antique and modern is not as clear cut in doll collecting as it is in other areas. In furniture, for instance, a piece must be at least 100 years old to be considered antique, whereas in car collecting a vehicle that is 25 years old is considered antique. In doll collecting the line is blurry although it generally falls somewhere in the neighborhood of 75 years. Dolls 30 to 75 years old are most often referred to as "collectible vintage" and dolls 30 years old or less are usually referred to as modern. Secondly, many doll making companies were in business for such long periods of time that they produced dolls which would now be considered antique as well as dolls that fall into the collectible vintage and modern categories. Thirdly, it is the belief of this author that by not creating barriers between dolls of different ages we see a more complete picture of the doll world and promote a better understanding of the history of the dolls we love and of our fellow collectors.

As stated previously this book is laid out in an alphabetical order by the manufacturer's name or by general type. Most dolls are marked in some way which indicates their maker. Wherever possible those markings have been included for reference. The general type headings include dolls made of like materials. Under these headings you will find dolls made by small companies, or about which little is known as well as unmarked, and as yet unattributable dolls.

The values listed in this book are compiled from several sources including auction prices, online auction prices, dealer asking prices, dealer prices realized, as well as other sources. These values are then compiled, analyzed and averaged. Although the collecting world is now much more global than it was even just a few years ago, there are still some regional differences in value which are generated by collector interest and doll availability in certain areas. This book is meant as a guide and is not the "definitive" word on doll value. Ultimately a doll is worth whatever a particular collector wishes to pay for it. Neither this author nor the publisher of this book take any responsibility for any decision or action taken by an individual on the basis of the information presented here. As stated earlier, this book is one more tool for the collector to use in their decision making process.

Finally I will say that study, evaluation, and value, although important, are not the bottom line in doll collecting. Ultimately we each need to "follow our bliss" as it were, and buy dolls that mean something to us and enrich our lives and collections.

Collectors seeking to learn more about dolls and exchange doll knowledge can turn to a national organization whose goals are education, research, preservation, and enjoyment of dolls. The United Federation of Doll Clubs can tell you if a doll club in your area is accepting members or tell you how to become a member-at-large. You may write for more information at:

United Federation of Doll Clubs, Inc.
10900 North Pomona Avenue
Kansas City, MO 64153
Phone: 816-891-7040
Fax: 816-891-8360
www.ufdc.org

CODES

RED (ALL CAPS)	MAIN CATEGORY
	EX: ADVERTISING DOLLS
Red (Roman)	First subcategory, usually a name of the doll, company, or material ex: **Gerber Baby**
Green (Italic)	Second subcategory ex: *1979 – 1985*
Black (Roman)	Third subcategory ex: **Talker**
Black (Indented-Italic)	Fourth subcategory

* at auction

ADVERTISING DOLLS

Dolls of various materials, made by a variety of manufacturers, to promote commercial brands or specific products. Doll in good condition with original clothing and accessories.

15" Aunt Jemima and Uncle Mose manufactured by Arnold Print Works for the Davis Milling Co. Pair shows some wear. $175.00. **Photo courtesy of Joan & Lynette Antique Dolls and Accessories.**

Aunt Jemima, cloth, Aunt Jemima, Uncle Moses, Diana, and Wade Davis
    16".................... $85.00 – 95.00
Button Nose, 1947, for Dan Rivers sheets, cloth mask face
    23".................... $30.00 – 35.00
Buster Brown Shoes
Composition head, cloth body, tag reads "Buster Brown Shoes"
    15".............. $250.00 – 300.00*
Colgate Fab Soap Princess Doll, ca. 1951
    5½".................... $12.00 – 18.00
Cream of Wheat, Rastus, printed cloth doll

    16".................. $90.00 – 100.00
Gerber Baby, 1936 to present. An advertising and trademark doll for Gerber Products, a baby food manufacturer located in Fremont, Michigan. More for black or special sets with accessories.
1936, cloth one-piece doll, printed girl or boy, holds can
    8".................... $450.00 – 500.00
1955 – 1958, Sun Rubber Company, designed by Bernard Lipfert, vinyl
    12" – 18"........ $100.00 – 125.00
1965, Arrow Rubber & Plastic Co., vinyl
    14".................. $125.00 – 150.00
1972 – 1973, Amsco, Milton Bradley, vinyl
    10".................... $75.00 – 90.00
    14" – 18"............ $55.00 – 65.00
1979 – 1985, Atlanta Novelty, vinyl, flirty eyes, cloth body
    17".................... $60.00 – 75.00
Talker
    17".................. $80.00 – 100.00
Collector Doll, christening gown, basket
    12".................... $75.00 – 90.00
Porcelain, limited edition
    17".................. $275.00 – 325.00
1989 – 1992, Lucky Ltd., vinyl
    6"........................ $12.00 – 18.00
    11".................... $35.00 – 40.00

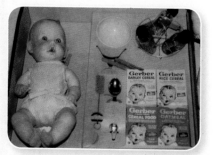

12" Gerber Baby made by Sun Rubber, c. 1955. MIB $200.00. **Photo courtesy of The Museum Doll Shop.**

14 – 16" .... $35.00 – 40.00
1994 –1996, Toy Biz, Inc., vinyl
    8" .... $12.00 – 15.00
    15" .... $20.00 – 25.00
Battery operated
    12 - 13" .... $20.00 – 25.00
Talker
    14" .... $35.00 – 40.00
    17" .... $45.00 – 50.00
Green Giant, Sprout, 1973
    10½" .... $18.00 – 25.00
Jolly Joan, Portland, Oregon, restaurant
    11" .... $100.00 – 125.00
Kellogg's cereals
Corn Flakes Red Riding Hood, printed cloth
    13½" .... $125.00 – 150.00
Goldilocks & Three Bears, set of four, printed cloth
    12" – 15" .... $240.00 – 265.00
Korn Krisp cereal
Miss Korn-Krisp, ca. 1900, cloth marked body
    24" .... $200.00 – 225.00
Little Debbie, 1972, made by Horsman, all vinyl with rooted hair
    11" .... $30.00 – 35.00
Mr. Peanut, 1940s, segmented wooden
    9" .... $125.00 – 150.00
Pepsodent toothpaste
Miss Pepsodent, vinyl doll on five-piece body,

16" vinyl Miss Pepsodent. $895.00 **Photo courtesy of Ziggy Zygarlowski.**

6" vinyl advertising doll for Prince Macaroni Co., 1960s. $20.00. **Photo courtesy of The Museum Doll Shop.**

rooted ponytail hair, doll's teeth are white when she is standing up and turn yellow when she is lying down
    16" .... $700.00 – 895.00
Prince Macaroni, mail-in premium dolls, vinyl, dressed in costumes from the provinces of Italy
    6¼" .... $15.00 – 20.00
Sunbeam Bread
Miss Sunbeam, by Horsman, all vinyl, rooted hair
    14" .... $25.00 – 30.00
"The Selling Fool," 1926, made by Cameo, wood segmented body, hat represents radio tube, composition advertising doll for RCA Radiotrons
    16" .... $1,000.00 – 1,200.00
Too few in database for a reliable range.
Uneeda Biscuit Boy, 1914, made by Ideal
    15" .... $400.00 – 450.00
The Yellow Kid, comic character drawn by R. F. Outcault, featured in *New York World* and later the *New York Journal,* composition doll with cloth torso
    13" .... $1,800.00 – 2,000.00
Too few in database for a reliable range.
ZuZu, 1916, composition doll made by Ideal to advertise ginger snaps made by the National Biscuit Co.
    14" .... $250.00 – 300.00

ALABAMA BABY

30" Alabama Baby. $4,750.00. **Photo courtesy of Joan & Lynette Antique Dolls and Accessories.**

1900 – 1925, Roanoke, Alabama. Ella Gauntt Smith, cloth over plaster doll, stitched on skull cap, painted features. Tab jointed at shoulders and hips, painted feet may be bare with stitched toes or have shoes painted in pink, blue, black, brown, or yellow.

Earlier model with applied ears

    11" – 14".. $1,600.00 – 1,900.00
    18" – 24".. $3,200.00 – 3,600.00

Wigged

    24"........... $2,900.00 – 3,500.00

Black

    14" – 18".. $5,500.00 – 6,000.00
    20" – 22".. $6,200.00 – 6,800.00

Later model with molded ears, bobbed hairstyle

    14" – 16".. $1,300.00 – 1,500.00
    18" – 22".. $1,700.00 – 2,000.00

Wigged

    30" $1,000.00

Black

    14" – 18".. $2,800.00 – 3,000.00
    20" – 22".. $3,800.00 – 5,800.00

MADAME ALEXANDER

1912 – present, New York City. In 1912 in New York City, Beatrice and Rose Alexander, known for making doll costumes, began the Alexander Doll Co. They began using the "Madame Alexander" trademark in 1928. Beatrice Alexander Behrman became a legend in the doll world with her long reign as head of the Alexander Doll Company. Alexander made cloth, composition, and wooden dolls, and eventually made the transition to hard plastic and vinyl. Dolls are listed by subcategories of the material of which the head is made. With Madame Alexander dolls, especially those made from 1950 on, condition as it relates to value is extremely important. **For the values listed here the doll must be in perfect condition with complete original clothing and tags. Dolls with incomplete or soiled costumes will bring one fourth to one third of the value of perfect examples.** Unusual dolls with presentation cases, trousseaux, or rare costumes may bring much more.

16" David Copperfield. $700.00. **Photo courtesy of Richard Withington, Inc.**

Cloth, 1930 – 1950 on

All-cloth head and body, mohair wig, flat or molded mask face, painted side-glancing eyes

Storybook characters such as Little Women, Dickens characters, Edith, and others

    16"................. $650.00 – 800.00

Alice in Wonderland

    Flat face .... $800.00 – 900.00

    Mask face,

    14" – 16" ....$700.00 – 800.00

Animals, such as March Hare, etc.

    15" – 16" .... $300.00 – 600.00

Baby

    13"................. $300.00 – 325.00

    17"................. $450.00 – 500.00

    24"................. $525.00 – 575.00

Funny, 1963 – 1977

    18"...................... $65.00 – 70.00

Little Shaver, 1940 – 1944, yarn hair

    7".................... $450.00 – 525.00

    10"................. $450.00 – 500.00

    15"................. $575.00 – 675.00

    22"................. $700.00 – 800.00

Muffin, ca. 1963 – 1977

    14"...................... $65.00 – 75.00

So Lite Baby or Toddler, 1930s – 1940s

    20"................. $375.00 – 425.00

Suzie Q, 1940 – 1942

    $600.00 – 700.00

Teeny Twinkle, 1946, disc floating eyes

    $475.00 – 550.00

Dionne Quintuplets, various materials

Cloth, 1935 – 1936

    16"................. $850.00 – 950.00

    24".......... $1,600.00 – 1,800.00

Composition, 1935 – 1945, all-composition, swivel head, jointed toddler or baby body, molded and painted hair or wigged, sleep or painted eyes. Outfit colors: Annette, yellow; Cecile, green; Emilie, lavender; Marie, blue; Yvonne, pink. Add more for extra accessories or in layette.

Baby

    8".................... $250.00 – 300.00

    Complete set.. $1,400.00 – 1,600.00

Set of five with wooden nursery furniture

    8"............. $2,000.00 – 2,250.00

Toddler

    8".................... $250.00 – 300.00

    Complete set .. $1,400.00 – 1,600.00

    11"................. $350.00 – 400.00

    Complete set .. $2,000.00 – 2,200.00

    14"................. $425.00 – 475.00

    Complete set .. $2,700.00 – 3,000.00

    20"................. $675.00 – 725.00

8" Dionne Quintuplets. $1,500.00 set.
Photo courtesy of Richard Withington, Inc.

Complete set.. $3,900.00 – 4,200.00
On cloth body
22".................. $650.00 – 750.00
 Complete set.. $3,400.00 – 3,700.00
Vinyl, 8", in carousel, 1998 75th
 anniversary set.. $375.00 – 425.00
Dr. Dafoe, 1937 – 1939
14".......... $1,200.00 – 1,400.00
Nurse
13" – 15"........ $900.00 – 975.00
Composition, 1930 – 1950
Babies, cloth body, sleep eyes, marked
"Alexander," dolls such as Baby Genius,
Butch, Baby McGuffy, Pinky, and others
10" – 12"........ $175.00 – 300.00
14" – 16"........ $175.00 – 275.00
22" – 24"........ $300.00 – 475.00
Baby Jane, 1935
16".............. $900.00 – 1,100.00
Child
Alice in Wonderland, 1930s, swivel waist
7" – 9"............ $375.00 – 425.00
11" – 14" .... $425.00 – 600.00
18" – 21"........ $700.00 – 950.00
Babs Skater, 1948, marked "ALEX" on head,
clover tag
18"........... $1,200.00 – 1,350.00
Carmen (Miranda), 1942, black hair
9" – 11".......... $300.00 – 375.00
14" – 17"........ $450.00 – 650.00
21"........... $1,400.00 – 1,800.00
Fairy Queen, ca. 1939 – 1946, clover wrist
tag, tagged gown
15 – 18" .... $600.00 – 700.00
21" – 22"........ $850.00 – 900.00
Flora McFlimsey, 1938, freckles, marked
"Princess Elizabeth"
14" – 17"........ $600.00 – 650.00
22"................. $800.00 – 900.00
Jane Withers, 1937 – 1939, green sleep
eyes, open mouth, brown mohair wig
12" – 13½".. $1,000.00 – 1,200.00

15" – 17"..... $900.00 – 1,300.00
18" – 19".. $1,450.00 – 1,550.00
20" – 22"... $1,700.00 – 1800.00
Jeannie Walker, tagged dress, closed mouth,
mohair wig
13" – 14"........ $675.00 – 750.00
14" MIB $2,200.00*
18".............. $800.00 – 1,000.00
Judy, original box, wrist tag, Wendy Ann
face, eye shadow
21"........... $3,200.00 – 3,400.00
Karen Ballerina, blue sleep eyes, closed
mouth, "Alexander" on head
15".............. $925.00 – 1,025.00
18"........... $1,200.00 – 1,300.00
Kate Greenaway, yellow wig, marked
"Princess Elizabeth"
13" – 15"........ $750.00 – 800.00
18"................ $850.00 – 900.00
24".............. $950.00 – 1,050.00
Little Betty, 1939 – 1943, side-glancing
painted eyes
9" – 11".......... $250.00 – 375.00
Little Colonel
Closed mouth
11" – 15"........ $625.00 – 850.00
Open mouth
14" – 17"........ $650.00 – 700.00
13" – 26"..... $950.00 – 1,300.00
Little Genius, blue sleep eyes, cloth body,
closed mouth, clover tag
12" – 14"........ $225.00 – 250.00
16" – 20"........ $250.00 – 275.00
Little Women, Meg, Jo, Amy, Beth
Set of four
7"......................... $375.00 each
9"......................... $350.00 each
13" – 15".$350.00 – 375.00 each
Madelaine DuBain, 1937 – 1944
14"................. $550.00 – 600.00
17"................. $625.00 – 650.00
Marcella, 1936, open mouth, wig, sleep eyes

21½" Margaret O'Brien. $1,495.00. Photo courtesy of Turn of the Century Antiques.

17" – 24" .... $650.00 – 900.00
Margaret O'Brien, 1946 – 1948
    14" – 17"..... $850.00 – 1,100.00
    19" – 24".. $1,300.00 – 1,600.00
McGuffey Ana, 1935 – 1937, sleep eyes, open mouth, tagged dress
    11" – 13"........ $650.00 – 750.00
    14" – 16"........ $650.00 – 875.00
    17" – 20"........ $700.00 – 900.00
    21" – 25"..... $750.00 – 1,600.00
    28"........... $1,000.00 – 1,400.00
    Painted eyes
    9" .... $375.00 – 475.00
Marionettes by Tony Sarg
    12"................. $450.00 – 550.00
Princess Elizabeth, 1937 – 1941
    Closed mouth
    13"................. $500.00 – 625.00
    Open mouth
    13" – 16"........ $500.00 – 600.00
    18" – 24"........ $650.00 – 800.00
    28"............. $950.00 – 1,000.00
Scarlett, 1937 – 1946, add more for rare costume
    11"................. $600.00 – 700.00
    14"............. $700.00 – 1,000.00
    18"........... $1,200.00 – 1,400.00

    21".......... $1,400.00 – 1,500.00
Snow White, 1939 – 1942, marked "Princess Elizabeth"
    13"................. $400.00 – 475.00
    16" – 18"........ $550.00 – 750.00
Sonja Henie, 1939 – 1942, open mouth, sleep eyes
    13", twist waist, MIB... $1,000.00*
    13" – 15"........ $650.00 – 700.00
    17" – 18"........ $875.00 – 950.00
    20" – 23".. $1,200.00 – 1,500.00
Tiny Betty, 1934 – 1943, side-glancing painted eyes
    7".................... $300.00 – 400.00
W.A.A.C. (Army), W.A.A.F. (Air Force), W.A.V.E. (Navy), ca. 1943 – 1944
    14"................. $725.00 – 775.00
Wendy Ann, 1935 – 1948, more for special outfit
    11" – 15"........ $400.00 – 600.00
    17" – 21"........ $700.00 – 950.00
    Painted eyes
    9" .... $350.00 – 375.00
    Swivel waist, molded hair or wig
    14" .... $450.00 – 500.00
Hard Plastic and Vinyl, 1948 on
Alexander-kins, 1953 on
1953, 7½" – 8", straight leg nonwalker
    Nude .... $350.00 – 375.00
    Dressed .... $400.00 – 650.00
1954 – 1955, straight leg walker
    Nude .... $250.00 – 300.00
    Dressed .... $375.00 – 500.00
1956 – 1965, bent-knee walker, after 1963 marked "Alex"
    Nude .... $150.00 – 200.00
    Dressed .... $425.00 – 72500.00
    1956
    FAO Schwarz trunk set .. $1,400.00
Too few in database for a reliable range.
1965 – 1972, bent-knee nonwalker, price depends on costume

Nude .... $75.00 – 95.00

Dressed .... $200.00 – 500.00

1973 – 1976, straight leg nonwalker, marked "Alex" on back of torso, price depends on costume

Dressed .... $75.00 – 250.00

1976 – 1994, straight leg nonwalker, marked "Alexander" on back of torso

Dressed .... $60.00 – 70.00

Babies

Baby Angel, #480, tagged tulle gown

8" $950.00

Too few in database for a reliable range.

Baby Brother or Sister, 1977 – 1982, vinyl

14" .... $65.00 – 80.00

Baby Clown, #464, seven-piece walker, leashed dog, Huggy

8" .... $900.00 – 1,100.00

Baby Ellen, 1965 – 1972, vinyl, rigid vinyl body, marked "Alexander 1965"

14" .... $100.00 – 125.00

Baby Precious, 1975, vinyl, cloth body

14" .... $100.00 – 125.00

Bonnie Toddler, 1954 – 1955, vinyl

19" .... $200.00 – 225.00

23" .... $250.00 – 275.00

Happy, 1970 only, vinyl

20" .... $175.00 – 200.00

Hello Baby, 1962 only

22" .... $150.00 – 175.00

Honeybun, 1951, vinyl

18" – 19" .... $200.00 – 225.00

Huggums

Big, 1963 – 1979

25" .... $85.00 – 100.00

Little, rooted hair, 1963 – 1988

12" .... $40.00 – 50.00

Little Bitsey, 1967 – 1968, all-vinyl

9" .... $130.00 – 150.00

Little Genius, 1956 – 1962, hard plastic, price depends on costume

8" .... $100.00 – 600.00

8" Little Genius. $500.00. **Photo courtesy of Masters Harris Auction Co.**

Littlest Kitten, vinyl

8" .... $150.00 – 200.00

Mary Cassatt, 1969 – 1970, vinyl

14" .... $150.00 – 175.00

20" .... $200.00 – 250.00

Pussy Cat, 1965 – 1985, vinyl

14" .... $45.00 – 55.00

Black, 1970 – 1976

14" .... $65.00 – 75.00

Rusty, 1967 – 1968 only, vinyl

20" .... $275.00 – 300.00

Sweet Tears, 1965 – 1974

9" .... $75.00 – 90.00

With layette

1965 – 1973... $150.00 – 175.00

Victoria, baby, 1967 – 1989

20" .... $60.00 – 70.00

Bible Character Dolls, 1954 only, hard plastic, original box made like Bible

8" .... $7,500.00+

Cissette, 1957 on 10", hard plastic head, synthetic wig, pierced ears, closed mouth, seven-piece adult body, jointed elbows and knees, high-heeled feet, mold later used for other dolls. Marks: None on body, clothes tagged "Cissette." doll's listed are in good condition with original clothing — value can be doubled for mint-in-box.

Basic doll

> *In undergarments*.. $175.00 – 225.00
> *In street dress*.... $300.00 – 450.00
> *In formal wear* .. $350.00 – 550.00

Gibson Girl

> 1962 – 1963... $800.00 – 900.00

Jacqueline

> 1961 – 1962... $700.00 – 800.00

Margot

> 1961 .... $525.00 – 625.00

Portrette

> 1968 – 1973... $375.00 – 450.00

Sleeping Beauty,1959, authorized Disney blue gown .... $325.00 – 375.00

Tinkerbelle, 1969 ..... $375.00 – 450.00

Cissy

1955 – 1959, 20", hard plastic, vinyl arms, jointed elbows and knees, high-heeled feet. Clothes are tagged "Cissy."

> *Basic doll in undergarments*
> $350.00 – 400.00
> *In street dress*.... $750.00 – 800.00
> *In formalwear*
> $1,000.00 – 2,500.00
> *With trunk and trousseau*
> $1,400.00+
> *Miss Flora McFlimsey,* 1953 only, Cissy, vinyl head, inset eyes
> 15"................. $725.00 – 800.00
> 15" MIB $1,500.00*

1996 on, 21", vinyl

> *Ebony & Ivory*
> 1996 .... $600.00 – 650.00
> *Legends Couture Collection*
> 1997 – 1998.. $350.00 – 600.00

Others

Alice in Wonderland, 1949 – 1952, hard plastic, Margaret and/or Maggie

> 14"................. $650.00 – 750.00
> 15", 18", 23" .. $450.00 – 1,000.00
> *1996,* vinyl
> 14"................... $85.00 – 100.00

20" Annabelle. $900.00. **Photo courtesy of McMasters Harris Auction Co.**

American Girl, 1962 – 1963, #388, seven-piece walker body, became McGuffey Ana in 1964 – 1965

> 8".................... $325.00 – 375.00

Annabelle, 1951 – 1952, Maggie head

> 14"................. $600.00 – 800.00
> 18" – 23"..... $800.00 – 1,000.00

Anne of Green Gables, 1993, in Concert dress

> 8"...................... $85.00 – 100.00

Babs Skater, 1948 – 1950, hard plastic, Margaret

> 15"........... $1,200.00 – 2,500.00
> 15" with crimped curls, wearing pink outfit........................... $5,500.00*
> 17" – 18".. $1,200.00 – 1,400.00

Bill/Billy, 1960, seven-piece walker body

> 8".................... $425.00 – 475.00

Binnie Walker, 1954 – 1955, Cissy face, value varies depending on how elaborate the costume is

> 15"................. $300.00 – 600.00
> 18"................. $425.00 – 675.00
> 25"................. $400.00 – 550.00

Bitsey, 1949 – 1951, hard plastic head, cloth body

> 11" – 16"........ $225.00 – 275.00

Brenda Starr, 1964 only, 12" hard plastic,

vinyl arms, red wig
> *In street dress*.... $250.00 – 300.00
> *In formalwear* ... $350.00 – 425.00

Bunny, 1962 only
> 18" .... $250.00 – 275.00

Caroline, 1961, #131, vinyl
> 15" .... $375.00 – 500.00
> MIB outfit only ... $75.00 – 125.00

Cinderella,
> *1950 – 1951,* Margaret face, 14",
hard plastic
> Ballgown
> 14" .... $850.00 – 950.00
> 18" .... $800.00 – 950.00
> Poor Cinderella, gray dress, original
> broom
> 14" .... $725.00 – 800.00

1967 – 1992, Mary Ann face, plastic and vinyl
> 14" .... $65.00 – 80.00

Cowgirl & Cowboy, 1967 – 1970, hard plastic, jointed knees
> 8" .... $300.00 – 350.00

Cynthia, 1952 only, hard plastic
> 15" .... $700.00 – 900.00
> 18" .... $900.00 – 1,200.00
> 23" .... $1,200.00 – 1,500.00

Edith, The Lonely Doll, 1958 – 1959, vinyl head, hard plastic body

14" Cynthia. $900.00. **Photo courtesy of McMasters Harris Auction Co.**

17" Elise ballerina. $350.00. **Photo courtesy of The Museum Doll Shop.**

> 8" .... $700.00 – 750.00
> 16" .... $300.00 – 350.00
> 22" .... $375.00 – 425.00
> *2003 – 2004,* vinyl, with 3" Mr. Bear
> 8" .... $75.00 – 80.00

Elise
> *1957 – 1964,* 16½", hard plastic body, vinyl arms, jointed ankles and knees
> Street dress ...... $450.00 – 550.00
> Ballerina .... $200.00 – 450.00
> Formalwear ...... $700.00 – 900.00
> *1963 only,* 18", hard plastic, vinyl arms, jointed ankles and knees
> Bouffant hairstyle.. $425.00 – 450.00
> *1966 – 1972,* 17", hard plastic, vinyl arms, jointed ankles and knees
> Street dress ...... $250.00 – 275.00
> Trousseau/trunk ..$650.00 – 800.00
> *1966 – 1987*
> Bride .... $100.00 – 130.00
> *1997,* vinyl
> 16" .... $95.00 – 125.00

Fairy Queen, 1948 – 1950, Margaret face
> 14½" .... $775.00 – 800.00

Fashions of a Century, 1954 – 1955, 14" – 18", Margaret face, hard plastic
> $2,400.00 – 3,000.00

First Ladies, 1976 – 1990
> *Set 1*
> 1976 – 1978.. $100.00 – 125.00 ea.
> *Set 2*
> 1979 – 1981.. $80.00 – 100.00 ea.
> *Set 3*
> 1982 – 1984.. $80.00 – 100.00 ea.
> *Set 4*
> 1985 – 1987.. $70.00 – 90.00 ea.
> *Set 5,* 1988 .... $70.00 – 90.00 ea.
> *Set 6*
> 1989 – 1990.. $50.00 – 75.00 ea.

Fischer Quints, 1964 only, vinyl, hard plastic body (Little Genius), one boy, four girls
> 7", set of five ... $500.00 – 550.00

Flower Girl, 1954, hard plastic, Margaret
> 15" .... $750.00 – 850.00

Glamour Girl Series, 1953 only, hard plastic, Margaret head, auburn wig, straight leg walker
> 18" .... $1,200.00 – 1,800.00

Godey Bride, 1950 – 1951, Margaret, hard plastic
> 14" .... $1,000.00 – 1,200.00

18" Glamour Girl. $1,700.00. **Photo courtesy of McMasters Harris Auction Co.**

> 14", MIB $3,700.00*
> 18" .... $1,300.00 – 1,500.00

Godey Lady, 1950 – 1951, Margaret, hard plastic
> 14" .... $1,400.00 – 1,600.00
> 14", MIB $4,500.00*

Godey Groom, 1950 – 1951, Margaret, hard plastic
> 14", MIB $3,600.00*
> 18" .... $1,200.00 – 1,400.00

Gold Rush, 1963 only, hard plastic, Cissette
> 10" .... $1,300.00 – 1,400.00

Grandma Jane, 1970 – 1972, #1420, Mary Ann, vinyl body
> 14" .... $200.00 – 225.00

Groom,
> *1949 – 1951,* Margaret, hard plastic
> 14" – 16" .... $750.00 – 850.00
> *1953 – 1955,* Wendy Ann, hard plastic
> 7½" .... $525.00 – 575.00

Jacqueline, 1961 – 1962, 21", hard plastic, vinyl arms
> *Street dress....* $850.00 – 1,000.00
> *Formalwear......* $900.00 – 950.00
> *Riding habit......* $825.00 – 875.00

Janie, 1964 – 1966, #1156, toddler, vinyl head, hard plastic body, rooted hair
> 12" .... $200.00 – 250.00

Jenny Lind, 1969 – 1970, hard plastic head
> 14" .... $300.00 – 350.00
> 21" .... $1,400.00 – 1,500.00

John Robert Powers Model, 1952, with oval beauty box, hard plastic
> 14" .... $1,700.00 – 2,000.00

Kathy Baby, 1954 – 1956, vinyl
> 13" – 15" .... $90.00 – 150.00

Kathy Cry, 1957 – 1958, nurser
> 11" – 15" .... $75.00 – 125.00
> 18" – 25" .... $100.00 – 225.00

Kelly
> *1959 only,* hard plastic, Lissy face
> 12" .... $400.00 – 500.00

20" Kelly. $300.00.
Photo courtesy of Richard Withington, Inc.

1958 – 1959, hard plastic, Marybel face
15" – 16"........ $200.00 – 300.00
1958
18" .... $350.00 – 375.00
1958 – 1959
22"................. $300.00 – 400.00
Leslie (black Polly), 1965 – 1971, 17", vinyl head, hard plastic body, vinyl limbs, rooted hair
Ballerina .... $375.00 – 400.00
Bride .... $300.00 – 350.00
Lissy, hard plastic, wigged
1956 – 1958, 12", elbow and knee joints
Street dress ...... $400.00 – 500.00
Formal............. $650.00 – 900.00
1959 – 1967, as above but no elbow and knee joints
Street dress ...... $200.00 – 275.00
2006, vinyl
12"................... $75.00 – 100.00
Little Shaver, 1963 – 1965, painted eyes, vinyl body
12"................. $200.00 – 250.00
Little Women,
1947 – 1956, Meg, Jo, Amy, Beth, plus Marme, Margaret and Maggie faces
14" – 15".$475.00 – 525.00 each
1955, Meg, Jo, Amy, Beth, plus Marme,

Wendy Ann, straight-leg walker
8".......................... $450.00 each
1956 – 1959, Wendy Ann, bent-knee walker
8".......................... $350.00 each
Set of four.. $1,500.00 – 1,600.00
1974 – 1992, straight leg, #411 – #415
8"...............$60.00 – 70.00 each
1957 – 1958, Lissy, jointed elbows and knees
12"................. $275.00 – 325.00
Set of 4 .... $1,500.00
1959 – 1968, Lissy, one-piece arms and legs
12"................. $225.00 – 250.00
1983 – 1989, Nancy Drew face
12"......................... $60.00 each
Lovey-Dove Ringbearer, 1951, hard plastic, five-piece toddler body, mohair wig, satin top, shorts
12"................. $350.00 – 450.00
Maggie Mixup, 1960 – 1961, hard plastic, freckles, price depends on outfit
8".................. $450.00 – 800.00

12" Lissy. $450.00. **Photo courtesy of Richard Withington, Inc.**

8" Maggie Mix-up. $400.00. **Photo courtesy of Richard Withington, Inc.**

Maggie Teenager, 1951 – 1953, hard plastic, price depends on outfit

15" – 18" ....$450.00 – 650.00

Maggie, hard plastic

1948 – 1954

20" – 21"........ $750.00 – 850.00

1949 – 1952

22" – 23"........ $800.00 – 900.00

1949 – 1953

17" – 18" .... $650.00 – 750.00

1949 – 1953, walker

15" – 18"........ $375.00 – 500.00

Margaret O'Brien, 1949 – 1951, hard plastic

14" .... $800.00 – 1,200.00

18" – 21"..... $600.00 – 1,100.00

Margot Ballerina, 1951 – 1953, Margaret and Maggie, dressed in various colored outfits

15" – 18"........ $650.00 – 850.00

Marlo Thomas as "That Girl," 1967 only, Polly face, vinyl........ $650.00 – 750.00

Mary Ellen, 1954 only, rigid vinyl walker

31"................. $625.00 – 675.00

Mary Ellen Playmate, 1965 only, bendable vinyl body

17"................. $300.00 – 350.00

Mary Martin, 1948 – 1952, South Pacific character Nell, two-piece sailor outfit, hard plastic

14" – 17"........ $750.00 – 950.00

Marybel, "The Doll That Gets Well," 1959 – 1965, rigid vinyl, in case with accessories

16"................. $300.00 – 325.00

1998

75th anniversary

re-issue .... $90.00 – 100.00

McGuffey Ana

1948 – 1950, hard plastic, Margaret

14" .... $1,000.00 – 1,200.00

18" .... $950.00 – 1,050.00

21" .... $1,200.00 – 1,400.00

MIB Fashion Academy Award winner in blue organdy

14" $5,600.00*

1956 only, hard plastic, #616, Wendy Ann face

8" .... $675.00 – 750.00

1963 only, hard plastic, rare doll, Lissy face

12" .... $2,500.00 – 3,000.00

12" Muffin, c. 1964, MIB. $100.00.
Photo courtesy of My Dolly Dearest.

12" Pamela in window box.
$1,300.00. **Photo courtesy of**
McMasters Harris Auction Co.

1999 – 2000, porcelain
15" .... $125.00 – 150.00
Melanie, 1966, "Coco," #2050, blue gown
21" .... $2,200.00 – 2,400.00
Melinda, 1962 – 1963, plastic/vinyl, cotton dress
14" – 22" .... $250.00 – 275.00
Muffin, 1989 – 1990, Janie face, vinyl
12" .... $50.00 – 60.00
Nancy Drew, 1967 only, vinyl body, Literature Series
12" .... $450.00 – 525.00
Nina Ballerina, 1949 – 1951, Margaret head, clover wrist tag
15" .... $700.00 – 750.00
19" .... $850.00 – 950.00
23" .... $850.00 – 900.00
Pamela, 1962 – 1963, Lissy face, changeable wigs
12", in window
box .... $1,000.00 – 1,300.00
Peter Pan, 1953 – 1954, Margaret
15" .... $600.00 – 800.00
1969, 14" Wendy (Mary Ann head), 12" Peter, Michael (Jamie head), 10" Tinkerbelle (Cissette head)
Peter, Wendy .... $200.00 – 225.00
Michael .... $225.00 – 250.00

Tinkerbelle .... $300.00 – 350.00
Set of four $1,000.00
Pink Champagne/Arlene Dahl, hard plastic, red hair, pink lace, rhinestone bodice gown
18" .... $7,000.00 – 8,000.00
Polly, 1965 only, 17"
Street dress .... $225.00 – 275.00
Pollyanna
1960 – 1961, vinyl, Marybel face
16" .... $400.00 – 450.00
1987 – 1988, Mary Ann face
14" .... $75.00 – 85.00
2000 – 2001, Wendy face
8" .... $60.00 – 70.00
Portraits, 1960 on, marked "1961," Jacqueline face, 21", early dolls have jointed elbows, later one piece. For models made over long periods the older dolls bring the higher end of the values listed, later dolls the lower end.
Agatha, 1967 – 1980
#2171 .... $250.00 – 650.00
Cornelia, 1972
#2191 .... $300.00 – 425.00
Gainsborough, 1968 – 1978
#2184 .... $300.00 – 650.00
Godey, Coco, 1966
#2063 ...... $2,300.00 – 2,500.00

15" Sonja Henie, vinyl $700.00. Photo courtesy of McMasters Harris Auction Co.

Godey, Jacqueline, 1969 – 1970
#2195 .... $300.00 – 600.00
Goya,1968
#2183 .... $500.00 – 550.00
Jenny Lind,1969 – 1970
#2193 ...... $1,400.00 – 1,500.00
Lady Hamilton,1968
#2182 .... $425.00 – 475.00
Madame,1966
#2060 ...... $2,300.00 – 2,400.00
Madame Alexander, 1985 – 1987
$225.00 – 250.00
Madame Pompadour, 1970
#2197 .... $400.00 – 500.00
Magnolia,1977
#2297 .... $3250.00 – 350.00
Melanie (Coco face), 1966
#2050 ...... $2,200.00 – 2,300.00
Melanie,1967 – 1980
$300.00 – 650.00
Renoir, 1965
#2154 .... $650.00 – 700.00
Scarlett,1965, green satin gown
#2152 ...... $1,900.00 – 2,100.00
Scarlett (Coco face), 1966,white gown
#2061 ...... $2,800.00 – 2,900.00

Southern Belle,1965
#2155 ...... $1,500.00 – 1,600.00
Prince Charles, 1957 only, #397, hard plastic, blue jacket, cap, shorts
8" .... $750.00 – 800.00
Prince Charming, 1948 – 1950, hard plastic, Margaret face, brocade jacket, white tights
14" .... $700.00 – 775.00
18" .... $825.00 – 875.00
Princess Margaret Rose
1949 – 1953, hard plastic, Margaret face
14" .... $750.00 – 800.00
18" .... $875.00 – 925.00
1953 only, #2020B, hard plastic, Beaux Arts Series, pink taffeta gown with red ribbon, tiara, Margaret face
18" .... $1,700.00 – 1,900.00
Queen, 1953, Margaret
18" .... $1,400.00 – 1,700.00
Quiz-Kin, 1953, hard plastic, back buttons, nods yes or no
8" .... $500.00 – 600.00
Renoir Girl, 1967 – 1968, vinyl body, Portrait Children Series
14" .... $100.00 – 125.00

17" Marlo Thomas as "That Girl." $650.00. Photo courtesy of McMasters Harris Auction Co.

Scarlett O'Hara
1950 on, hard plastic, Margaret face
14" – 16".. $1,500.00 – 1,700.00
1966 – 1972, jointed knees, Wendy
Ann face
8".................. $300.00 – 350.00
1969 – 1986, vinyl, Mary Ann face,
white gown
14"..................... $75.00 – 90.00
1970, #2180 green satin with white
trimmed jacket
21"................ $350.00 – 450.00
Shari Lewis, 1958 – 1959
14"................ $625.00 – 675.00
21"................ $800.00 – 850.00
Sleeping Beauty, 1959, Disneyland Special
10"................ $300.00 – 325.00
16"................ $600.00 – 650.00
21"................ $850.00 – 900.00
Smarty, 1962 – 1963, vinyl body
12"................ $225.00 – 300.00
Snow White
1967 – 1977, Disney authorized
14"................ $225.00 – 250.00
1990 – 1992, Wendy face, vinyl
8"...................... $65.00 – 80.00
2002 – 2004, Cissette face, came with
5" dwarves
10", complete set.. $225.00 – 250.00
Sonja Henie, 1951 only, Madeline face, vinyl head
15"................ $600.00 – 800.00
Sound of Music, 1965 – 1970 (large), 1971
– 1973 (small), vinyl
Brigitta
10" .... $175.00 – 200.00
14"................ $200.00 – 225.00
Friedrich
8" .... $150.00 – 175.00
10"................ $225.00 – 250.00
Gretl
8" .... $150.00 – 175.00
10"................ $200.00 – 225.00

Liesl
10" .... $225.00 – 250.00
14" .... $225.00 – 250.00
Louisa
10" .... $225.00 – 250.00
14" .... $225.00 – 250.00
Maria
12" .... $250.00 – 300.00
17" .... $250.00 – 275.00
Marta
8" .... $200.00 – 225.00
10" .... $200.00 – 225.00
Sugar Darlin', Lively, 1964, turn knob to
make limbs wiggle
14" – 24"....... $125.00 – 250.00
Timmy Toddler, 1960 – 1961, vinyl head,
hard plastic body
23"................ $125.00 – 150.00
1960 only
30"................ $200.00 – 250.00
Tommy Bangs, 1952 only, hard plastic, Little
Men Series
11"................ $825.00 – 875.00
**Wendy, Wendy Ann, Wendy-kin: See
Alexander-kins section.**
Special Event dolls, limited edition
Collector's United
Carnival Queen, 1999, limit 24
16"................ $275.00 – 300.00
Shea Elf, 1990, limit 1,000
8" .... $90.00 – 100.00
Disney
Alice in Wonderland, 1991, limit 750
10"................ $300.00 – 325.00
Cinderella, 1994, limit 900, Disney
catalog item
14"................ $175.00 – 200.00
Michael & Jane Banks, 1999, limit
200
8", pair .... $125.00 – 175.00
Madame Alexander Doll Club Convention
Briar Rose, 1989, Cissette head, limit

804
8".................. $225.00 – 250.00
Little Miss Bea, 2000, limit 500
8".................. $150.00 – 175.00
Southern Belle Cissy, 2003, limit 65
21".................. $450.00 – 500.00

U.F.D.C
Little Emperor, 1992, limit 400
8".................. $300.00 – 325.00
Miss Unity, 1991, limit 310
10".................. $300.00 – 325.00
Sailor Boy, limit 260
8".................. $450.00 – 500.00
Turn of Century Bathing Beauty, 1992,
R9 Conference, limit 300
10".................. $200.00 – 250.00
Columbian 1893 Sailor, 1993
12".................. $100.00 – 125.00
Gabrielle, 1998, limit 400
10".................. $200.00 – 225.00
Salon Salon, 2005, doll with two wigs
10"............................. $125.00

20" Phenix Bébé. $6,000.00. **Photo courtesy of Turn of the Century Antiques.**

Child, open mouth
16" – 18".. $2,100.00 – 2,400.00
20" – 24".. $2,400.00 – 2,800.00

HENRI ALEXANDRE

1888 – 1891, Paris. Succeeded by Tourrel in 1892 and in 1895 merged with Jules Steiner.
Incised HA model, bisque socket head, paperweight eyes, closed mouth with space between lips, straight wrist body
17" – 20".. $5,500.00 – 6,900.00
Bébé Phénix, trademarked in 1895, bisque socket head, paperweight eyes, pierced ears, composition body
Child, closed mouth
10" – 14".. $1,900.00 – 3,200.00
16" – 18" . $5,000.00 – 6,000.00
20" – 24".. $6,000.00 – 7,500.00

ALL-BISQUE FRENCH

1880 on, made by various French and German doll companies. Sold as French products. Most are unmarked, some have numbers only. Allow more for original clothes and tags, less for chips or repairs.
Glass eyes, swivel head, molded shoes or boots
2½" – 3½"...... $800.00 – 900.00
4" – 5"...... $1,500.00 – 1,800.00
6" – 7"...... $3,300.00 – 4,300.00
10"........... $6,300.00 – 6,500.00
Five-strap boots, glass eyes, swivel neck
5" – 6"...... $1,900.00 – 2,100.00

Painted eyes

2½" – 3½" ..... $500.00 – 600.00

4" .... $900.00 – 1,000.00

Bare feet

5" .... $2,300.00 – 2,600.00

6" .... $2,900.00 – 3,100.00

Later style, 1910 – 1920, glass eyes, molded shoes, swivel neck, long stockings

2½" .... $300.00 – 350.00

5" – 6" .... $575.00 – 625.00

7" .... $700.00 – 725.00

ALL-BISQUE GERMAN

1880s onward, made by various German doll companies including Alt, Beck & Gottschalk; Bähr & Pröschild; Hertel Schwab & Co.; Kämmer & Reinhardt; Kestner; Kling; Limbach; Bruno Schmidt; Simon & Halbig. Some incised "Germany" with or without

4½" all-bisque, stationary neck, painted side-glancing eyes. $175.00. **Photo courtesy of The Museum Doll Shop.**

numbers, others have paper labels glued onto their torsos. More for labels, less for chips and repairs.

All-Bisque, Black or Brown: See Black or Brown Section.

Painted eyes, 1880 – 1910, stationary neck, molded painted footwear, dressed or undressed, all in good condition

2" – 3" .... $100.00 – 150.00

4" – 5" .... $200.00 – 250.00

6" – 8" .... $225.00 – 350.00

Black or brown stockings, tan slippers

4" – 5" .... $375.00 – 450.00

6" .... $475.00 – 525.00

Ribbed hose or blue or yellow shoes

4" – 5" .... $275.00 – 325.00

6" .... $425.00 – 475.00

8" .... $825.00 – 875.00

Molded hair

4½" .... $150.00 – 175.00

6" .... $325.00 – 350.00

Early very round face

7" .... $2,100.00 – 2,300.00

Molded clothing, 1890 – 1910, jointed at shoulders only or at shoulders and hips, painted eyes, molded hair, molded shoes or bare feet, excellent workmanship, no breaks, chips, or rubs

3½" – 4" .... $115.00 – 145.00

5" – 6" .... $130.00 – 180.00

7" .... $165.00 – 225.00

Lesser quality

3" .... $65.00 – 75.00

4" .... $80.00 – 90.00

6" .... $100.00 – 120.00

Molded on hat or bonnet

5 – 6½" .... $365.00 – 395.00

8 – 9" .... $500.00 – 550.00

Stone bisque (porous)

4 – 5" .... $90.00 – 115.00

6 – 7" .... $125.00 – 145.00

Glass eyes, 1890 – 1910, stationary neck,

4½" all-bisque with molded clothing. $145.00. **Photo courtesy of Atlanta Antique Gallery.**

molded painted footwear, excellent bisque, open-closed mouth, sleep or set eyes, good wig, nicely dressed, molded one-strap shoes. Allow more for unusual footwear such as yellow or multi-strap boots.

3"	$225.00 – 275.00
5"	$300.00 – 350.00
7"	$400.00 – 600.00
9"	$600.00 – 750.00

Early style with unjointed hips, ribbed stockings or elaborate style shoes

3"	$325.00 – 350.00
4½"	$350.00 – 400.00
6" – 7"	$575.00 – 850.00
8" – 8½"	$1,200.00 – 1,300.00

Mold 100, 125, 150, 225 (preceded by 83/), rigid neck, fat tummy, jointed shoulders and hips, glass sleep eyes, open-closed mouth, molded black one-strap shoes with tan soles, white molded stockings with blue band. Similarly molded dolls, imported in 1950s by Kimport, have synthetic hair, lesser quality bisque. Add more for original clothing. Mold number appears as a fraction with the following size numbers under 83; Mold "83/100," "83/125," "83/150," or "83/225." One marked "83/100" has a green label on torso reading, "Princess// Made in Germany."

5½" – 6½"	$300.00 – 400.00
7½" – 8½"	$500.00 – 600.00

Swivel neck and glass eyes, 1880 – 1910, molded painted footwear, pegged or wired joints, open or closed mouth. Allow more for unusual footwear such as yellow or multi-strap boots or flirty eyes.

3" – 4"	$300.00 – 450.00
5" – 6"	$300.00 – 400.00
7" – 8"	$650.00 – 800.00
9" – 10"	$1,000.00 – 1,500.00

Simon & Halbig or Kestner types, closed mouth, excellent quality. Molds 130, 150, 160, 184, 208, 602, 881, 886, 890, and others

4" – 5"	$1,700.00 – 1,900.00
6" – 7"	$1,850.00 – 2,200.00
8"	$2,500.00 – 2,800.00
10"	$2,9 00.00 – 3,200.00

Jointed knees

6"	$3,500.00 – 4,000.00
8½"	$6,000.00 – 7,000.00

Bare feet

5"	$1,700.00 – 1,800.00
7½"	$2,400.00 – 2,600.00

Early round face

6"	$800.00 – 900.00
8"	$1,200.00 – 1,300.00

Mold 102, Wrestler (so called), fat thighs, arm bent at elbow, open mouth (can have two rows of teeth) or closed mouth, stocky

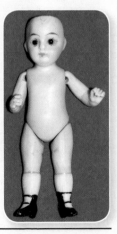

4" stationary neck, glass eyed with multi-strap boots. $325.00. **Photo courtesy of The Museum Doll Shop.**

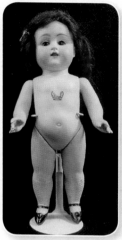

5½" Kestner mold 150. $300.00.
Photo courtesy of Richard Withington, Inc.

body, glass eyes, socket head, individual fingers or molded fist

6"............. $1,800.00 – 1,900.00
8"............. $2,100.00 – 2,300.00
9"............. $3,400.00 – 3,800.00

Slender dolls, 1900 on, stationary neck, slender arms and legs, glass eyes, molded footwear, usual wire or peg-jointed shoulders and hips. Allow much more for original clothes. May be in regional costumes. Add more for unusual color boots, such as gold, yellow, or orange, all in good condition.

3" – 4"............. $200.00 – 250.00
5" – 6"............. $275.00 – 325.00

Swivel neck, closed mouth

4"................. $275.00 – 300.00
5" – 6"............. $450.00 – 500.00
8½"................ $800.00 – 900.00
10"............ $1,100.00 – 1,300.00

Jointed knees and/or elbows with swivel waist

6"............. $1,950.00 – 2,050.00
8"............. $3,000.00 – 3,200.00

Swivel waist only

6"............. $2,000.00 – 2,200.00

Santa Claus, molded beard

2½"......................... $1,450.00*

Baby, 1900 on, jointed at hips and shoulders, bent limbs, molded hair, painted features

2½" – 3½"......... $80.00 – 90.00
5" – 6"............ $175.00 – 225.00

Character Baby, 1910 on, jointed at hips and shoulders, bent limbs, molded hair, painted features

Glass eyes, molds 391, 830, 833, and others

4" – 5" .... $275.00 – 375.00
6".................... $400.00 – 450.00
7½" in original wicker
cradle $1,700.00*
8".................. $625.00 – 650.00
11"................. $850.00 – 950.00

Painted eyes

3½".................. $90.00 – 100.00
4" – 5"............. $200.00 – 225.00
7".................. $300.00 – 350.00
8" .... $400.00 – 450.00

Swivel neck, glass eyes

5" – 6"............. $775.00 – 950.00
8" – 10".... $1,200.00 – 1,500.00

Swivel neck, painted eyes

5" – 6"............. $325.00 – 350.00
7" – 8"............. $550.00 – 600.00

10" Kestner 211. $1,695.00.
Photo courtesy of Joan & Lynette Antique Dolls and Accessories.

5" designed by Jeanne Orsini. $2,900.00. **Photo courtesy of Richard Withington, Inc.**

Baby Bo Kaye, mold 1394, designed by Kallus, distributed by Borgfeldt

5"............. $1,400.00 – 1,600.00
7" – 8"...... $1,800.00 – 1,900.00

Baby Bud, glass eyes, wig

6" – 7"...... $1,100.00 – 1,300.00

Baby Darling, mold 497, Kestner, 178, one-piece body, painted eyes

6".................... $850.00 – 950.00
8"................ $950.00 – 1,000.00
10"........... $1,100.00 – 1,200.00

Baby Peggy Montgomery, made by Louis Amberg, paper label, pink bisque with molded hair, painted brown eyes, closed mouth, jointed at shoulders and hips, molded and painted shoes/socks

3½"............... $325.00 – 375.00
5½"............... $525.00 – 575.00

Bonnie Babe, 1926 on, designed by Georgene Averill, glass eyes, swivel neck, wig, jointed arms and legs

5".................... $850.00 – 950.00
7"............. $1,400.00 – 1,500.00
8"............. $1,600.00 – 1,700.00

Bye-Lo: See Bye-Lo section.

Mildred (The Prize Baby), mold 880, 1914 on, made for Borgfeldt; molded, short painted hair; glass eyes; closed mouth; jointed at neck, shoulders, and hips; round paper label on chest; molded and painted footwear

5" – 7"...... $3,800.00 – 5,400.00

Our Darling, open mouth with teeth, glass eyes

5½"................ $160.00 – 200.00

Tynie Baby, made for E.I. Horsman, wigged or painted hair, glass eyes

8" – 10".... $1,600.00 – 2,200.00

Mold 231 (A.M.), toddler, swivel neck, with glass eyes

9"............. $1,300.00 – 1,400.00

Mold 369, 372

7".................. $650.00 – 725.00
9"............. $1,000.00 – 1,100.00
11"........... $1,400.00 – 1,500.00

Character Doll with Glass eyes, 1910

Molds 155, 156

5" – 6"........... $400.00 – 500.00
7".................. $625.00 – 650.00

Mold 602, swivel neck

5½" – 6"......... $575.00 – 650.00

Heubach, Ernst, 1913 – 1920s, jointed at shoulders and hips, molded painted hair, some with ribbons etc., intaglio eyes, Our Golden Three, molds such as 9557, 9558, 10134, 10490, 10499, 10511, others

3" – 3½" painted eye babies. $80.00 each.
Private collection.

3½" pair of later all-bisque dolls with painted eyes. $100.00 each. **Photo courtesy of Sharing My Dolls & Stuff.**

8" – 9"...... $1,800.00 – 2,000.00

9", swivel neck............. $2,400.00

Orsini, 1919 on, designed by Jeanne Orsini for Borgfeldt, produced by Alt, Beck & Gottschalk, Chi Chi, Didi, Fifi, Mimi, Vivi

Glass eyes

5"............. $2,800.00 – 3,000.00

7"............. $4,000.00 – 5,000.00

Painted eyes

5"............. $1,100.00 – 1,200.00

Our Fairy, mold 222, glass eyes

5"............... $800.00 – 1,000.00

8"............. $1,200.00 – 1,500.00

11"........... $1,800.00 – 2,000.00

Jointed animals, 1910 on, wire jointed shoulders and hips, crocheted clothing, makers such as Kestner, others.

2" – 3½"

Rabbit..................... $475.00 – 525.00

Bear .... $450.00 – 500.00

Frog, Monkey, Pig......... $600.00 – 700.00

Puss in Boots............ $350.00 – 400.00

Miniature dolls, painted eyes, crocheted clothing, various makers

1" – 1¾"........... $90.00 – 110.00

Character Dolls, painted eyes, 1913 on

Campbell Kids, molded clothes, Dutch bob

5"................... $210.00 – 245.00

Chin-chin, Gebruder Heubach, 1919, jointed arms only, triangular label on chest

4"................... $275.00 – 300.00

Happifats, designed by Kate Jordan for Borgfeldt, ca. 1913 – 1921

4"................... $400.00 – 450.00

HEbee, SHEbee

4" – 5"............ $675.00 – 800.00

7"................... $800.00 – 875.00

Max, Moritz, Kestner, 1914, jointed at the neck, shoulders, and hips, many companies produced these characters from the Wilhelm Busch children's story

4½" ..$1,300.00 – 1,400.00 each

Mibs, Amberg, 1921, molded blond hair, molded and painted socks and shoes, pink bisque, jointed at shoulders, legs molded to body, marked "C.//L.A.&S.192//GERMANY"

3"................... $200.00 – 250.00

5"................... $375.00 – 425.00

8"................... $500.00 – 575.00

Peterkin, 1912, one-piece baby, side-glancing googly eyes, molded and painted hair, molded blue pajamas on chubby torso, arms molded to body with hands clasping stomach

5" – 6"............ $275.00 – 350.00

1¾" painted bisque with crocheted clothing. $65.00. **Photo courtesy of The Museum Doll Shop.**

6½" flappers with molded loops for hair bows. $375.00 each. Photo courtesy of McMasters Harris Auction Co.

September Morn, jointed at shoulders and hips, Grace Drayton design, George Borgfeldt

4" – 5"...... $2,100.00 – 2,500.00
6"– 8"....... $2,600.00 – 3,000.00

Later issue with painted eyes, 1920 on, painted hair or wigged, molded painted single strap shoes, white stockings, makers such as Limbach, Hertwig & Co, others

3½"..................... $75.00 – 85.00
4" – 5"............ $110.00 – 125.00
6" – 7"............ $175.00 – 225.00

So-called Flapper, 1920, tinted bisque, molded bobbed hairstyle, painted features, molded single strap shoes

Child

3"................... $150.00 – 170.00

Adult

5½"............... $300.00 – 350.00

Molded loop for bow

5"................... $250.00 – 300.00
6" – 7"............ $350.00 – 400.00

Molded hat

4"................... $225.00 – 250.00

Aviatrix

5"................... $225.00 – 250.00

Swivel waist

4½"............... $375.00 – 400.00

Molded cap with rabbit ears

4½"............... $375.00 – 400.00

Wigged

3½"................... $95.00 – 125.00

Nodders, 1920 on, immobile body, head attached with elastic, makers such as Hertwig & Co., others, when their heads are touched, they "nod," molded clothes

Animals, cat, dog, rabbit

3" – 5" .... $100.00 – 150.00

Child/adult

3" – 4"............... $50.00 – 75.00

Comic characters

3" – 5"............ $120.00 – 135.00

Santa Claus or Indian

$200.00 – 225.00

Teddy Bear .... $200.00 – 225.00

Immobiles, 1920, one-piece doll with molded clothing, top layer of paint not fired on and the color can be washed off, some have molded hats

Baby

3½"..................... $40.00 – 50.00
5"....................... $50.00 – 60.00

Adults and Children

3"....................... $50.00 – 60.00
5"....................... $65.00 – 70.00

Bathing Beauties, 1910 – 1930s, various German porcelain factories made these bisque figures, painted features

3"................... $275.00 – 300.00
6"................... $550.00 – 600.00

Reclining woman, lying on stomach

2½"............... $135.00 – 165.00
4"................... $375.00 – 425.00

Mermaid tail

4"................... $300.00 – 325.00

Two figures molded together

4½" – 5½" ..$1,500.00 – 1,700.00

Wigged

    5".................. $700.00 – 7570.00

Wigged, seated, playing mandolin, molded stockings

    4"................................ $1,225.00

Too few in database for a reliable range.

Painted bisque child, 1920 – 1930s, all in original clothing

    3" – 4"................ $65.00 – 80.00

ALL-BISQUE JAPANESE

    1915 onward, made by a variety of Japanese companies. Quality varies widely, stationary dolls or jointed at shoulders and/or hips. Marked "Made in Japan" or "Nippon."

Fired bisque, fired on color, some jointed at shoulders, some immobile

Characters such as Que San Baby, Cho Cho San, etc.

    4" – 4½"......... $150.00 – 200.00

Painted bisque, top layer of paint not fired on and the color can be washed off, usually one-piece figurines with molded hair, painted features, including clothes, shoes, and socks, some have molded hats

Baby

    3" – 5"................ $15.00 – 25.00

    5" – 7"................ $30.00 – 40.00

Black baby, with pigtails

    4" – 5"................ $40.00 – 60.00

Bye-Lo Baby-type, fine quality

    3½".................... $70.00 – 85.00

    5".................... $120.00 – 140.00

Child

    3" – 5"................ $20.00 – 30.00

Child with molded clothes

    4½".................... $25.00 – 35.00

    6"........................ $40.00 – 50.00

Child, 1920s – 1930s, pink or painted bisque

3 ½" Que San baby by Morimura Bros. $200.00. **Photo courtesy of Sharing My Dolls & Stuff.**

with painted features, jointed at shoulders and hips, has molded hair or wig, excellent condition

    3"........................ $10.00 – 20.00

    4"........................ $15.00 – 35.00

Betty Boop, bobbed hair style, large eyes painted to side, head molded to torso

    4"........................ $20.00 – 30.00

    6"........................ $30.00 – 45.00

Bride & Groom, all original costume

    4"........................ $30.00 – 60.00

Happifats

    3½"................ $100.00 – 125.00

Hebee, Shebee

    4½".................... $70.00 – 90.00

Immobile characters, Indian, Pirate, etc.

    5"........................ $20.00 – 25.00

Skippy

    6".................... $110.00 – 135.00

Snow White

    5"...................... $90.00 – 110.00

Boxed with Dwarfs .... $450.00 – 650.00

Three Bears/Goldilocks

    Boxed set......... $325.00 – 400.00

Nippon mark

    5"........................ $75.00 – 85.00

Occupied Japan mark

    4"........................ $35.00 – 45.00

    7"........................ $45.00 – 55.00

Three bears in original box. $300.00. **Photo courtesy of Joan & Lynette Antique Dolls and Accessories.**

ALT, BECK & GOTTSCHALCK

1854, Nauendorf, Thüringia, Germany. Produced bisque and china headed dolls for a variety of companies including Bergmann and Borgfeldt.

Shoulder Heads, china, 1880 on. Mold 639, 698, 784, 870, 890, 912, 974, 990, 1000, 1008, 1028, 1032, 1044, 1046, 1064, 1112, 1123, 1127, 1142, 1210, 1222, 1234, 1235, 1254, 1304, cloth or kid body, bisque lower limbs, molded hair or wig, no damage and nicely dressed. Allow more for molded hat or fancy hairdo.

    15" – 18"........ $300.00 – 325.00
    19" – 22"........ $375.00 – 400.00
    23" – 26"........ $450.00 – 475.00
    28"................. $575.00 – 600.00

Shoulder Heads, bisque, 1880. Cloth or kid body, bisque lower arms, closed mouth, molded hair or wig. Molds such as 784, 911, 912, 916, 990, 1000, 1008, 1028, 1044, 1046, 1064, 1127, 1142, 1210, 1234, 1254, 1304. Allow more for molded hat or fancy hairdo.

Glass eyes, closed mouth
    9" – 11" .... $350.00 – 400.00
    15" –17".......... $500.00 – 700.00
    18" – 22"........ $800.00 – 900.00
Painted eyes, closed mouth
    14" – 18"........ $375.00 – 400.00
    21" – 23"........ $600.00 – 650.00

Turned Bisque Shoulder Heads, 1885, solid dome head or plaster pate, kid body, bisque lower arms, glass eyes, wigged, all in good condition, nicely dressed. Dolls marked 639, 698, 870, 1032, 1123, 1235, "DEP" or "Germany" after 1888. Some have "Wagner & Zetzsche" marked on head, paper label inside top of body. Allow more for molded bonnet or elaborate hairdo.

Closed mouth, glass eyes
    16" – 18"........ $600.00 – 700.00
    20" – 22"........ $750.00 – 850.00
Open mouth
    16" – 18"........ $300.00 – 375.00
    20" – 22"........ $475.00 – 550.00

Character Baby, 1910s on, open mouth, sleep eyes, bent limb body. Allow more for flirty eyes or toddler body. Molds such as 1322, 1342, 1346, 1352, 1361.

31" Sweet Nell. $980.00. **Photo courtesy of Sharing My Dolls & Stuff.**

10" – 12"........ $375.00 – 425.00
16" – 19"........ $575.00 – 650.00
22" – 24"........ $875.00 – 950.00
Mold 1407, Baby Bo-Kaye
8"............. $1,300.00 – 1,400.00
19"........... $2,300.00 – 2,500.00
Child, All-Bisque: See All-Bisque Section.
Child, 1880 onward, bisque socket head, ball-jointed composition body, glass eyes, wig, closed mouth
Mold 630, glass eyes, closed mouth, ca. 1880
20" – 22".. $1,800.00 – 2,000.00
Mold 911, 916, swivel head, closed mouth, ca. 1890
16" – 18".. $1,500.00 – 1,700.00
20" – 22".. $1,900.00 – 2,100.00
Mold 938, closed mouth
20" – 22" .. $4,200.00 – 4,500.00*
Mold 1362, ca. 1912, Sweet Nell, more for flapper body
14" – 16" .... $300.00 – 450.00
18" – 20"........ $400.00 – 450.00
22" – 24" .... $500.00 – 575.00
26" – 28"........ $600.00 – 700.00
29" – 32"..... $700.00 – 1,000.00
Character Child, ca. 1910 onward, bisque socket head, composition ball-jointed body
Mold 1357, ca. 1912, solid dome or

wigged, painted eyes, open mouth; mold 1358, ca. 1910, molded hair, ribbon, flowers, painted eyes, open mouth
15" – 20"..... $975.00 – 1,700.00
Mold 1322, 1342, 1352, 1361, glass eyes
10" – 12"........ $325.00 – 400.00
14" – 16"........ $425.00 – 500.00
18" – 20"........ $550.00 – 650.00
Mold 1367, 1368, ca. 1914
15"................. $450.00 – 475.00

LOUIS AMBERG & SONS

1878 – 1930, Cincinnati, Ohio, and New York City. Importer, wholesaler, and manufacturer. First company to manufacture all American-made composition dolls.
Newborn Babe, Bottle Babe, 1914 on, bisque head on cloth body, hands of celluloid, bisque, or rubber, sleep eyes, painted hair, closed or open mouth, molds such as 886, 371
Closed mouth
8" – 10".......... $300.00 – 325.00
12" – 14"........ $350.00 – 400.00
16" – 18"........ $500.00 – 550.00
Charlie Chaplin, 1915, composition head with molded moustache, cloth body, composition hands, cloth label on sleeve
14"................. $625.00 – 650.00
AmKid, 1918, composition shoulder head, kidolene body, composition arms, sleep eyes, wig
22"................. $100.00 – 150.00
Happinus, 1918, all-composition with head and torso molded in one piece, coquette-style, brown painted hair molded with hair ribbon
10"................. $275.00 – 325.00
Baby Peggy, portrait of child-actress Peggy Montgomery

Composition, 1923, composition head, arms, and legs, cloth body, molded bobbed hair painted brown, painted eyes

    18" – 20" .... $500.00 – 750.00

Bisque, 1924, bisque socket head, composition or kid body, sleep eyes, brown mohair wig

Molds 972, 973, socket head

    18" – 22" ..$1,800.00 – 2,000.00

Molds 982, 983, shoulder head

    18" – 22".. $1,100.00 – 1,400.00

Baby Peggy, All-Bisque: See All-Bisque, German Section.

Mibs, 1921, composition turned shoulder head, designed by Hazel Drukker, cloth body with composition arms and legs, painted eyes, molded painted hair, molded painted shoes and socks or barefoot mama-style leg

    16" .... $1,000.00 – 1,200.00

Mibs, All-Bisque: See All-Bisque, German Section.

Miss Victory, composition dolly faced doll, ball jointed composition body, wig, sleep eyes

    23" – 24" .... $250.00 – 300.00

Sunny Orange Maid, 1924, composition shoulder head, cloth body with composition arms and legs, head has molded "orange" bonnet

    14" .... $800.00 – 1,000.00

Vanta Baby, 1927 on, sold through Sears, advertising for Vanta baby clothes, bent-limb composition body, sleep eyes, open mouth with two teeth, painted hair

Bisque head

    18" – 22".. $1,100.00 – 1,275.00

Composition head

    10" – 14" .... $150.00 – 200.00

    18" – 23" .... $350.00 – 450.00

Edwina, Sue, or It, 1928, all-composition, painted features, molded side-part hair with swirl on forehead, body twist construction

    14" .... $475.00 – 500.00

Tiny Tots, Body Twists, 1929, all-composition, swivel waist ball attached to torso with a ball, molded hair, painted features, boy or girl

    7½" – 8½" ...... $125.00 – 175.00

Peter Pan, 1928, all-composition, round joint at waist, wearing original Peter Pan fashion dress

    14" .... $400.00 – 500.00

AMERICAN CHARACTER DOLL COMPANY

1919 – 1963, New York City. Made composition dolls, in 1923 registered the trademark "Petite" for mama and character dolls, later made cloth, rubber, hard plastic, and vinyl dolls. In 1960 the company name was changed to American Character Doll & Toy Co.

"A.C." or "Petite" marked composition doll, 1923, composition heads and limbs, cloth body

20" Little Love infant, c. 1942. $350.00. **Photo courtesy of Ruth Cayton.**

Baby
14"................. $125.00 – 175.00
18"................. $150.00 – 225.00
Mama doll, sleep eyes, human hair wig
16" – 18"........ $225.00 – 275.00
24" .... $325.00 – 350.00
Petite girls, 1930s, all-composition
16" – 18"........ $250.00 – 300.00
24"................. $325.00 – 350.00
Toddler
13"................. $200.00 – 225.00
Bottletot, 1926, composition head and bent limbs, cloth body, painted hair, open mouth, one arm molded to hold molded celluloid bottle
13"................. $200.00 – 225.00
18"................. $300.00 – 325.00
All-rubber, drink and wet, painted eye doll in layette case, labeled Bottletot, A Petite Baby, doll marked on back with Horsman horseshoe with "petite Dolls // Pt. Pending"
9½" .... $100.00 – 150.00
Puggy, 1928, all-composition, character face with frown and side-glancing painted eyes, molded painted hair, jointed at neck, shoulders, and hips, original outfits included baseball player, boy scout, cowboy, and newsboy. Mark: "A // Petite // Doll," clothes tagged "Puggy // A Petite Doll"
13"................. $400.00 – 475.00
Sally, 1930, Patsy-type, all-composition, molded hair or wig, marks: "Petite" or "American Char. Doll Co.," painted or sleep eyes
12"................. $175.00 – 225.00
14" – 16"........ $250.00 – 350.00
Sally, Shirley-type wig
24"................. $350.00 – 375.00
Sally-Joy, composition head on cloth body
18"................. $300.00 – 325.00
21"................. $325.00 – 350.00
24" .... $350.00 – 375.00
Carol Ann Beery, 1935, portrait doll of child-actor, daughter of Wallace Beery, all-com-

16" Tiny Tears, MIB with layette. $400.00.
Photo courtesy of Aunt Mary's Antique Dolls.

position, mohair wig with two braids drawn up across top of head, marks: "Petite Sally" or "Petite"
13"................. $400.00 – 500.00
16"................. $600.00 – 700.00
20"................. $675.00 – 750.00
Little Love (also called Newborn Babe), 1942, composition flange neck head and hands, cloth body, molded hair, sleep eyes, a Bye-Lo type doll
16" – 20"........ $250.00 – 350.00
Vinyl, sleep eyes, molded hair
16"................. $125.00 – 150.00
Tiny Tears, 1950s, hard plastic head with tear ducts, drink and wet doll
Rubber body
11½"............. $175.00 – 250.00
13½"............. $225.00 – 275.00
16"................. $250.00 – 350.00
18"................. $250.00 – 350.00
Clothing and accessories
Bottle $35.00
Bubble pipe $25.00
Bracelet................................... $30.00
Plastic cradle.......................... $200.00
Romper $35.00
All-vinyl, 1963
11½"............... $75.00 – 125.00
13½"............. $125.00 – 150.00

18" Sweet Sue bride. $300.00. **Photo courtesy of Turn of the Century Antiques.**

16" .... $150.00 – 200.00
20" .... $200.00 – 250.00
Danbury Mint, 2000, re-issue, porcelain, with layette
10" .... $50.00 – 75.00
Sweet Sue, 1953 – 1961, all-hard plastic or hard plastic and vinyl, saran wig, some on walker bodies others fully jointed including elbows, knees, and ankles, marks: "A.C." "Amer. Char. Doll" or "American Character" in a circle
15" .... $200.00 – 275.00
18" – 20" .... $275.00 – 350.00
22" – 25" .... $275.00 – 325.00
31" .... $350.00 – 435.00
Sweet Sue Sophisticate, vinyl head, earrings
20" .... $275.00 – 350.00
Annie Oakley, 1953, hard plastic walker
14" .... $400.00 – 450.00
Ricky Jr., 1954 –1956, personality doll based on character from I Love Lucy television show, baby
Hard plastic with rubber body, 1952
14" – 16" .... $350.00 – 500.00
All-vinyl, 1953 – 1956

13" .... $275.00 – 350.00
21" .... $275.00 – 350.00
Toodles, 1956, hard rubber drink and wet doll
Teeny Toodles
11" .... $225.00 – 275.00
18" – 20" .... $250.00 – 300.00
29" .... $325.00 – 350.00
Toodles Toddler, 1960, vinyl and hard plastic, "Peek-a-Boo" eyes
24" .... $325.00 – 400.00
30" .... $375.00 – 400.00
Eloise, 1955, cloth with molded mask face, yarn hair
22" .... $325.00 – 425.00
Toni, 1958, vinyl head with rooted hair
10½" .... $250.00 – 300.00
14" .... $275.00 – 350.00
20" .... $325.00 – 500.00
25" .... $500.00 – 600.00
Whimsies, 1960, all-vinyl characters
Dixie the Pixie, Hedda Get Bedda (three face), Miss Take, Tiller the Talker, Wheeler the Dealer, and others
19" – 20" .... $225.00 – 400.00

11" Tressy, grow-hair doll, $45.00. **Photo courtesy of The Museum Doll Shop.**

Astronaut

MIB $2,183.00*

Whimettes,1963 smaller doll modeled after the whimsies

7½" .... $200.00 – 275.00

Little Miss Echo, 1964, vinyl, recorder mechanism in torso

30" .... $200.00 – 250.00

Miss America, 1963 ..... $50.00 – 65.00

Tressy,1963 – 1965, vinyl, grow hair doll, marks: "American Doll & Toy Corp. // 19C.63" in a circle. MIB dolls will bring double the values here.

11" .... $50.00 – 75.00

Black .... $150.00 – 200.00

Pre-teen Tressy, 1963

15" .... $75.00 – 100.00

Tressy family and friends

Cricket

9" .... $35.00 – 40.00

Mary Make-Up, non-grow hair

11½" .... $35.00 – 55.00

Cartwrights, Ben, Hoss, Little Joe, 1966, personality dolls based on characters from the Bonanza television show. MIB dolls will bring double the values here.

9" .... $45.00 – 50.00

ANNALEE MOBILITEE DOLL CO.

1934 to present, Meredith, New Hampshire. Dolls originally designed by Annalee Thorndike, cloth with wire armature "mobilitee" body, painted features.

Early dolls, 1934 – 1960

9" – 10½" .... $350.00 – 450.00

Later dolls, must be in excellent condition with tags

8" skier 1950s. $450.00. Private collection.

10" Folk Hero dolls

Robin Hood & Johnny Appleseed

1983 – 1984... $100.00 – 150.00

Annie Oakley, 1985 .. $100.00 – 150.00

Mark Twain,1986..... $100.00 – 150.00

Ben Franklin, 1987 ... $100.00 – 150.00

Sherlock Holmes, 1988.. $100.00 – 150.00

Abraham Lincoln, 1989...$100.00 – 150.00

Betsy Ross, 1990 ..... $100.00 – 150.00

Christopher Columbus,

1991 .... $100.00 – 150.00

Uncle Sam, 1992 .... $100.00 – 150.00

Pony Express, 1993 .. $100.00 – 150.00

"50's Style" Bean Nose Santa,

1994 .... $100.00 – 150.00

Pocahontas, 1995 .... $100.00 – 150.00

Logo Kid dolls

Milk & Cookies, 1985 .... $675.00

Sweetheart, 1986....... $75.00 – 100.00

Naughty, 1987 .... $75.00 – 100.00

Raincoat, 1988.......... $75.00 – 100.00

Christmas Morning,

1989 .... $75.00 – 100.00

Reading, 1990 .... $75.00 – 100.00

Clown, 1991 .... $35.00 – 50.00

Back to School, 1992.... $35.00 – 50.00

Ice Cream, 1993.......... $35.00 – 50.00

Dress-Up Santa, 1994 .. $35.00 – 50.00
Goin' Fishin', 1995 ...... $35.00 – 50.00
Little Mae Flowers,
    1996 .... $18.00 – 22.00
Tea for Two?, 1997 ...... $18.00 – 22.00
15th Anniversary Kid,
    1998 .... $18.00 – 22.00
Mending My Teddy,
    1999 .... $18.00 – 22.00
Precious Cargo,
    2000 .... $18.00 – 22.00
Mother's Little Helper,
    2001 .... $18.00 – 22.00

MAX OSCAR ARNOLD

1877 – 1930, Neustadt, Thüringia, Germany. Made dressed dolls and mechanical dolls including phonograph dolls.

Baby, *bisque socket head,* composition body
    12"................. $125.00 – 125.00
    16"................. $245.00 – 265.00
    19"................. $430.00 – 480.00

Child

Shoulder head, kid body, open mouth, glass sleep eyes, wigged
    12" – 19"........ $350.00 – 425.00

Bisque socket head, composition body, glass sleep eyes, wigged, molds such as 200, 201, 250, or MOA

High quality bisque
    12"................. $225.00 – 275.00
    15" –18"......... $275.00 – 300.00
    21" – 24"........ $355.00 – 475.00
    32".................. $800.00 – 850.00

Low quality bisque
    15"................. $125.00 – 145.00
    18" – 20"........ $225.00 – 275.00
    24".................. $300.00 – 375.00

ARRANBEE DOLL CO.

8" composition My Dream Baby. $125.00. **Photo courtesy of The Museum Doll Shop.**

1922 – 1958, New York City. Sold to the Vogue Doll Company who continued to use their molds until 1961. Some bisque heads used by Arranbee were made by Armand Marseille and Simon & Halbig. The company also produced composition, rubber, hard plastic, and vinyl dolls.

12" Nancy. $250.00. **Photo courtesy of Joan & Lynette Antique Dolls and Accessories.**

12" Nancy, wigged, with wardrobe. $450.00. **Photo courtesy of American Beauty Dolls.**

My Dream Baby, 1924
Bisque head, made by Armand Marseille: See Armand Marseille section for values.
Composition head, 1927, composition, lower arms and legs, cloth body, metal sleep eyes

11" – 13"	$200.00 – 250.00
17" – 19"	$300.00 – 400.00

Composition
Baby

8"	$100.00 – 125.00
14"	$150.00 – 175.00
23"	$250.00 – 275.00

Bottletot, 1926, all-composition, molded bottle in hand

13"	$175.00 – 195.00
16"	$300.00 – 350.00

Child, 1930s and 1940s, all-composition, mohair wig, marks: "Arranbee" or "R & B"

9"	$100.00 – 125.00
15"	$225.00 – 3275.00

Debu Teen, 1938 on, all-composition

11"	$275.00 – 300.00
14"	$400.00 – 550.00
14", MIB	$2,025.00*
17"	$350.00 – 425.00
21"	$425.00 – 450.00

Skating costume

14"	$225.00 – 250.00
17"	$250.00 – 275.00
21"	$350.00 – 375.00

WAC

18"	$500.00 – 525.00

Kewty, 1934 – 1936, all-composition, mohair wig, marks: "Kewty"

14"	$225.00 – 275.00

Little Angel Baby, 1940s, composition head, cloth body, molded painted hair

11"	$150.00 – 160.00
16"	$275.00 – 300.00
18"	$325.00 – 350.00

Hard Plastic

18"	$325.00 – 350.00

Nancy, 1930s, Patsy-type, all-composition, marks: "Arranbee" or "Nancy"

18" Deb'uteen, all original. $400.00.
Photo courtesy of My Dolly Dearest.

Molded hair, painted eyes

         12".................. $250.00 – 300.00
         17" – 21"........ $300.00 – 450.00

Nancy Lee, all-composition, mohair wig, sleep eyes

         12" – 14"........ $350.00 – 475.00
         16" – 17"........ $400.00 – 575.00

Storybook dolls, 1935, composition dolls

11" Littlest Angel, mint with hang tag. $225.00.
Photo courtesy of McMasters Harris Auction Co.

dressed as storybook charactors

         8½" – 10"....... $175.00 – 195.00

Little Bo Peep with papier-mâché lamb .. $150.00 – 175.00

Hard Plastic & Vinyl

Cinderella, 1952, hard plastic

         14".................. $225.00 – 275.00
         20".................. $375.00 – 400.00

Coty Girl, 1958, vinyl, high heel fashion doll, allow more for rare outfits

         10½".............. $160.00 – 180.00

Lil Imp, 1960, vinyl with red hair and freckles

         10"................... $75.00 – 100.00

14" Nancy Lee Cinderella. $400.00. **Photo courtesy of McMasters Harris Auction Co.**

Littlest Angel, 1956, hard plastic, bent knee walker, mark: "R & B"

         11".................. $125.00 – 200.00

MIB set with storybook............ $425.00*

My Angel, 1961, hard plastic and vinyl

         17"..................... $35.00 – 45.00
         22"..................... $60.00 – 70.00
         36"................. $155.00 – 165.00

Walker, 1957 – 1959

         30"................. $130.00 – 150.00

14" Nanette Walker. $300.00. **Photo courtesy of McMasters Harris Auction Co.**

Vinyl head on oilcloth body, 1959
22".................... $50.00 – 60.00
Nanette, 1949 – 1959, hard plastic, synthetic wig, sleep eyes, closed mouth
14"................. $325.00 – 400.00
17"................. $325.00 – 400.00
Nanette Walker, 1957 – 1959
17"................. $300.00 – 350.00
20"................. $400.00 – 450.00
Nancy, 1951 – 1952, vinyl head with hard plastic body, wigged
14"................. $125.00 – 150.00
18"................. $170.00 – 190.00
Nancy Lee, 1950 – 1959, hard plastic
14" .... $375.00 – 425.00
17"................. $425.00 – 475.00
20"................. $500.00 – 600.00
Nancy Lee Baby, 1952, painted eyes, crying face
15"................. $125.00 – 145.00
Taffy, 1956, Cissy-type
23"................. $145.00 – 165.00

ARTIST DOLLS

Original artist dolls may be one-of-a-kind pieces or limited edition pieces made by the designing artist. Production artist dolls are artist series produced in workshop or factory settings, worked on by people other than the designing artist, often limited edition. Values listed reflect secondary market prices, retail from the artist will differ.

Original Artist Dolls
Martha Armstrong-Hand, porcelain
Babies.............. $1,200.00 – 1,300.00
Children
Brandon, Elizabeth
$450.00 – 500.00
Bob and June Beckett, wood
Children.................. $325.00 – 400.00
Roberta Bell, wood
Historic figures .... $400.00 – 600.00
Halle Blakeley, high-fire clay
Lady dolls............... $600.00 – 700.00
Carol Bowling, cloth over molded form
Child
13"................. $400.00 – 450.00
Frances Bringloe, wood
Pioneer Children
6¼"............... $300.00 – 350.00
Muriel Bruyere, low-fire porcelain
Children
8".................. $200.00 – 250.00

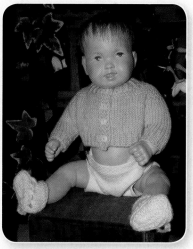

9½" latex baby by Dewees Cochran. $1,800.00. **Photo courtesy of Turn of the Century Antiques.**

9" Andy, wooden doll by Helen Bullard. $400.00. Photo courtesy of Richard Withington, Inc.

Helen Bullard, wood
Original artist dolls ... $350.00 – 500.00
Production artist dolls
  Holly, Barbry Allen
    $200.00 – 250.00
  Tennessee Mountain Kids
    $50.00 – 60.00
Emma Clear, porcelain
China or bisque ladies
    $300.00 – 500.00
George & Martha Washington
  Painted eyes ..... $450.00 – 500.00
  Glass eyes..$700.00 – 800.00 pair
Dewees Cochran, various media: latex composition
Grow Up Series
  18".......... $2,500.00 – 2,600.00
Look Alikes, portrait children
  15" – 16".. $1,000.00 – 1,500.00
  18" – 20".. $1,700.00 – 1,900.00
Production doll, Cindy
  15"................. $500.00 – 600.00
Judith Congdon, porcelain
Black children.......... $250.00 – 400.00
Dianne Dengel, cloth

3½"............... $125.00 – 150.00
20" – 24"....... $225.00 – 275.00
Gertrude Florian, ceramic, composition
Ladies..................... $250.00 – 375.00
Dorothy Heizer, cloth
20th Century Fashion Ladies
    $1,600.00 – 2,000.00
Historic Figures, 10" – 11"
  Men and more simple costumes
    $2,200.00 – 3,200.00
  More elaborate costume (queens, etc.)
    $3,000.00 – 5,000.00
Maggie Head Kane, porcelain
    $400.00 – 450.00
Avis Lee, wood
Americanettes
  11"................. $500.00 – 600.00
Maryanne Oldenburg, porcelain
Children.................. $200.00 – 250.00
Irma Park, wax
Wax over porcelain miniatures
    $200.00 – 375.00
Frances & Bernard Ravca, various media
Crepe paper
  6" – 7".............. $90.00 – 120.00
Cloth, needlesculpted
  Peasants
  10" – 14"........ $100.00 – 150.00
  Other figures
  10" – 14"........ $125.00 – 175.00
Composition, cloth and paper
  Historical figures
  10" – 14".......... $75.00 – 125.00
Kathy Redmond, porcelain
East Indian man with applied turban
  16".......................... $3,550.00*
Ladies
  13" – 14"........ $300.00 – 500.00
Regina Sandreuter, wood
    $550.00 – 650.00
Madeline Saucier, cloth
  15"................. $250.00 – 300.00

Sherman Smith, wood, 5" – 6"
Simple style.............. $250.00 – 325.00
More elaborate .... $375.00 – 500.00
Bisque head on wooden boy
$300.00 – 400.00
Lewis Sorenson, wax
Ladies
14" – 25"........ $800.00 – 900.00
Peddler
18" – 25".. $1,000.00 – 2,000.00
Tamara Steinheil
Victorian lady .... $400.00 – 500.00
Martha Thompson, porcelain
Betsy .... $550.00 – 650.00
Caroline & John .. $525.00 – 575.00 each
Fashion plate ladies
8" – 14".... $1,200.00 – 4,000.00
Little Women .....$600.00 – 800.00 each
Ellery Thorpe, porcelain
Children.................. $400.00 – 500.00
Vargas, wax
Ethnic figures
10" – 11"........ $600.00 – 700.00

Betsy, porcelain by Martha Thompson. $600.00.
Private collection.

Faith Wick, porcelain
$2,500.00 – 2,700.00
Fawn Zeller, porcelain
One-of-a-Kind.... $1,000.00 – 2,000.00
US Historical Society
Holly .... $200.00 – 300.00
Polly II .... $175.00 – 225.00
Production Artist Dolls
Sabine Esche, vinyl by Sigikid
22".................. $250.00 – 300.00
Hildegard Gunzel, various media
Porcelain for Seymour Mann, limited 1,200
26".................. $100.00 – 140.00
Vinyl
Children
24" – 30"........ $150.00 – 200.00
Sonja Hartmann, various media
Porcelain
20".................. $275.00 – 300.00
Vinyl
23".................. $150.00 – 200.00
Philip Heath, vinyl
World of Children Collection
$375.00 – 450.00
Karin Heller, cloth
Children.................. $200.00 – 250.00
Annette Himstedt, 1986 on. Distributed by Timeless Creations, a division of Mattel, Inc. Swivel rigid vinyl head with shoulder plate, cloth body, vinyl limbs, inset eyes, real lashes, molded eyelids, holes in nostrils, human hair wig, bare feet, original in box.
Barefoot Children, 1986, 26"
Bastian .... $275.00 – 375.00
Beckus .... $275.00 – 375.00
Ellen................ $275.00 – 375.00
Fatou............... $275.00 – 375.00
Kathe .... $275.00 – 375.00
Lisa .... $275.00 – 375.00
Paula............... $275.00 – 375.00
The World Children Children, 1988, 31"
Friederike......... $625.00 – 700.00

Miami Miss by Fawn Zeller for UFDC Convention. $200.00. **Photo courtesy of The Museum Doll Shop.**

Kasimir .... $625.00 – 700.00
Makimura .... $625.00 – 700.00
Malin .... $625.00 – 700.00
Michiko .... $625.00 – 700.00
Reflections of Youth, 1989 – 1990, 26"
Adrienne.......... $425.00 – 500.00
Jule, 1992 .... $425.00 – 500.00
Kai.................. $425.00 – 500.00
Mia Yin............ $425.00 – 500.00
Neblina .... $425.00 – 500.00
Tara .... $425.00 – 500.00
Anna I, 1998

26" .... $300.00 – 350.00
World Children's Summit, 2005, Nia, limited 377
35" .... $900.00 – 1,000.00
Ai Lien, 2005
35½" $2,600.00
Too few in database for a reliable range.
Maggie Iacono, cloth
Children .... $500.00 – 650.00
Lee Middleton, vinyl
Babies & toddlers.......... $75.00 – 85.00
Bubba Chubbs
22" .... $175.00 – 200.00
Lynn & Michael Roche, porcelain and wood
Children
17" – 22"..... $800.00 – 1,000.00
Robert Tonner, vinyl
Fashion Models
19" .... $175.00 – 225.00
Robin Woods, 1980s on. Creative designer for various companies, including Le Petit Ami, Robin Woods Company, Madame Alexander (Alice Darling), Horsman, and Playtime Productions.
Cloth
1985, clowns .... $40.00 – 50.00

Golli by R. John Wright, limited edition club doll for 1997. $500.00. **Private collection.**

Vinyl

  2000, Halle Angel, for Home Shopping
  Network
    14".................... $40.00 – 50.00
R. John Wright, cloth
Early Adult Peasant characters
            $900.00 – 1,100.00
Children............... $750.00 – 1,000.00
Christopher Robin and Pooh, 1st edition,
1985
    18".......... $1,200.00 – 1,500.00
Kewpies.................. $450.00 – 500.00
Raggedy Ann........... $500.00 – 525.00
U.F.D.C. Souvenir dolls, various artists for
special events
Xanthos Kontis, 1953, Pa Pitt
    9".................... $125.00 – 150.00
Kathy Redmond, Little Women, porcelain
    12" ....$300.00 – 500.00 each
R. John Wright, felt, 2006 Becassine
            $625.00 – 750.00
Fawn Zeller, porcelain,1961, Miss Miami
            $175.00 – 225.00

ASHTON-DRAKE

Located in Niles, Illinois, Ashton-
Drake is a division of Bradford Industries.
Manufactures dolls designed by a number of
well-known artists. Sells its doll lines through
distributors or via direct mail-order sales to
the public. Doll in perfect condition with
original clothing and tags.
Yolanda Bello
Picture Perfect Babies
Jason, 1985............ $100.00 – 150.00
Heather, 1986 .... $20.00 – 35.00
Jennifer, 1987 .... $20.00 – 35.00
Matthew, 1987 .... $20.00 – 35.00
Amanda, 1988............ $20.00 – 35.00
Sarah, 1989 .... $20.00 – 35.00
Jessica, 1989 .... $20.00 – 35.00

Gene wearing
Mandarin Mood.
$60.00. Photo cour-
tesy of The Museum Doll
Shop.

Michael, 1990............. $20.00 – 35.00
Lisa, 1990 .... $20.00 – 35.00
Emily, 1991................ $20.00 – 35.00
Danielle, 1991............. $20.00 – 35.00
Playtime Babies, 1994
Lindsey........................ $25.00 – 30.00
Shawna .... $25.00 – 30.00
Todd .... $25.00 – 30.00
Lullaby Babies.............. $20.00 – 25.00
Brigitte Duval
Fairy Tale Princesses series
    18"..................... $40.00 – 50.00
Diana Effner
Heroines of Fairy Tale series, 16"
Cinderella................ $100.00 – 120.00
Snow White............. $100.00 – 120.00
Goldilocks .... $100.00 – 120.00
Red Ridinghood........ $100.00 – 120.00
Rapunzel.................. $100.00 – 120.00
What Little Girls Are Made of series, 15"
Sunshine & Lollipops ..... $60.00 – 75.00
Peaches & Cream .... $60.00 – 75.00
Christmas & Candy Canes
            $60.00 – 75.00
Mother Goose series, 14"
Mary Mary................. $60.00 – 75.00

Curl with a Curl .... $60.00 – 75.00
Curly Locks .... $60.00 – 75.00
Snips & Snails .... $60.00 – 75.00
Julie Good-Krueger
Amish Blessings series
Rebeccah .... $40.00 – 50.00
Rachel......................... $40.00 – 50.00
Adam .... $40.00 – 50.00
Joan Ibarolle
Little House on the Prairie series, 1992
– 1995
Laura......................... $60.00 – 100.00
Mary......................... $60.00 – 100.00
Carrie........................ $60.00 – 100.00
Ma & Pa .... $60.00 – 100.00
Baby Grace .... $100.00 – 150.00
Nellie......................... $70.00 – 110.00
Almanzo .... $75.00 – 80.00
Wendy Lawton
Little Women, set of 5,
   16".................. $225.00 – 250.00
Mary Had a Little Lamb . $30.00 – 35.00
Little Bo Peep................ $35.00 – 40.00
Little Miss Muffet........... $35.00 – 40.00
Jenny Lundy
Simple Pleasures series
Gretchen .... $50.00 – 60.00
Molly.......................... $50.00 – 60.00
Others
Josephine, Memoirs of the Original Gibson
Girl, limited 400, vinyl
   15½".............. $325.00 – 375.00
Patty Playpal Re-issues
   35" – 37"........ $150.00 – 200.00
Princess Diana, porcelain
   19".................. $75.00 – 150.00
Mel Odom
GENE
1995, designed by Mel Odom marketed
through Ashton Drake
   Premier, 1st
   1995 .... $350.00 – 450.00

Monaco, 2nd
   1995 .... $40.00 – 50.00
Red Venus, 3rd
   1995 .... $40.00 – 50.00
Other Genes
Bird of Paradise
   1997 .... $60.00 – 75.00
Blue Goddess........ $60.00 – 75.00
Breathless
   1999 .... $60.00 – 75.00
Iced Coffee........... $45.00 – 55.00
Midnight Romance
   1997 .... $50.00 – 65.00
Song of Spain
   1999 .... $50.00 – 75.00
White Hyacinth
   1997 .... $60.00 – 80.00
Gene Specials
Champagne Flight MDCC, limited edition
250
   2002 .... $150.00 – 200.00
Covent Garden, NALED
   1998 .... $40.00 – 55.00
Diamond Evening
   2001 .... $175.00 – 225.00
Dream Girl, Convention
   1998 .... $225.00 – 250.00
Holiday Benefit Gala, limited editon 25
   1998 .... $245.00 – 265.00
King's Daughter, NALED
   1997 .... $60.00 – 75.00
Madra, Gene convention centerpiece, limited
edition100
   2005 .... $300.00 – 320.00
Moments to Remember, MDCC, limited
edition 250
   2000 .... $125.00 – 175.00
Night at Versailles, FAO Schwarz
   1997 .... $50.00 – 90.00
On the Avenue, FAO Schwarz
   1998 .... $100.00 – 130.00
Priceless, FAO Schwarz exclusive

1999 .... $75.00 – 90.00
Sparkling Seduction, NALED
1997 .... $50.00 – 80.00
Titus Tomescu
From This Day Forward bridal series,
1994 .... $60.00 – 70.00
Barely Yours Series
Snug as a Bug in a Rug . $60.00 – 70.00
Clean as a Whistle .... $50.00 – 65.00
Cool as a Cucumber ...... $65.00 – 80.00
Cute as a Button, 1993 .. $60.00 – 70.00
Pretty as a Picture, 1996 . $60.00 – 80.00
Special Delivery .... $50.00 – 65.00
I Am the Way, the Truth, and the Life Collection
Footprints in the Sand
17" .... $65.00 – 85.00

AUTOMATONS

Various manufacturers used many different mediums including bisque, wood, wax, cloth, and others to make dolls that performed some action. More complicated models performing more or complex actions bring higher prices. The unusual one-of-a-kind dolls in this category make it difficult to provide a good range. All these auction prices are for mechanicals in good working order.

Autoperipatetikos, 1860 – 1870s
Bisque, china, or papier-mâché by American Enoch Rice Morrison, key wound mechanism
12" .... $1,100.00 – 1,500.00
With French poupée head. $17,000.00*
Ballerina
Bisque Simon & Halbig mold 1159, key rotates head and arms lower, leg extends, key wound, Leopold Lambert, ca. 1900
20" $4,000.00
Bébé Cage
Bisque Jumeau mold 203, key wound, turns head, hand gives berry to bird, bird flies,

8" keywind clown on a donkey. $2,000.00.
Photo courtesy of Turn of the Century Antiques.

one tune, Leopold Lambert, ca. 1890
19" $13,500.00
Bébé Eventail
Bisque Tété Jumeau, key wound, moves head, lifts flower and fan, plays "La Mascotte," blue silk costume, Leopold Lambert, ca. 1890
19" $12,500.00
Bébé with Fan and Flowers
Bisque Tété Jumeau, key wound, moves hand, fans herself, sniffs flower, plays "Le Petit Bleu," Leopold Lambert, ca. 1892
19" $16,500.00
Bicyclist Coquette by Roullet et Decamps
$12,500.00
Blackamoor musician
Jean Roullet, key wound, plays instrument
Pair $450,000.00*
Clown Équilibriste
Roullet et Descamps, Jumeau head, clown raises his body to do a handstand on the back of the chair, turns head, lifts one arm.
25" $8,812.50
Edison Phonograph Doll
Simon Halbig or Jumeau bisque head doll with mechanism in torso of composition body
Simon Halbig head mold 719
23" .... $4,900.00 – 5,400.00

Garden Tea Party

Three bisque children, painted eyes, move head and arms at tea table on 9" x 9" base

12"............................ $3,050.00

Girl with Hankie

Bisque head by FG, raises hankie to face, head turns and body sways back and forth as music plays, Leopold Lambert, ca. 1890

16"............................ $2,500.00

Laughing Girl with Kitten

Bisque laughing Jumeau socket head, carton torso, key wound mechanism, turns head, smells flower, kitten pulls ribbon, Leopold Lambert, ca. 1890

20"............................ $10,000.00

Little Girl with Marionette Theater

French bisque socket head, key wound, head moves, lifts curtain, stage rotates, shows five different players, Renou, ca. 1900

16½".......................... $16,500.00

Mandolin Player

Girl with a Jumeau head

21" automaton with Simon & Halbig head. $4,700.00.
Photo courtesy of Turn of the Century Antiques.

14"......... $7,000.00 – 10,000.00

Monkey Smoker

Papier-mâché head, smokes a cigarette, Roullet et Descamps

30"....... $18,000.00 – 22,000.00

Nègre Buveur

Roullet et Descamps, papier-mâché head, boy drinking brandy while holding a monkey on his lap

30"............................ $28,200.00

Pushing a Carriage, key wind toy with pressed fabric doll head

Goodwin ... $1,400.00 – 1,600.00

Riding Toy, key wind, fur covered horse with doll, metal with German bisque head, when wound the horse gallops across the floor, heads such as Cowboys, Indians, George Washington

6"................... $450.00 – 500.00

Waltzing Lady, by Steiner

16"........... $5,000.00 – 7,000.00

Walking doll

Roullet et Descamps. Simon Halbig 1078 head

23"........... $2,000.00 – 2,400.00

Steiner

15"......... $8,000.00 – 10,000.00

GEORGENE AVERILL

1913 – 1960s, New York City. Georgene and James Averill began their doll business dressing dolls. Georgene was the designer, James the businessman. They began as Averill Manufacturing Company. In 1915 they trademarked the name "Madame Hendron" for doll designs. In 1923 the Averills ended their association with Averill Manufacturing which continued to make dolls designed by other artists. The Averills also continued to manufacture their own dolls under the name Georgene Novelties.

Allie Dog, bisque head by Alt, Beck & Gottschalk, glass eyes, open mouth with tongue and teeth, mold 1405

    12" – 15".. $7,000.00 – 7,500.00

Baby Dawn, 1950, vinyl with cloth body

    19"................. $300.00 – 325.00

Baby Georgene or Baby Hendron, composition head, arms, and legs, cloth body, marked with name on head

    16"................. $175.00 – 225.00
    20"................. $275.00 – 300.00
    26"................. $475.00 – 525.00

Body Twists, 1927, composition with bale swivel joint in torso

Dimmie & Jimmie

    14½"............. $425.00 – 475.00

Bonnie Babe, 1926 – 1930s, bisque heads made in Germany by Alt, Beck and Gottschalk, cloth bodies made in the USA by K&K toys.

Bisque head, open mouth with two lower teeth, composition or celluloid lower arms and legs, cloth body, molds 1368, 1402

    12"............. $900.00 – 1,000.00
    15"........... $1,000.00 – 1,100.00
    18"........... $1,100.00 – 1,200.00
    22"........... $1,500.00 – 1,600.00

Celluloid head

20" Bonnie Babe. $1,350.00. **Photo courtesy of McMasters Harris Auction Co.**

    10"................. $450.00 – 500.00
    16"................. $625.00 – 675.00

All-bisque Bonnie Babe: See All-bisque, German section.

Brownies, Girl Scouts: See Girl Scout section.

Character animals such as Uncle Wiggley, Nurse Jane, Krazy Kat, and others

    18"................. $450.00 – 550.00

Character or ethnic doll, 1915 on, composition head, cloth or composition body, character faces, painted features

Indian, Sailor, Dutch Boy, etc.

    12"................. $125.00 – 150.00
    16"................. $225.00 – 275.00

Black

    14"................. $375.00 – 400.00

Cloth, 1920s on, molded mask face, painted features, sometimes inset hair eyelashes, yarn hair, cloth body, many dressed in international costumes

    12" – 15"........ $100.00 – 150.00
    18"................. $175.00 – 200.00

Comic Characters, 1944 – 1965, cloth, molded mask face, cloth body, appropriate character clothing

Alvin, Nancy, Sluggo, Little Lulu, etc.

    14"................. $400.00 – 500.00

Becassine, 1950s, French character doll

    13"................. $650.00 – 700.00

Dolly Reckord, 1922 – 1928, composition head, arms, and legs, cloth body with record player inside, human hair wig, sleep eyes, open mouth with teeth

    26"................. $750.00 – 900.00

Grace Drayton designs, 1923, flat faced cloth dolls with painted features, some with yarn hair

Chocolate Drop

    10"................. $350.00 – 400.00
    14"................. $500.00 – 550.00

Dolly Dingle

    11"................. $375.00 – 400.00

Becassine with cloth mask face. $675.00. **Photo courtesy of The Museum Doll Shop.**

15".................. $525.00 – 550.00
Maude Tausey Fangel designs, 1938, flat faced cloth dolls with painted features
Sweets, Snooks, etc.
12" – 14"........ $500.00 – 600.00
15" – 17"........ $625.00 – 675.00
21".................. $750.00 – 800.00
Kris Kringle, cloth mask face
14".................. $175.00 – 200.00
Little Cherub, designed by Harriet Flanders, composition with painted eyes
16".................. $300.00 – 400.00
Mama doll, 1918 on, composition head, arms and swing style legs, cloth body, voice box in torso, molded hair or mohair wig, painted or sleep eyes
15" – 18"........ $200.00 – 300.00
20" – 22"........ $400.00 – 475.00
Peaches, 1928 on, Patsy-type, all-composition, jointed at hips and shoulders, molded hair or wigged, painted eyes or glass, open mouth or closed
14".................. $325.00 – 350.00
17".................. $400.00 – 425.00

Snookums, 1927, child actor at Universal Stern Brothers studio, composition, laughing mouth with two rows of teeth
14".................. $350.00 – 375.00
Sunny Girl, 1927, celluloid head, cloth body, turtle mark
15".................. $375.00 – 425.00
Tear Drop Baby, designed by Dianne Dengel, cloth mask face, molded tear on cheek
16".................. $200.00 – 250.00
Whistling doll, 1925 – 1929, doll made a whistling noise when its head was pushed down
Whistling Dan, etc.
14" – 15"........ $350.00 – 450.00

18" Uncle Wiggley. $500.00. **Photo courtesy of My Dolly Dearest.**

BABYLAND RAG DOLL

Babyland Rag dolls were a line of dolls sold by Horsman from 1893 to 1928. The actual manufacturer of these dolls is still unknown. The dolls were originally marked with paper tags which read "Genuine// Babyland//Trade//Mark." Dolls had flat

20" Babyland rag with hand-painted face. Exceptional condition. $1,900.00.
Photo courtesy of Turn of the Century Antiques.

cloth faces, cloth body, some with mohair wigs. Dolls listed are in good, clean condition with original clothing. Faded, stained or worn examples can bring half the values listed.

Painted face
12" – 15"........ $650.00 – 750.00
18" – 22"..... $800.00 – 1,000.00
30".......... $1,700.00 – 2,000.00
Black
15" – 17"........ $850.00 – 950.00
20" – 22".. $1,300.00 – 1,600.00
Topsy-Turvy
13" – 15"........ $700.00 – 800.00
Lithographed face, 1907 on
12" – 15"........ $450.00 – 500.00
24" – 30"..... $550.00 – 1,000.00
Topsy-Turvy
14"................. $650.00 – 700.00

BADEKINDER

1860 – 1940. Most porcelain factories made china and bisque dolls in one-piece molds with molded or painted black or blond hair, and usually undressed. Sometimes called Bathing Dolls, they were dubbed "Frozen Charlotte" from a song about a girl who went dancing dressed lightly and froze in the snow. They range in size from under 1" to over 19". Some were reproduced in Germany in the 1970s to the present. Allow more for pink tint, extra decoration, or hairdo.

All china
2" – 3"........... $150.00 – 200.00
4" – 5"........... $215.00 – 230.00
6" – 7"........... $245.00 – 265.00
9" – 10"......... $275.00 – 300.00
14" – 15"........ $500.00 – 575.00
Black china
5" – 6"........... $190.00 – 250.00
Blond hair, flesh tones head and neck
9" – 12".......... $500.00 – 800.00
14" – 15"..... $800.00 – 1,000.00
Molded boots
4".................... $225.00 – 225.00
8".................... $275.00 – 300.00
Molded clothes or hats
1½" – 3"......... $250.00 – 375.00
6".................... $300.00 – 350.00
8".................... $425.00 – 475.00
Pink tint, hairdo
3".................... $250.00 – 375.00
5".................... $400.00 – 425.00
13" – 14"........ $600.00 – 700.00
Pink tint, bonnet-head
3".................... $400.00 – 425.00

11½" china. $600.00.
Photo courtesy of Joan & Lynette Antique Dolls and Accessories.

5" .... $500.00 – 550.00
Bisque
Good quality
5" .... $200.00 – 275.00
Fancy hair, molded boots
4" – 5" .... $275.00 – 300.00
Stone bisque, molded hair, one piece
3" .... $18.00 – 25.00
6" .... $30.00 – 40.00
Parian-type, 1860
5" .... $200.00 – 225.00
7" .... $250.00 – 275.00

12" mold 585. $600.00. **Photo courtesy of McMasters Harris Auction Co.**

BÄHR & PRÖSCHILD

1871 – 1930s, Orhdruf, Thüringia, Germany. Porcelain factory that made its own dolls as well as providing heads for companies such as Kley & Hahn, Bruno Schmidt, Heinrich Stier, and others.
Belton-type, 1880 on. Solid dome head with flat crown with small stringing holes in it, closed mouth, paperweight eyes, pierced ears, straight wrists, composition or kid body, molds in the 200 series
12" .... $1,700.00 – 1,800.00
14" – 16".. $1,900.00 – 2,100.00
18" – 20".. $2,500.00 – 2,800.00
Child, 1888, bisque head, open or closed mouth, human hair or mohair wig, composition body in German or French style or kid body, molds 204, 224 239, 246, 252, 273, 275, 277, 286, 289, 293, 297, 309, 325, 332, 340, 343, 379, 394
11" – 14"..... $700.00 – 1,100.00
16" – 18"..... $900.00 – 1,200.00
22" – 24"..... $950.00 – 1,050.00
Kid body
13" – 16"........ $250.00 – 375.00
24" .... $625.00 – 675.00
Mold 224, with dimples
14" – 16"..... $975.00 – 1,025.00
22" – 24".. $1,200.00 – 1,300.00
Character Child
Mold 247, open/closed mouth
26" $2,100.00
Mold 520, closed mouth
13" $2,500.00
Mold 531
19" $2,600.00
Mold 536
18" – 20" ....$3,750.00 – 3,800.00
Mold 592
12" $2,800.00
Mold 604
11" – 14".. $1,100.00 – 1,200.00
18" – 22".. $1,200.00 – 1,500.00
Mold 624, open mouth
17" $2,700.00
Too few in database for a reliable range.
Character Baby, 1909 on, bisque socket head, solid dome or wigged, sleep eyes, open mouth, bent limb body, molds: 585, 586, 587, 602, 604, 619, 620, 624, 630, 641, 678

18" Bahr & Pröschild mold 289. $1,000.00. **Photo courtesy of Cybermogul Dolls.**

9" – 10".......... $300.00 – 425.00
12" – 14"........ $600.00 – 700.00
17" – 19"........ $650.00 – 700.00
22" – 24"........ $825.00 – 900.00
Toddler body
10" – 12"..... $900.00 – 1,000.00
18" – 20".. $1,100.00 – 1,200.00

BARBIE®

Barbie®, 1959 to present, Hawthorne, California, 11½" fashion doll manufactured by Mattel Inc. Values listed are for perfect condition dolls in original clothing and bearing all appropriate tags. Played with and undressed dolls should be valued at one-fourth to one-third the value of perfect. Mint-in-box examples will bring double the values listed here.

Lilli, 1955 – 1964, a German cartoon character, created by Reinhard Beuthien for the tabloid *Bild-Zeitung* in Hamburg, Germany, inspiration for Barbie design
7½ "......... $2,000.00 – 2,600.00
12"........... $2,600.00 – 2,800.00

#1 Barbie®, 1959, heavy, solid vinyl torso, faded to pale white color, white irises, pointed arch eyebrows, soft texture ponytail hairstyle, black and white swimsuit, gold hoop earrings, metal lined holes in bottom of feet and shoes to accept doll stand
Blond............... $5,500.00 – 6,000.00
Brunette............. $6,000.00 – 6,500.00
#2 Barbie®, 1959, doll same as previous doll, but with no holes in feet, some wore pearl earrings
Blond............... $3,300.00 – 3,600.00
Brunette............. $3,600.00 – 3,800.00
#3 Barbie®, 1960, same as previous doll, but now has blue irises and curved eyebrows
Blond...................... $800.00 – 900.00
Brunette................ $900.00 – 1,000.00
#4 Barbie®, 1960, same as previous doll, but torso now has a flesh-tone color
Blond or brunette...... $250.00 – 300.00
#5 Barbie®, 1961, same as previous, but now has a hollow, hard plastic torso, hair is now firmer texture saran
Blond or brunette...... $275.00 – 325.00

12" Bild Lilli, the inspiration for Barbie®. $2,400.00. **Private collection.**

11½" #2 Barbie®. $3,000.00.
Photo courtesy of McMasters Harris Auction Co.

Red-head .... $325.00 – 350.00
#6 Barbie®, 1962, same as previous, but now the doll is available in many more hair and lipstick colors and wears a red swimsuit
$275.00 – 300.00
Swirl Ponytail, 1964, smooth bangs swirled across forehead and to the side instead of the curly bangs of the previous ponytail dolls
$350.00 – 450.00
Bubblecut Barbie®, 1961, same doll as others of this year but with new bubble cut hairstyle
Brown .... $450.00 – 500.00
White Ginger .... $300.00 – 350.00
Others .... $225.00 – 275.00
Side-part bubblecut... $325.00 – 375.00
Barbie® Fashion Queen, 1963, doll has molded hair with a hair band and three interchangeable wigs, gold and white striped swimsuit and turban
$175.00 – 200.00
Miss Barbie®, 1964, doll has molded bendable legs, hair with a hair band and three interchangeable wigs, sleep eyes
$450.00 – 600.00
American Girl Barbie®, 1965, bobbed hairstyle with bangs, bendable legs
$400.00 – 600.00
Side-part American girl with box
$1,800.00*

Color Magic Barbie®, 1966, dolls hair can change color
Blond .... $600.00 – 700.00
Midnight to ruby red . $750.00 – 850.00
Twist N' Turn Barbie®, 1967, swivel jointed at waist .... $300.00 – 450.00
Talking Barbie®, 1968, doll now has pull-string talker .... $150.00 – 175.00
Living Barbie®, 1970, joints at neck, shoulder, elbow, wrist, hip, knee, and ankle
$120.00 – 140.00
Other Barbie® dolls. Dolls listed are in excellent condition, wearing original clothing, Mint-in-box can bring double the values listed.
Angel Face
1983 .... $16.00 – 20.00
Ballerina
1976 .... $35.00 – 45.00
Barbie Baby-sits
1974 .... $20.00 – 40.00
Beach Party
1980 .... $25.00 – 45.00
Beautiful Bride
1976 .... $95.00 – 120.00
Beauty Secrets
1980 .... $20.00 – 30.00
Bicyclin'
1994 .... $15.00 – 20.00
Busy Barbie
1972 .... $95.00 – 130.00
Dance Club
1989 .... $15.00 – 20.00
Day-To-Night
1985 .... $25.00 – 35.00
Doctor
1988 .... $22.50 – 30.00
Dream Barbie
1995 .... $20.00 – 30.00
Fashion Jeans, black
1982 .... $16.00 – 22.00
Fashion Photo

1978 .... $22.50 – 28.00
Free Moving
1975 .... $55.00 – 75.00
Gold Medal Skater
1975 .... $32.50 – 40.00
Golden Dream w/coat
1981 .... $35.00 – 5.00
Growin' Pretty Hair
1971 .... $125.00 – 175.00
Hair Fair
1967 .... $75.00 – 100.00
Hair Happenin's
1971 .... $375.00 – 550.00
Happy Birthday
1981 .... $17.50 – 25.00
Ice Capades, 50th
1990 .... $15.00 – 20.00
Kellogg Quick Curl
1974 .... $25.00 – 32.00
Kissing
1979 .... $15.00 – 20.00
Live Action on Stage
1971 .... $90.00 – 120.00
Loving You
1983 .... $25.00 – 32.00
Magic Curl
1982 .... $17.50 – 25.00
Magic Moves
1986 .... $25.00 – 32.00
Malibu (Sunset)
1971 .... $25.00 – 32.00
My First Barbie
1981 .... $10.00 – 15.00
My Size
1993 .... $55.00 – 75.00
Newport the Sport's Set
1973 .... $62.50 – 82.00
Peaches 'n Cream
1985 .... $18.00 – 22.00
Pink & Pretty
1982 .... $15.00 – 20.00
Rappin' Rockin'

1992 .... $22.50 – 30.00
Rocker
1986 .... $20.00 – 24.00
Roller Skating
1980 .... $22.50 – 30.00
Secret Hearts
1993 .... $12.50 – 18.00
Sensations
1988 .... $25.00 – 30.00
Silkstone Barbie, 2000
Lingerie .... $50.00 – 75.00
Sun Lovin' Malibu
1979 .... $16.00 – 22.00
Sun Valley, The Sports Set
1973 .... $32.50 – 42.00
Super Fashion Fireworks
1976 .... $45.00 – 62.00
Super Size, 18"
1977 .... $100.00 – 130.00
Superstar Promotional
1978 .... $32.50 – 45.00
Talking Busy
1972 .... $130.00 – 162.00
Twinkle Lights
1993 .... $25.00 – 30.00
Walking Lively
1972 .... $100.00 – 130.00

11½" #4 Barbie®.
$275.00. Photo courtesy of
McMasters Harris Auction Co.

11½" Swirl Ponytail Barbie®. $450.00. Photo courtesy of McMasters Harris Auction Co.

Western (3 hairstyles)
1981 .... $25.00 – 30.00
Gift Sets
Mint-in-box prices; add more for NRFB (never removed from box), less for worn or faded.
Barbie Hostess
1966 .... $4,750.00
Beautiful Blues, Sears
1967 .... $3,300.00
Color Magic Gift Set, Sears
1965 .... $2,000.00
Fashion Queen Barbie & Friends
1963 .... $2,250.00
Fashion Queen & Ken Trousseau
1963 .... $2,600.00
Little Theatre Set
1964 .... $5,500.00
On Parade
1960 .... $2,350.00
Party Set
1960 .... $2,300.00
Pink Premier
1969 .... $1,600.00
Round the Clock
1964 .... $5,000.00
Sparkling Pink
1964 .... $2,500.00

Travel in Style, Sears
1964 .... $2,400.00
Trousseau Set
1960 .... $2,850.00
Wedding Party
1964 .... $3,000.00
Store Specials or Special Editions, mint-in-box
Avon Winter Velvet
1996 .... $20.00
Billy Boy Feelin' Groovy
1986 .... $80.00
Bloomingdales
Savvy Shopper
1994 .... $35.00
Donna Karan
1995 .... $45.00
Ralph Lauren
1996 .... $40.00
Bob Mackie
Gold
1990 .... $200.00
Platinum
1991 .... $175.00
Starlight Splendor, black
1992 .... $200.00
Empress
1992 .... $500.00
Neptune Fantasy
1992 .... $300.00
Masquerade Ball
1993 .... $175.00
Queen of Hearts
1994 .... $125.00
Goddess of the Sun
1995 .... $125.00
Moon Goddess
1996 .... $75.00
Madame du Barbie®
1997 .... $300.00
Classique Series
Benefit Ball
1992 .... $30.00

City Style

    1993 .... $35.00

Opening Night

    1994 .... $30.00

Evening Extravaganza

    1994 .... $25.00

Uptown Chic

    1994 .... $30.00

Midnight Gala

    1995 .... $40.00

Disney

Euro Disney

    1992 .... $40.00

Disney Fun

    1993 .... $15.00

Disney World, 25th anniversary

    1996 .... $15.00

FAO Schwarz

Golden Greetings

    1989 .... $40.00

Winter Fantasy

    1990 .... $90.00

Night Sensation

    1991 .... $40.00

Madison Avenue

    1991 .... $50.00

Rockette

    1993 .... $50.00

Silver Screen

    1994 .... $50.00

Jeweled Splendor

    1995 .... $45.00

Great Eras

Gibson Girl

    1993 .... $25.00

Flapper

    1993 .... $30.00

Southern Belle

    1994 .... $25.00

French Lady

    1996 .... $20.00

Hallmark

11½" Bubblecut Barbie®. $275.00.
Photo courtesy of McMasters Harris Auction Co.

Victorian Elegance

    1994 .... $20.00

Sweet Valentine

    1996 .... $20.00

Hills

Party Lace

    1989 .... $25.00

Evening Sparkle

    1990 .... $25.00

Moonlight Rose

    1991 .... $30.00

Blue Elegance

    1991 .... $35.00

Holiday Barbie®

1988, red gown...................... $550.00

1989, white gown................... $125.00

1990, fuchsia gown $75.00

1991, green gown $70.00

1992, silver gown $45.00

1993, red/gold gown $40.00

1994...................................... $38.00

1995...................................... $20.00

1996...................................... $20.00

1997...................................... $20.00

1998...................................... $18.00

1999...................................... $22.00

2000...................................... $35.00

11½" side-part American Girl Barbie®. Sold for $1,800.00 at auction. Photo courtesy of McMasters Harris Auction Co.

2001 .... $38.00
2002 .... $95.00
2003 .... $95.00
2004 .... $95.00
2005 .... $55.00
2006 .... $40.00
2007 .... $40.00

Hollywood Legends
Scarlett O'Hara, red
    1994 .... $40.00
Dorothy, Wizard of Oz
    1994 .... $30.00
Glinda, Good Witch
    1995 .... $35.00
Maria, Sound of Music
    1995 .... $20.00
Home Shopping Club
Evening Flame
    1991 .... $25.00
J.C. Penney
Evening Elegance
    1990 .... $55.00
Enchanted Evening
    1991 .... $55.00

Golden Winter
    1993 .... $35.00
Night Dazzle, blond
    1994 .... $35.00
K-Mart
Peach Pretty
    1989 .... $40.00
Pretty in Purple
    1992 .... $35.00
Little Debbie
    1993 .... $35.00
Mervyns
Ballerina
    1983 .... $75.00
Fabulous Fur
    1986 .... $70.00
Montgomery Ward
#1 Replica, shipping box
    1972 .... $710.00
#1 Replica, pink box
    1972 .... $840.00
Nostalgia Series
35th Anniversary
    1994 .... $50.00
Solo in the Spotlight
    1994 .... $30.00

11½" Live Action Barbie®. $120.00. Photo courtesy of McMasters Harris Auction Co.

Busy Gal
1995 .... $40.00
Enchanted Evening
1996 .... $35.00
Poodle Parade
1996 .... $30.00
Fashion Luncheon
1997 .... $45.00
Prima Ballerina Music Box
Swan Lake, music box
1991 .... $30.00
Nutcracker, music box
1992 .... $30.00
Sears
Celebration, 100th Anniversary
1986 .... $25.00
Star Dream
1987 .... $20.00
Blossom Beautiful
1992 .... $50.00
Ribbons & Roses
1995 .... $20.00
Service Merchandise
Blue Rhapsody
1991 .... $45.00
Satin Nights
1992 .... $30.00
City Sophisticate
1994 .... $30.00
Sea Princess
1996 .... $20.00
Spiegel
Sterling Wishes
1991 .... $30.00
Regal Reflections
1992 .... $50.00
Royal Invitation
1993 .... $30.00
Theatre Elegance
1994 .... $50.00
Target
Gold 'n Lace

Bob Mackie Queen of Hearts.
$125.00. Photo courtesy of My Dolly Dearest.

1989 .... $30.00
Party Pretty
1990 .... $20.00
Golden Evening
1991 .... $35.00
35th Anniversary Barbie
1997 .... $20.00
Barbie & Kelly Easter Egg Hunt set
1997 .... $12.00
Timeless Creations, Stars & Stripes Collection
Air Force
1990 .... $20.00
Navy
1991 .... $25.00
Marine
1992 .... $30.00
Army Gift Set
1993 .... $40.00
Air Force Gift Set
1994 .... $40.00
Toys R Us
Dance Sensation
1985 .... $40.00
Pepsi Spirit
1989 .... $30.00

11½" bendable leg Francie.
$280.00 MIB. Photo courtesy
of McMasters Harris Auction Co.

Vacation Sensation
1989 .... $25.00
Radiant in Red
1992 .... $16.00
Very Violet
1992 .... $25.00
Moonlight Magic
1993 .... $16.00
Harley-Davidson, #1
1997 .... $225.00
Firefighter
1995 .... $75.00
WalMart
Pink Jubilee, 25th Anniversary
1987 .... $25.00
Frills & Fantasy
1988 .... $25.00
Dream Fantasy
1990 .... $25.00
Wholesale Clubs
Party Sensation
1990 .... $20.00
Fantastica
1992 .... $20.00
Royal Romance
1992 .... $65.00
Season's Greetings

1994 .... $55.00
Winter Royale
1994 .... $35.00
After the Walk, Sam's Club
1997 .... $35.00
Country Rose, Sam's Club
1997 .... $40.00
Woolworths
Special Expressions, white
1989 .... $30.00
Sweet Lavender
1992 .... $25.00
Family and other related dolls. Dolls listed
are in excellent condition, wearing original
clothing. Mint-in-box can bring double the
values listed.
Alan, 1964 – 1967
Straight leg .... $75.00 – 100.00
Bendable leg .... $125.00 – 150.00
Buffy & Mrs. Beasley
$75.00 – 100.00
Cara, Quick Curl, 1974, African-American
$75.00 – 85.00
Casey, Twist 'N Turn
1967 .... $75.00 – 85.00
Chris, brunette, bendable leg
1967 .... $70.00 – 90.00
Francie
Bendable leg
1966 .... $125.00 – 140.00
Straight leg
1966 .... $125.00 – 150.00
Twist 'N Turn
1967 .... $150.00 – 165.00
Black
1967 .... $850.00 – 950.00
Malibu
1971 .... $20.00 – 25.00
Growin' Pretty Hair
1971 .... $100.00 – 125.00
Jamie, Walking
1970 .... $150.00 – 170.00

Julia, Twist 'N Turn
1969 .... $130.00 – 150.00
Talking
1969 .... $100.00 – 110.00
Kelly
Quick Curl
1973 .... $70.00 – 80.00
Yellowstone
1974 .... $125.00 – 145.00
Ken, #1, straight leg, blue eyes, hard plastic hollow body, flocked hair, 12", mark: "Ken® MCMLX//by//Mattel//Inc."
1961 .... $110.00 – 150.00
Molded hair
1962 .... $60.00 – 70.00
Bendable legs
1965 .... $75.00 – 100.00
Talking
1968 .... $60.00 – 70.00
Mod Hair
1968 .... $30.00 – 35.00
Busy Talking
1971 .... $80.00 – 100.00
Midge
Straight leg
1963 .... $85.00 – 100.00
No freckles
1963 .... $170.00 – 190.00
Bendable legs
1965 .... $125.00 – 175.00
P.J. Talking
1970 .... $90.00 – 110.00
Twist 'N Turn
1970 .... $110.00 – 130.00
Live Action/Stage
1971 .... $75.00 – 85.00
Ricky, straight legs
1965 .... $75.00 – 85.00
Skipper
Straight leg
1964 .... $85.00 – 100.00
Bendable leg

1965 .... $100.00 – 125.00
Twist 'N Turn
1968 .... $80.00 – 100.00
Living
1969 .... $95.00 – 120.00
Growing Up
1975 .... $35.00 – 40.00
Skooter
Straight leg
1965 .... $65.00 – 75.00
Bendable leg
1966 .... $100.00 – 120.00
Stacey
Talking
1968 .... $100.00 – 120.00
Twist 'N Turn
1968 .... $120.00 – 150.00
Todd, bendable, posable
1966 .... $60.00 – 80.00
Tutti, bendable, posable
1967 .... $100.00 – 150.00
Twiggy, Twist 'N Turn
1967 .... $160.00 – 170.00
Barbie Accessories
Animals
All American (horse)
1991 .... $35.00

11½" straight-leg Midge. $100.00. **Photo courtesy of The Museum Doll Shop.**

11½" bendable-leg Midge. $350.00 MIB.
Photo courtesy of McMasters Harris Auction Co.

Blinking Beauty (horse)
   1988 .... $25.00
Champion (horse)
   1991 .... $40.00
Dancer (horse)
   1971 .... $100.00
Fluff (kitten)
   1983 .... $20.00
Ginger (giraffe)
   1988 .... $30.00
Prancer (horse)
   1984 .... $35.00
Prince (poodle)
   1985 .... $35.00
Snowball (dog)
   1990 .... $35.00
Tahiti (bird w/cage)
   1985 .... $20.00
Cases
Fashion Queen, black, zippered
   1964 .... $150.00
Fashion Queen, round hatbox
   1965 .... $250.00

Miss Barbie, zippered
   1964 .... $160.00
Vanity, Barbie & Skipper
   1964 .... $200.00
Clothing
Name of outfit, stock number; price for mint in package, much less for loose.
Aboard Ship
   1631 .... $550.00
All That Jazz
   1848 .... $350.00
Arabian Knights
   874 .... $495.00
Barbie in Japan
   821 .... $500.00
Beautiful Bride
   1698 .... $2,100.00
Benefit Performance
   1667 .... $1,400.00
Black Magic Ensemble
   1609 .... $420.00
Bride's Dream
   947 .... $350.00
Busy Gal
   981 .... $450.00
Campus Sweetheart
   1616 .... $1,750.00
Cinderella
   872 .... $550.00
Commuter Set
   916 .... $1,400.00
Country Club Dance
   1627 .... $490.00
Dancing Doll
   1626 .... $525.00
Debutante Ball
   1666 .... $1,300.00
Dog 'n Duds
   1613 .... $350.00
Drum Majorette
   875 .... $265.00
Easter Parade

971 .... $4,500.00
Evening Enchantment
1695 .... $595.00
Fabulous Fashion
1676 .... $595.00
Formal Occasion
1697 .... $550.00
Fashion Editor
1635 .... $850.00
Formal Luncheon
1656 .... $1,400.00
Garden Wedding
1658 .... $575.00
Gay Parisienne
964 .... $4,300.00
Glimmer Glamour
1547 .... $5,000.00
Gold 'n Glamour
1647 .... $1,750.00
Golden Glory
1645 .... $495.00
Here Comes the Bride
1665 .... $1,200.00
Holiday Dance
1639 .... $625.00
International Fair
1653 .... $500.00
Intrigue
1470 .... $425.00
Invitation to Tea
1632 .... $600.00
Junior Prom
1614 .... $695.00
Knitting Pretty, pink
957 .... $450.00
Let's Have a Ball
1879 .... $325.00
Little Red Riding Hood
880 .... $625.00
Magnificence
1646 .... $625.00
Make Mine Midi

1861 .... $350.00
Masquerade
944 .... $250.00
Maxi 'n Midi
1799 .... $375.00
Midnight Blue
1617 .... $850.00
Miss Astronaut
1641 .... $700.00
On the Avenue
1644 .... $575.00
Open Road
985 .... $385.00
Pajama Pow
1806 .... $300.00
Pan American Stewardess
1678 .... $5,000.00
Patio Party
1692 .... $375.00
Picnic Set
967 .... $365.00
Plantation Belle
966 .... $600.00
Poodle Parade
1643 .... $985.00

12" straight-leg Ken, molded hair. $70.00.
Photo courtesy of The Museum Doll Shop.

9½" bendable-leg Skipper. $250.00 MIB.
Photo courtesy of McMasters Harris Auction Co.

Rainbow Wraps
  1798 .... $350.00
Reception Line
  1654 .... $600.00
Red Fantastic, Sears
  1817 .... $850.00
Riding in the Park
  1668 .... $625.00
Roman Holiday
  968 .... $5,000.00
Romantic Ruffles
  1871 .... $250.00
Satin 'n Rose
  1611 .... $395.00
Saturday Matinee
  1615 .... $950.00
Sears Pink Formal
  1681 .... $2,450.00
Shimmering Magic
  1664 .... $1,550.00
Sleeping Pretty
  1636 .... $375.00
Smasheroo

1860 .... $275.00
Solo in the Spotlight $200.00
Sorority Meeting
  937 .... $300.00
Suburban Shopper
  969 .... $350.00
Sunday Visit
  1675 .... $595.00
Swirley-Cue
  1822 .... $300.00
Trailblazers
  1846 .... $250.00
Travel Togethers
  1688 .... $300.00
Tunic 'n Tights
  1859 .... $300.00
Under Fashions
  1655 .... $695.00
Velveteens, Sears
  1818 .... $850.00
Weekenders, Sears
  1815 .... $950.00

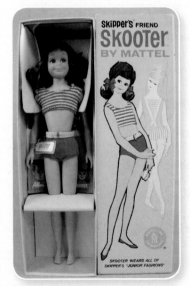

9½" straight-leg Skooter. $150.00 MIB.
Photo courtesy of McMasters Harris Auction Co.

Wedding Wonder
1849 ....$375.00
Wild 'n Wonderful
1856 ....$300.00
Furniture, Suzy Goose
Canopy Bed, display box
1960s $250.00
Chifferobe, cardboard box
1960s $250.00
Queen Size Bed, pink
1960s $600.00
Vanity, pink $75.00
Vehicles
Austin Healy, beige
1964 ....$3,300.00
Beach Bus
1974 ....$45.00
Mercedes, blue-green
1968 ....$450.00
Speedboat, blue-green
1964 ....$1,100.00
Sport Plane, blue
1964 ....$3,000.00
Sun 'n Fun Buggy
1971 ....$150.00
United Airlines
1973 ....$75.00

E. BARROIS

1846 – 1877, Paris, France. Assembled, sold, and distributed lady-type dolls with bisque heads, closed mouths, on kid and cloth bodies. It is still largely unknown which French and German porcelain factories made heads for Barrois, although it is known that the heads Barrois supplied to Steiner and Blampoix were made by Frayon.
Mark: EB
Poupée (Fashion-type)
Painted eye
14" – 16".. $1,800.00 – 2,200.00

19" – 21".. $2,600.00 – 3,000.00
Glass eye
14" – 16".. $4,000.00 – 4,800.00
19" – 21".. $4,000.00 – 4,400.00
23" – 24".. $4,600.00 – 4,800.00

BELTON-TYPE

1875 on, made by various German manufacturers including Bähr & Pröschild, Kestner, Simon & Halbig, and others. Solid dome bisque socket head doll with small holes in crown for stringing and/or wig application. Paperweight eyes, straight wristed wood and composition body, closed mouth, pierced ears. Belton-type is a name applied to this type of doll by modern doll collectors and is not a reference to a specific maker. Mark: none or mold numbers only.
Bru-look face
12" – 14".. $2,000.00 – 2,200.00
French-Trade, dolls with a French look that were manufactured for the French market, some mold 137, 138
9" – 15".... $1,100.00 – 3,000.00
18" – 20".. $1,800.00 – 3,000.00

20" French-trade Belton. $3,000.00.
Photo courtesy of Richard Withington, Inc.

22" – 24" .... $3,000.00 – 3,200.00
German look dolls
  8" .... $800.00 – 850.00
  12" – 15" ..... $900.00 – 1,250.00
  18" – 20" .. $1,800.00 – 2,000.00
Mold 200: See Bähr & Pröschild listing.

C.M. BERGMANN

1888 – 1931, Walterhausen, Thuringia, Germany. Doll factory that distributed in the United States through L. Wolfe & Co. Bergmann had bisque doll heads made for them by Alt, Beck & Gottschalk, Armand Marseille, Simon & Halbig, and others. Registered trademarks: Cinderella 1897, Columbia 1904, My Gold Star 1926. Dolls listed are in good condition, appropriately dressed.

Character Babies, bisque socket head on bent-limb composition body
Open mouth
  12" – 14" .... $275.00 – 325.00
  15" – 18" .... $375.00 – 575.00
Mold 612, open/closed mouth
  15" .... $2,000.00 – 2,200.00
Mold 134, character toddler
  12" .... $950.00 – 1,000.00

25" C.M. Bergman doll. $450.00. **Photo courtesy of Atlanta Antique Gallery.**

Child, bisque socket head, open mouth, wigged, sleep or set eyes, ball-jointed composition body, mold 1916 or others, some marked with Simon Halbig/Bergman mark
  10" .... $150.00 – 275.00
  14" – 16" .... $325.00 – 350.00
  20" – 24" .... $400.00 – 600.00
  26" – 28" .... $500.00 – 575.00
  30" – 32" .... $400.00 – 525.00
  42" .... $1,100.00 – 1,300.00
Flapper-type body
  12" .... $625.00 – 650.00
  16" .... $1,100.00 – 1,200.00
Eleonore
  18" .... $550.00 – 600.00
  25" .... $700.00 – 800.00

BETSY MCCALL

Dolls based on *McCall's Magazines* paper doll Betsy McCall. Dolls listed are in excellent condition wearing original clothing, mint-in-box can bring double the values listed.

Ideal Toy Corp., 1952 – 1953
Doll with vinyl head, on a hard plastic Toni body, saran wig
  14" .... $150.00 – 200.00
1958, vinyl, four hair colors, rooted hair, flat feet, slim body, round sleep eyes, may have swivel waist or one-piece torso, mark: "McCall 19©58 Corp." in circle
  14" .... $100.00 – 200.00
1959, vinyl, rooted hair, slender limbs, some with flirty eyes, one-piece torso, mark: "McCall 19©58 Corp." in a circle
  19" – 20" .... $200.00 – 275.00
1961, vinyl, five colors of rooted hair, jointed wrists, ankles, waist, blue or brown sleep eyes, four to six outfits available, mark: "McCall 19©61 Corp." in a circle
  22" .... $125.00 – 175.00

29"................. $200.00 – 225.00

American Character Doll Co., 1957 to 1963, 8" hard plastic doll with jointed knees, sleep eyes, molded eyelashes, metal barrettes in hair. First year these dolls had mesh cap saran wigs and plastic pin joints in knees. Second year they had vinyl skull-caps on their wigs and metal knee pins.

11½" Betsy by Uneeda Doll Co. $200.00. **Photo courtesy of McMasters Harris Auction Co.**

In undies .... $225.00 – 250.00
In street dress .... $225.00 – 300.00
In formalwear .... $325.00 – 375.00
Doll in bedroom carrying case
$1,000.00*

8" doll clothing
Dresses .... $35.00 – 65.00
Shoes and socks .... $28.00 – 30.00
Boxed outfit .... $100.00 – 125.00
Vinyl doll, 1958 on, jointed at shoulder, neck & hip, sleep eyes

14"................. $350.00 – 475.00
20"................. $350.00 – 450.00
30"................. $550.00 – 600.00
36"................. $650.00 – 750.00

Additional joints at wrists, waist, knees, and ankles

22"................. $300.00 – 375.00
29"................. $400.00 – 475.00

Companion-size Betsy McCall, 1959, vinyl, rooted hair, mark: "McCall Corp//1959" on head

14" Betsy by Ideal Novelty & Toy Co, vinyl head hard plastic Toni body. $175.00. **Photo courtesy of McMasters Harris Auction Co.**

34"................. $400.00 – 500.00
Linda McCall (Betsy's cousin), 1959, vinyl, Betsy face, rooted hair, mark: "McCall Corp//1959" on head

34"................. $400.00 – 500.00
Sandy McCall (Betsy's brother), 1959, vinyl, molded hair, sleep eyes, red blazer, navy shorts, mark: "McCall 1959 Corp."; tag reads "I am Your Life Size Sandy McCall"

35"................. $450.00 – 550.00

Uneeda
1964, vinyl, rooted hair, rigid vinyl body, brown or blue sleep eyes, slim pre-teen body, wore mod outfits, some mini-skirts, competitor of Ideal's Tammy, mark: none

11½".............. $125.00 – 225.00

Horsman
1974, vinyl with rigid plastic body, sleep eyes, came in Betsy McCall Beauty Box with extra hair piece, brush, bobby pins on card, eye pencil, blush, lipstick, two sponges, mirror, and other accessories, mark: "Horsman Doll Inc.//19©67" on head; "Horsman Dolls Inc." on torso

12½"................. $35.00 – 50.00

1974, vinyl with rigid plastic teen type body, jointed wrists, sleep eyes, lashes, rooted hair with side part (some blond with pony-tails), closed mouth, original clothing marked "BMc" in two-tone blue box marked "©1974//Betsy McCall — she WALKS with you," marks: "Horsman Dolls 1974"

29".................. $200.00 – 225.00

Rothchild

1986, 35th anniversary Betsy, hard plastic, sleep eyes, painted lashes below eyes, single stroke eyebrows, tied ribbon emblem on back, marks: hang tag reads "35th Anniversary//BetsyMcCall//by Rothschild (number) 'Betsy Goes to a Tea Party,' or 'Betsy Goes to the Fair,'" box marked "Rothchild Doll Company//Southboro, MA 01722"

8"....................... $25.00 – 35.00

Robert Tonner

1996 to present, vinyl (some porcelain), rooted hair, rigid vinyl body, glass eyes, closed smiling mouth, mark: "Betsy McCall//by//Robert Tonner//©Gruner & Jahr USA PUB." Values below are secondary market prices, dolls still available at retail as well.

8"

In undies.............. $20.00 – 30.00
Dressed .... $35.00 – 60.00
14"...................... $40.00 – 75.00
29"...................... $70.00 – 85.00

BING ART DOLLS

8" boy by Bing. $325.00.
Doll courtesy of Elaine Holda.

Germany, 1921 – 1932. Gebrüder Bing was founded in 1882. In 1921 it became a part of a conglomerate called the Bing Werke Corporation, this is when they began making their cloth "art dolls." Molded cloth face, sometimes with a heavy coating of gesso giving a composition appearance, cloth head and body, oil-painted features, wigged or painted hair, pin-jointed at neck, shoulders, and hips, seams down front of legs, mitt hands.

Painted hair or wigged, cloth or felt, unmarked or "Bing" on bottom of foot

8" – 10".......... $325.00 – 400.00
13"................. $450.00 – 500.00
15"................. $750.00 – 850.00

BISQUE, UNKNOWN OR LITTLE KNOWN MAKERS

Various manufacturers of bisque headed child dolls working from 1870 on. No separate listing for these makers. No damage, appropriately dressed.

French

Unknown Maker

Early desirable very French-style face, marks such as "J.D.," "J.M. Paris," and "H. G." (possibly Henri & Granfe-Guimonneau)

17"....... $17,000.00 – 18,000.00
21"....... $19,000.00 – 21,000.00
27"....... $25,000.00 – 27,000.00

Jumeau or Bru style face, may be marked "W. D." or "R. R."

13" – 14".. $3,000.00 – 3,400.00
19"........... $3,000.00 – 3,500.00
24"........... $4,600.00 – 4,900.00

27".......... $5,000.00 – 5,250.00
Closed mouth, marks: "J," "137," "136," or others
    Excellent quality, unusual face
    10" – 12".. $3,200.00 – 3,600.00
    15" – 17".. $4,200.00 – 5,200.00
    23" – 25".. $6,200.00 – 8,000.00
    Standard quality, excellent bisque
    13".......... $2,200.00 – 2,450.00
    18".......... $3,200.00 – 3,450.00
    23".......... $4,300.00 – 4,500.00
    Lesser quality, may have poor painting and/or blotches on cheeks
    15".......... $1,100.00 – 1,200.00
    21".......... $1,600.00 – 1,800.00
    26".......... $2,100.00 – 2,300.00
Open mouth
    Excellent quality, ca. 1890 on, French body
    15".......... $1,300.00 – 1,500.00
    18".......... $2,100.00 – 2,300.00
    21".......... $2,300.00 – 2,400.00
    24".......... $3,000.00 – 3,100.00
High cheek color, ca. 1920s, may have five-piece papier-mâché body
    15".................. $575.00 – 625.00
    19".................. $750.00 – 800.00
    23".................. $900.00 – 950.00
Known Makers
Danel et Cie., 1889 – 1895, Paris, France. Bisque socket head on composition body, paperweight eyes, wigged, pierced ears
    Paris Bébé
    15".......... $4,000.00 – 4,500.00
    18".......... $5,000.00 – 5,500.00
    22".......... $6,500.00 – 7,000.00
    24".......... $8,000.00 – 8,500.00
    28"....... $10,000.00 – 12,000.00
    Bébé Francaise
    14".......... $3,500.00 – 3,600.00
    20".......... $4,300.00 – 4,400.00
Delcroix, Henri, 1887, Paris and Montreuil

13½" W.D. closed mouth doll. $3,000.00.
Photo courtesy of Richard Withington, Inc.

sous Bois. Pressed bisque socket head, closed mouth, paperweight eyes, marked Pan Bébé
    12"....... $10,000.00 – 14,000.00
    18" ...... $15,000.00 – 20,000.00
Falck & Roussel, 1880s, socket head, closed mouth, paperweight eyes, wood and composition body, marked: F.R.
    15" – 16"..$12,000.00 – 14,000.00
    18"....... $16,000.00 – 17,000.00
Halopeau, A., 1881 – 1889, Paris, pressed bisque socket head, closed mouth, paperweight eyes, cork pate, French wood and composition body, marked: H
    16" – 18"..$60,000.00 – 70,000.00
    21" – 24".. $95,000.00 – 125,000.00
Lefebvre et Cie., Alexander, 1975, pressed bisque socket head, closed mouth, paperweight eyes, French wood and composition body, marked: A.L.
    22"......................... $35,000.00
Too few in database for a reliable range.
Joanny, Joseph Louis, 1888, pressed bisque socket head, closed mouth, paperweight eyes, French wood and composition body, marked: J.

12" – 15".. $5,400.00 – 7,500.00
17" – 18".. $8,000.00 – 8,300.00
23"........... $9,500.00 – 9,600.00

J.M. Bébé 0, 1880s, pressed bisque socket head, closed mouth, paperweight eyes, French wood and composition body, marked: J.M.

19".............................$3,222.00
26" $9,000.00

Too few in database for a reliable range.

M. Bebe, 1890s, pressed bisque socket head, closed mouth, paperweight eyes, pierced ears, French wood and composition body, marked: M with size number

12" – 14".. $3,000.00 – 4,000.00
19" – 23".. $2,900.00 – 3,900.00

Marque, Albert, 1914, fewer than 100 dolls are believed to have been made

21" – 22"..... $175,000.00 and up

May Frères Cie, 1890 – 1897, later Steiner (1898 on), closed mouth paperweight eyes, pierced ears, composition body, marked: Bébé Mascotte

19" – 20".. $4,000.00 – 6,000.00

Mothereau, Alexandre, 1880 – 1895, pressed bisque socket head, closed mouth, paperweight eyes, French wood and composition body, marked: B.M.

12" – 15"..$16,000.00 – 18,000.00
22" – 24"..$20,000.00 – 22,000.00
28" – 29"..$23,000.00 – 25,000.00

Pannier, 1875, pressed bisque socket head, closed mouth, paperweight eyes, French wood and composition body, marked: C.P.

20"............................$59,000.00

Too few in database for a reliable range.

Petite et Dumontier, 1878 – 1890, Paris. Pressed bisque socket head, closed mouth, paperweight eyes, French wood and composition body, some with metal hands, marked: P. D. with size number

16"....... $10,000.00 – 11,000.00

18" – 19"..$12,000.00 – 14,000.00
23"....... $15,000.00 – 16,000.00

Pintel et Godchaux, 1880 – 1889, Montreuil, France, pressed bisque socket head, closed mouth, paperweight eyes, French wood and composition body, trademark: Bébé Charmant

20" – 22".. $4,000.00 – 5,000.00

Open mouth

18" – 20".. $1,700.00 – 1,900.00

German

Various German manufacturers of bisque headed dolls working from 1870 on. No separate listing for these makers. Marks: May be unmarked or only a mold or size number or Germany.

Baby

Character Baby, 1910 on, solid dome or wigged, open mouth, glass eyes, bent-limb composition body, marks: G.B., P.M. (Porzellanfabrik Mengersgereuth), F.B., or unmarked

9" – 12".......... $300.00 – 500.00
14" – 16"........ $525.00 – 600.00
19" – 21"........ $650.00 – 700.00

11" bisque shoulder head doll marked "Made in Germany." $175.00. **Photo courtesy of The Museum Doll Shop.**

My Sweet Baby
23" toddler ..$1,100.00 – 1,200.00
Newborn Baby, 1924, bisque head on cloth body, bisque or celluloid hands, marks: Baby Weygh, IV, others.
    10" – 12"........ $225.00 – 275.00
    14" – 17"........ $400.00 – 425.00
    Gerling Baby
    17"................. $575.00 – 625.00
Dolly face child, 1880 on, bisque socket-head, wigged, glass eyes, open mouth, ball-jointed composition body or kid body with bisque lower arms, mark: G.B., K inside H, L.H.K., P.Sch, D.& K., and or unmarked
    8" – 10" .... $200.00 – 300.00
    12" – 15"........ $300.00 – 350.00
    18" – 20"........ $400.00 – 475.00
    23" – 25"........ $425.00 – 475.00
    Mold 50, 51, square teeth
    14" – 16".. $1,000.00 – 1,100.00
    Mold 422, 444, 457, 478
    17"................. $600.00 – 650.00
    23"................. $800.00 – 825.00
    My Girlie, My Dearie, Pansy, Princess,
    Special, Sweetheart, Viola, G.&S.,
    MOA, A.W.
    13"................. $350.00 – 375.00
    18" – 20"........ $275.00 – 325.00
    22" – 24" .... $350.00 – 400.00
    26" – 28" .... $425.00 – 475.00
    32"................. $550.00 – 600.00
Shoulder head, wigged, 1880 – 1890, glass eyes, open mouth, kid or cloth body, special and other molds or no mold mark
    10" – 12"........ $150.00 – 250.00
    15" – 17"........ $250.00 – 350.00
    20" – 23"........ $275.00 – 375.00
Closed mouth
    Mold 50, shoulder head
    14" – 16"........ $450.00 – 650.00
    22" – 24".. $1,200.00 – 1,275.00
    Mold 120, 126, 132, Bru-look

7" German bisque socket head dolly faced doll on five-piece composition body. $400.00. **Photo courtesy of The Museum Doll Shop.**

    13".......... $2,500.00 – 2,600.00
    19" – 21".. $3,800.00 – 4,000.00
    Mold 51, swivel neck shoulder head
    17".............. $950.00 – 1,100.00
    German-look doll, composition body
    11" – 13".. $1,200.00 – 1,300.00
    16" – 18".. $1,600.00 – 1,800.00
    Mold 136, French-look
    12" – 14".. $1,900.00 – 2,000.00
    19" – 20".. $1,600.00 – 1,700.00
    E.G., maker Ernst Grossman
    16".......... $2,500.00 – 2,600.00
Shoulder head with molded hair, 1880 on
    American Schoolboy-type
    12" – 14"........ $375.00 – 425.00
    18" – 20"........ $500.00 – 650.00
Small Child, 1890 to mid 1910s, bisque socket head, open mouth, set or sleep eyes, five-piece composition body
    High quality bisque
    5"................... $350.00 – 400.00
    8"................... $400.00 – 450.00
    Fully jointed body
    7" – 8"............ $600.00 – 650.00
    Closed mouth
    4" – 5"............ $475.00 – 500.00

16" PM baby by P.M. Porzellanfabrik Mengersgereuth. $550.00. **Photo courtesy of Cybermogul Dolls.**

8"..................... $750.00 – 800.00
Character, 1910 on, glass eyes, open or open/closed mouth, solid dome or wigged, composition body
Mold 125, smiling
　13"........... $6,000.00 – 6,500.00
Mold 159
　23"........... $1,100.00 – 1,200.00
Mold 213, 214, maker Bawo & Dotter
　13" – 14".. $4,900.00 – 5,200.00
Mold 221, toddler
　16"........... $2,500.00 – 2,600.00
Mold 411, shoulder head lady
　14"............................. $3,500.00
Too few in database for a reliable range.
Mold 838, P.M. Coquette
　11"................. $550.00 – 575.00
K&K Mama doll, 1924, German bisque shoulder head, American made cloth Mama style body with composition limbs, glass eyes, made for George Borgfeldt
　15" – 23"........ $250.00 – 375.00
Wolfe, Louis & Co., 1870 – 1930 on,

Sonneberg, Germany, Boston, and New York City. Made and distributed dolls, also distributed dolls made for them by other companies such as Hertel Schwab & Co. and Armand Marseille. They made composition as well as bisque dolls and specialized in babies and Red Cross nurses before World War I. May be marked "L.W. & C."
Baby, open or closed mouth, sleep eyes
　12"................. $400.00 – 475.00
　22" toddler body
　　　$1,000.00 – 1,100.00
　26"................. $675.00 – 725.00
　Sunshine Baby, solid dome, cloth body, glass eyes, closed mouth
　15"........... $1,000.00 – 1,300.00
Too few in database fro a reliable range.
Japanese
1915 on, Japan. Bisque head dolls often in imitation of the German bisque dolls. Distributed in the United States by companies such as Morimura Brothers, Yamato

26" doll marked LWC 152 for Louis Wolfe. $725.00. **Photo courtesy of Cybermogul Dolls.**

19" Morimura Bros. character baby. $250.00.
Photo courtesy of The Museum Doll Shop.

Importing Co., and others, marks: 1915 to 1921 marked Nippon, after 1921 marked Japan.

Character baby, bisque socket head, solid dome or wigged, open mouth with teeth, bent limb composition body

```
11" – 12"........ $200.00 – 300.00
13" – 15"........ $175.00 – 225.00
19" – 21"........ $300.00 – 375.00
```

Hilda look-alike

```
13".................................$600.00
19"................................$900.00
```

Heubach pouty look-alike, 300 series

```
17" ................ $800.00 – 900.00
```

Child, bisque head, mohair wig, glass sleep eyes, open mouth, composition or kid body

```
9" – 11".......... $175.00 – 250.00
13" – 15"........ $250.00 – 275.00
19" – 21"........ $300.00 – 500.00
```

BLACK OR BROWN DOLLS

Dolls both homemade and made by various European and American manufacturers. Shades range from black to tan. Sometimes Caucasian mold in dark color, other times ethnic sculpted mold was used. Dolls listed are in good condition, appropriately dressed.

All-bisque

Glass eyes, wigged

```
4" – 5"............ $450.00 – 575.00
```

Hertwig, character

```
2½"................... $85.00 – 100.00
```

Gebruder Kunlenz

```
3½" – 5"......... $650.00 – 750.00
```

Kestner, swivel neck

```
6".............. $1,800.00 – 1,900.00
```

Simon & Halbig, 886

```
5" – 7"...... $1,400.00 – 1,800.00
```

Bisque, 1880 on, French and German makers. Bisque socket head, painted black or black color in slip, brown composition or kid body

French

Poupée (Fashion-type), kid body

Unmarked

```
14" – 15".. $3,000.00 – 3,400.00
```

14" Armand Marseille 341. $825.00.
Photo courtesy of Richard Withington, Inc.

8" Hanna South Sea Baby by Schoenau Hoffmeister. $425.00. **Photo courtesy of The Museum Doll Shop.**

FG
14".......... $3,400.00 – 3,600.00
Bru
14"......................... $19,000.00*
17"......... $9,500.00 – 10,000.00
Jumeau
15".......... $8,500.00 – 9,000.00
Bébé
B.M., closed mouth
15" portrait.............. $24,000.00*
Bru
Circle Dot
17" – 19"
$30,000.00 – 50,000.00
Bru Jne
23"....... $33,000.00 – 35,000.00
Danel et Cie
19"............................ $6,250:00*
E.D., open mouth
16".......... $2,300.00 – 2,400.00
22".......... $2,600.00 – 2,700.00
Eden Bebe, open mouth
15".......... $2,300.00 – 2,500.00
Gaultier, Francois, closed mouth
12".......... $5,000.00 – 6,000.00
Hulss, Adolf
Mold 156 baby
15"............................. $850.00*
Jumeau

E.J., closed mouth
15" – 17".. $8,200.00 – 9,300.00
Tété, open mouth
10".......... $1,800.00 – 2,100.00
15".......... $2,500.00 – 2,700.00
20".......... $3,200.00 – 3,300.00
Tété, closed mouth
15".......... $4,500.00 – 4,700.00
18".......... $4,900.00 – 5,100.00
22" – 24".. $5,200.00 – 6,500.00
DEP, open mouth
16".......... $2,400.00 – 2,600.00
Lanternier
18" – 20".. $1,000.00 – 1,300.00
Mothereau
15" – 16"..$16,500.00 – 18,000.00
Paris Bebe, closed mouth
13".......... $3,900.00 – 4,300.00
16".......... $4,500.00 – 4,600.00
19".......... $5,300.00 – 5,500.00
S.F.B.J.
Molds 226, 235
15" – 17".. $2,600.00 – 3,000.00
Mold 237 .... $16,500.00*
Molds 301, 60 (Unis France mark .
also), jointed composition body, open
mouth
8" – 10".......... $225.00 – 375.00

8" Kämmer & Reinhardt. $400.00 **Doll courtesy of Elaine Holda.**

7" German bisque American Indian, maker unknown. $175.00.
Photo courtesy of The Museum Doll Shop.

14" – 17"........ $450.00 – 675.00
Steiner
Figure A series, closed mouth
10" – 11".. $4,000.00 – 4,800.00
14"............................ $5,000.00
18" – 22".. $6,500.00 – 7,000.00
Open mouth
13".......... $4,200.00 – 4,400.00
16".......... $4,600.00 – 4,900.00
Series C
18".......... $6,000.00 – 6,200.00
21".......... $6,400.00 – 6,600.00
No mold #
15"......................... $10,500.00*
German
Unmarked
Closed mouth
10 – 11"......... $325.00 – 375.00
14"................. $425.00 – 475.00
17"................. $575.00 – 625.00
21"................. $825.00 – 875.00
Open mouth
10"................. $550.00 – 600.00
13"................. $700.00 – 750.00
15"................. $900.00 – 950.00
Painted bisque
Closed mouth
16"................. $400.00 – 450.00
19"................. $550.00 – 600.00
23".............. $900.00 – 1,000.00

Open mouth
14"................. $325.00 – 375.00
18"................. $525.00 – 575.00
Ethnic features
15".......... $3,000.00 – 3,200.00
18".......... $3,800.00 – 4,000.00
Bähr & Pröschild, open mouth, mold 277, ca. 1891
10"................. $850.00 – 900.00
12".......... $1,100.00 – 1,300.00
Mold 244, Indian or native
14" – 16".. $2,100.00 – 2,300.00
Bye-Lo Baby
16".......... $2,700.00 – 3,000.00
Handwerck, Heinrich, mold 79, 119
Open mouth
12"................. $800.00 – 900.00
18" – 21".. $1,600.00 – 1,900.00
29".......... $2,500.00 – 2,600.00
Heubach, Ernst (Koppelsdorf)
Mold 271, 1914, shoulder head,
painted eyes, closed mouth
10"................. $425.00 – 475.00
Mold 320, 339, 350
10"................. $375.00 – 425.00
13"................. $500.00 – 525.00
18"................. $650.00 – 700.00

22" Kämmer & Reinhardt. $1,400.00.
Photo courtesy of Cybermogul Dolls.

18" Schoenau & Hoffmeister mold 1909. $750.00. Photo courtesy of Joan & Lynette Antique Dolls and Accessories.

Mold 399, allow more for toddler

10" – 14"........ $475.00 – 575.00

17"................. $650.00 – 700.00

Mold 414

9"................... $340.00 – 450.00

14"........................... $1,100.00*

17"................. $715.00 – 950.00

Mold 418 (grin)

9"................... $675.00 – 725.00

14"................. $850.00 – 900.00

Mold 444, 451

9"................... $250.00 – 300.00

14"................. $550.00 – 600.00

Mold 452, brown

7½"............... $425.00 – 475.00

10"................. $525.00 – 600.00

15"................. $675.00 – 700.00

Mold 458

10"................. $465.00 – 495.00

15"................. $700.00 – 775.00

Mold 463

12"................. $650.00 – 750.00

16"............. $950.00 – 1,050.00

Mold 473

13"................. $425.00 – 475.00

Mold 1900

14"................. $500.00 – 600.00

17"................. $675.00 – 775.00

Heubach, Gebruder, Sunburst mark

Boy, eyes to side, open-closed mouth

12" – 14".. $2,300.00 – 2,500.00

Mold 7657, 7658, 7668, 7671

9"............... $975.00 – 1,200.00

13"........... $1,400.00 – 1,700.00

Mold 7620, 7661, 7686

10"........... $1,800.00 – 2,100.00

14"........... $3,500.00 – 4,000.00

17"........... $4,100.00 – 4,200.00

Molds 8457, 9467, Indians

14"........... $2,400.00 – 2,500.00

Kämmer & Reinhardt (K * R)

Child, no mold number

14" –16"...... $800.00 – 1,000.00

17" – 19".. $1,000.00 – 1,200.00

Mold 100

10" – 11"........ $850.00 – 950.00

17" – 20".. $1,600.00 – 1,900.00

Mold 101, painted eyes

15" – 18".. $3,300.00 – 3,500.00

Mold 101, glass eyes

15" – 17".. $4,300.00 – 4,800.00

Mold 114

13"........... $5,000.00 – 5,500.00

Mold 116, 116a

15"........... $4,000.00 – 4,500.00

19"........... $5,900.00 – 6,200.00

Mold 122, 126, baby body

12"................. $700.00 – 750.00

18" homemade black cloth doll. $1,600.00. Photo courtesy of Richard Withington, Inc.

1996 Molly Golli and Peg made by Steiff. Limited Edition of 2,500. $450.00. **Private Collection.**

18"........... $1,000.00 – 1,125.00
Mold 126, toddler
18"........... $1,400.00 – 1,600.00
Mold 192, open mouth child
12".............. $900.00 – 1,100.00
Kestner, J. D.
   Baby, no mold number, open mouth, teeth
   10"............................... $1,500.00
Too few in database for a reliable range.
   Hilda, mold 245
   12" – 14".. $2,800.00 – 3,100.00
   18"........... $4,000.00 – 4,500.00
   Child, no mold number
   Closed mouth
   14".............. $900.00 – 1,100.00
   17"........... $1,500.00 – 1,700.00
   Open mouth
   12"............... $550.00 – 6255.00
   16" – 18"..... $750.00 – 1,100.00
   Five-piece body
   9".................... $285.00 – 300.00
   12"................. $350.00 – 400.00
   Long face with letter mark, open mouth
   18" – 19".. $2,000.00 – 2,500.00
Knoch, Gebruder, mold 185 dolly face child, five-piece composition body
   8" – 10".......... $100.00 – 125.00
Koenig & Wernicke (KW/G)

14"................................ $900.00
18"................ $750.00 – 800.00
Too few in database for a reliable range.
   Ethnic features
   17".......... $1,000.00 – 1,100.00
Kuhnlenz, Gebruder
   Closed mouth
   15"................ $675.00 – 900.00
   18".......... $1,350.00 – 1,800.00
   Open mouth, mold 34.14, 34.16, 34.24, etc.
   7" – 9"......... $900.00 – 1,100.00
   12"........... $1,300.00 – 1,400.00
   Ethnic features
   16"........... $3,800.00 – 4,000.00
Marseille, Armand
   No mold number, ebony
   11"................................ $850.00
Too few in database for a reliable range.
   Mold 341, 351, 352, 362
   8" – 10".......... $550.00 – 650.00
   14" – 16"........ $825.00 – 950.00
   20"........... $1,100.00 – 1,200.00
   Mold 390, 390n
   16"................ $550.00 – 600.00
   19"................ $775.00 – 825.00

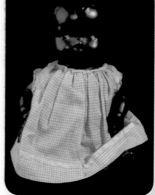

10" Patsy Baby by Effanbee. $600.00. **Photo courtesy of Richard Withington, Inc.**

23" .... $895.00 – 920.00
28" .... $1,100.00 – 1,200.00
Mold 966, 970, 971, 992, 995 (some in composition)
9" .... $265.00 – 290.00
14" .... $550.00 – 600.00
18" .... $875.00 – 900.00
Mold 1894, 1897, 1902, 1912, 1914
12" .... $500.00 – 550.00
14" .... $700.00 – 750.00
18" .... $800.00 – 850.00
Recknagel, marked "R.A.," mold 126, 138
16" .... $800.00 – 950.00
22" .... $1,275.00 – 1,430.00
Schmidt, Franz
Mold 1255, baby
21" .... $900.00 – 1,000.00
Closed mouth child, glass eyes, wig
15" .... $2,300.00 – 3,000.00
Schoenau Hoffmeister (S PB H)
Hanna
7" – 8" .... $475.00 – 550.00
10 – 12" .... $600.00 – 650.00
15" .... $750.00 – 800.00
18" .... $900.00 – 950.00
Mold 1909
16" .... $575.00 – 625.00
19" .... $750.00 – 850.00

6" Japanese painted bisque flange neck doll. $65.00. **Photo courtesy of The Museum Doll Shop.**

Simon & Halbig
Mold 126
8" toddler body.... $875.00 – 925.00
Mold 639
14" .... $6,400.00 – 6,800.00
18" .... $9,000.00 – 10,000.00
Mold 739, open mouth
16" .... $1,500.00 – 1,800.00
22" .... $2,80.00 – 3,000.00
Closed mouth
13" $1,500.00
Too few in database for reliable range.
17" .... $2,400.00 – 2,600.00
Mold 939
Closed mouth
18" .... $3,000.00 – 3,300.00
21" .... $4,300.00 – 4,500.00
Open mouth
13" .... $2,300.00 original outfit
Too few in database for reliable range.
Mold 949
Closed mouth
18" .... $3,200.00 – 3,400.00
21" .... $3,750.00 – 3,950.00
Open mouth
15" .... $2,600.00 – 2,800.00
Mold 1009, 1039, 1078, 1079, 1248
Open mouth
11" – 12".. $1,000.00 – 1,200.00
15" – 16".. $1,400.00 – 1,500.00
18" – 19".. $1,900.00 – 2,100.00
34" .... $1,900.00 – 2,000.00
Pull-string sleep eyes
19" .... $2,200.00 – 2,300.00
Mold 1248, open mouth
15" .... $1,400.00 – 1,500.00
18" .... $1,600.00 – 1,800.00
Mold 1272
20" .... $1,800.00 – 2,000.00
Mold 1302, closed mouth, glass eyes, character face
18" .... $9,000.00 – 10,000.00

Indian, sad expression, brown face
18"........... $7,000.00 – 7,400.00
Mold 1303, Indian, thin face, man or woman
15" – 16".. $6,000.00 – 6,500.00
21".......... $7,800.00 – 8,000.00
Mold 1339, 1368
16".......... $5,700.00 – 5,900.00
Mold 1348
15".......... $5,000.00 – 6,000.00
Mold 1358
15".......... $6,500.00 – 7,000.00
19" – 24"..$7,500.00 – 10,000.00
Papier-mâché, shoulder head on cloth body
10" – 13"........ $375.00 – 425.00

China
Frozen Charlie/Charlotte
3".................... $100.00 – 135.00
6".................... $225.00 – 250.00
8 – 9"............. $300.00 – 350.00
Jointed at shoulder
3".................... $150.00 – 200.00
6".................... $300.00 – 350.00

Celluloid
All-celluloid
10"................. $150.00 – 200.00
15"................. $275.00 – 350.00
18"................. $500.00 – 600.00
Celluloid shoulder head, kid body, add more for glass eyes
17"................. $s75.00 – 350.00
21"................. $375.00 – 450.00
French-type, marked "SNF"
14"................. $300.00 – 350.00
18"................. $550.00 – 600.00
Kämmer & Reinhardt, mold 775, 778
11"................. $175.00 – 200.00
18"................. $425.00 – 475.00

Cloth
Alabama Baby: See Alabama section.
Babyland Rag Doll: See Babyland section.
Brazilian, embroidered features, shell fingernails

18" Saralee, by Ideal. $325.00.
Photo courtesy of My Dolly Dearest.

17" – 19"........ $500.00 – 700.00
Bruckner: See Bruckner section.
Homemade, painted, embroidered, or appliquéd features, values vary according to the skill of the maker and the charm of the doll
Mid nineteenth century – early twentieth century
15" – 20"..... $400.00 – 1,600.00
1900 – 1920
15" – 18"........ $250.00 – 500.00
1920 – 1940
15" – 18"........ $175.00 – 250.00
1930s Mammy-type
14"................. $400.00 – 500.00
18"................. $500.00 – 600.00
Chase: See Chase section.
Golliwog, 1895 to present. Character from 1895 book *The Adventures of Two Dutch Dolls and a Golliwogg,* all-cloth, various English makers. See also Deans Rag.
1895 – 1920
13"................. $750.00 – 800.00
1930 – 1950
11"................. $400.00 – 475.00
15"................. $500.00 – 600.00
1950 – 1970s
13" – 18"........ $250.00 – 325.00
Steiff, 1996
Molly Golli & Peg $450.00

8" Effanbee Fluffy Brownie
Scout. $70.00. Photo courtesy
of Ebay-Babe408.

Mask face, 1920 – 1930s, American
13" – 18"............ $65.00 – 100.00
Stockinette Baby (often mis-called Black
Beecher), embroidered features, glass eyes
20" – 22".. $3,300.00 – 4,000.00
Composition, doll in good condition with
original clothing
Effanbee
Baby Grumpy
16"................. $525.00 – 600.00
Bubbles
17" – 22"........ $650.00 – 750.00
Candy Kid, original shorts, robe, and gloves
12"................. $300.00 – 350.00
Patsy baby
10"................. $575.00 – 625.00
Skippy, with original outfit
14"................................$900.00
Too few in database for reliable range.
Horsman
12".................. $225.00 – 250.00
Ideal
Marama, Shirley Temple body, from the
movie, Hurricane

13".............. $900.00 – 1,000.00
Koenig & Wernicke, mold 134
14".................. $450.00 – 500.00
Leo Moss type .... $2,500.00 – 8,000.00
Patsy-type
13" – 14"........ $275.00 – 325.00
Skookum Apple character head, googly look
14"................................. $300.00
Too few in database for reliable range.
Tony Sarg Mammy with baby
18".............. $900.00 – 1,100.00
Topsy-type, cotton pigtails
10" – 12"........ $175.00 – 225.00
Rubber
Amosandra, from Amos & Andy radio show
10".................. $175.00 – 225.00
Hard Plastic
Terri Lee
Benji, painted plastic, brown, 1946 – 1962,
black lamb's wool wig
16"........... $1,800.00 – 2,000.00
Patty Jo, 1947 – 1949
16"........... $1,200.00 – 1,500.00
Bonnie Lou, black
16"........... $1,200.00 – 1,800.00
Vinyl
Dee & Cee, 1960– 1970s, Canada, vinyl
head and body, rooted hair. See also Vinyl.
12" – 15".......... $90.00 – 110.00
Effanbee Fluffy, 1957 on
8"....................... $30.00 – 40.00
FloJo, Florence Griffin Joyner, made by LJN
11½"................... $15.00 – 20.00
Gotz
World of Children Series
23"................. $150.00 – 180.00
Mindy, 1957, Earl Pullan Co. Canada, vinyl
head with molded braids, stuffed vinyl body
15"................. $200.00 – 250.00
Sara Lee, Ideal, 1950, vinyl head and limbs,
cloth body, sleep eyes
17"................. $325.00 – 375.00

BLEUETTE

Bleuette SFBJ 60 with set black eyes full length. $2,400.00. **Doll courtesy of Agnes Sura.**

1905 – 1960, France. This premium doll was first made in bisque and later in composition for a weekly children's periodical, *La Semanine De Suzette* (The Week of Suzette), that also produced patterns for Bleuette. Premiere Bleuette was a bisque socket head, Tété Jumeau, marked only with a "1" superimposed on a "2," and 10⅝" tall. She had set blue or brown glass eyes, open mouth with four teeth, wig, and pierced ears. The composition jointed body was marked "2" on back and "1" on the sole of each foot. This mold was made only in 1905. S.F.B.J., a bisque socket head, began production in 1905, using a Fleischmann and Bloedel mold marked "6/0," blue or brown glass eyes, wig, open mouth, and teeth. S.F.B.J. mold marked "SFBJ 60" or "SFBJ 301 1" was a bisque socket head, open mouth with teeth, wig, and blue or brown glass eyes. All Bleuettes were 10⅝" tall prior to 1933, after that all Bleuettes were 11⅜".

Bisque
Premiere, 1905, Jumeau head

10⅝" .... $3,800.00 – 7,000.00
SFJB 6/0, 1905 – 1915, head made in Germany by Fleischman
    10⅝" .... $2,800.00 – 3,100.00
SFBJ 60 8/0, 1916 – 1933
    10⅝" .... $2,000.00 – 2,800.00
SFBJ 301 1
    10⅝" .... $2,500.00 – 3,000.00
71 Unis France 149 60 8/0
    10⅝" .... $1,800.00 – 2,500.00
71 Unis France 149, 1933 on
    11⅜" .... $1,200.00 – 1,800.00
Composition, 1930 – 1933
SFBJ 301 or 71 Unis France 149 251, 1930 – 1933
    10⅝" .... $1,500.00 – 1,700.00
SFBJ or 71 Unis France 149 251, 1933 on
    11⅜" .... $500.00 – 800.00

BONNET HEAD

1860s – 1940s on, dolls made of a variety of materials by numerous manufacturers, all with molded bonnets or hats.

All-bisque, German immobiles, painted eyes
    5" .... $175.00 – 200.00
    7" – 8" .... $275.00 – 325.00
    10" .... $350.00 – 375.00

18" china with molded bonnet with applied flowers. $900.00. **Photo courtesy of Richard Withington, Inc.**

4" – 5" bisque dolls with molded bonnets.
$275.00 each. **Dolls courtesy Jean Grout.**

Stone bisque immobile
    3½" – 5" .... $22.00 – 35.00
Bisque, socket or shoulder head, five-piece
composition body, kid body or cloth body
Painted eyes
    5" – 8" .... $200.00 – 275.00
    11" – 14" .... $400.00 – 500.00
    18" – 20" .... $500.00 – 600.00
Glass eyes
    7" – 9" .... $225.00 – 350.00
    12" – 15" .... $500.00 – 750.00
Alt, Beck & Gottschalk
Painted eye
    16" .... $1,500.00 – 2,000.00
Glass eye
    18" $1,530.00
Too few in database for a reliable range.
China, blond or black hair, painted eyes
Common style and quality
    10" – 13" .... $175.00 – 225.00
    18" with applied flowers
                    $875.00 – 975.00
High quality
    10½" .... $3,000.00 – 4,000.00
Handwerck, Max, WWI military figure,
painted eyes, mark: Elite
Bisque socket head, glass eyes, molded helmet

    10" – 14" .. $1,900.00 – 2,200.00
Heubach, Gebruder
Mold 7975, "Baby Stuart," ca. 1912, glass
eyes, removable molded bisque bonnet
    9" – 13" .... $1,600.00 – 3,000.00
Molds 7877, 7977, "Baby Stuart," ca. 1912,
molded bonnet, closed mouth, painted eyes
    8" – 9" .... $975.00 – 1,025.00
    11" – 13" .. $1,400.00 – 1,600.00
    15" .... $1,600.00 – 1,700.00
Hertwig, molded bonnet, jointed shoulders
    2½" – 4" .... $75.00 – 100.00
    18" .... $425.00 – 475.00
Japan
    8" – 9" .... $85.00 – 95.00
    12" .... $125.00 – 145.00
Molded shirt or top
    15" .... $750.00 – 850.00
    21" .... $1,200.00 – 1,305.00
Recknagel, Bonnet head baby, painted eyes,
open-closed mouth, teeth. Molds 22, 28, 44,
molded white boy's cap, bent-leg baby body
    8" – 9" .... $300.00 – 400.00
    11" – 12" .... $550.00 – 600.00
Stone bisque
    8" – 9" .... $125.00 – 175.00
    12" – 15" .... $200.00 – 300.00

Parian-type lady
Painted eye
7" – 9"............ $600.00 – 700.00
Glass eye
18".......... $2,000.00 – 3,800.00
Too few in database for reliable range.
Wax-over composition, cloth body with composition or wood lower limbs, glass eyes
7" – 13".......... $250.00 – 400.00
15"................. $575.00 – 650.00
19" – 23".. $1,400.00 – 1,800.00
29".......... $2,000.00 – 2,200.00

BOUDOIR DOLLS

1915 – 1940s, made in France, Italy, and United States usually. Long limbed dolls of a variety of materials, used primarily as decorative items, fancy costumes, usually 28" – 30".
Cloth mask face, 1920s
High quality with silk floss hair
$350.00 – 650.00
Average quality........ $400.00 – 450.00
Composition head, 1920 – 1940s
Smoker .... $550.00 – 700.00

26" cloth mask faced boudoir doll. $400.00.
Photo courtesy of The Museum Doll Shop.

High quality............. $350.00 – 500.00
Average quality........ $125.00 – 500.00
Hard plastic, 1940s
$100.00 – 180.00

BRU

1866 – 1899, Bru Jne. & Cie, Paris and Montreuil-sous-Bois, France. Bru eventually became one of the members of the S.F.B.J. syndicate (1899 – 1953). Bébés Bru with kid bodies are some of the most collectible dolls, highly sought after because of the fine quality of bisque, delicate coloring, and fine workmanship. Brus are made of pressed bisque and have a metal spring stringing mechanism in the neck. Add more for original clothes and rare body styles.
Poupée (Fashion-type lady), 1866 –1877, pressed bisque socket head attached to bisque shoulder plate with metal spring stringing, painted or glass eyes, pierced ears, cork pate, mohair wig, kid body, mark: numbers only, some marked B. Jne et Cie on shoulder plate
12" – 13".. $3,900.00 – 4,200.00
15" – 17".. $3,200.00 – 3,500.00
15" with trunk and wardrobe
$16,500.00*
20" – 21".. $4,200.00 – 4,800.00
Wooden lower arms
16" – 17".. $5,700.00 – 6,000.00
Wooden body
15" – 16".. $5,900.00 – 6,500.00
Smiler, 1873 on, closed smiling mouth, mark: size letters A through O
Kid body with kid or bisque lower arms
11".......... $3,800.00 – 4,000.00
13" – 15".. $4,100.00 – 5,000.00
20" – 21".. $7,000.00 – 8,000.00
Wooden lower arms
16" – 19".. $5,500.00 – 7,500.00

12" smiling Bru Poupée. $4,000.00.
Photo courtesy of The Museum Doll Shop.

Wooden body
15" – 16".. $7,100.00 – 8,500.00
18" – 21"..$10,000.00 – 15,000.00
Surprise Doll, poupée with two faces
13"....... $12,000.00 – 15,000.00
Bru Breveté, 1879 – 1880, pressed bisque socket head on bisque shoulder plate, paperweight eyes, multi-stroked eyebrows, closed mouth with space between the lips, full cheeks, pierced ears, cork pate, skin wig, kid or wood articulated body, mark: size number only on head
11"....... $19,000.00 – 21,000.00
14" – 16"..$20,000.00 – 22,000.00
19" – 22"..$25,000.00 – 30,000.00
Circle Dot or Crescent mark Bru, 1879 – 1884, pressed bisque socket head on bisque shoulder plate, paperweight eyes, multi-stroked eyebrows, open/closed mouth with molded, painted teeth, full cheeks, pierced ears, cork pate, mohair or human hair wig, gusseted kid body with bisque lower arms
11" – 12"..$14,000.00 – 18,000.00
13" – 14"..$17,000.00 – 20,000.00

18" – 19"..$23,000.00 – 25,000.00
22" – 24"..$23,000.00 – 29,000.00
31"....... $32,000.00 – 35,000.00
Bru Jne, 1880 – 1891, pressed bisque socket head on bisque shoulder plate with deeply molded shoulders, paperweight eyes, multi-stroked eyebrows, open/closed mouth with molded, painted teeth, pierced ears, cork pate, mohair or human hair wig, gusseted kid body with wood upper arms, bisque lower arms and kid or wood lower legs
10" ...... $34,000.00 – 36,000.00
12" – 14"..$25,000.00 – 30,000.00
15" – 17"..$32,000.00 – 36,000.00
22" – 24"..$37,000.00 – 40,000.00
Bru Jne R, 1891 – 1899, pressed bisque socket head on bisque shoulder plate with deeply molded shoulders, paperweight eyes, multi-stroked eyebrows, open/closed mouth with four to six teeth, pierced ears, cork pate, mohair or human hair wig, articulated wood and composition body
Open mouth
12"........... $1,800.00 – 2,000.00

18" Circle Dot Bru.
$23,000.00. **Photo courtesy of Richard Withington, Inc.**

18" – 21".. $3,100.00 – 3,400.00
Closed mouth
    10½"........ $4,000.00 – 4,500.00
    12" – 13".. $4,500.00 – 5,000.00
    19" – 21".. $7,000.00 – 8,000.00
    27" – 29".. $8,500.00 – 9,500.00
Mechanical Specialty Dolls
Bébé Teteur (nursing), 1879 –1898, open mouth for insertion of bottle, screw key at back of head allowed doll to drink
    13" .... $8,500.00 – 9,000.00
    15" – 17".. $6,000.00 – 7,800.00
    19" – 24".. $8,500.00 – 9,000.00
Bébé Gourmand (eating), 1880 on, open mouth with tongue, bisque lower legs, when fed food pellets went in through mouth and out through holes on the bottom of the feet, special shoes with a flap opening on the bottom allowed for food removal
    16" – 18"..$44,000.00 – 54,000.00
Bébé Modele, 1880 on, Breveté face, carved wood body
    16" – 19"..$30,000.00 – 40,000.00
Bébé Automate (breathing, talking), 1892 on, key or lever in torso activates mechanism to simulate chest movement

19".......... $4,600.00 – 4,800.00
24"....... $11,000.00 – 17,000.00
Bébé Baiser (kiss throwing), 1892 on, pull string mechanism raises dolls arm and simulates throwing a kiss
    11".......... $4,100.00 – 4,200.00
    15".......... $4,300.00 – 4,400.00
    22".......... $5,500.00 – 6,000.00
Bru shoes
    $700.00 – 900.00

ALBERT BRUCKNER

1901 – 1930 on, Jersey City, New Jersey. Made some dolls for the Horsman Babyland line. These dolls had molded cloth mask faces, cloth bodies and printed features. Later made flat faced cloth dolls.
Molded cloth, mask faces
    12" – 14"........ $250.00 – 300.00
Black .... $500.00 – 550.00
Topsy-Turvy.............. $600.00 – 650.00
Flat faced, printed, 1925 on, such as Dollypop, Pancake Baby, others
    12" – 13"........ $250.00 – 275.00

19" Bru Jne. $37,000.00. **Photo courtesy of Richard Withington, Inc.**

12½" Bruckner Topsy-Turvy doll. $650.00. **Photo courtesy of The Museum Doll Shop.**

10" flat-faced Bruckner baby doll. $200.00. **Photo courtesy of The Museum Doll Shop.**

Jiggs, Mutt & Jeff, others
$450.00 – 500.00
Becassine .... $800.00 – 1,000.00

BUDDY LEE

1920 – 1962, United States. Made by the H.D. Lee Co., Inc. as an advertising doll to spotlight their overalls and work gear. Doll with molded hair, painted side-glancing eyes, jointed shoulders, legs molded apart, all original clothing, mark: embossed Buddy Lee.

BUCHERER

1921 –1930s, Armisil, Switzerland. Metal bodies with metal ball joints, composition head, hands and feet, mark: "MADE IN SWITZERLAND PATENTS APPLIED FOR"
6½" – 7"......... $350.00 – 450.00
Regional and characters such as baseball player, fireman, military, Pinocchio, others
$400.00 – 600.00
Comic characters such as Charlie Chaplin, Happy Hooligan, Katzenjammers, Maggie &

13" composition Buddy Lee. $225.00. **Photo courtesy of Marie Novocin.**

Composition, 1920 –1948, 13"
Engineer, Cowboy, Phillips 66
$450.00 – 550.00
Football uniform, Minneapolis Moline uniform
$1,400.00 – 1,800.00
Too few in database for reliable range.
Hard Plastic, 1949 – 1962
13".................. $350.00 – 400.00

BURGARELLA

1925 to WWII, Rome, Italy. Made by Gaspare Burgarella, designed by Ferdinando Stracuzzi. Mark: cloth label sewn into outfit BURGARELLA Made in Italy.

6½" & 8" Mutt & Jeff by Bucherer. $800.00 pair. **Photo courtesy of McMasters Harris Auction Co.**

Child, high quality composition, expressively painted eyes with heavy shading, high quality human hair or mohair wig, jointed at neck, shoulders, hips, and knees.

16" – 18"..... $900.00 – 1,200.00
22"........... $1,300.00 – 1,400.00

BYE-LO BABY

1922 – 1952. Baby doll designed by Grace Storey Putnam to represent a three-day old infant. Distributed by George Borgfeldt & Co. Bisque heads made by German makers such as Hertel & Schwab, Kestner, Kling, others. Cloth bodies made by K & K in the United States. Composition bodies made by Koenig & Wernicke in Germany. Composition head made by Cameo Doll Co.
All-bisque, 1925 on, made by Kestner, some with pink or blue booties, mark: G. S. Putnam on back, paper sticker on chest reads Bye-Lo Baby
Painted eye

4" – 5" .... $350.00 – 450.00
6" .... $500.00 – 550.00

9" Bye-Lo baby. $400.00. **Doll courtesy Elaine Holda.**

8".................... $700.00 – 750.00
Glass eye, wigged
5" – 6"............ $650.00 – 700.00
8"............. $1,400.00 – 1,500.00
Swivel neck, glass eyes
5".................... $650.00 – 700.00
8"............. $1,250.00 – 1,350.00
Bisque head, flange neck head on cloth body with "frog" style legs or straight legs, closed mouth, molded, painted hair, blue sleep eyes, celluloid or composition hands, mark: head incised, some bodies stamped Bye-Lo Baby
Head circumference

8" – 9"............ $350.00 – 400.00
11" – 13"........ $400.00 – 500.00
18" – 22"........ $550.00 – 650.00
13" mold 1548 smiling Bye-lo
              $3,400.00*
Socket head on composition body
13"........... $2,000.00 – 2,400.00
Composition head, 1924 on, molded painted hair, sleep or painted eyes, closed mouth, cloth body
Head circumference

12".................. $350.00 – 425.00
16".................. $500.00 – 550.00
Celluloid, made by Karl Standfuss, Saxony, Germany
All-celluloid

5" all-bisque Bye-Lo baby. $650.00. **Photo courtesy of Richard Withington, Inc.**

4".................. $150.00 – 200.00
6".................. $225.00 – 275.00
Celluloid head on cloth body
   10"................. $300.00 – 350.00
   12"................. $425.00 – 450.00
Wax, 1925, sold in New York boutiques
   18" – 20".. $1,500.00 – 2,000.00
Wood, 1925, made by Schoenhut
           $1,700.00 – 2,000.00
Vinyl, Horsman, 1972, mark: Grace Storey Putnam on head
   14" – 16"............ $40.00 – 60.00
Other Putnam dolls
Fly-Lo, 1926 –1930. Bisque, ceramic, or composition head, glass or metal sleep eyes, molded painted hair, flange neck on cloth body, celluloid hands, satin wings in pink, green, or gold, mark: "Corp. by //Grace S. Putnam" on head
Bisque, less for ceramic
   10" – 11".. $3,000.00 – 4,000.00
Composition
   12" – 14"........ $500.00 – 700.00

CABBAGE PATCH KIDS

   1978 to present, initially designed by Xavier Roberts as an all-cloth needle-sculpted doll. The dolls were made in varying skin tone and hair and eye color combinations giving them each a unique look and "personality." Kids were 22", Newborns 17", and Preemies 15". Later licensing agreement led to vinyl headed dolls made by Coleco. In 1988 rights for the vinyl headed dolls went to Hasbro and in 1994 to Mattel. In 2004 rights for vinyl production were sold Play Along Toys and 4Kids Entertainment. Dolls listed are in perfect condition with original clothing and tags or paperwork.

Coleco Preemie. $28.00. **Photo courtesy of The Museum Doll Shop.**

1978 on, Babyland General Hospital, Cleveland, GA, cloth, needle sculpture, signature color changes year to year.
"A" blue edition
   1978 .... $1,300.00 – 1,400.00
"B" red edition
   1978 .... $1,000.00 – 1,100.00
"C" burgundy edition
   1979 .... $800.00 – 900.00
"D" purple edition
   1979 .... $700.00 – 800.00
"E" bronze edition
   1980 .... $300.00 – 400.00
Preemie edition
   1980 .... $300.00 – 400.00
New Ears edition
   1981 .... $300.00 – 400.00
Ears edition
   1982 .... $300.00 – 400.00
Green edition
   1983 .... $300.00 – 400.00
"KP" dark green edition
   1983 .... $300.00 – 400.00
"KPR" red edition
   1983 .... $300.00 – 400.00
"KPB" burgundy edition

1983 .... $300.00 – 400.00
"KPZ" edition
1983 – 1984..... $80.00 – 200.00
Champagne edition
1983 – 1984..... $80.00 – 200.00
"KPP" purple edition
1984 .... $80.00 – 200.00
"KPF," "KPG," "KPH," "KPI," "KPJ" editions
1984 – 1985..... $80.00 – 200.00
Emerald edition
1985 .... $80.00 – 200.00
Aquamarine
1988 .... $80.00 – 200.00
1989 through 1990s
Kid, Newborn, or Preemie
$200.00 – 300.00
1993, 27" girl
$300.00 at online auction
2004 on
Kid.................. $200.00 – 400.00
Coleco Cabbage Patch Kids, 1983 on, vinyl
head, cloth body, black signature stamp
Kid, Newborn, or Preemie
$12.00 – 40.00
Red Hair boys, fuzzy hair
$50.00 – 75.00
Popcorn hairdos, rare
$85.00 – 200.00
Cornsilk Kid.................. $30.00 – 50.00
Porcelain, 1985, made by Shaders
Kid.................... $60.00 – 150.00

CAMEO DOLL CO.

1922 – 1930 on, New York City, Port
Allegheny, Pennsylvania. Joseph L. Kallus's
company made composition dolls, some with
wood segmented bodies and cloth bodies.
All dolls listed are in good condition with
original clothing, allow less for crazed or
undressed dolls.
Bisque

10" Pinkie by Cameo. $300.00. **Photo
courtesy of The Museum Doll Shop.**

Baby Bo Kaye
Bisque head, made in Germany, molded hair,
open mouth, glass eyes, cloth body, composition limbs, good condition, mark: "J.L. Kallus:
Corp. Germany//1394/30"
17" – 20".. $2,300.00 – 2,400.00
All-bisque, molded hair, glass sleep eyes,
open mouth, two teeth, swivel neck, jointed
arms and legs, molded pink or blue shoes,
socks, unmarked, some may retain original
round sticker on body
5"............. $1,400.00 – 1,600.00
7" – 8"...... $1,800.00 – 1,900.00
Celluloid
Baby Bo Kaye
Celluloid head, made in Germany, molded
hair, open mouth, glass eyes, cloth body
12" – 16"........ $650.00 – 750.00
Composition
Annie Rooney, 1926, Jack Collins, designer,
all-composition, yarn wig, legs painted black,
molded shoes
13"................. $475.00 – 500.00
17"................. $650.00 – 700.00
Baby Blossom, 1927, "DES, J.L.Kallus," composition upper torso, cloth lower body and
legs, molded hair, open mouth

11" Popeye, composition and wood. $450.00. Photo courtesy of Turn of the Century Antiques.

19" – 20"........ $550.00 – 650.00

Baby Bo Kaye

Composition head, molded hair, open mouth, glass eyes, light crazing

14"................. $650.00 – 675.00

Bandy, 1929, composition head, wood segmented body, marked on hat "General Electric Radio," designed by J. Kallus

18½"............. $800.00 – 900.00

Betty Boop, 1932, composition head character, wood segmented body, molded hair, painted features, label on torso

11"................. $600.00 – 700.00

Champ, 1942, composition with freckles

16"................. $575.00 – 600.00

Felix the Cat, composition and wood segmented doll

13"................. $200.00 – 275.00

Giggles, 1946, "Giggles Doll, A Cameo Doll," composition with molded loop for ribbon

12" – 14"........ $425.00 – 475.00

Ho-Ho, 1940, painted plaster, laughing mouth

5½"............... $175.00 – 200.00

Joy, 1932, composition head character, wood segmented body, molded hair, painted features, label on torso

10"................. $300.00 – 350.00
15"................. $425.00 – 500.00

15" all original $860.00*

Margie, 1929, composition head character, wood segmented body, molded hair, painted features, label on torso

10"................. $200.00 – 225.00
15"................. $375.00 – 425.00
17"................. $500.00 – 550.00

Pete the Pup, 1930 – 1935, composition head character, wood segmented body, molded hair, painted features, label on torso

9"................... $375.00 – 425.00

Pinkie, 1930 – 1935, composition head character, wood segmented body, molded hair, painted features, label on torso

10"................. $275.00 – 300.00

Popeye, 1935, composition head character, wood segmented body, molded hair, painted features, label on torso

14"................. $600.00 – 650.00

Pretty Bettsie, composition head, molded hair, painted side-glancing eyes, open/closed mouth, composition one-piece body and limbs, wooden neck joint, molded and painted dress with ruffles, shoes, and socks, triangular red tag on chest marked "Pretty Bettsie//Copyright J. Kallus"

15" Scootles, 1925 on. $400.00. Doll courtesy of Ruth Cayton.

18".................. $450.00 – 500.00
Scootles, 1925 on, Rose O'Neill design, all-composition, no marks, painted side-glancing eyes, paper wrist tag
   7" – 8"............ $425.00 – 475.00
   12".................. $400.00 – 450.00
   15".................. $500.00 – 550.00
   22"........... $1,000.00 – 1,000.00
Composition, sleep eyes
   15".................. $650.00 – 700.00
Black composition
   12".................. $650.00 – 750.00
Hard Plastic and Vinyl, dolls listed here are in good condition wearing original clothing, allow double for mint-in-box.
Baby Mine, 1962 – 1964, vinyl and cloth, sleep eyes
   16".................. $100.00 – 125.00
   19".................. $150.00 – 200.00
Ho Ho, "Rose O'Neill," laughing mouth, squeaker, tag
White
   7".................... $150.00 – 200.00
Black
   7".................... $225.00 – 275.00
Miss Peep, 1957 – 1970s, pin jointed shoulders and hips, vinyl
   15"..................... $35.00 – 55.00
   18"................... $65.00 – 100.00
Black
   18".................. $110.00 – 125.00
1984, Jesco re-issue, all vinyl
   16"..................... $25.00 – 30.00
Miss Peep, Newborn, 1962, vinyl head and rigid plastic body
   14" – 18"............ $30.00 – 40.00
Pinkie, 1950s
   10" – 11"........ $125.00 – 150.00
Scootles, 1964, vinyl
   14".................. $175.00 – 195.00
   20".................. $350.00 – 375.00
1980s, Jesco

   12"..................... $25.00 – 30.00
   16"..................... $40.00 – 50.00
   19"..................... $60.00 – 80.00

CATTERFELDER PUPPENFABRIK

1906 on, Catterfeld, Thuringia, Germany. Had heads made by Kestner. Trademark: My Sunshine
C.P. Child, 1902 on, dolly face, bisque socket head, glass sleep eyes, wigged, open mouth with teeth, ball-jointed composition body
Mold 264
   9"................... $550.00 – 600.00
   14" – 16"........ $700.00 – 800.00
   25" – 28"..... $900.00 – 1,000.00
C.P. Character child, 1910 on, bisque socket head, painted eyes, wigged, open mouth with teeth, ball-jointed composition body
Mold: 207, 210, 215, 219, 217, others
   15" –16"... $8,500.00 – 9,000.00
Mold 220, glass eyes
   14"........... $8,300.00 – 8,500.00

18" mold 201 by Catterfelder Puppenfabrik. $950.00. **Doll courtesy of Lucy DiTerlizzi.**

Character Baby, 1910 on, bisque socket head, molded hair or wig, painted or glass sleep eyes, composition baby body
Mold: 200, 201, 207, 208, others
  8" – 10"......... $650.00 – 750.00
  14" – 16"........ $850.00 – 900.00
  19" – 21"..... $975.00 – 1,025.00
201, toddler
  8" – 10"....... $900.00 – 1,200.00
Mold 262, 263
  15" – 17"........ $450.00 – 500.00
  20" – 22"........ $650.00 – 700.00
262 toddler, five-piece composition body
  18".................. $800.00 – 825.00

CELLULOID

Early form of plastic made from nitrocellulose and a plasticizer such as camphor. Came into use in 1869 and an improved version became popular about 1905.

Made in numerous countries:

England — Wilson Doll co., Cascelliod Ltd. (Palitoy)

France — Petitcollin (profile of eagle head), Widow Chalory, Convert Cie, Parisienn Cellulosine, Neuman & Marx (dragon), Société Industrielle de Celluloid (SIC), Société Nobel Francaise (SNF in diamond), Sicoine, others.

Germany — Bähr & Pröschild, Buschow & Beck (helmet Minerva), Catterfelder Puppenfibrik Co., Cuno & Otto Dressel, E. Maar & Sohn (3M), Emasco, Kämmer & Reinhardt, Kestner, Koenig & Wernicke, A. Hagendorn & Co., Hermsdorfer Celluloidwarenfabrik (lady bug), Dr. Paul Hunaeus, Kohn & Wengenroth, Rheinsche Gummi und Celluloid Fabrik Co. later known as Schildkröte (turtle mark), Max Rudolph, Bruno Schmidt, Franz Schmidt & Co., Schoberl & Becker (mermaid) who used Cellba as a trade name, Karl Standfuss, Albert Wacker, others.

USA — Averill, Bo-Peep (H.J. Brown), DuPont Viscaloid Co., Horsman, Irwin, Marks Bros., Parsons-Jackson (stork mark), Celluloid Novelty Co. others.

All Celluloid
Baby, 1910 on, painted eyes
  4" – 8"................. $65.00 – 95.00
  12" – 15"........ $150.00 – 175.00
  19" – 21"........ $225.00 – 275.00

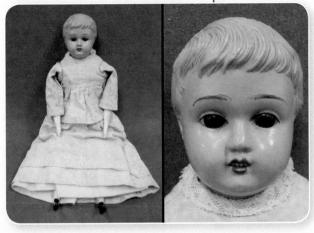

15" Turtle mark shoulder-head doll by Rheinsche Gummi und Celluloid Fabrik Co. $200.00.
Photo courtesy of William J. Janack Estate Appraisals & Auctioneers.

6" pair of celluloid children, by Schoberl & Becker, 1930s. $100.00. **Dolls courtesy of Elaine Holda.**

Marked France

5" – 9"............ $120.00 – 250.00

16" – 18"........ $350.00 – 450.00

Marked German character baby

12".................. $275.00 – 325.00

Marked Japan

4" – 5"................ $18.00 – 22.00

8" – 10".............. $65.00 – 75.00

13" – 15"........ $145.00 – 165.00

Occupied Japan

24".................. $150.00 – 175.00

Child, painted eyes, jointed at shoulder and hips

5" – 7"................ $50.00 – 75.00

11" – 14"........ $125.00 – 150.00

18" – 20"........ $200.00 – 225.00

Glass eyes

12" – 13"........ $175.00 – 200.00

15" – 16"........ $225.00 – 250.00

Marked France

7" – 9"............ $150.00 – 175.00

15" – 18"........ $300.00 – 325.00

Marked Japan

With molded clothing

3" – 4"................ $50.00 – 60.00

8" – 9"............ $125.00 – 150.00

Jointed shoulders only

3" – 4"................ $18.00 – 22.00

8" – 10".............. $30.00 – 40.00

Occupied Japan

6" – 8".............. $90.00 – 100.00

In regional costume, tagged LeMinor, Poupée Magali, others

8"...................... $60.00 – 75.00

12" – 15"........ $150.00 – 175.00

19"................. $250.00 – 275.00

Carnival-type, may have feathers glued on head or body

8" – 12".............. $35.00 – 45.00

Kewpie: See Kewpie listing.

Shoulder head child, 1900 on, German, molded hair or wig, open or open/closed mouth, kid or cloth body, sometimes arms of other materials

Painted eye

11" – 14".......... $75.00 – 100.00

16" – 18"........ $150.00 – 175.00
Glass eye
16" – 18"........ $235.00 – 250.00
Bye-Lo Baby: See Bye-Lo listing.
Socket-head child, 1910 on, open mouth, glass sleep eyes, wig, composition body
French, such as Petitcolin, others, glass eyes, wigged
18" – 19"........ $350.00 – 400.00
Jumeau
13"................ $450.00 – 500.00
16"................ $575.00 – 600.00
German, various makers
Molded hair, painted eyes
11" – 13"....... $200.00 – 300.00
16" – 19"........ $225.00 – 325.00
Glass eyes
14" – 17"........ $200.00 – 400.00
Heubach Koppelsdorf, mold 399
11".................. $75.00 – 100.00
Kämmer & Reinhardt
Baby, mold 721, 728
17" – 21"........ $350.00 – 450.00
Toddler, flirty eyes
17"................ $700.00 – 800.00
Child, socket head, mold 701, 717
13" – 18"........ $500.00 – 600.00
Kestner, mold 203 character baby
12"................ $425.00 – 450.00
Koenig & Wernicke (K & W)
Toddler
15" – 19"........ $375.00 – 500.00
Max & Moritz
7"............$300.00 – 350.00 each
American
Parsons-Jackson (stork mark)
Baby
12"................ $250.00 – 275.00
14"................ $300.00 – 350.00
Toddler
15"................ $375.00 – 400.00
Black

14"................ $475.00 – 500.00
Petitcolin
18"................ $375.00 – 400.00

CENTURY DOLL CO.

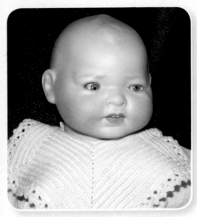

18" Century doll by Kestner. $700.00. **Photo courtesy of The Museum Doll Shop.**

1909 – 1930, New York City. Founded by Max Scheuer and sons, used bisque heads on many later dolls. In about 1929, Century merged with Domec to become the Doll Corporation of America. Some heads were made by Kestner, Herm Steiner, and other firms for Century. Dolls listed here are in good condition, with original clothes or appropriately dressed. More for boxed, tagged, or labeled exceptional doll.

Bisque
Baby, 1926, by Kestner, bisque head, molded and painted hair, sleep eyes, open-closed mouth, cloth body
13"................ $525.00 – 575.00
16" – 18"........ $600.00 – 700.00
Mold 275, solid dome, glass eyes, closed mouth, cloth body, composition limbs
14"................ $900.00 – 950.00

Child
Molds 285, 287, by Kestner, bisque socket head, glass eyes, wig, ball-jointed body
14".................. $625.00 – 675.00
19" – 24"........ $600.00 – 650.00
Composition
Child, composition shoulder head, cloth body, composition arms and legs, molded hair, painted eyes
13" – 17"........ $175.00 – 225.00
Century Baby, 1920s, composition flange head and hands, cloth baby body
13" – 15"........ $125.00 – 175.00
Chuckles, 1927 – 1929, composition shoulder head, arms, and legs, cloth body with crier, open mouth, molded short hair, painted or sleep eyes, two upper teeth, dimples in cheeks, came as a bent-leg baby or toddler
14" – 16"........ $125.00 – 200.00
18" – 22"........ $200.00 – 300.00
Mama dolls, 1922 on, composition head, tin sleep eyes, cloth body, with crier, swing legs and arms of composition
16".............. $1755.00 – 200.00
23".................. $300.00 – 325.00
Bisque shoulder head, mold 281
21".................. $650.00 – 750.00

CHAD VALLEY

1917 – 1930s, Harbonne, England. Founded by Johnson Bros. in 1897, in 1917 began making all types of cloth dolls, early ones had stockinette faces, later felt, with velvet body, jointed neck, shoulders, hips, glass or painted eyes, mohair wig, used designers such as Mabel Lucie Atwell and Norah Wellings.
Animals
Cat
12".................. $215.00 – 230.00

18" Chad Valley Princess Elizabeth, glass eyes. $1,000.00. **Photo courtesy of Richard Withington, Inc.**

Bonzo, cloth dog with painted eyes, almost closed and smile
4".................... $210.00 – 230.00
12".................. $750.00 – 800.00
Bonzo, eyes open
5½".................. $275.00 – 300.00
14".................. $575.00 – 600.00
Dog, plush
12".................. $260.00 – 280.00
Characters
Captain Blye, Fisherman, Long John Silver, Pirate, Policeman, Train Conductor, etc.
Glass eyes
10" – 12"........ $225.00 – 250.00
18" – 20"..... $900.00 – 1,100.00
Painted eyes
13" – 15"........ $375.00 – 400.00
18" – 20"........ $675.00 – 775.00
Ghandi/India
13".................. $625.00 – 675.00
Rahmah-Jah
26".................. $850.00 – 900.00
Child
Glass eyes

10" Chad Valley Beefeater, painted eyes. $200.00. **Doll courtesy of Ruth Cayton.**

14"................	$400.00 – 500.00
16"................	$450.00 – 575.00
18"................	$625.00 – 675.00

Painted eyes

9" – 10".........	$150.00 – 200.00
12" – 15"........	$200.00 – 275.00
18"................	$375.00 – 425.00

Royal Family, all with glass eyes, 16" – 18"
Princess Alexandra
$1,400.00 – 1,500.00
Prince Edward, Duke of Windsor
$900.00 – 1,100.00
Princess Elizabeth
$1,200.00 – 1,400.00
Princess Margaret Rose
$1,200.00 – 1,400.00

Story Book Dolls
Dong Dell
14"................ $300.00 – 375.00
My Elizabeth, My Friend
14"................ $500.00 – 575.00
Snow White & Dwarfs
Dwarf, 6½"............. $225.00 – 250.00
Set 10" dwarves, 16" Snow White
$2,000.00 – 2,500.00
Red Riding Hood

14" – 19"........ $350.00 – 500.00
Golliwog
14" – 16"........ $100.00 – 125.00

CHASE DOLL COMPANY

1889 to 1981, Pawtucket, Rhode Island. Founded by Martha Chase, earlier dolls had heads of molded stockinette with heavily painted features including thick lashes, closed mouth, painted textured hair, jointed shoulder, elbows, knees, and hips, later dolls jointed only at shoulders and hips, later dolls had latex heads on vinyl coated bodies, all in good condition with original or appropriate clothing.

Baby or child, short hair with curls around face

12" – 16"........	$600.00 – 850.00
17" – 20"........	$650.00 – 750.00
22 " – 24"	$850.00 – 950.00
26" – 30"..	$1,100.00 – 1,300.00

Hospital-type, weighted doll with pierced nostrils and ear canals

25" Chase baby. $1,000.00. **Photo courtesy of Richard Withington, Inc.**

14" bobbed hair
Chase. $1,200.00.
Photo courtesy of The
Museum Doll Shop.

20".................. $500.00 – 550.00
29".................. $450.00 – 550.00
Child
Molded bobbed hair
    12" – 15".. $1,200.00 – 1,400.00
    20" – 22".. $1,700.00 – 2,000.00
Side-part painted hair
    15" – 16".. $2,600.00 – 3,000.00
Characters, 1905 to 1920s, produced
characters based on Alice in Wonderland,
Dickens, Joel Chandler Harris books, and
George Washington
Alice in Wonderland Characters
    12"............ $67,000.00* set of six
Dickens Characters, needlesculpted hairstyles
including buns, curls, etc.
    15"
Lady .... $1,100.00 – 1,500.00
Little Nell, braids .. $1,400.00 – 1,600.00
George Washington
    15" .... $5,500.00 – 6,500.00
Black Child, ethnic features
    13"......................... $16,450.00*
Mammy

26"........... $6,000.00 – 6,500.00
Later Dolls, latex heads
Hospital Baby
    14" – 15"........ $200.00 – 250.00
    19"................. $300.00 – 400.00
Baby
    12"................. $150.00 – 200.00
Black
    12"................. $200.00 – 250.00
Child
    15"................. $175.00 – 225.00
Black
    15" .... $275.00 – 300.00

CHINA OR GLAZED PORCELAIN HEAD

1840 on. Most china shoulder head
dolls were made in Germany by various
firms. Prior to 1880, most china heads were
pressed into the mold; later ones poured.
Pre-1880, most china heads were sold
separately with purchaser buying commercial

20" Kinderkopf, pink tint, 1840s style.
$4,000.00. Photo courtesy of The Museum
Doll Shop.

20" bald head china, 1850s style.
$2,800.00. Photo courtesy of Richard
Withington, Inc.

body or making one at home. Original commercial costumes are rare; most clothing was homemade. Early unusual features are glass eyes or eyes painted brown. After 1870, pierced ears and blond hair were found and, after 1880, more child chinas with shorter hair and shorter necks were popular. Most common in this period were flat tops and low brows and the latter were made until the mid-1900s. Later innovations were china arms and legs with molded boots. Most heads are unmarked or with size or mold number only, usually on the back shoulder plate. Identification tips: hair styles, color, complexion tint, and body help date the doll. Dolls listed are in good condition with original or appropriate clothes. More for exceptional quality.

1840 Styles

China shoulder head with long neck, painted features, black or brown molded hair, may have exposed ears and pink complexion, with red-orange facial detail, may have bust modeling, cloth, leather, or wood body, nicely dressed, good condition.

Early marked china (Nuremberg, Rudolstadt)
    14".......... $2,500.00 – 3,000.00
    17".......... $3,500.00 – 4,000.00
Covered Wagon
Center part, combed back to form sausage curls, pink tint complexion
    7" – 10".......... $375.00 – 550.00
    14" – 17"........ $600.00 – 800.00
    20" – 25".. $1,000.00 – 1,200.00
    31".......... $1,400.00 – 1,500.00
Pink complexion, bun or coronet
    13" – 15".. $4,000.00 – 4,600.00
    18" – 21".. $5,200.00 – 6,000.00
Kinderkopf (child-head)
Pink tint child head doll, brush strokes around face
    12" – 16".. $1,500.00 – 3,000.00
K.P.M. (Königliche Porzellanmanufaktur Berlin), 1840s – 1850s on, made china doll heads marked KPM inside shoulder plate.
Pink tint lady
    14".......... $3,000.00 – 4,000.00
    19" – 22".. $5,300.00 – 6,000.00
Brown hair man, marked
    16" – 18".. $4,700.00 – 5,200.00
    22" – 23".. $7,100.00 – 8,100.00

13" "spill curls" china, 1860s style.
$1,100.00. Photo courtesy of Richard
Withington, Inc.

Brown hair lady with bun, marked
　　16" – 18".. $6,500.00 – 7,500.00
1850 Styles
China shoulder head, painted features, bald with black spot or molded black hair, may have pink complexion, cloth, leather, or wood body, china arms and legs, nicely dressed, good condition.
Alice in Wonderland, snood, headband
　　12" – 14"........ $675.00 – 775.00
　　16" – 18"........ $875.00 – 975.00
　　20" – 22".. $1,150.00 – 1,300.00
Bald head (so-called Biedermeier style), glazed china with black spot, human hair or mohair wig
　　12".............. $950.00 – 1,000.00
　　14" – 16".. $1,200.00 – 1,400.00
　　20" – 24".. $2,800.00 – 3,400.00
Baderkinder (Frozen Charlies or Charlottes): See that section.
Greiner-type with painted black eyelashes, various hairdos
Painted eyes
　　14" – 15".. $1,100.00 – 1,300.00
　　18" – 22".. $1,800.00 – 2,100.00
Glass eyes
　　13" – 15".. $3,700.00 – 4,200.00
　　21" – 22".. $4,900.00 – 5,100.00
French, 1850s on, some heads may have been made in Germany for the French makers.
Morning Glory, brown hair with molded morning glories
　　21" – 24"..$8,000.00 – 10,250.00
Poupée-type, glass or painted eyes, open crown, cork pate, wig, kid body, china arms
　　12" – 14".. $4,500.00 – 5,000.00
　　17" – 21".. $8,500.00 – 9,000.00
Jacob Petit, pink tint to skin, black painted pate
　　22"........................... $3,300.00
Sophia Smith, straight sausage curls ending

in a ridge around head, rather than curved to head shape
　　19" – 22".. $2,200.00 – 2,400.00
Young Queen Victoria, molded braids looped around ears, bun in back
　　16" – 18".. $2,400.00 – 2,600.00
　　22" – 23".. $2,700.00 – 2,800.00
Wooden body, simple hair, pink complexion, on pin jointed wooden body, with china hands
　　4½" .... $2,500.00 – 4,000.00
1860 Styles
China shoulder head, center part, smooth black curls, painted features, seldom brush marks or pink tones, all-cloth bodies or cloth with china arms and legs, may have leather arms. Decorated chinas with fancy hair styles embellished with flowers, ornaments, snoods, bands, ribbons, may have earrings.
Flat top Civil War
Black hair, center part, with flat top, curls on sides and back
　　5" – 7"............. $250.00 – 300.00
　　10" – 14"........ $300.00 – 375.00
　　18" – 22"........ $325.00 – 475.00
　　24" – 26"........ $475.00 – 550.00

22" "Adelina Patti" china, 1870s style. $800.00. **Photo courtesy of Richard Withington, Inc.**

34".................. $625.00 – 675.00
Swivel neck
15"........... $1,300.00 – 1,500.00
Molded necklace
21" – 24"........ $700.00 – 800.00
Highbrow, curls, high forehead, round face
12" – 13"........ $150.00 – 200.00
15" – 18"........ $400.00 – 500.00
19" – 22"........ $300.00 – 400.00
25" – 32"........ $250.00 – 350.00
Conta & Boehme, pierced ears
14" – 16"..... $900.00 – 1,100.00
18" – 20".. $1,400.00 – 1,700.00
Curly Top
12".................. $700.00 – 800.00
Currier & Ives, long hair lying on shoulders
15" – 17"........ $700.00 – 800.00
Dagmar, curls on forehead, curls gathered at
nape with barrette
13" – 18".. $1,600.00 – 1,900.00
Dolley Madison, with molded bow
9".................... $250.00 – 300.00
14" – 16"........ $550.00 – 600.00
20" – 24"........ $750.00 – 950.00
Kling, marked with bell and number
13".................. $350.00 – 450.00
16".................. $475.00 – 500.00
22".................. $525.00 – 550.00
Man or boy with curls
17" – 19".. $1,300.00 – 1,800.00
Grape Lady, with cluster of grape leaves and
blue grapes
15" – 18".. $2,000.00 – 2,500.00
Mary Todd Lincoln, black hair, gold snood,
gold luster bows at ears
14" – 15"........ $850.00 – 900.00
18" – 21".. $1,100.00 – 1,200.00
Blond with snood
15" – 16".. $1,000.00 – 1,100.00
18" – 21".. $1,600.00 – 1,900.00
Spill Curls, with or without headband, a lot of
single curls across forehead, around back to

ringlets in back
13" – 15".. $1,100.00 – 1,200.00
18" – 20".. $1,200.00 – 1,400.00
24" – 26".. $1,600.00 – 1,800.00
1870 Styles
China shoulder head, poured, finely painted,
well molded, black or blond hair, cloth or
cloth and leather bodies, now with pink
facial details instead of earlier red-orange.
14" – 16"........ $350.00 – 400.00
18" – 24"........ $425.00 – 475.00
Adelina Patti, hair pulled up and away,
center part, brush-stroked at temples, partly
exposed ears, ringlets across back of head
13" – 15"........ $450.00 – 500.00
18" – 22"........ $700.00 – 800.00
26"........... $1,200.00 – 1,500.00
Bangs, full cut across forehead, sometimes
called Highland Mary
Black hair
14" – 16"........ $400.00 – 475.00
19" – 21"........ $525.00 – 600.00
Blond hair
14" – 18"........ $400.00 – 550.00
Jenny Lind, black hair pulled back into a bun
or coronet
12" – 15"..... $900.00 – 1,400.00
20" – 24".. $1,300.00 – 1,500.00
1880 Styles
Now may also have many blond as well as
black hair examples, more curls, and overall
curls, narrower shoulders, fatter cheeks, irises
outlined with black paint, may have bangs,
china legs have fat calves and molded boots
Child, short black or blond curly hairdo with
exposed ears, makers such as Alt, Beck &
Gottschalk, Kling, and others.
14" – 18"........ $300.00 – 425.00
20" – 24"........ $500.00 – 600.00
27".................. $575.00 – 625.00
Bawo & Dotter, patented 1880
14".................. $150.00 – 175.00

18" – 20"........ $325.00 – 400.00

1890 Styles

Shorter fatter arms and legs, may have printed body with alphabet, emblems, flags **Common or low brow,** black or blond center part wavy hairdo that comes down low on forehead

4" – 8".............. $75.00 – 125.00
10" – 14"........ $150.00 – 250.00
16"................. $200.00 – 300.00
19" – 23"........ $275.00 – 350.00
27" – 28"........ $400.00 – 500.00

With jewel necklace

8"................... $160.00 – 190.00
20" – 22"........ $425.00 – 475.00

Pet Names, 1899 – 1930 on

Agnes, Bertha, Daisy, Dorothy, Edith, Esther, Ethel, Florence, Helen, Mabel, Marion, Pauline, and Ruth, made for Butler Brothers by various German firms, china head and limbs on cloth body, molded blouse marked in front with name in gold lettering, molded blond or black allover curls

9"................... $125.00 – 150.00
12" – 14"........ $200.00 – 275.00
17" – 21"........ $325.00 – 400.00

Japanese, 1910 – 1920, marked or unmarked, black or blond hair

10"................. $100.00 – 125.00
15"................. $160.00 – 190.00

CLOTH

Various American and European manufacturers of cloth headed dolls working from 1850 on. No separate listing for these makers. Marks: Many are unmarked or carried paper hang tags.

Becassine, French comic character, originally drawn by Emile Joseph Porphyre Pinchon for La Semaine de Suzette. Made in doll form by various makers, needle sculpted nose, painted features.

Reine Dégrais, 1947 – 1972,
8" – 14".......... $200.00 – 450.00

Minerve, 1972 on
12" – 16"........ $250.00 – 350.00

See Averill section for additional listing.

Homemade, nineteenth and early twentieth centuries. Makers unknown, many one-of-a-kind type dolls. Embroidered or painted features. Dolls vary greatly according to the skill of the maker. Values may differ substantially for individual examples.

16" – 24"..... $700.00 – 1,200.00

Known Makers

Baps, 1946 on, Burgkunstadt, Germany. Made by Edith von Arps. Felt doll with felt over wire armature body, yarn hair, metal feat, painted features. Many represent storybook characters.

2½" – 6"

Set of four such as Goldilocks and bears, 3 little pigs and wolf.... $200.00 – 250.00

Peter Rabbit set of five figures
$350.00 – 400.00

Single figures .... $75.00 – 200.00

Blossom, 1920s on, New York, NY. Made cloth, mask faced dolls depicting children as

8" Becassine by Minerve, MIB $125.00. **Doll courtesy of Alfred Edward.**

well as long limbed lady dolls (See Boudoir dolls section)

11".................... $50.00 – 75.00

Hol-Le Toy, 1950s, New York, NY. Eloise, cloth mask face based on the fictional character created by Kay Thompson

21"................. $175.00 – 225.00

Maggie Bessie dolls, 1890s on, Salem, N.C. Margaret and Elizabeth Pfohl made cloth dolls with oil painted faces in three sizes, 13/14", 17/18", and 20/22"

13" – 18"..$12,000.00 – 15,000.00

Molded cloth shoulder head dolls, mid nineteenth century on. Makers such as George H. Hawkins, Carl Weigand, and others both known and unknown. Dolls resemble the china and papier-mâché dolls of the era.

19" – 24"........ $600.00 – 750.00

11" Orange Girl by Blossom Doll Co. $75.00. **Photo courtesy of The Museum Doll Shop.**

Nelke, 1917 to 1930, Philadelphia, Pennsylvania. Harry Nelke founded the Elke Knitting Mills Co. in 1901 and began making stockinette crib dolls in 1917. The dolls were made of a silky stockinette fabric with painted features. Clothing integral to body, added band of stockinette around

10" Nelke. $85.00. **Photo courtesy of The Museum Doll Shop.**

neck, and/or added collars, hats, etc. Doll in clean, un-faded condition.

8" – 10".............. $75.00 – 95.00

13" – 15"........ $125.00 – 150.00

Tebbetts Sisters, 1922 on, Pittsburg, Pennsylvania, Mary, Elizabeth, Marion, and Ruth Tebbetts patented and made cloth dolls **Petiekins,** cloth mask face, crepe or flannel body

6½"................ $375.00 – 475.00

Baby Sister, needle-sculpted stockinette doll with painted features, wigged

18"......... $1,5000.00 – 2,000.00

Tiny Town, 1949 into the 1950s, San Francisco, California. Alma LeBlane took

6½" Sweet Petiekins by the Tebbetts sisters. $400.00. **Photo courtesy of The Museum Doll Shop.**

out a patent under the business name of Lenna Lee's Tiny Town Dolls for these dolls. The dolls have felt faces with painted features, mohair wigs, and wrapped wire armature bodies with metal feet

4" – 7".............. $45.00 – 55.00
(double for MIB)

Worsted dolls, 1878 – 1900s, Emil Wittzack of Gotha, Thuringia, Germany. Woolen crib dolls with needle-sculpted features, bead eyes, chenille embroidered designs on bodies, some had bells sewn on them

7" – 10".......... $100.00 – 125.00
15" – 18"........ $150.00 – 200.00

19" & 13½" pair of Colonial dolls by Art Fabric Mills. $135.00. **Photo courtesy of Joan & Lynette Antique Dolls and Accessories.**

10" worsted doll. $125.00. **Photo courtesy of The Museum Doll Shop.**

16" – 18"........ $175.00 – 225.00
20" – 24"........ $250.00 – 275.00
30"................. $300.00 – 325.00

Punch and Judy, pair
27"................. $550.00 – 650.00

Brownies,1892 – 1907, produced by Aronld Printworks. Printed cloth dolls based on copyrighted figures of Palmer Cox; 12 different figures, including Canadian, Chinaman, Dude, German, Highlander, Indian, Irishman, John Bull, Policeman, Sailor, Soldier, and Uncle Sam

Single Doll
7½"................. $125.00 – 175.00

Printed underwear, Dolly Dear, Flaked Rice, Merry Marie, etc.
7" – 9".............. $95.00 – 115.00
16" – 18"........ $125.00 – 175.00
20" – 24"........ $175.00 – 225.00

Child with printed clothing, 1903
12" – 14"........ $175.00 – 225.00
17" – 19"........ $250.00 – 300.00

Columbian Sailor, Arnold Printworks, 1892

CLOTH, PRINTED

1876 on. Made by various American, British, and German firms including Arnold Print Works, North Adams, MA , Cocheco Manufacturing Co., Art Fabric Mills, and other lesser or unknown firms who printed fabric for making cutout dolls to be sewn together and stuffed. Dolls listed are in good, clean condition, uncut sheets bring double the values listed here.

Improved Life Size Doll, with printed underwear

Mother's Congress Baby Stuart, designed by Made Meade, excellent condition. $1,100.00. **Doll courtesy Jean Grout.**

16".................. $250.00 – 300.00
Foxy Grandpa
    18".................. $200.00 – 225.00
Gutsell, Ida, 1893 on, made by Cocheco Manufacturing. Designed and patented by Ida Gutsell of Ithaca, New York. Printed boy doll with a center-seam face, removable clothing with printed detail
    16".................. $500.00 – 600.00
Mother's Congress, 1900 on, Philadelphia, PA. Designed and patented by Madge L. Meade. The uniquely styled pattern piece used for the head included a round section to produce the crown and several darts in the neck area. Unbleached muslin doll with lithographed facial features, blond hair with a blue bow and black Mary Jane style shoes, marked with a stamp: "Mother's Congress Doll//Baby Stuart//Children's Favorite// Philadelphia, Pa.//Pat. Nov. 6, 1900"
    17" – 24"........ $500.00 – 800.00
Our Soldier Boys ...... $125.00 – 150.00
Red Riding Hood ...... $150.00 – 175.00
Peck, 1886 Santa Claus/St. Nicholas
    15".................. $250.00 – 300.00

COLUMBIAN

1891 on, Oswego, NY. Emma E.

Adams designed and made rag dolls, sold directly or through stores such as Marshall Field & Co. Won awards at the 1893 Chicago World Fair. Succeeded by her sister, Marietta Adams Ruttan. Cloth dolls had hand–painted features, stitched fingers and toes. Values are for dolls in good condition wearing appropriate clothing, exceptional condition examples will sell for more.
    14" – 15".. $5,000.00 – 5,600.00
    19" – 23".. $5,800.00 – 6,200.00
    28"........... $7,000.00 – 9,000.00

18" Columbian rag doll. $5,700.00. **Private collection.**

COMPOSITION

Dolls listed are in good condition with original or appropriate dress. Allow more for exceptional dolls with elaborate costume or accessories.
American
Animal head doll, 1930s, all-composition on Patsy-type five-piece body, could be wolf, rabbit, cat, monkey
    10".................. $300.00 – 350.00
Baby, 1910 on, wigged or molded hair, painted or sleep eyes, composition or cloth body with bent legs

12" – 14"........ $175.00 – 225.00

18" – 20"........ $250.00 – 300.00

Bester Doll Company, 1918 – 1921, Bloomfield and Newark, New Jersey. Composition doll in the style of German dolly faced dolls, ball-jointed body, sleep eyes, wigged

18" – 22"........ $425.00 – 475.00

Child, costumed in ethnic or theme outfit, all-composition, sleep or painted eyes, mohair wig, closed mouth, original costume

Lesser quality

9" – 11"............... $65.00 – 75.00

Better quality

9" – 11".......... $125.00 – 145.00

16"................. $250.00 – 300.00

Coleman Walker

24" – 28"........ $200.00 – 225.00

Denny Dimwitt, Toycraft Inc, 1948, all-composition, nodder, painted clothing

11½".............. $200.00 – 225.00

Early child, 1910 – 1920, all-composition, unmarked, painted features, may have molded hair

12"................. $145.00 – 165.00

18" – 19"........ $200.00 – 250.00

Character face, 1910 – 1920, unmarked, cork-stuffed cloth body, painted features, may have molded hair

12" – 15"........ $150.00 – 200.00

18" – 20"........ $250.00 – 300.00

24"................. $375.00 – 400.00

Jackie Robinson, complete in box

13".............. $900.00 – 1,000.00

Kewty, 1930, made by Domec of Canada, all-composition Patsy-type, molded bobbed hair, closed mouth, sleep eyes, bent left arm

13½".............. $300.00 – 350.00

Lone Ranger, "TLR Co, Inc.//Doll Craft Novelty Co. NYC," cloth body, hat marked

20"................. $800.00 – 900.00

Louis Vuitton, 1955, ceramic, composition,

21" composition Miss Curity. $500.00. **Photo courtesy of Sharing My Dolls & Stuff.**

with labeled case and wardrobe

19"............................. $2,200.00

Too few in database for a reliable range.

Maiden America, "1915, Kate Silverman," all-composition, patriotic ribbon

8½"................. $165.00 – 185.00

Mama doll, 1922 on, wigged or painted hair, sleep or painted eyes, cloth body, with crier and swing legs, lower composition legs and arms

16" – 18"........ $225.00 – 250.00

20" – 22"........ $300.00 – 325.00

24" – 26"........ $375.00 – 400.00

Miss Curity, composition, eye shadow, nurse's uniform

18"................. $475.00 – 500.00

Patsy-type girl, 1928 on, molded and painted bobbed hair, sleep or painted eyes, closed pouty mouth, composition or hard stuffed cloth body

9" – 10".......... $125.00 – 150.00

14" – 16"........ $225.00 – 275.00

19" – 20"........ $275.00 – 300.00

With molded hair loop

12" – 15"........ $150.00 – 200.00

Pinocchio, composition and wood character

16½" .... $400.00 – 425.00

Puzzy, 1948, "H of P"

    15"................. $350.00 – 400.00

Quintuplets, 1934 on, all-composition, jointed five-piece baby or toddler body, molded hair or wig, with painted or sleep eyes, closed or open mouth

    7" – 8"............ $140.00 – 160.00

    13"................. $225.00 – 250.00

Refugee, Madame Louise Doll Co., 1945, represents victims of WWII

    20".......................$550.00* MIB

Santa Claus, composition molded head, composition body, original suit, sack

    19"................. $400.00 – 425.00

Shirley Temple-type girl, 1934 on, all-composition, five-piece jointed body, blond curly wig, sleep eyes, open mouth, teeth, dimples

    16" – 19"........ $250.00 – 300.00

Sizzy, 1948, "H of P"

    14"................. $250.00 – 300.00

Thumbs-Up, to raise money for ambulances during WWII, see photo first edition

    8"................... $140.00 – 155.00

Uncle Sam, various makers

All original, cloth body

    13"................................$900.00

Too few in database for reliable range.

Ca. 1918, straw-filled

    30" $450.00

Too few in database for reliable range.

Whistler, composition head, cotton body, composition arms, open mouth

    14½".............. $200.00 – 225.00

Canadian, Pullan

Little Lulu

    14"................. $350.00 – 450.00

German, composition head, composition or cloth body, wig or molded and painted hair, closed or open mouth with teeth, dressed, may be Amusco, Sonneberger Porzellanfabrik, Winkler, or others

Character Baby

Cloth body

    18"................. $275.00 – 325.00

Composition baby body, bent limbs

    16"................. $275.00 – 325.00

Child

Composition shoulder head, cloth body, composition arms

    20"................. $275.00 – 300.00

Socket head, all-composition body

    12" – 14"........ $200.00 – 300.00

    19" – 21"........ $425.00 – 450.00

Japanese

Quintuplets

    7" – 9"............ $175.00 – 250.00

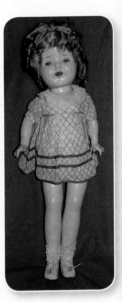

22" unmarked composition, made in imitation of Ideal's Shirley Temple. $300.00. **Photo courtesy of The Museum Doll Shop.**

COSMOPOLITAN DOLL & TOY CORP.

1950s on, Jackson Heights, New York. Dolls listed are in perfect condition with original clothing. Mint-in-box can be double the values listed here, naked dolls bring one-third the values listed here.

8" Ginger gift set. $200.00. **Photo courtesy of McMasters Harris Auction Co.**

Ginger, 1955 on, 7½", hard plastic
Painted lash straight leg walker
$60.00 – 75.00
1954, wearing Disney Safari outfit
$315.00 online auction
Molded lash straight leg walker
$50.00 – 65.00
Bent knee walker .... $40.00 – 60.00
Vinyl head .... $25.00 – 35.00
Boxed outfit .... $50.00 – 60.00
Cardboard house and furniture
$130.00 – 150.00
Miss Ginger, 1957 on, vinyl, rooted hair, sleep eyes, teen doll, tagged clothes
10½" .... $50.00 – 75.00
Boxed outfit .... $80.00 – 90.00
Little Miss Ginger, 1958 on, vinyl, rooted hair, sleep eyes, teen doll, tagged clothes
8" .... $60.00 – 75.00

CRÈCHE

Figures of various materials made especially for religious scenes such as the Christmas manger scene. Usually not jointed, some with elaborate costumes. Some early created figures were gesso over wood head and limbs, fabric covered bodies with wire frames, later figures made of terra-cotta or other materials, some with inset eyes.

Wood, carved
Man or woman, shoulder head, glass eyes, wire body
8" .... $400.00 – 500.00
10" – 14" .... $500.00 – 900.00
Angel
10" – 16" .. $2,000.00 – 2,800.00
Too few in database for reliable range.

12" crèche angel. $2,200.00. **Doll courtesy of Lynda Christian.**

Terra Cotta, mid nineteenth century, shoulder head, wire frame
Man or woman
15".................. $400.00 – 900.00

DE FUISSEAUX

1909 – 1912, Baudour, Belgium. Porcelain heads, often highly colored. Marked with D.F.B, or F1 (and other #s), D1 (and other numbers).

19" doll marked F2, by De Fuisseaux. $2,500.00. **Photo courtesy of Joan & Lynette Antique Dolls and Accessories.**

Open mouth dolly face, sleep eyes, wig, cardboard and composition ball-jointed body
18" – 22"........ $325.00 – 400.00
Character doll
Painted eyes, resembles Kämmer & Reinhardt 101, various body types
8"................... $400.00 – 450.00
Glass eyes, resembles Heubach, ball-jointed composition body
12" – 18".. $1,200.00 – 1,800.00
Portrait style girl or lady, cloth body
19" – 23".. $2,100.00 – 2,600.00

DEANS RAG BOOK CO.

16" painted eye doll by Dean's Rag Book Co. $600.00. **Photo courtesy of Richard Withington, Inc.**

1905 on, London. Subsidiary of Dean & Son, Ltd., a printing and publishing firm, used "A1" to signify quality, made Knockabout Toys, Tru-to-Life, Evripoze, and others. An early designer was Hilda Cowham.
Child, painted eyes
10"................. $275.00 – 300.00
16" – 17"........ $500.00 – 600.00

13" cloth dancing dolls. $110.00. **Photo courtesy of The Museum Doll Shop.**

24"................. $600.00 – 700.00
Printed cloth, cut and sew type
9" – 10".............. $85.00 – 95.00
15" – 16"........ $175.00 – 225.00
Mask face, velvet, with cloth body and limbs
12" – 15"........ $125.00 – 175.00
18" – 24"........ $275.00 – 350.00
30" – 34"........ $475.00 – 550.00
40"................ $625.00 – 675.00
Dancing Dolls, cloth dolls sewn together at hands to look like a dancing couple, on a string.
12" – 14"........ $110.00 – 125.00
Lupino Lane
12"................. $250.00 – 300.00
Mickey Mouse
12" – 13"........ $700.00 – 800.00
Golliwogs (English black character doll)
11" – 13"........ $225.00 – 275.00
15"................. $400.00 – 450.00

DELUXE READING

1955 – 1972, Elizabeth, NJ. Also used the names Deluxe Toy Creations, Deluxe Premium Corp., Deluxe Topper, Topper Toys, and Topper Corp. Dolls listed are complete, all original, in good condition, wearing original clothes, hard plastic or vinyl, allow double for mint-in-box.

Baby

Baby Boo, 1965, battery operated
21"..................... $75.00 – 90.00
Baby Catch A Ball, 1969 (Topper Toys), battery operated
18"..................... $50.00 – 60.00
Baby Magic, 1966, blue sleep eyes, rooted saran hair, magic wand has magnet that opens/closes eyes
18"..................... $40.00 – 50.00
Baby Peek 'N Play, 1969, battery operated
18"..................... $20.00 – 25.00
Baby Tickle Tears
14"..................... $18.00 – 20.00
Nancy Nurse, 1963
21"..................... $25.00 – 30.00
Suzy Cute, move arm and face changes expressions

6" Angie & Dawn, MIB. $40.00 each. **Photo courtesy of McMasters Harris Auction Co.**

7".......................... $35.00 – 45.00

Child or Adult

Betty Bride, 1957, also called Sweet Rosemary, Sweet Judy, Sweet Amy, one-piece vinyl body and limbs, more if many accessories

    30"...................... $40.00 – 60.00

Candy Fashion, 1958, made by Deluxe Premium, a division of Deluxe Reading, sold in grocery stores, came with three dress forms, extra outfits

    21"...................... $60.00 – 85.00

Dawn Series, circa 1969 – 1970s, all-vinyl doll with additional friends, Angie, Daphne, Denise, Glori, Jessica, Kip, Long Locks, Majorette, Maureen, black versions of Van and Dale, accessories available, included Apartment, Fashion Show, outfits

Dawn and friends

    6"........................ $18.00 – 20.00

Dawn & other outfits

    Loose, but complete.......... $10.00+

    NRFP................... $35.00 – 45.00

    Fashion Show Stage in box

        $65.00 – 75.00

Go Gos, 1965, soft vinyl bendable body. Cool Cat, Private Ida, Tom Boy

8" Penny Brite. $18.00.
Photo courtesy of The Museum Doll Shop.

6"........................ $25.00 – 30.00

Little Miss Fussy, battery operated

    18"...................... $15.00 – 20.00

Little Red Riding Hood, 1955, vinyl, synthetic hair, rubber body, book, basket

    23"...................... $50.00 – 75.00

Penny Brite, 1963 on, all-vinyl, rooted blond hair, painted eyes, bendable and straight legs, extra outfits, case, furniture available, marks: "A – 9/B150 (or B65) DELUXE READING CORP.//c. 1963"

    8"........................ $15.00 – 20.00

Outfit, NRFP .... $30.00 – 40.00

Kitchen set .... $50.00 – 60.00

Suzy Homemaker, 1964, hard plastic and vinyl, jointed knees, mark: "Deluxe Reading Co."

    21"...................... $35.00 – 45.00

Suzy Smart, ca. 1962, vinyl, sleep eyes, closed mouth, rooted blond ponytail, hard plastic body, The Talking School Doll, desk, chair, easel

    25"................. $100.00 – 125.00

Sweet Rosemary, vinyl head, soft vinyl body, high-heel foot

    28"...................... $75.00 – 95.00

DEP

The "DEP" mark on the back of bisque heads stands for the French "Depose" or the German "Deponirt," which means registered claim. Some dolls made by Simon & Halbig have the "S&H" mark hidden above the "DEP" under the wig. Bisque head, swivel neck, appropriate wig, paperweight eyes, open or closed mouth, good condition, nicely dressed on French style wood and composition body. Dolls listed are in good condition with original or appropriate clothing.

Closed mouth

    15"........... $2,100.00 – 2,250.00

    18" – 20".. $2,550.00 – 2,850.00

20" DEP on Jumeau body with original box. $2,000.00. **Photo courtesy of Dolls & Lace.**

23" – 25".. $3,150.00 – 3,800.00
Open mouth, including those marked Jumeau
13" – 15"........ $925.00 – 975.00
18" – 20".. $1,400.00 – 1,800.00
23" – 25".. $1,600.00 – 1,900.00
28" – 30".. $1,900.00 – 2,200.00

DOLLHOUSE DOLLS

Small German dolls generally under 8" usually dressed as member of a family or in

6" German dollhouse man with molded moustache. $325.00. **Photo courtesy of The Museum Doll Shop.**

household-related occupations, often sold as a group. Made of any material, but usually bisque head by 1880. Dolls listed are in good condition with original clothes.

Bisque
Adult, man or woman,
Painted eyes, molded hair, wig
6".................. $200.00 – 225.00
Glass eyes
  Molded hair
  6".................. $350.00 – 400.00
  Wigged
  6".................. $500.00 – 550.00

4½" pair of German dollhouse dolls from the 1920s. $475.00. **Photo courtesy of The Museum Doll Shop.**

Black man or woman, molded hair, original clothes
  6".................. $400.00 – 475.00
Chauffeur, molded cap
  6".................. $245.00 – 285.00
Grandparents, or with molded on hats
  6".................. $235.00 – 265.00
Military man, mustache, original clothes
  6".................. $475.00 – 575.00
With molded-on helmet
  6".................. $700.00 – 775.00

Children, all-bisque
4"..................... $75.00 – 100.00
China
With early hairdo
4"..................... $300.00 – 400.00
With low brow or common hairdo, 1900 on
4"..................... $150.00 – 175.00
Composition, papier-mâché, plaster, etc.
5"..................... $150.00 – 200.00

DOOR OF HOPE

1901 – 1950, Shanghai, China. Cornelia Bonnell started the Door of Hope Mission in Shanghai to help poor girls sold by their families. As a means to learn sewing skills, the girls dressed carved pear wood heads from Ning-Po. The heads and hands were natural finish, stuffed cloth bodies were then dressed in correct representation for 26 different Chinese classes. Carved wooden head with cloth or wooden arms, original handmade costumes, in very good condition. Dolls listed are in good condition with clean, bright clothing. Exceptional dolls could be higher. Values are lower for dolls in faded costumes.

Adult, man or woman
11" – 13".. $1,400.00 – 2,000.00
Amah with Baby
$1,900.00 – 2,100.00
Boy with western hairstyle
8" – 9"............ $800.00 – 950.00
Bride & Groom
12"....$1,300.00 – 1,600.00 each
Farmer in bamboo raincoat
12"........... $2,200.00 – 2,800.00
Kindergarten child
6"............. $4,025.00 – 4,200.00
Manchu Lady
12"......................... $9,200.00*
Policeman
11½"....................... $5,400.00*
Schoolchild
7" – 8"...... $1,600.00 – 2,000.00

12" Door of Hope Bride & Groom. $3,000.00. **Photo courtesy of Richard Withington, Inc.**

CUNO & OTTO DRESSEL

1857 – 1943, Sonneberg, Thüringia, Germany. The Dressel family began its business in the early 1700s and was dealing in toys from a very early date. Cunno & Otto became involved in the 1880s. The Dressels made wood, wax, wax-over-composition, papier-mâché, composition, china, and bisque heads for their dolls which they produced, distributed, and exported. Their bisque heads were made by Simon & Halbig, Armand Marseille, Ernst Heubach, Schoenau & Hoffmeister, and others. Dolls listed are in good condition with appropriate clothing.
Bisque

Baby, 1910 on, character face, marked "C.O.D.," more for toddler body

12" – 14"........	$325.00 – 375.00
15" – 17"........	$375.00 – 425.00
19" – 23"........	$550.00 – 600.00

Child, mold 1912, others, open mouth, jointed composition body

14" – 16"........	$300.00 – 350.00
18" – 24"........	$375.00 – 400.00

Shoulder head child

Molds 93, 1896, or no mold #, bisque, wigged, open mouth, kid or cloth body, glass eyes

13" – 15"........	$150.00 – 200.00
18" – 24"........	$200.00 – 275.00

Bisque, closed mouth, molded hair, kid or cloth body, glass eyes

14".................	$300.00 – 325.00

Child, character face, closed mouth, jointed child or toddler body

Painted eyes

14" – 16"..	$1,200.00 – 1,300.00
18" – 20"..	$1,500.00 – 1,7000.00

Glass eyes

15"...........	$2,200.00 – 2,500.00
18" – 20"..	$3,200.00 – 3,500.00

Flapper, mold 1469, lady doll, closed mouth, five-piece composition body with thin legs and high heel feet, painted on hose up entire leg, mold 1469

12" – 15"..	$3,500.00 – 4,000.00

Composition

Holz-Masse, 1875 on, shoulder head, wigged or molded hair, painted or glass eyes, cloth body, composition limbs, molded on boots

13" – 15"........	$350.00 – 400.00
18" – 20"........	$450.00 – 525.00
24" – 29"........	$575.00 – 650.00

Glass eyes

12".................	$400.00 – 500.00
16" – 18"........	$550.00 – 650.00

8" Admiral Dewey by Cunno & Otto Dressel. $800.00. **Photo courtesy of The Museum Doll Shop.**

Wigged

18"..................	$650.00 – 750.00

Jutta

Baby open mouth, bent-leg body

16" – 18"........	$625.00 – 675.00
21" – 24"....	1,150.00 – 1,300.00

Child, 1906 – 1921, open mouth, marked with "Jutta" or "S&H" mold 1914, 1348, 1349, etc.

14" – 16"........	$450.00 – 525.00
17" – 19"........	$550.00 – 625.00
21" – 24"........	$825.00 – 875.00
25" – 29".....	$950.00 – 1,100.00

Toddler

8"...................	$525.00 – 550.00
14" – 16"........	$575.00 – 625.00
17" – 19"........	$700.00 – 750.00

Portrait dolls, 1896 on, bisque head, glass eyes, composition body

Admiral Dewey, Admiral Byrd

8"....................	$750.00 – 825.00
12" – 14"..	$1,550.00 – 1,900.00

Buffalo Bill

10".................	$700.00 – 750.00

Farmer, Old Rip, Witch

8"...................	$650.00 – 750.00
12"...........	$1,900.00 – 2,200.00

The Professor (old Rip head, dressed in

tuxedo)

15".......................... $4,250.00*

Father Christmas

12"........................... $1,500.00+

Uncle Sam

13" – 15½" .. $1,200.00 – 1,500.00

E.D.

28" closed mouth E.D., maker Etienne Denamur. $4,200.00. **Photo courtesy of Richard Withington, Inc.**

1857 – 1899, Paris. E.D. Bébés marked with "E.D." and a size number and the word "Depose" were made by Etienne Denamur. It is important to note that other dolls marked E.D. with no Depose mark were made when Emile Douillet was director of Jumeau and should be priced as Jumeau Tété face dolls. Denamur had no relationship with the Jumeau firm and his dolls do not have the spiral spring used to attach heads used by Jumeau. Denamur bébés have straighter eyebrows, the eyes slightly more recessed, large lips, and lesser quality bisque. Smaller sizes of Denamure E.D. bébés may not have the Depose mark. Dolls listed are in good condition, appropriately dressed. Allow more for exceptional clothing.

Closed mouth

11" – 15".. $3,000.00 – 4,000.00

18" – 22".. $5,000.00 – 6,500.00

25" – 28".. $4,100.00 – 4,300.00

Open mouth

14" – 16".. $1,600.00 – 1,800.00

18" – 21".. $1,900.00 – 2,100.00

25" – 27".. $2,500.00 – 2,600.00

EDEN BÉBÉ

1890 – 1899, made by Fleischmann & Bloedel; 1899 – 1953, made by Société Francaise de Fabrication de Bébés & Jouet (S.F.B.J.). Dolls had bisque heads, jointed composition bodies. Dolls listed are in good condition, appropriately dressed.

Closed mouth, pale bisque

14" – 16".. $2,400.00 – 2,900.00

18" – 24".. $3,600.00 – 4,400.00

High color, five-piece body

13".............. $900.00 – 1,200.00

19"........... $1,600.00 – 1,800.00

22"........... $2,100.00 – 2,300.00

Open mouth

15" – 18".. $1,700.00 – 1,900.00

20" – 26".. $2,100.00 – 2,500.00

17" Eden Bébé. $3,200.00. **Photo courtesy of Joan & Lynette Antique Dolls and Accessories.**

EEGEE

1917 on, Brooklyn, NY. Owned by E. G. Golderberger, assembled and made dolls, some of their dolls had bisque heads imported from Armand Marseille. Eegee also made their own heads and complete dolls of composition, hard plastic, and vinyl. Dolls listed are in all original, good condition. Add more for exceptional doll, tagged, extra outfits, or accessories.

11½" Dolly Parton, c. 1978. $20.00. **Doll courtesy of Talona Griffin.**

Composition

Baby, cloth body, bent limbs

16"................. $100.00 – 125.00

Child, open mouth, sleep eyes

14"................. $145.00 – 160.00

18"................. $200.00 – 220.00

MaMa Doll, 1920s – 1930s, composition head, sleep or painted eyes, wigged or molded hair, cloth body with crier, swing legs, composition lower arms and legs

16"................. $225.00 – 250.00

20"................. $325.00 – 350.00

Miss Charming, 1936, all-composition, Shirley Temple look-alike

19"................. $475.00 – 550.00

Pin-back button $50.00

Hard Plastic and Vinyl

Andy, 1963, vinyl, teen-type, molded and painted hair, painted eyes, closed mouth

12"..................... $25.00 – 35.00

Annette, 1963, vinyl, teen-type fashion, rooted hair, painted eyes

11½".................. $45.00 – 55.00

Child, 1966, marked "20/25 M/13"

19"..................... $40.00 – 50.00

Child, walker, all-vinyl rooted long blond hair or short curly wig, blue sleep eyes, closed mouth

25"..................... $40.00 – 50.00

28"..................... $55.00 – 65.00

36"..................... $75.00 – 85.00

Babette, 1970, vinyl head, stuffed limbs, cloth body, painted or sleep eyes, rooted hair

15"..................... $30.00 – 40.00

25"..................... $55.00 – 65.00

Baby Care, 1969, vinyl, molded or rooted hair, sleep or set glassine eyes, drink and wet doll, with complete nursery set

18"..................... $35.00 – 45.00

Baby Carrie, 1970, rooted or molded hair, sleep or set glassine eyes with plastic carriage or carry seat

24"..................... $50.00 – 60.00

Baby Luv, 1973, vinyl head, rooted hair, painted eyes, open/closed mouth, marked "B.T. Eegee," cloth body, pants are part of body

14"..................... $30.00 – 40.00

Baby Susan, 1958, marked "Baby Susan" on head

8½"..................... $20.00 – 20.00

Baby Tandy Talks, 1963, pull string activates talking mechanism, vinyl head, rooted hair, sleep eyes, cotton and foam-stuffed body and limbs

14"..................... $25.00 – 35.00

20"..................... $55.00 – 65.00

20" Tandy Talks by Eegee, c. 1961. $65.00.
Photo courtesy of Steve Carissimo.

Ballerina
1964, vinyl head and hard plastic body
31".................... $75.00 – 100.00
1967, vinyl head, foam-filled body
18".................... $30.00 – 40.00
Barbara Cartland, painted features, adult
15".................... $45.00 – 52.00
Beverly Hillbillies, Clampett family from 1960s TV sitcom
Car $350.00
Granny Clampett, gray rooted hair
14".................... $55.00 – 65.00
Fields, W. C., 1980, vinyl ventriloquist doll by Juro, division of Goldberger
30"................. $150.00 – 200.00
Flowerkins, 1963, marked "F–2" on head; seven dolls in series
Boxed
16".................... $50.00 – 60.00
Gemmette, 1963, rooted hair, sleep eyes, jointed vinyl, dressed in gem colored dress, includes child's jeweled ring
Misses Amethyst, Diamond, Emerald, Ruby, Sapphire, and Topaz
15½"............................ $50.00
Georgie, Georgette, 1971, vinyl head, cloth

bodies, redheaded twins
22"..................... $40.00 – 50.00
Gigi Perreau, 1951, early vinyl head, hard plastic body, open/closed smiling mouth
17"................. $550.00 – 700.00
Honey, 1949, hard plastic
12"................. $125.00 – 150.00
Karena Ballerina, 1958, vinyl head, rooted hair, sleep eyes, closed mouth, hard plastic body, jointed knees, ankles, neck, shoulders, and hips, head turns when walks
21"..................... $45.00 – 55.00
Little Debutantes, 1958, vinyl head, rooted hair, sleep eyes, closed mouth, hard plastic body, swivel waist, high-heeled feet
18" – 20"............ $80.00 – 90.00
28"................. $100.00 – 125.00
My Fair Lady, 1958, all-vinyl, fashion type, swivel waist, fully jointed
20"..................... $65.00 – 75.00
Parton, Dolly, 1978
11½"................. $20.00 – 25.00
18"..................... $40.00 – 45.00
Posi Playmate, 1969, vinyl head, foam-filled vinyl body, bendable arms and legs, painted or rooted hair, sleep or painted eyes
12"..................... $15.00 – 20.00
Puppetrina, 1963 on, vinyl head, cloth body, rooted hair, sleep eyes, pocket in back for child to insert hand to manipulate doll's head and arms
22"..................... $70.00 – 80.00
Shelly, 1964, Tammy-type, grow hair
12"..................... $12.00 – 18.00
Sniffles, 1963, vinyl head, rooted hair, sleep eyes, open/closed mouth, marked "13/14 AA–EEGEE"
12"..................... $15.00 – 20.00
Susan Stroller, 1955, vinyl head, hard plastic walker body, rooted hair, closed mouth
20"..................... $60.00 – 70.00
23"..................... $75.00 – 85.00

26"...................... $85.00 – 90.00

Tandy Talks, 1961, vinyl head, hard plastic body, freckles, pull string talker

20"...................... $75.00 – 85.00

Ventriloquist dolls, 1960s, vinyl and cloth

Lester

25"...................... $50.00 – 60.00

Charlie McCarthy

30"................. $125.00 – 150.00

Bozo

31"...................... $70.00 – 80.00

Winky the Wurlitzer Walking doll, vinyl

36"................. $100.00 – 125.00

EFFANBEE

1910 to present, New York City. Founded by Bernard Fleischaker and Hugo Baum. This company began selling composition headed dolls, these heads were made for them by Otto Ernst Denivelle (marked Deco). Effanbee eventually did their own manufacturing, by the late 1920s they were one of the leading manufacturers of American composition dolls. They went on to make dolls of hard plastic and vinyl. In 2002 the company was purchased by Robert Tonner. The new management of the company is currently re-issuing many of the designs from the past as well as new pieces. Values shown are for early dolls in good condition with original clothing, dolls from 1950 on in perfect condition with appropriate tags. More for exceptional doll with wardrobe or accessories.

Bisque/ Composition

Mary Jane, 1920, dolly-faced doll to compete with German bisque. Some with bisque heads, others composition; bisque head, manufactured by Lenox Potteries, NJ, for Effanbee, sleep eyes, composition body, wooden arms and legs, also kid body with wood and composition limbs

Composition shoulder head marked Effanbee on kid body (marked with Effanbee sticker), wooden ball-jointed arms and legs, composition hands, wigged, sleep eyes

24" .... $450.00 – 500.00

Early Composition

Babies

Baby Bud, 1918 on, all-composition, painted features, molded hair, open/closed mouth, jointed arms, legs molded to body, one finger goes into mouth

6".................... $175.00 – 195.00

Black.............. $200.00 – 225.00

Baby Dainty, 1912 on, name given to a variety of dolls, with composition heads, cloth bodies, some toddler types, some mama-types with crier

12" – 14"........ $150.00 – 170.00

15"................. $175.00 – 200.00

Vinyl

10"..................... $30.00 – 40.00

Baby Effanbee, 1925, composition head, cloth body

12" – 13"........ $165.00 – 185.00

Baby Evelyn, 1925, composition head, cloth body

17"................. $250.00 – 275.00

12" Coquette, composition head, 1912 on. $400.00. **Photo courtesy of Joan & Lynette Antique Dolls and Accessories.**

21" Bubbles baby doll. $400.00.
Photo courtesy of Joan & Lynette Antique Dolls and Accessories.

Baby Grumpy, 1915 on, also later variations, composition character, heavily molded and painted hair, frowning eyebrows, painted intaglio eyes, pin-jointed limbs, cork-stuffed cloth body, gauntlet arms, pouty mouth

Mold #172, 174, 176
12" – 16"........ $400.00 – 450.00
Black.............. $525.00 – 600.00

Baby Grumpy Gladys, 1923, composition shoulder head, cloth body, marked in oval, "Effanbee//Baby Grumpy// corp. 1923"
15"................. $300.00 – 350.00

Grumpy Aunt Dinah, black, cloth body, striped stocking legs
14½"............. $400.00 – 425.00

Grumpykins, 1927, composition head, cloth body, composition arms, some with cloth legs, others with composition legs
12"................. $200.00 – 250.00
Black.............. $325.00 – 375.00

Grumpykins, Pennsylvania Dutch Dolls, 1936, dressed by Marie Polack in Mennonite, River Brethren, and Amish costumes
12"................. $225.00 – 250.00

Bubbles, 1924 on, composition shoulder head, open/closed mouth, painted teeth, molded and painted hair, sleep eyes, cloth body, bent-cloth legs, some with composition toddler legs, composition arms, finger of left hand fits into mouth, wore heart necklace, various marks including "Effanbee// Bubbles//Copr. 1924//Made in U.S.A."
16" – 18"........ $375.00 – 425.00
20" – 22"........ $475.00 – 525.00
24" – 26"........ $700.00 – 800.00

Lamkin, 1930 on, composition molded head, sleep eyes, open mouth, cloth body, crier, chubby composition legs, with feet turned in, fingers curled, molded gold ring on middle finger
16"................. $400.00 – 425.00

Lovums, 1928 on, child doll, composition swivel head, shoulder plate, and limbs, cloth body, sleep eyes, molded and painted hair or wigged, can have bent baby legs or toddler legs
16" – 18"........ $375.00 – 425.00
20" – 22"........ $400.00 – 450.00
25" – 28"........ $450.00 – 500.00

Pat-o-Pat, 1925 on, composition head, painted eyes, cloth body with mechanism which, when pressed causes hands to clap
13"................. $200.00 – 250.00
15"................. $250.00 – 275.00

Cloth mask faced
15"................. $575.00 – 600.00

Character Children, 1912 on, composition, heavily molded hair, painted eyes, pin-jointed cloth body, composition arms, cloth or composition legs, some marked "Deco"

Cliquot Eskimo, 1920, painted eyes, molded hair, felt hands, mohair suit
18"................. $525.00

Coquette, Naughty Marietta, 1915, composition girl, molded bow in hair, side-glancing eyes, cloth body
12"................. $375.00 – 425.00

Harmonica Joe, 1923, cloth body, with rubber ball, when squeezed provides air to open mouth with harmonica

15"................ $425.00 – 450.00

Irish Mail Kid, 1915, or Dixie Flyer, composition head, cloth body, arms sewn to steering handle of wooden wagon

10"................ $300.00 – 325.00

Johnny Tu-face, 1912, composition head with face on front and back, painted features, open/closed crying mouth, closed smiling mouth, molded and painted hair, cloth body, red striped legs, cloth feet, dressed in knitted romper and hat

16"................ $375.00 – 425.00

Pouting Bess, 1915, composition head with heavily molded curls, painted eyes, closed mouth, clothcork stuffed body, pin jointed, mark: "162" or "166" on back of head

15"................ $300.00 – 325.00

Whistling Jim, 1916, composition head, with heavily molded hair, painted intaglio eyes, perforated mouth, cork stuffed cloth body, black sewn-on cloth shoes, wears red striped shirt, blue overalls, mark, label: "Effanbee//Whistling Jim//Trade Mark"

15"................ $300.00 – 325.00

MaMa Dolls, 1921 on, including Rosemary and Marilee, composition shoulder head, painted or sleep eyes, molded hair or wigged, cloth body, swing legs, crier, with composition arms and lower legs

14"................ $275.00 – 300.00

17" – 19"........ $300.00 – 375.00

24" – 27"........ $350.00 – 400.00

Late Composition

American Children, 1936 – 1939 on, all-composition, designed by Dewees Cochran, open mouth, separated fingers can wear gloves, marks: heads may be unmarked, "Effanbee//Anne Shirley" on body

Babyette, 1943, eyes molded closed

20" painted eye American Children girl, designed by Dewees Cochran. $1,900.00. Photo courtesy of Richard Withington, Inc.

13"................ $350.00 – 400.00

Barbara Joan, Barbara Ann

14" – 17"........ $600.00 – 750.00

Barbara Lou

21"................ $900.00 – 925.00

Closed mouth, separated fingers, sleep or painted eyes, marks: "Effanbee// American//Children" on head; "Effanbee// Anne Shirley" on body

Painted eye such as Peggy Lou and others

14" – 17".. $1,300.00 – 1,700.00

19" – 21".. $1,800.00 – 2,000.00

Sleep eye such as Gloria Ann and others

17" – 21".. $1,800.00 – 2,000.00

Anne Shirley, 1936 – 1940, never advertised as such, same mold used for Little Lady, all-composition, more grown-up body style, mark: "EFFANBEE//ANNE SHIRLEY"

14" – 15"........ $200.00 – 225.00

17" – 18"........ $250.00 – 275.00

21"................ $300.00 – 375.00

27"................ $450.00 – 500.00

Movie Anne Shirley, 1935 – 1940. 1934

14" Historical replica doll. $595.00. **Photo courtesy of American Beauty Dolls.**

RKO movie character, Anne Shirley from Anne of Green Gables movie, all-composition, marked "Patsy" or other Effanbee doll, red braids, wearing Anne Shirley movie costume and gold paper hang tag stating "I am Anne Shirley." The Anne Shirley costume changes the identity of these dolls.

Mary Lee/Anne Shirley, open mouth, head marked "©Mary Lee," on marked "Patsy Joan" body

16"................. $450.00 – 500.00

Patsyette/Anne Shirley, body marked "Effanbee// Patsyette// Doll"

9½"................. $325.00 – 375.00

Patricia/Anne Shirley, body marked "Patricia"

15"................. $500.00 – 550.00

Patricia-kin/Anne Shirley, head marked "Patricia-kin," body marked "Effanbee// Patsy Jr.," hang tag reads "Anne Shirley"

11½"............. $325.00 – 375.00

Bright Eyes, 1940, composition head, hands, legs, cloth body, molded hair

14" – 16"........ 4250.00 – 350.00

Brother or Sister, 1943, composition head, hands, cloth body, legs, yarn hair, painted eyes

12" – 16" .... $200.00 – 250.00

Butin-nose: See Patsy family, and vinyl.

Candy Kid, 1946 on, all-composition, sleep eyes, toddler body, molded and painted hair, closed mouth

13" .... $500.00 – 550.00

Charlie McCarthy, 1937, composition head, hands, feet, painted features, mouth opens, cloth body, legs, marked: "Edgar Bergen's Charlie McCarthy//An Effanbee Product"

17" – 19"........ $400.00 – 450.00

Happy Birthday Doll, 1940, music box in body, heart bracelet

17"................. $450.00 – 550.00

Historical Dolls, 1939 on, all-composition, jointed body, human hair wigs, painted eyes, made only three sets of 30 dolls depicting history of apparel, 1492 – 1939, very fancy original costumes, metal heart bracelet, head marked "Effanbee//American//Children," on body, "Effanbee//Anne Shirley"

21"........... $2,250.00 – 2,500.00

Historical Replicas, 1939 on, all-composition, jointed body, copies of sets above, but smaller, human hair wigs, painted eyes, original costumes

14"................. $450.00 – 600.00

Honey, 1947 – 1948, all-composition jointed body, human hair wig, sleep eyes, closed mouth

18" – 21"........ $200.00 – 375.00

All hard plastic, ca. 1949 – 1955, see Vinyl and Hard Plastic later in this category.

Ice Queen, 1937 on, composition, open mouth, skater outfit

17"................. $625.00 – 750.00

Little Lady, 1939 on, used Anne Shirley mold, all-composition, wigged, sleep eyes, more grown-up body, separated fingers, gold paper hang tag, many in formals, as brides, or fancy gowns with matching parasol, during war years yarn hair was used, may have gold hang tag with name, like Gaye or Carole

15".................. $275.00 – 325.00
18".................. $350.00 – 400.00
21".................. $375.00 – 425.00
27".................. $450.00 – 475.00

Mae Starr, 1928, talking doll, composition shoulder head, cloth body, open mouth, four teeth, with cylinder records, marked: "Mae// Starr// Doll"

29".................. $600.00 – 700.00

Marionettes, 1937 on, puppets designed by Virginia Austin, composition, painted eyes
Clippo, clown

15".................. $175.00 – 225.00

Emily Ann

14".................. $175.00 – 225.00

Lucifer, black

15".............. $525.00* mint-in-box

Portrait Dolls, 1940 on, all-composition, Bo-Peep, Ballerina, Bride, Groom, Gibson Girl, Colonial Maid, etc.

12".................. $275.00 – 350.00

Suzanne, 1940, all-composition, jointed body, sleep eyes, wigged, closed mouth, may have magnets in hands to hold accessories, more for additional accessories or wardrobe

14".................. $400.00 – 475.00

Suzette, 1939, all-composition, fully jointed, painted side-glancing eyes, closed mouth, wigged

12".................. $300.00 – 325.00

Sweetie Pie, 1939 on, also called Baby Bright Eyes, Tommy Tucker, Mickey, composition bent limbs, sleep eyes, caracul wig, cloth body, crier, issued again in 1952+ in hard plastic, cloth body, and vinyl limbs, painted hair or synthetic wigs, wore same pink rayon taffeta dress with black and white trim as Noma doll

16" – 18"........ $275.00 – 325.00
20" – 24"........ $350.00 – 450.00

W. C. Fields, 1929 on, composition shoulder

22" composition Bright Eyes, flirty eyed. $750.00. **Photo courtesy of Dollyology Vintage Dolls.**

head, painted features, hinged mouth, painted teeth

1980, vinyl, Legend Series, marked: "W.C. Fields//An Effanbee Product"

17½".............. $900.00 – 950.00

Patsy Family, 1928 on, composition through 1947, later issued in vinyl and porcelain, many had gold paper hang tag and metal bracelet that read "Effanbee Durable Dolls," more for black, special editions, costumes, or with added accessories

Babies

Patsy Baby, 1931, painted or sleep eyes, wigged or molded hair, composition baby body, advertised as Babykin, came also with cloth body, in pair, layettes, trunks, marks: on head, "Effanbee//Patsy Baby"; on body, "Effanbee //Patsy// Baby"

10" – 11"........ $275.00 – 325.00

Patsy Babyette, 1932, sleep eyes, marked on head "Effanbee," on body "Effanbee//Patsy //Babyette"

9".................... $325.00 – 400.00

Patsy Baby Tinyette, 1934, painted eyes, bent-leg composition body, marked on head "Effanbee," on body "Effan-bee//Baby//

17" composition Little Lady. $325.00. Photo courtesy of McMasters Harris Auction Co.

Tinyette"

7".................. $300.00 – 375.00

Quints, 1935, set of five Patsy Baby Tinyettes in original box, from FAO Schwarz, organdy christening gowns and milk glass bottles, excellent condition

Set of five

7"............. $1,750.00 – 2,200.00

Children

Patsy

1924, cloth body, composition legs, open mouth, upper teeth, sleep eyes, painted or human hair wig, with composition legs to hips, marked in half oval on back shoulder plate: "Effanbee//Patsy"

15"................. $300.00 – 350.00

1928, all-composition jointed body, painted or sleep eyes, molded headband on red molded bobbed hair, or wigged, bent right arm, with gold paper hang tag, metal heart bracelet, marked on body: "Effanbee//Patsy// Pat. Pend.//Doll"

14"................. $600.00 – 650.00

Oriental with black painted hair, painted eyes, in fancy silk pajamas and matching shoes

14"................. $750.00 – 800.00

1946, all-composition jointed body, bright facial coloring, painted or sleep eyes, wears pink or blue checked pinafore

14"................. $450.00 – 500.00

Patsy Ann, 1929, all-composition, closed mouth, sleep eyes, molded hair, or wigged, marked on body:"Effanbee//'Patsy-Ann'//©//Pat. #1283558"

19"................. $450.00 – 500.00

1959, limited edition, vinyl, sleep eyes, white organdy dress, with pink hair ribbon, marked "Effanbee//Patsy Ann//©1959" on head, "Effanbee" on body

15"................. $245.00 – 285.00

Patsyette, 1931, composition

9".................. $325.00 – 375.00

Black, Dutch, George & Martha Washington

9" ....$350.00 – 400.00 each

Patsy Fluff, 1932, all-cloth, with painted features, pink checked rompers and bonnet

16"............................ $1,000.00

Too few examples in database for reliable range.

Patsy Joan, 1931, composition

16"............... $4500.00 – 475.00

1946, marked "Effanbee" on body, with extra "d" added

17"................. $325.00 – 425.00

Patsy Jr., 1931, all-composition, advertised as Patsykins, marks: "Effanbee//Patsy Jr.// Doll"

11½"............. $300.00 – 325.00

Patsy Lou, 1930, all-composition, molded red hair or wigged, marks: "Effanbee//Patsy Lou" on body

22"................. $400.00 – 475.00

Patsy Mae, 1934, shoulder head, sleep eyes, cloth body, crier, swing legs, marks: "Effanbee//Patsy Mae" on head, "Effanbee// Lovums//c//Pat. No. 1283558" on shoulder plate

    29".......... $1,500.00 – 1,600.00

Patsy Ruth, 1934, shoulder head, sleep eyes, cloth body, crier, swing legs, marks: "Effanbee//Patsy Ruth" on head, "Effanbee//Lovums//©//Pat. No. 1283558" on shoulder plate

    26".......... $1,600.00 – 1,700.00

Patsy Tinyette Toddler, 1935, painted eyes, marks: "Effanbee" on head, "Effanbee// Baby//Tinyette" on body

    7¾"................ $325.00 – 375.00

Tinyette Toddler, tagged "Kit & Kat"

    In Dutch costume.. $800.00 for pair

Wee Patsy, 1935, head molded to body, molded and painted shoes and socks, jointed arms and hips, advertised only as "Fairy Princess," pin back button, marks on body: "Effanbee//Wee Patsy"

    5¾"................ $400.00 – 450.00

Related items

    Metal heart bracelet, reads "Effanbee Durable Dolls"................... $25.00

    Metal personalized name bracelet for Patsy family....................... $65.00

    Patsy Ann, Her Happy Times, ca. 1935, book by Mona Reed King... $75.00

    Patsy For Keeps, c 1932, book by Ester Marian Ames $125.00

Patricia Series, 1935, all sizes advertised in Patsytown News, all-composition slimmer bodies, sleep eyes, wigged, later WWII-era Patricia dolls had yarn hair and cloth bodies

Patricia, wig, sleep eyes, marked, "Effanbee Patricia" body

    15"................ $375.00 – 425.00

Patricia Ann, wig, marks unknown

    19"................ $600.00 – 650.00

Patricia Joan, wig, marks unknown, slimmer legs

5¾" Wee Patsy. $275.00. Photo courtesy of The Museum Doll Shop.

    16"................ $500.00 – 550.00

Patricia-Kin, wig, mark: "Patricia-Kin" head; "Effanbee//Patsy Jr." body

    11½".............. $350.00 – 400.00

Patricia Lou, wig, marks unknown

    22"................ $475.00 – 525.00

Patricia Ruth, head marked: "Effanbee// Patsy Ruth," no marks on slimmer composition body

    27".......... $1,200.00 – 1,350.00

Patsy Related Dolls and Variants

Betty Bee, 1932, all-composition, short tousle wig, sleep eyes, marked on body: "Effanbee//Patsy Lou"

    22"................ $375.00 – 400.00

Betty Bounce, tousle head, 1932 on, all-composition, sleep eyes, used Lovums head on body, marked: "Effanbee//'Patsy Ann'/ /©//Pat. #1283558"

    19"................ $350.00 – 400.00

Betty Brite, 1932, all-composition, short tousle wig, sleep eyes, some marked: "Effanbee// Betty Brite" on body and others marked on head "© Mary-Lee," on body "Effanbee Patsy Joan," gold hang tag reads "This is

Betty Brite, The lovable Imp with tiltable head and movable limb, an Effanbee doll."

16".................. $300.00 – 350.00

Butin-nose, 1936 on, all-composition, molded and painted hair, features, distinct feature is small nose, usually has regional or special costume

8".................... $275.00 – 300.00

Cowboy .... $325.00 – 350.00

Dutch pair, with gold paper hang tags reading: "Kit and Kat"

8".................... $500.00 – 525.00

Oriental, with layette

8".................................. $525.00

Mary Ann, 1932 on, composition, sleep eyes, wigged, open mouth, marked: "Mary Ann" on head, "Effanbee//'Patsy Ann'//©//Pat. #1283558" on body

19"................. $350.00 – 375.00

Mary Lee, 1932, composition, sleep eyes, wigged, open mouth, marked: "©//Mary Lee" on head, "Effanbee//Patsy Joan" on body

16½"............. $325.00 – 350.00

Patsy/Patricia, 1940, used a marked Patsy head on a marked Patricia body, all-composition, painted eyes, molded hair, may have magnets in hands to hold accessories, marked on body: "Effanbee//'Patricia'"

15"................. $400.00 – 450.00

Skippy, 1929, advertised as Patsy's boyfriend, composition head, painted eyes, molded and painted blond hair, composition or cloth body, with composition molded shoes and legs, marked on head: "Effanbee//Skippy//©//P. L. Crosby," on body "Effanbee//Patsy//Pat. Pend// Doll"

14"

Military outfit .... $400.00 – 425.00

Boy's outfit.............. $600.00 – 650.00

11" Dy-Dee doll, all original exceptional condition. $1,099.00. **Photo courtesy of Dollyology Vintage Dolls.**

Rubber

Dy-Dee, 1934 on, hard rubber head, sleep eyes, jointed rubber bent-leg body, drink/ wet mechanism, molded and painted hair. Early dolls had molded ears, after 1940 had applied rubber ears, nostrils, and tear ducts, later made in hard plastic and vinyl, marked: "Effanbee//Dy-Dee Baby" with four patent numbers

Dy-Dee Wee

9"..................	$275.00 – 300.00
11"..................	$200.00 – 225.00
13"..................	$225.00 – 250.00
15"..................	$375.00 – 400.00
20"..................	$425.00 – 450.00

Dy-Dee in Layette Trunk, with accessories

15".................	$550.00 – 575.00

Hard Plastic and Vinyl, dolls listed are all in good condition wearing original clothing, allow more for MIB

Alyssa, 1960 – 1961, vinyl head, hard plastic jointed body, walker, including elbows, rooted saran hair, sleep eyes

23".................	$200.00 – 225.00

Baby Lisa, 1980, vinyl, designed by Astri Campbell, represents a three-month-old baby, in wicker basket with accessories

11".....................	$65.00 – 75.00

Baby Lisa Grows Up, 1983, vinyl, toddler body, in trunk with wardrobe

	$75.00 – 85.00

Butterball, 1969, all vinyl, molded hair, sleep eyes

12".....................	$40.00 – 45.00

Button Nose, 1968 – 1971, vinyl head, cloth body

18".....................	$25.00 – 35.00

Champagne Lady, 1959, vinyl head and arms, rooted hair, blue sleep eyes, lashes, hard plastic body, from Lawrence Welk's TV show, Miss Revlon-type

21".................	$225.00 – 275.00

23".................	$250.00 – 300.00

Currier & Ives, vinyl and hard plastic

12".....................	$35.00 – 45.00

Disney dolls, 1977 – 1978, Snow White, Cinderella, Alice in Wonderland, and Sleeping Beauty

14".................	$145.00 – 185.00
16½"..............	$300.00 – 325.00

Fluffy, 1954+, all-vinyl

8".......................	$15.00 – 20.00
11".....................	$35.00 – 40.00

Black .... $40.00 – 45.00

*Grand Dames,*1970 on, vinyl, sleep eyes, rooted hair elaborate costumes

11".....................	$20.00 – 25.00
15".....................	$30.00 – 35.00
18".....................	$20.00 – 25.00

Gumdrop, 1962 on, vinyl, jointed toddler, sleep eyes, rooted hair

16".....................	$25.00 – 30.00

Hagara, Jan, designer, all-vinyl, jointed, rooted hair, painted eyes, Christina 1984, Larry 1985, Laurel 1984, Lesley 1985

15".....................	$40.00 – 65.00

Half Pint, 1966 – 1983, all-vinyl, rooted hair, sleep eyes, lashes

11".....................	$25.00 – 30.00

Happy Boy, 1960, vinyl, molded hair, tooth, freckles, painted eyes

11".....................	$45.00 – 50.00

Hibel, Edna, designer, 1984 only, all-vinyl

Flower Girl .... $75.00 – 95.00

Contessa .... $75.00 – 95.00

Honey, 1949 – 1958, hard plastic (see also composition), saran wig, sleep eyes, closed mouth, marked on head and back, "Effanbee," had gold paper hang tag that read: "I am//Honey//An//Effanbee// Sweet/ /Child"

Honey, 1949 – 1955, all hard plastic, closed mouth, sleep eyes

14".................	$300.00 – 325.00

18" Grand Dames, Topaz. $25.00. **Doll from private collection.**

Cinderella, 14" $650.00*
Prince Charming, 14" $725.00*
18" .... $450.00 – 500.00
In tagged Schiaparelli gown
18" $700.00*
24" .... $500.00 – 525.00
Honey Walker, 1952 on, all hard plastic with walking mechanism, Honey Walker Junior Miss, 1956 – 1957, hard plastic, extra joints at knees and ankles permit her to wear flat or high-heeled shoes, add $50.00 for jointed knees, ankles
14" .... $275.00 – 300.00
19" .... $400.00 – 425.00
Humpty Dumpty, 1985 .. $55.00 – 75.00
Katie, 1957, molded hair
8½" .... $40.00 – 50.00
Legend Series, vinyl, 15½", allow double for MIB
1980, W.C. Fields .... $45.00 – 50.00
1981, John Wayne, cowboy

$50.00 – 60.00
1982, John Wayne, cavalry
$50.00 – 60.00
1982, Mae West .... $20.00 – 25.00
1983, Groucho Marx ... $20.00 – 25.00
1984, Judy Garland, Dorothy
$40.00 – 45.00
1985, Lucille Ball .... $50.00 – 60.00
1986, Liberace .... $20.00 – 25.00
1987, James Cagney.... $20.00 – 25.00
Lil Sweetie, 1967, nurser with no lashes or brow
16" .... $40.00 – 45.00
Limited Edition Club, vinyl
1975, Precious Baby .. $150.00 – 175.00
1976, Patsy Ann ...... $160.00 – 180.00
1977, Dewees Cochran.. $65.00 – 75.00
1978, Crowning Glory .. $40.00 – 50.00
1979, Skippy .... $150.00 – 175.00
1980, Susan B. Anthony ..$40.00 – 50.00
1981, Girl with Watering Can
$60.00 – 70.00
1982, Princess Diana ..$100.00 – 125.00
1983, Sherlock Holmes. $65.00 – 75.00
1984, Bubbles .... $45.00 – 50.00
1985, Red Boy .... $35.00 – 40.00
1986, China head .... $25.00 – 30.00
1987 – 1988, Porcelain Grumpy (2,500)
$100.00 – 125.00
Vinyl Grumpy .... $40.00 – 50.00
Martha and George Washington, 1976 – 1977, all-vinyl, fully jointed, rooted hair, blue eyes, molded lashes
11" pair .... $50.00 – 75.00
Mickey, 1956 – 1972, all-vinyl, fully jointed, some with molded hat, painted eyes
10" .... $35.00 – 45.00
Miss Chips, 1966 – 1981, all-vinyl, fully jointed, side-glancing sleep eyes, rooted hair
17" .... $35.00 – 45.00
Black

17".................... $45.00 – 55.00

Most Happy Family, 1958, vinyl, 21" mother, 10" brother and sister, 8" baby

Set................. $125.00 – 175.00

Noma, The Electronic Doll, 1950, hard plastic, cloth body, vinyl limbs, battery-operated talking doll, wore pink rayon taffeta dress with black and white check trim

27"................. $350.00 – 375.00

Polka Dottie, 1954, vinyl head, with molded pigtails on fabric body, or with hard plastic body

21".................. $145.00 – 165.00

Latex body

11".................. $100.00 – 120.00

Personality Series

1984, Sir Winston Churchill

$50.00 – 60.00

1984, Louis Armstrong.. $65.00 – 75.00

1984, Mark Twain .... $50.00 – 60.00

1985, Eleanor Roosevelt.. $45.00 – 50.00

Presidents, 1984 on

Abraham Lincoln

18"...................... $40.00 – 45.00

George Washington

16".................... $40.00 – 45.00

Teddy Roosevelt

17"................... $60.00 – 65.00

Franklin D. Roosevelt

1985 .... $45.00 – 50.00

Andrew Jackson

1989 .... $45.00 – 50.00

Princess Diana, 1982, vinyl

18"...................... $20.00 – 25.00

Pun'kin, 1966 – 1983, all-vinyl, fully jointed toddler, sleep eyes, rooted hair

11"..................... $15.00 – 20.00

Rootie Kazootie, 1954, vinyl head, cloth or hard plastic body, smaller size has latex body

11"................. $100.00 – 120.00

21" .... $145.00 – 165.00

Santa Claus, 1982 on, designed by Faith Wick, "Old Fashioned Nast Santa," No. 7201, vinyl head, hands, stuffed cloth body, molded and painted features, marked "Effanbee//7201 c//Faith Wick"

18"...................... $65.00 – 75.00

Sugar Pie, 1960, vinyl nurser, rooted or molded hair, sleep eyes

14" – 16"............ $30.00 – 40.00

Suzie Sunshine, 1961 – 1979, designed by Eugenia Dukas, all-vinyl, fully jointed, rooted hair, sleep eyes, lashes, freckles on nose, add $25.00 more for black

18"...................... $40.00 – 50.00

Sweetie Pie, 1952, hard plastic

27"................. $300.00 – 325.00

Tintair, 1951, hard plastic, hair color set, to compete with Ideal's Toni

15"................. $350.00 – 400.00

MIB $780.00*

Wicket Witch, 1981 – 1982, designed by Faith Wick. No. 7110, vinyl head, blond rooted hair, painted features, cloth stuffed body, dressed in black, with apple and basket, head marked: "Effanbee//Faith Wick//7110 19cc81"

18"...................... $65.00 – 75.00

FARNELL-ALPHA TOYS

1915 – 1930s, Acton, London. Cloth dolls with molded felt or velvet heads, cloth bodies, painted features, mohair wigs.

Baby

15"................. $350.00 – 400.00

18"................. $450.00 – 550.00

Child

10"................. $350.00 – 400.00

15" King George VI, pressed felt face. $550.00. **Photo courtesy Glenda Antique Dolls & Collectables.**

14" – 15" .... $450.00 – 500.00
Black
13" .... $800.00 – 850.00
Too few in database for reliable range.
Characters such as Islanders, pirates etc.
15" .... $400.00 – 450.00
Long Limbed Lady doll
26" .... $800.00 – 850.00
Too few in database for reliable range.
King George VI, "H.M. The King"
15" .... $450.00 – 550.00
Palace Guard, "Beefeater"
15" .... $400.00 – 500.00

FRANKLIN MINT

The Franklin Mint, 1964 on, began to make legal tender coins for foreign countries, as well as commemorative medallions, casino tokens, and precious metal ingots. Eventually, the product line was expanded to include the sculptures, deluxe games, precision die-cast models, and collector dolls. Since 2003 the doll lines have been reduced in production, some phased out completely. Values are for secondary market dolls in perfect condition wearing original clothing, many are still available retail.

Vinyl
Cinderella
15½" .... $75.00 – 85.00
Marilyn Monroe
16" .... $75.00 – 100.00
Princess Diana
15½" .... $130.00 – 150.00
Porcelain
Arwen Evenstar
22" .... $125.00 – 140.00
Country Store Advertising Logo Dolls, 1986 on
13" .... $20.00 – 40.00
Gibson girl
21" .... $55.00 – 75.00
Jackie Kennedy
15" .... $70.00 – 80.00
With trunk and wardrobe
$200.00 – 300.00

15" porcelain Jackie Kennedy in bridal gown. $70.00. **Private collection.**

Marilyn Monroe
19"................... $75.00 – 150.00
Scarlett O'Hara, in wedding gown
19"................. $225.00 – 250.00
Princess Diana
18½"............... $75.00 – 100.00

FRENCH POUPÉE

15" Poupée Peau, swivel neck. $6,000.00. **Photo courtesy of Richard Withington, Inc.**

1869 on. Glass eyes, doll modeled as an adult lady, with bisque shoulder head, stationary or swivel neck, closed mouth, earrings, kid or kid and cloth body, nicely dressed, good condition. Add more for original clothing, special body such as Gesland, Kintzbach, Terrenne, black, or exceptional doll.

Poupée Peau (kid body), unmarked or with size number only
Glass eyes
    12" – 14" ... $3,000.00 – 6,000.00
    16" – 18" ... $6,000.00 – 8,000.00
    21"........... $7,000.00 – 7,500.00
    27"........... $8,000.00 – 9,000.00
Painted eyes, kid body
    14" – 16".. $1,600.00 – 1,900.00

Poupée Bois (wood body), unmarked or with size number only, articulated body, glass eyes
    13"........... $6,500.00 – 9,000.00
    15"........... $7,000.00 – 8,500.00
    18"........... $7,500.00 – 8,000.00
Kid-over wood body
    15" – 17" ... $4,800.00 – 8,000.00
Barrois: See Barrios section.
B.S., Blampoix
    12" – 14" ... $1,800.00 – 2,200.00
    16" – 17" ... $2,600.00 – 2,900.00
A. Dehors, 1860, swivel neck, bisque lower arms
Generic face, wooden body
    14"........... $2,400.00 – 2,500.00
    17" – 20" ... $5,000.00 – 9,000.00
Portrait face
    17" – 18"...$17,000.00 – 20,000.00
L.D., Louis Doleac, kid body
    17" – 20" ... $3,000.00 – 5,300.00
Too few in database for a reliable range.

17" Poupée Peau with bisque arms. $7,500.00. **Photo courtesy of Richard Withington, Inc.**

18" china head Poupée. $9,000.00.
Photo courtesy of Richard Withington, Inc.

Simonne
Kid body
16" – 17".. $5,000.00 – 6,000.00
Wood body
14".......... $6,500.00 – 7,500.00
18"......... $9,500.00 – 11,000.00
Fortune Teller Dolls, fashion-type head with swivel neck, glass or painted eyes, kid body, skirt made to hold many paper "fortunes," exceptional doll may be more
Closed mouth
15"........................... $4,100.00+
Open mouth
18"........................... $3,100.00+
China, glazed finish, 1870 – 1880 hairstyle
14" – 15" ...$5,000.00 – 5,500.00
18".......... $8,500.00 – 9,000.00
Accessories
Dress .... $500.00+
Shoes marked by maker .... $500.00+
Unmarked $250.00
Trunk .... $250.00+
Wig .... $250.00+

RALPH A. FREUNDLICH

1924 – 1945, New York City, later Clinton, Massachusetts. Ralph Freundlich worked for Jeanette Doll Co. then opened Silver Doll & Toy Manufacturing Co. in 1923. In 1924 became Ralph Freundlich Inc. and made composition dolls. Dolls listed are in good condition wearing original clothing.
Baby Sandy, 1939 – 1942, all-composition, jointed toddler body, molded hair, painted or sleep eyes, smiling mouth
8".................... $200.00 – 250.00
12"................. $300.00 – 350.00
15"................. $400.00 – 450.00
20"................. $625.00 – 700.00
Dummy Dan, ventriloquist doll, Charlie McCarthy look-alike
15"..................... $50.00 – 75.00
21"................... $75.00 – 100.00

17" Baby Sandy. $600.00. Photo courtesy of Emmie's Antique Doll Castle.

General Douglas MacArthur, 1942, all-composition, jointed body, bent arm salutes, painted features, molded hat, jointed, in khaki uniform, with paper tag
   18"................. $300.00 – 400.00
Military dolls, 1942+, all-composition, molded hats, painted features, original clothes, with paper tag Soldier, Sailor, WAAC, or WAVE
   15"................. $300.00 – 350.00
Orphan Annie and her dog, Sandy
   12"................. $525.00 – 625.00
Pig Baby, 1930s, composition pig head, with painted features on unmarked five-piece body, freundlich presumed maker of similar composition cat, rabbit, and monkey dolls
   9"................... $350.00 – 400.00
Pinocchio, composition and cloth, with molded hair, painted features, brightly colored cheeks, large eyes, open/closed mouth, tagged: "Original as portrayed by C. Collodi"
   16"................. $425.00 – 500.00
Red Riding Hood, Wolf, Grandma, 1934, composition, set of three, in schoolhouse box, original clothes
Set of three
   9"................... $775.00 – 875.00
Trixbe (Patsy-type), all-composition girl,

painted features, molded painted hair with bow pined into head
   11"................. $100.00 – 125.00

FULPER POTTERY CO.

1918 – 1921, Flemington, New Jersey. Made dolls with bisque heads and all-bisque dolls. Sold dolls to Amberg, Colonial Toy Mfg. Co., and Horsman. "M.S." monogram stood for Martin Stangl, in charge of production. Dolls listed are in good condition with original or appropriate clothes.
Baby, bisque socket head, glass eyes, open mouth, teeth, mohair wig, bent-leg body
   14" – 16"........ $300.00 – 400.00
   17" – 22"........ $375.00 – 475.00
Toddler
   16" – 18"........ $575.00 – 625.00
Child, socket-head, glass eyes, open mouth
Kid body
   18" – 22"........ $275.00 – 300.00

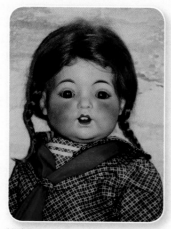

17" bisque character baby on toddler body by Fulper Pottery Co. $600.00.
Photo courtesy of Fine Antique Dolls & Accessories.

27" mold 513.. $400.00 – 500.00
Composition body
16" – 18"........ $350.00 – 400.00
22" – 24"........ $450.00 – 525.00

GABRIEL

The Lone Ranger Series, vinyl action figures with horses, separate accessory sets available. Doll in very good condition with original clothing and accessories. Mint-in-box can bring double values listed.
Dan Reed on Banjo, blond hair, figure on palomino horse
9"........ $40.00 – 50.00
Butch Cavendish on Smoke, black hair, mustache, on black horse
9"........ $50.00 – 55.00
Lone Ranger on Silver, masked figure on white horse
9"........ $45.00 – 50.00
Little Bear, Indian boy
6"........ $50.00 – 55.00
Red Sleeves, vinyl Indian figure, black hair, wears shirt with red sleeves
9"........ $50.00 – 55.00
Tonto on Scout, Indian on brown and white horse
9"........ $45.00 – 50.00

GANS & SEYFARTH PUPPENBABRIK

1908 – 1922, Waltershausen, Thüringia. Made bisque dolls; had a patent for flirty and googly eyes. Partners separated in 1922, Otto Gans opened his own factory.
Baby, bent-leg baby, original clothes or appropriately dressed
16"........ $400.00 – 450.00
20"........ $525.00 – 575.00

25"........ $650.00 – 725.00
Child, open mouth, composition body, original clothes, or appropriately dressed, no mold number or molds 120, 6589
13" – 15"........ $325.00 – 425.00
21" – 24"........ $450.00 – 500.00
28"........ $650.00 – 700.00

FRANCOIS GAULTIER

1860 – 1899. After 1899, became part of S.F.B.J., located near Paris. They made bisque doll heads and parts for lady dolls and for bébés and sold to many French makers of dolls including Gesland, Jullien, Petite et Dumontier, Rabery et Delphieu, and Thuillier. Also made all-bisque dolls marked "F.G." Dolls listed are in good condition, appropriately dressed.
Poupée (fashion-type), 1860 on, F.G., marked swivel head on bisque shoulder plate, kid body, may have bisque lower arms
Glass eyes
10" – 11" ... $1,700.00 – 1,900.00
12" – 13" ... $2,100.00 – 2,600.00
15" – 17" ... $3,750.00 – 4,500.00
18" – 20" ... $4,800.00 – 5,000.00
23" – 24" ... $6,000.00 – 6,200.00
Painted eyes
16" – 17" ... $1,800.00 – 2,000.00
Wood body
16" – 18"...$10,000.00 – 10,200.00
Later one-piece shoulder head, kid body, often in regional dress
Painted eyes
12" – 15"........ $700.00 – 900.00
Glass eyes
18"........ $900.00 – 1,000.00
Bébé (child), "F.G." in block letters, 1879 – 1887, closed mouth, excellent quality bisque

13" bébé marked F. 3 G. (block letters) on a kid body. $4,000.00. **Photo courtesy of The Museum Doll Shop.**

socket head, glass eyes, pierced ears, cork pate

Composition and wood body with straight wrists

10" – 11"	...$6,500.00 – 7,000.00
13" – 16"	...$5,000.00 – 7,500.00
18" – 22"	...$6,000.00 – 7,000.00
27" – 28"	...$7,000.00 – 8,000.00

Kid body, may have bisque forearms

10" – 12"	...$4,000.00 – 4,200.00
12" with trunk and wardrobe	$8,500.00*
13" – 15"	...$4,200.00 – 4,800.00
17" – 19"	...$4,800.00 – 5,400.00

Bébé (child), "F.G." inside scroll, 1887 – 1900, composition body, closed mouth

13"	...$3,200.00 – 4,000.00
15" – 17"	...$3,200.00 – 4,000.00
22" – 24"	...$4,000.00 – 4,200.00
28"	...$5,000.00 – 5,500.00

Composition body, open mouth

14" – 16"	...$1,700.00 – 1,900.00
20" – 24"	...$2,100.00 – 2,700.00

GESLAND

1860 – 1928, Paris. Made, repaired, exported, and distributed dolls, patented a doll body, used heads from Francois Gaultier with "F.G." block or scroll mark. In 1926 became part of the Société Industrielle de France. Gesland's doll's body had metal articulated armature covered with padding and stockinette, with bisque or wood/composition hands and legs. Dolls listed are in good condition, appropriately dressed. Allow more for exceptional original clothing.

Poupée (fashion-type) Gesland, stockinette covered metal articulated fashion-type body, bisque lower arms and legs

14"	...$4,000.00 – 5,500.00
16" – 17"	...$4,000.00 – 5,000.00
23" – 24"	...$5,000.00 – 5,500.00

Bébé (child) on marked Gesland body, closed mouth

12" – 15"	...$6,000.00 – 7,000.00
17" – 20"	...$5,500.00 – 6,000.00
22" – 24"	...$5,700.00 – 6,200.00
28" – 30"	...$4,900.00 – 6,200.00

14½" French poupée with Gesland body. $4,200.00. **Photo courtesy of Atlanta Antique Gallery.**

RUTH GIBBS

7" Godey lady doll by Ruth Gibbs. $80.00.
Doll courtesy of Elaine Holda.

1946 on, Flemington, New Jersey. Made dolls with china heads and limbs on cloth bodies. The dolls were designed by Herbert Johnson. Dolls listed are in good condition wearing original clothing, in original box can bring double the values listed.

Godey's Lady Book Dolls, pink-tint or white shoulder head, cloth body

7"........................ $65.00 – 80.00
12".................... $90.00 – 110.00

Blond special for G Fox 100th anniversary CT,
12" MIB $150.00*

With molded necklace
12"................. $100.00 – 135.00

Black
12"................. $145.00 – 155.00

Caracul wig, original outfit
10"................. $225.00 – 275.00

GILBERT TOYS

1909 – 1966, New Haven, Connecticut. company founded on the invention of the Erector Set, went on to make dolls based on popular television characters. Dolls listed are in very good condition with all original clothing and accessories, mint-in-box can bring double the value listed.

Honey West, 1965, vinyl head and arms, hard plastic torso and legs, rooted blond hair, painted eyes, painted beauty spot near mouth, head marked "K73" with leopard

11½".............. $200.00 – 225.00
Accessories MOC........ $80.00 – 90.00

The Man From U.N.C.L.E. characters from TV show of the 1960s

Ilya Kuryakin (David McCallum)
12¼".............. $200.00 – 250.00

Napoleon Solo (Robert Vaughn)
12¼".............. $100.00 – 125.00

James Bond, Secret Agent 007, character from James Bond movies

12¼".............. $100.00 – 125.00

GIRL SCOUT DOLLS

1917 on, listed chronologically. Dolls made for the Girl Scouts of America, various manufacturers. Dolls listed are in good condition with original clothing, MIB can

11" Effanbee Fluffy Brownie. $75.00.
Photo courtesy of The Museum Doll Shop.

bring double the values listed.

1917, all-composition doll, painted features, mohair wig

6½".............. $225.00 – 250.00

1920s Girl Scout doll in camp uniform, pictured in Girls Scout 1920 handbook, all-cloth, mask face, painted features, wigged, gray green uniform

13"...............................$600.00+

Grace Corry, Scout 1929, composition shoulder head, designed by Grace Cory, cloth body with crier, molded hair, painted features, original uniform, mark on shoulder plate: "by Grace Corry," body stamped "Madame Hendren Doll//Made in USA"

13"................. $550.00 – 675.00

Averill Mfg. Co, 1936, all-cloth, printed and painted features

16"................. $350.00 – 400.00

Georgene Novelties

1940 – 1946, all-cloth, flat-faced painted features, yellow yarn curls, wears original silver green uniform with red triangle tie, hang tag reads: "Genuine Georgene Doll//A product of Georgene Novelties, Inc., NY//Made in U.S.A."

15"................. $300.00 – 350.00

1946 – 1955, all-cloth, mask face, painted features and string hair

13½".............. $225.00 – 250.00

1955 – 1957, same as previous listing, but now has a stuffed vinyl head

13"................. $200.00 – 250.00

Terri Lee, 1949 – 1958, hard plastic, felt hats, oilcloth saddle shoes

16"................. $600.00 – 700.00

Outfit only..................... $160.00*

Tiny Terri Lee, 1955 – 1958, hard plastic, walker, sleep eyes, wig, plastic shoes

10"................. $125.00 – 175.00

Ginger, 1956 – 1958, made by

8" Effanbee Fluffy in a Camp Fire Girl uniform. $70.00. **Photo courtesy of The Museum Doll Shop.**

Cosmopolitan for Terri Lee, hard plastic, straight-leg walker, synthetic wig

7½" – 8"......... $150.00 – 200.00

Effanbee Honey, 1949 – 1957, hard plastic, mohair wig

14"................. $125.00 – 150.00

18"................. $250.00 – 300.00

Vogue, Painted Lash Walker Ginny, 1954, hard plastic

8"................... $225.00 – 275.00

Nancy Ann Storybook, 1957, Muffie, hard plastic

8"................... $150.00 – 175.00

Effanbee, Patsy Ann, 1959 on, all-vinyl jointed body, saran hair, with sleep eyes, freckles on nose, Brownie or Girl Scout

15"................. $300.00 – 325.00

Effanbee Suzette, ca. 1960, jointed vinyl body, sleep eyes, saran hair, thin body, long legs

15"................. $350.00 – 400.00

Uneeda, 1961 – 1963, Ginny look-alike, vinyl head, hard plastic body, straight-leg walker, Dynel wig, marked "U" on head

8"................... $100.00 – 125.00

Effanbee Fluffy, 1964 – 1972, vinyl dolls, sleep eyes, curly rooted hair, Brownie had blond wig, Junior was brunette, box had

8" PLW Ginny. $250.00. **Photo courtesy of Dolls & Lace.**

clear acetate lid, printed with Girl Scout trademark, and catalog number

8".................... $75.00 – 100.00

Related, Fluffy Camp Fire Girl

8" .... $75.00 – 100.00

Effanbee Fluffy Cadette, 1965, vinyl, rooted hair, sleep eyes

11"................. $400.00 – 500.00

Effanbee Pun'kin Jr., 1974 – 1979, all-vinyl, sleep eyes, long straight rooted hair Brownie and Junior uniforms

11½"................. $70.00 – 85.00

Related, Fluffy Camp Fire Girl

11½"................ $85.00 – 100.00

Hallmark, 1979, all-cloth, Juliette Low, from 1916 handbook, wearing printed 1923 uniform

6½"..................... $45.00 – 50.00

Jesco, 1985, Katie, all-vinyl, sleep eyes, long straight rooted hair, look-alike Girl Scout, dressed as Brownie and Junior

9"....................... $55.00 – 65.00

Dakin, Ginny, 1986 – 1995, all vinyl

8"..................... $90.00 – 110.00

Madame Alexander, 1992, vinyl, unofficial Girl Scout, sleep eyes

8"..................... $80.00 – 100.00

GLADDIE

1928 – 1930 on. Trade name of doll designed by Helen Webster Jensen, made in Germany, body made by K&K, for Borgfeldt. Flange heads made of bisque or biscaloid (a ceramic imitation of bisque), with molded hair, glass or painted eyes, open-closed mouth with two upper teeth and laughing expression, composition arms, lower legs, cloth torso, some with crier and upper legs, mark "copyriht" (misspelled). Dolls listed are in good condition, appropriately dressed.

Biscaloid ceramic head

18" – 20" ...$1,000.00 – 1,100.00

23" – 24" ...$1,200.00 – 1,400.00

29"........... $1,500.00 – 1,900.00

Bisque head

14"........... $2,600.00 – 2,800.00

18" – 20" ...$3,800.00 – 4,800.00

23" biscaloid Gladdie, open/closed mouth. $1,200.00. **Photo courtesy of The Museum Doll Shop.**

WM. AND F. & W. GOEBEL

5½" Goebel character. $275.00. **Photo courtesy The Museum Doll Shop.**

1867 – 1930 on, Oeslau, Thüringia. Made porcelain and glazed china dolls, as well as bathing dolls, Kewpie-types, and others. Earlier mark was triangle with half moon. Supplied heads to other doll makers including Max Handwerck. Dolls listed are in good condition appropriately dressed. Exceptional dolls may be more.

Child, 1895
Socket head, open mouth, composition body, sleep or set eyes, no mold number or mold 120
10".................. $100.00 – 135.00
12" – 16"........ $275.00 – 350.00
17" – 23"........ $375.00 – 425.00
Baby body
13".................. $200.00 – 275.00
Shoulder head, open mouth, kid or cloth body, glass eyes
24".................. $195.00 – 210.00
Character Child, after 1909
Molded hair, may have flowers or ribbons, painted features, with five-piece papier-mâché body
6".................. $275.00 – 300.00
9".................. $350.00 – 400.00

Molded on bonnet or hat, closed mouth, five-piece papier-mâché body, painted features
9".................. $475.00 – 525.00
Character Baby, after 1909, open mouth, sleep eyes, five-piece bent-leg baby body
13" – 15"........ $325.00 – 400.00
18" – 21"........ $450.00 – 550.00
Toddler body
14".................. $425.00 – 500.00

GOOGLY

Popular 1900 – 1925, various manufacturers. Doll with exaggerated side-glancing eyes. Round eyes were painted, glass, tin, or celluloid, when they move to side they are called flirty eyes. Most doll manufacturers of the period made dolls with googly eyes. With painted eyes, they could be painted looking to side or straight ahead; with inserted eyes, the same head can be found with and without flirty eyes. May have closed smiling mouth, composition or papier-mâché body, molded hair or wigged. Dolls listed are in good condition appropriately dressed. Exceptional dolls can be more.

6" Kestner mold 189. 2,000.00. **Photo courtesy of Turn of the Century Antiques.**

8" Ernst Heubach, mold 262. $800.00. **Photo courtesy of Richard Withington, Inc.**

All-Bisque, jointed shoulders, hips, molded shoes, socks
Painted intaglio eyes, no maker's mark
  3".................. $350.00 – 400.00
  5".................. $500.00 – 600.00
Rigid neck, glass eyes, no maker's mark
  3".................. $325.00 – 375.00
  5".................. $525.00 – 600.00
  7".................. $675.00 – 800.00
Marked by maker, Molds 217, 330, 501
  4" – 5"............ $700.00 – 750.00
  6" – 7"............ $900.00 – 950.00
Swivel neck, glass eyes, no maker's mark
  5".................. $575.00 – 650.00
  7".................. $875.00 – 950.00
Marked by maker, Molds 189, 292
  4" – 5"...... $1,000.00 – 1,200.00
  6" – 7"...... $1,400.00 – 1,600.00
No mold number, jointed knees
  7"............ $2,500.00 – 2,800.00
Hertwig, molded clothing, wire jointed at shoulders and hips, painted eyes
  4" – 7"............ $100.00 – 125.00
Kestner Mold 111, jointed knees and elbows
  4½".......... $1,000.00 – 1,400.00

7½ "......... $2,200.00 – 2,600.00
Mold 211, with jointed elbows, knees, neck
  5"............. $2,800.00 – 3,000.00
Too few in database for reliable range.
  7"............. $3,750.00 – 4,200.00
Too few in database for reliable range.
Our Fairy, mold 222, ca. 1914, wigged, glass eyes
  4½" – 5"........ $500.00 – 600.00
  7"............. $1,400.00 – 1,800.00
  11"........... $3,600.00 – 3,800.00
Painted eyes, molded hair
  5".................... $450.00 – 550.00
  8".................... $750.00 – 850.00
  12".............. $950.00 – 1,500.00
Mold 292, 192, glass eyes, watermelon smile
  5"............. $1,000.00 – 1,200.00
Limbach, painted eyes, stiff neck baby, resemble Campbell kids
  5½" – 7"......... $300.00 – 350.00
Peek-a-boo kids, designed by Chloe Preston, 1914 on, bisque immobile with painted features including wide lashes
  4" – 5"............ $335.00 – 250.00
Bisque Head, painted or glass eye, composition body
Bähr & Pröschild, marked "B.P.," mold 686, ca. 1914, glass eyes
  10"........... $4,000.00 – 4,200.00
Demacol, made for Dennis Malley & Co., London, bisque socket head, glass eyes, closed watermelon mouth, mohair wig, five-piece composition toddler body
  10" – 13"..... $950.00 – 1,200.00
Goebel
Painted eyes
  6" – 7"............ $600.00 – 650.00
  9" – 10".......... $800.00 – 850.00
  12"............... $900.00 – 1000.00
Glass eyes
  7" – 8"......... $900.00 – 1,100.00

9" glass eye Googly doll marked 573. $1,200.00. **Photo courtesy of William Jenack Estate Appraisers and Auctioneers.**

10" – 11".. $1,500.00 – 1,600.00
13"........... $2,200.00 – 2,500.00
Round open/closed mouth, molded painted hair, toddler body, resembles Recknagel mold 50
   Painted eyes
   7"............................ $1,700.00*
   Glass eyes
   9½" $3,600.00*
Handwerck, Max
Marked "Elite," bisque socket head, glass eyes, molded helmet, closed mouth
   10" – 14".. $1,900.00 – 2,100.00
Molded Military helmet, painted eye, open mouth
   12"............................ $1,700.00*
Bellhop style molded hat
   12"............................ $3,000.00*
Uncle Sam, painted eye
   12"............................ $2,000.00*
Two-faced with molded military caps, painted eyes
   12"............................ $3,200.00*
Set with 5 changeable heads,
   MIB........................... $5,750.00*
Hertel Schwab & Co., 1914 on
Mold 163, solid dome, glass eyes, molded hair, closed smiling mouth, toddler body
   12"........... $4,000.00 – 4,500.00
   16"........... $6,700.00 – 7,200.00

21½"....................... $13,000.00
Mold 165, Jubilee, socket head, glass eyes, closed smiling mouth
   Baby
   11" – 12".. $3,500.00 – 3,800.00
   16"........... $5,000.00 – 5,400.00
   Toddler
   11" – 12".. $4,900.00 – 5,400.00
   15" – 16".. $6,500.00 – 8,000.00
Mold 172, solid dome, glass eyes, closed smiling mouth, baby body
   15"........... $6,500.00 – 7,000.00
Mold 173, solid dome, glass eyes, closed smiling mouth
   Baby
   10" – 11".. $3,500.00 – 3,800.00
   16"........... $5,800.00 – 6,200.00
   Toddler
   10" – 12".. $4,000.00 – 5,000.00
   16"........... $7,000.00 – 7,400.00
Heubach, Ernst
   Molds 262, 264, ca. 1914, "EH" painted eyes, closed mouth
   6" – 8"............ $500.00 – 600.00
   10" – 12"..... $700.00 – 1,000.00
Mold 291, ca. 1915, "EH" glass eyes, closed mouth
   7" – 9"...... $1,200.00 – 1,400.00
Mold 318, ca. 1920, "EH" character, closed mouth

6½" mold 46 by Recknagel. $350.00. Photo courtesy of Joan & Lynette Antique Dolls and Accessories.

11".......... $1,100.00 – 1,285.00
14".......... $1,900.00 – 2,050.00

Mold 319, ca. 1920, "EH" character, painted eyes, tearful features
   8"................... $500.00 – 575.00
   11".......... $1,050.00 – 1,150.00

Mold 322, ca. 1915, character, glass eyes, closed smiling mouth
   8" – 10".... $1,300.00 – 1,700.00

Heubach, Gebruder

No mold number, painted eyes
   6" – 7"............ $575.00 – 650.00
   9"................... $700.00 – 800.00
   13".......... $1,500.00 – 1,700.00

Mold 8556, painted eyes
   16".........................$23,000.00*

Mold 8676, painted eyes
   9"................... $800.00 – 850.00
   11".............. $950.00 – 1,050.00

Mold 8678, glass eyes
   6" – 7"......... $900.00 – 1,000.00
   9" – 11".... $1,400.00 – 1,600.00

Mold 8723, 8995, glass eyes
   13".......... $2,600.00 – 2,900.00

Mold 8764, Einco, shoulder head, glass eyes, closed mouth, for Eisenmann & Co.
   11".......... $4,500.00 – 5,000.00
   18" – 20"..$11,500.00 – 13,500.00

Mold 9056, ca. 1914, square, painted eyes closed mouth
   8"................... $650.00 – 700.00

Mold 9058, painted eyes, closed watermelon mouth
   7"............................$1,700.00*

Mold 9573, glass eyes
   6" – 8"...... $1,000.00 – 1,100.00
   9" – 11".... $1,500.00 – 2,000.00

Mold 9578, painted eyes, molded hair, closed mouth
   7"............................$1,700.00*

Mold 9594, painted eyes, molded hair
   6½"............................$600.00*

Mold 9743, sitting, open-closed mouth, top-knot, star shaped hands
   7"................... $500.00 – 600.00

Elisabeth, glass eyes, wigged, tiny mouth
   7" $4,000.00*

Winker, one eye painted closed
   7" .... $950.00 – 1,100.00
   14".......... $2,100.00 – 2,300.00

Mold 10342, glass eyes, wigged, rosebud mouth
   8" $1,600.00*

Kämmer & Reinhardt

Mold 131, ca. 1914, "S&H//K*R," glass eyes, closed mouth
   8½" toddler.. $6,500.00 – 6,800.00
   13".......... $5,500.00 – 6,000.00
   15" – 16"..$10,000.00 – 12,000.00

Kestner

Mold, 221, ca. 1913, "JDK ges. gesch," character, glass eyes, smiling closed mouth
   11" – 13".. $5,700.00 – 6,700.00
   14" – 16"..$12,000.00 – 14,000.00

Kley & Hahn, mold 180, ca. 1915, "K&H" by Hertel Schwab & Co. for Kley & Hahn, character, glass eyes, laughing open-closed mouth
   15".......... $2,700.00 – 3,000.00

17".......... $3,400.00 – 3,500.00

Lenci: See Lenci category.

Limbach, marked with crown and cloverleaf, socket head, large round glass eyes, pug nose, closed smiling mouth

7" – 8"...... $1,800.00 – 2,100.00

Armand Marseille

Mold 200, ca. 1911, glass eyes, closed mouth

8"............. $1,250.00 – 1,500.00

11".......... $2,000.00 – 2,500.00

Mold 210, ca. 1911, painted intaglio eyes, character, solid-dome head, painted eyes, closed mouth

6" – 8"........... $300.00 – 500.00

Mold 223, ca. 1913, character, closed mouth

7"................... $700.00 – 750.00

11"................ $900.00 – 950.00

Mold 240, ca. 1914, "AM" dome, glass eyes, painted, closed mouth

10" – 11".. $3,000.00 – 3,100.00

Mold 252, "AM 248," ca. 1912, solid dome, painted intaglio eyes, molded tuft, painted eyes, closed mouth

9"............. $1,100.00 – 1,300.00

12" – 15".. $1,900.00 – 2,000.00

Mold 253, "AM Nobbikid Reg. U.S. Pat. 066 Germany," ca. 1925

6" – 7"......... $950.00 – 1,100.00

9" – 11".... $1,700.00 – 2,800.00

Mold 254, ca. 1912, "AM" dome, painted eyes, closed mouth

6½" .... $750.00 – 800.00

10"................ $750.00 – 800.00

Mold 320, "AM 255," ca. 1913, dome, painted eyes

9"................ $900.00 – 1,000.00

12".......... $1,200.00 – 1,300.00

Mold 322, "AM," ca. 1914, dome, painted eyes

8"................... $600.00 – 675.00

7¼" mold 208 by Walthur & Sohn. $400.00. **Photo courtesy of McMasters Harris Auction Co.**

11"................ $800.00 – 875.00

Mold 323, 1914 – 1925, glass eyes, also composition

7" – 8"......... $800.00 – 1,000.00

10" – 11".. $1,100.00 – 1,300.00

13".......... $2,000.00 – 2,200.00

Mold 325, ca. 1915, character, closed mouth

9"................... $675.00 – 725.00

14"............. $900.00 – 1,000.00

Nippon, baby, painted eyes, five-piece body

6½"................. $75.00 – 100.00

P.M. Porzellanfabrik Mengersgereuth, ca. 1926, "PM" character, closed mouth, previously thought to be made by Otto Reinecke, mold 950

7" – 11".... $1,400.00 – 2,800.00

Recknagel, no mold number, glass eyes

7" – 8"......... $900.00 – 1,100.00

10" – 11".. $1,500.00 – 1,600.00

13".......... $2,200.00 – 2,500.00

Mold 43, intaglio eyes, molded hat & hair tufts, closed mouth

7" – 8"............ $700.00 – 900.00
Mold 45, 46, 49, intaglio eyes, molded hair, closed mouth
7" – 8"............ $400.00 – 450.00
Mold 50, round open/closed mouth, intaglio eyes, molded hair
7" – 8"............ $600.00 – 850.00
S.F.B.J.
Mold 245, glass eyes
7" – 8"...... $4,000.00 – 6,000.00
Fully jointed body
10"........... $5,800.00 – 6,500.00
Steiner, Herm, mold 133, ca. 1920, "HS," closed mouth, papier-mâché body
7" – 8"............ $750.00 – 800.00
Walthur & Sohn, mold 208, ca. 1920, "W&S" closed mouth, five-piece papier-mâché body, painted socks/shoes
7" – 9" .... $400.00 – 700.00
Composition Face, 1911 – 1914, all-composition head or composition mask face, cloth body, includes Hug Me Kids, Little Bright Eyes, and others.
9" – 12".......... $800.00 – 900.00

LUDWIG GREINER

1840 – 1874. Succeeded by sons, 1890 – 1900, Philadelphia, Pennsylvania. Papier-mâché shoulder head dolls, with molded hair, painted/glass eyes, usually made up to be large dolls. Dolls listed are in good condition appropriately dressed. Some wear is acceptable for these dolls but highly worn condition examples will bring half the value of good condition examples.

With "1858" label
12" – 13".. $1,200.00 – 1,400.00
15" – 17"..... $950.00 – 1,050.00
20" – 23".. $1,200.00 – 1,600.00
28" – 30".. $1,600.00 – 2,000.00

29" Greiner with 1858 label. $1,800.00.
Photo courtesy of Joan & Lynette Antique Dolls and Accessories.

Glass eyes
21"........... $2,100.00 – 2,200.00
26"........... $2,500.00 – 2,800.00
With "1872" label
15"................. $300.00 – 400.00
18" – 24"........ $600.00 – 775.00
26" – 30"........ $750.00 – 800.00
32" – 33"........ $700.00 – 750.00

GUND

1898 on, Connecticut and New York. Adolph Gund founded the company making stuffed toys.
Character
Cloth mask face, painted features, cloth body
19"................. $250.00 – 300.00
Little Lulu
16"..................... $40.00 – 50.00
Flat faced cloth
6½".................... $20.00 – 25.00
Plastic mask face, 1940s – 1950s, cloth body, Perki and others
14" – 16"............ $25.00 – 35.00
21"..................... $35.00 – 45.00
Vinyl mask face, 1950s – 1960s, on plush body, included characters such as Popeye, Disney Pinocchio, Seven Dwarves, and others

9" – 12" .... $35.00 – 45.00

Christopher Robin, cloth body

18" .... $95.00 – 110.00

The Now Kids, 1970s, cloth dolls, yarn hair, hippies named Desmond and Rhoda

Pair .... $50.00 – 60.00

HALF DOLLS

1900 – 1930s, Germany, Japan. Half dolls can be made of bisque, china, composition, or papier-mâché, and were used not only for pincushions but on top of jewelry or cosmetic boxes, brushes, lamps, and numerous other items of decor. The hardest to find have arms molded away from the body as they were easier to break with the limbs in this position and thus fewer survived. Dolls listed are in good condition, add more for extra attributes. Rare examples may bring more.

Arms Away

China or bisque figure, bald head with wig

4" .... $125.00 – 140.00

4½" $400.00

6" .... $185.00 – 210.00

Child, molded hair

2½" .... $80.00 – 90.00

Goebel mark, dome head, wig

5" .... $175.00 – 195.00

Galluba and Hoffman, unglazed area at base which flares out, wigged

5" – 7½" ...... $800.00 – 1,600.00

Holding items, such as letter, flower

4" .... $250.00 – 350.00

6" .... $500.00 – 600.00

Marked by maker or mold number

4" .... $185.00 – 200.00

6" .... $275.00 – 300.00

8" .... $375.00 – 400.00

12" .... $850.00 – 900.00

Flapper

4" – 5" .... $400.00 – 600.00

2¾" German china half doll, arms molded to body. $70.00.
Photo courtesy of The Museum Doll Shop.

Holding punch doll, made by Fasold & Stauch

5" .... $778.00 at online auction

One Arm Away and back to body, common German type

4" – 4½" .... $200.00 – 400.00

Arms In

Close to figure, bald head with wig

4" .... $65.00 – 80.00

6" .... $100.00 – 115.00

Both arms away and back to body

3" .... $25.00 – 35.00

5" .... $35.00 – 45.00

7" .... $60.00 – 70.00

Decorated bodice, necklace, fancy hair or holding article

3" .... $100.00 – 125.00

4¾" ... $305.00* holding tray, cups

Marked by maker or mold number

5" .... $125.00 – 135.00

6" .... $145.00 – 155.00

With legs, dressed, fancy decorations

5" .... $275.00 – 300.00

7" .... $375.00 – 400.00

Papier-mâché or composition

4" .... $25.00 – 35.00

6" .... $60.00 – 80.00

Jointed Shoulders

China or bisque, molded hair

5" .... $125.00 – 145.00

6" German china half doll, arms molded away from body, all original. $500.00. Photo courtesy of The Museum Doll Shop.

7"..................... $175.00 – 200.00
Solid dome, mohair wig
    4".................. $200.00 – 220.00
    6".................. $350.00 – 400.00
Man or Child
    4".................. $100.00 – 120.00
    6".................. $130.00 – 160.00
Marked Germany
    4".................. $175.00 – 200.00
    6".................. $300.00 – 400.00

5" doll with both arms away, made by Galluba & Hoffman. $850.00. Photo courtesy of Dolls & Lace.

Marked Japan
    3"....................... $15.00 – 25.00
    6"....................... $40.00 – 50.00
Other Items
Brush, with porcelain figurine for handle, molded hair, may be holding something
    9"....................... $65.00 – 75.00
Dresser box
Unmarked, with figurine on lid
    7".................. $325.00 – 350.00
    9".................. $425.00 – 450.00
Marked with mold number, country, or manufacturer
    5".................. $265.00 – 285.00
    6".................. $325.00 – 350.00

HEINRICH HANDWERCK

1855 – 1932, Waltershausen, Thüringia, Germany. Made composition doll bodies, sent Handwerck molds to Simon & Halbig to make bisque heads. Trademarks included an eight-point star with French or German wording, a shield, and "Bébé Cosmopolite," "Bébé de Reclame," and "Bébé Superior." Sold dolls through Gimbels, Macy's, Montgomery Wards, and others. Bodies marked "Handwerk" in red on lower back torso. Patented a straight wrist body. Dolls listed are in good condition appropriately dressed. Exceptional dolls may be more.

Socket Head Child, 1885 on. Open mouth, sleep or set eyes, ball-jointed body, bisque socket head, pierced ears, appropriate wig, nicely dressed

Molds 69, 79, 89, 99, 109, 119, or No Number
    10" – 12"........ $700.00 – 900.00
    14" – 16"........ $675.00 – 750.00
    18" – 24"........ $700.00 – 850.00

17" mold 109 by Heinrich Handwerck. $725.00. **Photo courtesy of William Jenack Estate Appraisers and Auctioneers.**

26" – 28"..... $900.00 – 1,000.00
30" – 33"..... $950.00 – 1,200.00
39"........... $1,800.00 – 1,900.00
Mold 79, 89 closed mouth
15"........... $1,700.00 – 1,800.00
18" – 20".. $2,200.00 – 2,400.00
24"........... $2,800.00 – 3,000.00
Mold 189, open mouth
15"................. $800.00 – 850.00
18" – 22"..... $950.00 – 1,100.00
Bébé Cosmopolite
19"................. $1,000.00* boxed
28" .... $1,500.00* boxed
33"............................ $2,2500.00
Shoulder Head Child, 1885 on, open mouth, glass eyes, kid or cloth body
Molds 139 or no numbers
12"................. $125.00 – 150.00

15" – 16"........ $175.00 – 225.00
18" – 22"........ $250.00 – 300.00
24" – 25"........ $325.00 – 350.00

MAX HANDWERCK

1899 – 1928, Waltershausen, Thüringia, Germany. Made dolls and doll bodies, registered trademark, "Bébé Elite." Used heads made by Goebel.

Child

Bisque socket head, open mouth, sleep or set eyes, jointed composition body. Size numbers only or molds 283, 285, 286, 291, 297, 307, and others
16" – 18"........ $350.00 – 375.00
22" – 26"........ $450.00 – 750.00
31" – 32"........ $650.00 – 700.00

26" Heinrich Handwerck doll with inset fur eyebrows. $900.00. **Photo courtesy of William Jenack Estate Appraisers and Auctioneers.**

Bébé Elite, 1900 on, bisque socket head, mohair wig, glass sleep eyes, mohair lashes, open mouth, pierced ears, jointed composition/wood body, marks: "Max Handwerck Bébé Elite 286 12 Germany" on back of head

    15".................. $375.00 – 425.00
    19" – 21"........ $475.00 – 550.00
    27" – 29"........ $625.00 – 700.00

Googly: See Googly category.

18" open mouth dolly faced doll by Max Handwerck. $325.00. **Private collection.**

HARD PLASTIC

Hard plastic was developed during WWII and became a staple of the doll industry after the war ended. Numerous companies made hard plastic dolls from 1948 through the 1950s; dolls have all hard plastic jointed bodies, sleep eyes, lashes, synthetic wig, open or closed mouths. Marks: none, letters, little known, or other unidentified companies.

Hard Plastic Child, 1950s, maker unknown, some marked U.S.A., original clothing and wig

    14" – 16"........ $250.00 – 275.00
    18" – 20"........ $300.00 – 350.00

Advance Doll & Toy Company, 1954 on. Made heavy walking hard plastic dolls, metal rollers on molded shoes, named Winnie and Wanda, later models had vinyl heads

    18" – 24"........ $150.00 – 175.00

Artisan Novelty Company, 1950s, hard plastic, wide crotch

Raving Beauty

    20"................. $100.00 – 125.00

Black .... $225.00 – 275.00

Duchess Doll Corporation, 1948 – 1950s, made small hard plastic adult dolls, mohair wigs, painted or sleep eyes, jointed arms, stiff or jointed neck, molded and painted shoes, about 7" – 7½" tall, costumes stapled onto body, elaborate costumes, exceptional dolls may be more

    7"...................... $15.00 – 20.00

Fortune Doll Company, a subsidiary of the Beehler Arts Company

Pam (Ginny-type), hard plastic, sleep eyes, synthetic wig, closed mouth

    8"...................... $55.00 – 75.00

18" hard plastic doll by Royal Doll Co. $200.00.
Photo courtesy of My Dolly Dearest.

Furga, Italy

Simonna outfit, MIB

1967 .... $300.00 – 330.00

Imperial Crown Toy Co. (Impco), 1950s, made hard plastic or vinyl dolls, rooted hair, synthetic wigs

Hard Plastic Walker

14" .... $45.00 – 55.00

20" .... $85.00 – 100.00

Vinyl

16" .... $55.00 – 65.00

Kendall Company

Miss Curity, 1953, hard plastic, jointed only at shoulders, blond wig, blue sleep eyes, molded-on shoes, painted stockings, uniform sheet vinyl, "Miss Curity" marked in blue on hat

7½" .... $40.00 – 50.00

Nun Doll, all hard plastic, sleep eyes, unmarked

12" .... $45.00 – 65.00

17" .... $100.00 – 125.00

Roberta Doll Co.

Walker

17" .... $45.00 – 55.00

Roddy of England, 1950 – 1960s, made by D.G. Todd & Co. Ltd., Southport, England, hard plastic walker, sleep or set eyes

12½" .... $80.00 – 100.00

Walking Princess, tagged

11½" .... $40.00 – 50.00

Rosebud of England, 1950s – 1960s, started in Raunds, Northamptonshire, England, by T. Eric Smith shortly after WWII

Miss Rosebud, hard plastic, various shades of blue sleep eyes, glued-on mohair wig, jointed at the neck and hips, marked "Miss Rosebud" in script on her back and head and "MADE IN ENGLAND" on her upper back, more for rare examples or mint-in-box dolls

7½" .... $95.00 – 115.00

Ross Products

8" Lolly Pop by Virga. $75.00. **Photo courtesy of The Museum Doll Shop.**

Tina Cassini, designed by Oleg Cassini, hard plastic, marked on back torso, "TINA CASSINI," clothes tagged "Made in British Crown Colony of Hong Kong"

12" .... $175.00 – 200.00

Costume, MIB .... $100.00 – 125.00

Royal Doll Co.

Hard plastic girl, 1950s, similar to Sweet Sue by American Character

Wearing formal

20" .... $200.00 – 225.00

Virga, a subsidiary of the Beehler Arts Company, marketed Ginny type dolls under various lines such as Playmates, Lolly Pop, Play-Pals, Lucy, and Schiaparelli GoGo

Lolly Pop dolls, hair colors such as pink, blue, bright yellow

8" .... $60.00 – 80.00

HARTLAND PLASTICS

1954 – 1963, Hartland, Wisconsin. Made action figures and horses, many figures from Warner Brothers television productions. Purchased by Revlon Cosmetics in 1963 and stopped making toys. Others have bought the molds and make these products today. Dolls discussed here are the 1954 to 1963 dolls.

Television or Movie Characters, 8"

Annie Oakley, 1953 – 1956, played by Gail Davis in *Annie Oakley*

8" ... $160.00 – 200.00 with horse

Bret Maverick, ca. 1958, played by James Garner in *Maverick*

8" .... $350.00 – 400.00

Clint Bonner, 1957 – 1959, played by John Payne in *The Restless Gun*

8" .... $135.00 – 160.00

Colonel Ronald MacKenzie, ca. 1950s, played by Richard Carlson in *Mackenzie's Raiders*

8" .... $650.00 – 700.00 with horse

Dale Evans, ca. 1958, #802, with horse, Buttermilk from *The Roy Rogers Show*

8" .... $375.00* MIB

Davy Crockett, 1956 played by Fess Parker

8" .... $320.00 – 370.00 with horse

Jim Hardie, 1958, played by Dale Robertson in *Tales of Wells Fargo*

8" .... $250.00 – 275.00

Josh Randall, ca. 1950s, played by Steve McQueen in *Wanted Dead or Alive*

8" .... $600.00 – 650.00 with horse

Major Seth Adams, 1957 – 1961, #824, played by Ward Bond in *Wagon Train*

8" .... $200.00 with horse

Paladin, 1957 – 1963, played by Richard Boone in *Have Gun, Will Travel*

8" .... $160.00 – 220.00 with horse

Roy Rogers, ca. 1955, and Trigger from *The Roy Rogers Show*

8" .... $485.00* MIB with Trigger

The Rifleman, Chuck Connors

8" .... $200.00 – 250.00

Sgt. Lance O'Rourke RCMP

8" .... $180.00 – 200.00 with horse

Sgt. William Preston, ca. 1958, #804, played by Richard Simmons in *Sgt. Preston of the Yukon*

8" .... $490.00 – 525.00 with horse

Tom Jeffords, ca. 1958 – 1961 played by John Lupton

8" .... $325.00 – 350.00 with horse

Other Figures

Brave Eagle, #812, and his horse, White Cloud

Buffalo Bill, #819, Pony Express Rider

Chief Thunderbird, and horse, Northwind

Cochise, #815, with pinto horse from Broken Arrow

Jim Bowie, #817, with horse, Blaze

General George Custer, #814, and horse, Bugler

General George Washington, #815 and horse, Ajax

General Robert E. Lee, #808, and horse, Traveler

Lone Ranger, #801, and horse, Silver

Tonto, #805, and horse, Scout

8" .... $380.00 – 425.00

All others

8" .... $125.00 – 225.00

Baseball 8" Figures

Babe Ruth .... $120.00 – 140.00

Ernie Banks, #920 .... $175.00 – 225.00

Hank Aaron, #912 ... $175.00 – 225.00

Mickey Mantle .... $200.00 – 250.00

Willie Mays .... $165.00 – 195.00

Yogi Berra .... $120.00 – 140.00

Ted Williams .... $130.00 – 150.00

CARL HARTMANN

1889 – 1930s, Neustadt, Germany. Made and exported bisque and celluloid dolls, especially small dolls in regional costumes, called Globe Babies.

Child, bisque socket head, open mouth, jointed composition and wood body

22" – 24" .... $500.00 – 700.00

Globe Baby, bisque socket head, glass sleep

eyes, open mouth, four teeth, mohair or human hair wig, five-piece papier-mâché or composition body with painted shoes and stockings

    8".................. $325.00 – 400.00
    12"................ $425.00 – 475.00

24" doll by Carl Hartmann. $700.00. **Photo courtesy of McMasters Harris Auction Co.**

KARL HARTMANN

1911 – 1926, Stockheim, Germany. Doll factory, made and exported dolls. Advertised ball-jointed dolls, characters, and papier-mâché dolls. Marked "KH."

Child, bisque socket head, open mouth, glass eyes, composition body

    18" – 22"........ $300.00 – 350.00
    24" – 26"........ $400.00 – 450.00
    27" – 32"........ $575.00 – 625.00

HASBRO

1923, Pawtucket, Rhode Island. Founded by the Hassenfeld Brothers. Began making toys in 1943. One of their most popular toys was the G.I. Joe series which came out in 1964. Dolls listed are in good condition with original clothing and accessories, mint-in-package usually brings double the value listed. Dolls in played with condition bring one-third to one-half the value of complete examples.

Aimee, 1972, rooted hair, amber sleep eyes, jointed vinyl body, long dress, sandals, earrings

    18"..................... $20.00 – 30.00

Bridal Sewing Set, 1950s, hard plastic dolls (6"), boxed with fabric and sewing supplies

    Complete set.... $135.00 – 165.00

Charlie's Angels, 1977, vinyl, Jill, Sabrina, Kelly, Kris

    8½"..................... $25.00 – 30.00
    Set of three ...... $100.00 – 125.00

Dolly Darling, 1965

    4½" .... $30.00 – 60.00

Sport series.................. $65.00 – 75.00

Flying Nun

    4⅞"..................... $50.00 – 60.00
    12"................. $125.00 – 135.00

Jem: See Jem section.

Leggie, 1972

    10"..................... $30.00 – 40.00

Black .... $50.00 – 60.00

Little Miss No Name, 1965

    15"................. $100.00 – 125.00

Maxie, 1987, vinyl fashion doll

    11½".................. $15.00 – 20.00

My Buddy, 1985, vinyl and cloth

    24"..................... $25.00 – 30.00

My Buddy, 1985, vinyl & cloth boy

    24".................... $75.00 – 100.00

Peteena Poodle, 1966, vinyl fashion doll poodle

    9½"................. $175.00 – 200.00

Pippi Longstocking, 1973, vinyl

    12"..................... $20.00 – 30.00

Real Baby, 1984, designed by J. Turner

    18"..................... $30.00 – 40.00

Show Biz Babies, 1967, 4"

18" *Aimee.* $25.00. **Photo courtesy of My Dolly Dearest.**

Mama Cass Elliott..... $150.00 – 180.00
Denny Doherty......... $100.00 – 125.00
Monkees
Individual .... $75.00 – 80.00
Set of four .... $325.00 – 350.00
Storykins, 1967, 3", includes Cinderella, Goldilocks, Prince Charming, Rumpelstiltskin, Sleeping Beauty....$40.00 – 50.00 each
Snow White and Dwarfs
Set...................... $60.00 – 75.00
Sweet Cookie, 1972, vinyl, with cooking accessories
18".................. $100.00 – 125.00
That Kid, 1967
21"...................... $85.00 – 95.00
World of Love Dolls, 1971,
Love, Peace, Flower
9"...................... $35.00 – 45.00
Soul (black).................. $50.00 – 60.00
Adam .... $30.00 – 40.00
G.I. Joe Action Figures, 1964, hard plastic head with facial scar, painted hair and no beard. Dolls listed are in good condition with original clothing and accessories, MIB can bring double the values listed.
G.I. Joe Action Soldier, flocked hair, Army fatigues, brown jump boots, green plastic cap, training manual, metal dog tag, two sheets of stickers

11½"............. $250.00 – 275.00
Painted hair .... $275.00 – 300.00
Black............... $575.00 – 600.00
Green Beret, teal green fatigue jacket, four pockets, pants, Green Beret cap with red unit flashing, M-16 rifle, 45 automatic pistol with holster, tall brown boots, four grenades, camouflage scarf, and field communication set
11"................. $375.00 – 500.00
G.I. Joe Action Marine, camouflage shirt, pants, brown boots, green plastic cap, metal dog tag, insignia stickers, and training manual
11"................. $300.00 – 340.00
G.I. Joe Action Sailor, blue chambray work shirt, blue denim work pants, black boots, white plastic sailor cap, dog tag, rank insignia stickers .... $300.00 – 330.00
G.I. Joe Action Pilot, orange flight suit, black boots, dog tag, stickers, blue cap, training manual .... $375.00 – 500.00
Dolls only, nude .... $100.00 – 125.00
G.I. Joe Action Soldier of the World, 1966, figures in this set may have any hair and eye color combination, no scar on face, hard plastic heads
Australian Jungle Fighter
$395.00 – 450.00
British Commando, boxed
$525.00 – 600.00
French Resistance Fighter
$425.00 – 500.00
German Storm Trooper
$500.00 – 600.00
Japanese Imperial Soldier
$500.00 – 600.00
Russian Infantryman .. $475.00 – 500.00
Talking G.I. Joe, 1967 – 1969, talking mechanism added, semi-hard vinyl head, marks: "G.I. Joe®//Copyright 1964//By Hasbro®//Pat. No. 3,277,602//Made in U.S.A. "

Talking G.I. Joe Action Soldier, green fatigues, dog tag, brown boots, insignia, stripes, green plastic fatigue cap, comic book, insert with examples of figure's speech
$330.00 – 360.00

Talking G.I. Joe Action Sailor, denim pants, chambray sailor shirt, dog tag, black boots, white sailor cap, insignia stickers, Navy training manual, illustrated talking comic book, insert examples of figure's speech
$475.00 – 500.00

Talking G.I. Joe Action Marine, camouflage fatigues, metal dog tag, Marine training manual, insignia sheets, brown boots, green plastic cap, comic, and insert
$385.00 – 400.00

Talking G.I. Joe Action Pilot, blue flight suit, black boots, dog tag, Air Force insignia, blue cap, training manual, comic book, insert
$460.00 – 500.00

G.I. Joe Action Nurse, 1967, vinyl head, blond rooted hair, jointed hard plastic body, nurse's uniform, cap, red cross armband, white shoes, medical bag, stethoscope, plasma bottle, two crutches, bandages, splints, marks: "Patent Pending//©1967 Hasbro®//Made in Hong Kong"
$900.00 – 1,000.00

G.I. Joe, Man of Action, 1970 – 1975, flocked hair, scar on face, dressed in fatigues with Adventure Team emblem on shirt, plastic cap, marks: "G.I. Joe®//Copyright 1964// By Hasbro®//Pat. No. 3, 277, 602//Made in U.S. A."
Kung Fu Grip .... $250.00 – 325.00
Talking .... $300.00 – 400.00

G.I. Joe, Adventure Team, marks: "©1975 Hasbro ®//Pat. Pend. Pawt. R.I.," flocked hair and beard, six team members:
Air Adventurer, orange flight suit
$265.00 – 285.00
Astronaut, talking, white flight suit, molded

4½" Dolly Darlings, Sugar 'N Spice by Hasbro, MOC. $75.00. Photo courtesy of The Museum Doll Shop.

scar, dog tag pull string
$300.00 – 400.00
Land Adventurer, black, tan fatigues, beard, flocked hair, scar ..... $300.00 – 350.00
Land Adventurer, talking, camouflage fatigues .... $400.00 – 450.00
Sea Adventurer, light blue shirt, navy pants
$250.00 – 300.00
Talking Adventure Team Commander, flocked hair, beard, green jacket, and pants
$400.00 – 450.00
G.I. Joe Land Adventurer, flocked hair, beard, camouflage shirt, green pants
$100.00 – 150.00
G. I. Joe Negro Adventurer, flocked hair
$700.00 – 750.00
G. I. Joe, "Mike Powers, Atomic Man"
$45.00 – 55.00
G.I. Joe Eagle Eye Man of Action
$100.00 – 125.00
G.I. Joe Secret Agent, unusual face, mustache
$400.00 – 450.00
Sea Adventurer w/Kung Fu Grip
$125.00 – 145.00
Bulletman, muscle body, silver arms, hands,

9" Love & Adam, from The World of Love, c. 1971. $40.00 & $35.00. Photo courtesy of The Museum Doll Shop.

helmet, red boots ..... $100.00 – 125.00

Others

G.I. Joe Air Force Academy, Annapolis, or West Point Cadet ..... $350.00 – 400.00

G.I. Joe Frogman, Underwater Demolition Set .... $250.00 – 300.00

G.I. Joe Secret Service Agent, limited edition of 200 .... $225.00 – 275.00

Accessory sets, mint, no doll included

Adventures of G.I. Joe

   Adventure of the Perilous Rescue
     $250.00

   Eight Ropes of Danger Adventure
     $200.00

   Fantastic Free Fall Adventure
     $275.00

   Hidden Missile Discovery Adventure
     $150.00

   Mouth of Doom Adventure.. $150.00

   Adventure of the Shark's Surprise
     $200.00

Accessory Packs or Boxed Uniforms and Accessories

Air Force, Annapolis, West Point Cadet
     $200.00

Action Sailor............................ $350.00

Astronaut $250.00

Crash Crew Fire Fighter $275.00

Deep Freeze with Sled $250.00

Deep Sea Diver $250.00

Frogman Demolition Set............ $375.00

Fighter Pilot, no package........ $285.00*

Green Beret $450.00

Landing Signal Officer.............. $250.00

Marine Jungle Fighter............... $850.00

Marine Mine Detector............... $275.00

Military Police $325.00

Pilot Scramble Set $275.00

Rescue Diver $350.00

Secret Agent $150.00

Shore Patrol............................ $300.00

Ski Patrol................................ $350.00

G.I. Joe Vehicles and Other Accessories, mint in package

Amphibious Duck, green plastic, Irwin
     $600.00

Armored Car, green plastic, one figure
     $150.00

Crash Crew Fire Truck, blue.... $1,400.00

Desert Patrol Attack Jeep, tan, one figure
     $1,400.00

Footlocker, with accessories .... $400.00+

Iron Knight Tank, green plastic
     $1,400.00

Jet Aeroplane, dark blue plastic
     $550.00

Jet Helicopter, green, yellow blades
     $350.00

Motorcycle and Side Car, by Irwin
     $225.00

Personnel Carrier and Mine Sweeper
     $700.00

Sea Sled and Frogman $400.00

Space Capsule and Suit, gray plastic
     $425.00

Staff Car, four figures, green plastic, Irwin
$900.00

Jem, 1986 – 1987

Jem dolls were patterned after characters in the animated Jem television series, ca. 1985 – 1988, and include a line of 27 dolls. All-vinyl fashion type with realistically proportioned body, jointed elbows, wrists, and knees, swivel waist, rooted hair, painted eyes, open or closed mouth, and hole in bottom of each foot. All boxes say "Jem" and "Truly Outrageous!" Most came with cassette tape of music from Jem cartoon, plastic doll stand, poster, and hair pick. All 12½" tall, except Starlight Girls, 11".

Dolls listed are in excellent condition, wearing complete original outfit.

Jem and Rio

Jem/Jerrica 1st issue
4000 .... $25.00 – 30.00
Jem/Jerrica, star earrings
$30.00 – 40.00
Glitter 'n Gold Jem
4001 .... $55.00 – 65.00
Rock 'n Curl Jem
4002 .... $25.00 – 30.00
Flash 'n Sizzle Jem
4003 .... $48.00 – 56.00
Rio, 1st issue
4015 .... $25.00 – 30.00
Glitter 'n Gold Rio
4016 .... $25.00 – 30.00
Glitter 'n Gold Rio, pale vinyl
4016 .... $125.00 – 150.00
Holograms
Synergy
4020 .... $40.00 – 50.00
Aja, 1st issue
4201/4005 .... $40.00 – 50.00
Aja, 2nd issue
4201/4005 .... $100.00 – 125.00
Kimber, 1st issue

4202/4005 .... $40.00 – 50.00
Kimber, 2nd issue
4202/4005 .... $60.00 – 70.00
Shana, 1st issue
4203/4005 .... $65.00 – 75.00
Shana, 2nd issue
4203/4005 .... $200.00 – 225.00
Danse
4208 .... $45.00 – 50.00
Video
4209 .... $20.00 – 25.00
Raya
4210 .... $125.00 – 150.00
Starlight Girls, 11", no wrist or elbow joints
Ashley
4211/4025 .... $30.00 – 40.00
Krissie
4212/4025 .... $25.00 – 35.00
Banee
4213/4025 .... $25.00 – 35.00
Misfits
Pizzazz, 1st issue
4204/4010 .... $40.00 – 50.00
Pizzazz, 2nd issue
4204/4010 .... $45.00 – 55.00
Stormer, 1st issue
4205/4010 .... $50.00 – 60.00
Stormer, 2nd issue
4205/4010 .... $60.00 – 80.00
Roxy, 1st issue
4206/4010 .... $60.00 – 80.00
Roxy, 2nd issue
4206/4010 .... $40.00 – 50.00
Clash
4207/4010 .... $25.00 – 35.00
Jetta
4214 .... $30.00 – 40.00
Accessories
Glitter 'n Gold Roadster
$200.00 – 250.00
Rock 'n Roadster........... $75.00 – 90.00
JEM Guitar .... $30.00 – 40.00

New Wave Waterbed.... $40.00 – 50.00

Backstager................... $30.00 – 35.00

Star Stage .... $40.00 – 45.00

MTV jacket (promo) .. $100.00 – 125.00

Jem Fashions

Prices reflect NRFB (never removed from box or card), with excellent packaging. Damaged boxes or mint and complete, no packaging prices are approximately 25 percent less.

$30.00 – 60.00

HERTEL SCHWAB & CO.

1910 – 1930s, Stutzhaus, Germany. Porcelain factory founded by August Hertel and Heinrich Schwab, both designed doll heads used by Borgfeldt, Kley and Hahn, Koenig & Wernicke, Louis Wolf, and others. Made china and bisque heads as well as all-porcelain, most with character faces. Molded hair or wig, painted blue or glass eyes (often blue-gray), open mouth with tongue or closed mouth, socket or shoulder heads. Usually marked with mold number and "Made in

13" Hertel & Schwab mold 142. $375.00.
Photo courtesy of The Museum Doll Shop.

Germany" or mark of company that owned the mold.

Baby, 1910 on, bisque head, molded hair or wig, open or open-closed mouth, teeth, sleep or painted eyes, bent-leg baby composition body

Mold 130, 142, 150, 151, 152, 159

 9" – 12".......... $300.00 – 375.00

 15" – 16"........ $350.00 – 400.00

 19" – 21"........ $525.00 – 600.00

 22" – 24"........ $600.00 – 650.00

Toddler body

 14"................. $450.00 – 500.00

 20"................. $750.00 – 850.00

Mold 1125 (so-called Patsy Baby)

 12".............. $975.00 – 1,025.00

Mold 126 (so-called Skippy Baby)

 9".................... $825.00 – 875.00

Child

Mold 127, ca. 1915, character face, solid dome with molded hair, sleep eyes, open mouth, Patsy-type

 15".......... $1,350.00 – 1,450.00

 17".......... $2,000.00 – 2,400.00

Mold 131, ca. 1912, character face, solid dome, painted closed mouth

 18"............................. $1,300.00

Too few in database for reliable range.

Mold 134, ca. 1915, character face, sleep eyes, closed mouth

 15".......... $3,500.00 – 4,000.00

Mold 136, ca. 1912, "Made in Germany," character face, open mouth

 7".................. $325.00 – 375.00

 18" – 20"........ $500.00 – 550.00

 24" – 25" .... $600.00 – 700.00

Mold 140, ca. 1912, character, glass eyes, open-closed laughing mouth

 12" – 15".. $3,400.00 – 4,200.00

Mold 141, ca. 1912, character, painted eyes, open-closed mouth

 12" – 14".. $2,800.00 – 3,300.00

17" – 18".. $7,400.00 – 9,000.00
Mold 149, ca. 1912, character, glass eyes, closed mouth, ball-jointed body

17"........... $8,500.00 – 9,500.00

Googly: See Googly category.

HERTWIG & CO.

1864 – 1940s, Kutzhütte, Thüringia, Germany. Porcelain factory producing china and bisque dolls. Some distributed by Butler Brothers.

Half-Bisque Dolls, 1911 on, bisque head and torso, molded clothing, lower body cloth, lower arms and legs bisque

Child

4½"................ $200.00 – 225.00

9"................................$900.00*

Adult

6½"................ $325.00 – 350.00

All Bisque: See All-Bisque section.

China Name Dolls: See China section.

Bisque Bonnet-Head: See Bonnet-Head section.

ERNST HEUBACH

1887 – 1930s, Köppelsdorf, Germany. In 1919, the son of Armand Marseille married the daughter of Ernst Heubach and merged the two factories. Mold numbers range from 250 to 452. They made porcelain heads for Dressel (Jutta), Revalo, and others. Dolls listed are in good condition, appropriately dressed.

Child, 1888 on

Mold 1900, 225, 275, or Horseshoe Mark, shoulder head, open mouth, glass eyes, kid or cloth body

10" – 12"........ $125.00 – 150.00

18" – 22"........ $225.00 – 275.00

26"................. $350.00 – 400.00

Molds 250, 251, 302, and others, socket head, composition body, open mouth, glass eyes

8" – 10".......... $200.00 – 275.00

8" – 9" on flapper body

$300.00 – 350.00

13" – 15"........ $225.00 – 250.00

16" – 19"........ $300.00 – 375.00

Hertwig Co salesman sample card of all-bisque dolls. $2,500.00. **Photo courtesy of Atlanta Antique Gallery.**

23" – 25"........ $350.00 – 400.00
27" – 32"........ $600.00 – 675.00
36"................. $700.00 – 750.00

Painted bisque
8" – 12".......... $140.00 – 160.00
16"................. $200.00 – 225.00

Baby, 1910 on, open mouth, glass eyes, socket head, wig, five-piece bent-leg composition body, add more for toddler body, flirty eyes
Molds 300, 320, 321, 342, and others
5" – 6½"......... $250.00 – 275.00
8" – 11".......... $200.00 – 275.00
14" – 17"........ $300.00 – 375.00
19" – 21"........ $400.00 – 475.00
25" – 27"........ $525.00 – 650.00

Painted bisque, flirty eyes
24"................. $375.00 – 425.00

Character Child, 1910 on, painted eyes
Molds 261, 262, 271, and others, bisque shoulder head, cloth body
12"................. $300.00 – 400.00
Mold 312 (for Seyfarth & Reinhard)
14"................. $300.00 – 325.00
18"................. $400.00 – 425.00
28"................. $600.00 – 650.00

Mold 417, glass eyes, resembles Armand Marseille Just Me
11" – 12".. $1,200.00 – 1,400.00

Baby, Newborn, 1925 on solid dome, molded and painted hair, glass eyes, closed mouth,

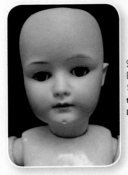

26" mold 250 by Ernst Heubach. $375.00. **Photo courtesy of Cybermogul Dolls.**

cloth body, composition or celluloid hands
Molds 338, 339, 340, 348, 349
10" – 12"........ $375.00 – 425.00
14" – 16"........ $475.00 – 575.00
17"................. $600.00 – 650.00
Black, mold 444
12"................. $375.00 – 425.00

GEBRÜDER HEUBACH

1910 – 1938, Lichte, Thüringia, Germany. Porcelain factory founded in 1804 but did not make dolls until 1910. Made bisque heads and all-bisque dolls, characters, either socket or shoulder head, molded hair or wigs, sleeping or intaglio eyes, in heights from 4" to 26". Provided heads to other companies including Bauersachs, Cuno & Oto Dressel, Eisemann & Co., and Gebruder Ohlhaver. Mold numbers from 556 to 10633. Sunburst or square marks, more dolls with square marks. Dolls listed are in good condition, appropriately dressed.

Marked "Heubach," no mold number
Closed mouth, intaglio eyes, wigged
8"................. $900.00 – 1,000.00
Closed mouth pouty, intaglio eyes
14" .... $500.00 – 600.00
Smile, painted eyes
15"........... $3,400.00 – 3,500.00
Lady doll, open or closed mouth, glass eyes, mold 76325, 7635, others
10" – 11".. $2,400.00 – 2,600.00
14" – 16".. $3,500.00 – 4,000.00
Animal head, bears, cats, etc on five-piece composition child doll bodies
6" – 8"...... $1,500.00 – 1,600.00
Marked Heubach Googly: See **Googly category.**
Character Child

8" Heubach teddy bear.
$1,600.00. **Photo courtesy of Dolls & Lace.**

Shoulder Head

Mold 5777, Dolly Dimple, shoulder head version
    17" – 19".. $1,300.00 – 1,500.00
Mold 6692, ca. 1912, shoulder head version, sunburst, intaglio eyes, closed mouth pouty
    14" – 16"........ $550.00 – 650.00
    20"................. $875.00 – 900.00
Mold 6736, ca. 1912, square mark, painted eyes, laughing mouth
    12" – 13"........ $500.00 – 700.00
    16".......... $1,100.00 – 1,200.00
Mold 6894, ca. 1912
    13"................. $600.00 – 700.00
Mold 7345, ca. 1912, sunburst, pink-tinted closed mouth
    17".......... $1,000.00 – 1,150.00
Mold 7644, ca. 1910, "Our Pet," sunburst or square mark, painted eyes, open-closed laughing mouth
    9" – 10".......... $300.00 – 350.00
    14"................. $750.00 – 850.00
    17".......... $1,000.00 – 1,100.00
    20".......... $1,450.00 – 1,550.00

Mold 7850, ca. 1912, "Coquette," open-closed mouth
    11" – 12"........ $450.00 – 500.00
    15"................. $650.00 – 700.00
Mold 7852, ca. 1912, molded hair in coiled braids
    16"............................ $2,200.00
Too few in database for reliable range.
Mold 7853, ca. 1912, downcast eyes
    14".......... $1,600.00 – 1,800.00
Mold 7925, ca. 1914, mold 7926, ca. 1912, lady, glass eyes, smiling open mouth
    11" – 15".. $1,400.00 – 2,000.00
    18" – 20" . $2,900.00 – 3,100.00
Too few in database for reliable range.
Mold 8191, baby, solid dome with molded hair, open/closed mouth, intaglio eyes
    11"................. $900.00 – 950.00
Mold 8221, square mark, dome, intaglio eyes, open-closed mouth
    14"................. $650.00 – 700.00
Too few in database for reliable range.
Mold 8306, open, closed mouth laughing, intaglio eyes, molded hair
    13".......... $1,200.00 – 1,400.00
Mold 8457, Princess Angeline, Native American woman, wrinkled face, downcast eyes, wigged believed to be a portrait of the daughter of Chief Seattle
    13"......... $7,500.00 – 10,000.00
Mold 9355, ca. 1914, square mark, glass eyes, open mouth
    13"................. $800.00 – 850.00
    19".......... $1,100.00 – 1,250.00
Mold 9722, character with molded spiked helmet
    14" .... $6,200.00 – 6,400.00
Socket-Head
Mold 5636, ca. 1912, glass eyes, open-closed laughing mouth, teeth
    12" – 13".. $1,700.00 – 1,800.00
    15" – 18".. $2,300.00 – 2,600.00

12½" Heubach lady. $3,000.00. **Photo courtesy of The Museum Doll Shop.**

Mold 5689, ca. 1912, sunburst mark, smiling open mouth

    14"........... $1,600.00 – 1,700.00
    17"........... $2,000.00 – 2,100.00
    22"........... $2,700.00 – 2,800.00

Mold 5730, "Santa," ca. 1912, sunburst mark, made for Hamburger & Co.

    16"........... $1,600.00 – 1,700.00
    19" – 22".. $1,900.00 – 2,100.00
    24" – 26".. $2,400.00 – 2,600.00

Mold 5777, "Dolly Dimple," ca. 1913, open mouth, for Hamburger & Co.

    12" – 14".. $2,700.00 – 2,800.00
    16" – 19".. $3,100.00 – 3,600.00
    22" – 24".. $3,700.00 – 3,900.00

Mold 6894, intaglio eyes, closed mouth

    20"................. $825.00 – 875.00

Mold 6969, ca. 1912, socket head, square mark, glass eyes, closed mouth

    7" – 9"...... $1,050.00 – 1,250.00
    12" – 13".. $2,100.00 – 2,200.00
    16" – 18".. $3,300.00 – 3,700.00
    20" – 24".. $3,900.00 – 4,100.00

Mold 6970, ca. 1912, sunburst, glass eyes, closed mouth

    7" – 9"........... $850.00 – 950.00
    12" – 13".. $2,800.00 – 3,000.00
    16" – 18".. $3,000.00 – 3,300.00
    20" – 24".. $3,500.00 – 3,900.00

Mold 6971, ca. 1912, intaglio eyes, closed smiling mouth in original costume box

    11"............................. $1,200.00

Too few in database for reliable range.

Molds 7246, 7247, 7248, ca. 1912, sunburst or square mark, closed mouth, glass eyes

    7" – 10".... $1,100.00 – 1,200.00
    12" – 13".. $2,100.00 – 2,400.00
    16" – 18".. $3,200.00 – 3,600.00
    20" – 24".. $4,100.00 – 4,400.00
    26" – 28".. $4,500.00 – 6,000.00

Mold 7407, character, glass eyes, open-closed mouth

    7" – 9"............ $850.00 – 950.00
    12" – 13".. $2,100.00 – 2,400.00
    16" – 18".. $3,100.00 – 3,500.00
    20" – 24".. $4,100.00 – 4,900.00

Mold 7602, 7603, ca. 1912, molded hair tufts, intaglio eyes

    10" – 11"........ $300.00 – 400.00
    15" – 18".. $1,100.00 – 1,300.00

Mold 7604, ca. 1912, open-closed mouth, intaglio eyes

    12" – 14"........ $650.00 – 700.00
    20"........... $1,100.00 – 1,200.00

Mold 7608, pouty

    9".................... $400.00 – 500.00

Mold 7622, 7623, ca. 1912, intaglio eyes, closed or open-closed mouth

    16" – 18".. $1,100.00 – 1,300.00

Mold 7633, ca. 1912, laughing child, glass eyes

    12" – 13".. $1,700.00 – 1,800.00
    15" – 18".. $2,300.00 – 2,600.00

Mold 7681, dome, intaglio eyes, closed mouth

    10" – 12" .... $500.00 – 575.00

Mold 7711, ca. 1912, glass eyes, open mouth, flapper body

    9" – 10".... $1,000.00 – 1,200.00
    18"........... $6,000.00 – 7,000.00

Mold 7746, ca. 1912, open/closed mouth w/two teeth, ears sticking out from head

    14"............................. $6,200.00

Too few in database for a reliable range.

Mold **7759,** ca. 1912, dome, painted eyes, closed mouth

12" .... $800.00 – 900.00

Molds **7763, 7788, 7850** (Coquette), ca. 1912, molded hair with bow

11" .... $900.00 – 950.00

14" – 15".. $1,100.00 – 1,300.00

20" .... $1,500.00 – 1,600.00

Mold **7911,** ca. 1912, intaglio eyes, laughing open-closed mouth

9" – 11" .... $625.00 – 700.00

15" .... $850.00 – 950.00

Mold **8191,** "Crooked Smile," ca. 1912, square mark, intaglio eyes, laughing mouth

11½" .... $1,200.00 – 1,300.00

14" .... $1,500.00 – 1,600.00

16" .... $2,800.00 – 3,000.00

Mold **8192,** ca. 1914, sunburst or square mark, sleep eyes, open mouth

11" – 13" .... $750.00 – 950.00

18" – 20".. $1,275.00 – 1,450.00

Mold **8316,** "Grinning Boy," ca. 1914, wig, open-closed mouth, eight teeth, glass eyes

16" .... $3,200.00 – 3,400.00

19" .... $4,600.00 – 4,800.00

Mold **8381,** "Princess Juliana," molded hair, ribbon, painted eyes, closed mouth

14" – 16" ..$10,000.00 – 13,000.00

Mold **8413,** ca. 1914, wig, sleep eyes, open-closed mouth, molded tongue, upper teeth

8" .... $1,000.00 – 1,150.00

Mold **8429,** square mark, closed mouth

15" $2,500.00

Too few in database for reliable range.

Mold **8686,** glass eyes, open-closed mouth

14" $3,200.00

Too few in database for reliable range.

Mold **8774,** "Whistling Jim," ca. 1914, smoker or whistler, square mark, flange neck, intaglio eyes, molded hair, cloth body, bellows

9" .... $1,200.00 – 1,400.00

13" mold 8457, Princess Angeline, character doll by Gebruder Heubach. $10,000.00. **Photo courtesy of Richard Withington, Inc.**

13" – 14".. $1,100.00 – 1,200.00

Mold **8950,** laughing girl, blue hair bow

18" .... $6,900.00 – 7,200.00

Mold **8970,** closed mouth, intaglio eyes, wigged

9" .... $1,200.00 – 1,300.00

Mold **9055,** intaglio eyes, closed mouth

11" $375.00

Too few in database for reliable range.

Mold **9457,** ca. 1914, square mark, dome, intaglio eyes, closed mouth, Eskimo

15" .... $2,300.00 – 2,500.00

18" .... $3,800.00 – 4,000.00

Mold **9746,** square mark, painted eyes, closed mouth

7½" .... $700.00 – 800.00

Mold **10532,** ca. 1920, square mark, open mouth, five-piece toddler body

8½" .... $1,000.00 – 1,100.00

13½" .... $1,450.00 – 1,550.00

20" – 22".. $1,900.00 – 2,100.00

25" .... $2,400.00 – 2,500.00

Mold **11173,** "Tiss Me," socket head, wig

8" .... $1,900.00 – 2,000.00

Too few in database for reliable range.

Character Baby, socket head, 1911 on, bisque head, bent-limb body

9" mold 7975, Baby Stuart, with removable bisque bonnet. $1,800.00. **Photo courtesy of Richard Withington, Inc.**

Mold 6894, 6897, 7759, 7602, 7604, all ca. 1912, sunburst or square mark, intaglio eyes, closed mouth, molded hair

6" – 7"............ $350.00 – 450.00

9" – 12".......... $525.00 – 600.00

15"................. $600.00 – 700.00

20".............. $900.00 – 1,000.00

Toddler

14"................. $850.00 – 950.00

Molds 7877, 7977, "Baby Stuart," ca. 1912, molded bonnet, closed mouth, painted eyes

8" – 9"...... $1,100.00 – 1,200.00

11" – 13".. $1,500.00 – 1,700.00

15"........... $1,900.00 – 2,100.00

Mold 7975, "Baby Stuart," ca. 1912, glass eyes, removable molded bisque bonnet

9" – 13".... $1,700.00 – 2,100.00

Mold 8420, ca. 1914, square mark, glass eyes, closed mouth

10"................. $650.00 – 750.00

15"........... $1,200.00 – 1,400.00

Mold 9072, molded curly baby hair, intaglio eyes, open/closed mouth with one lower tooth

9" – 10".... $1,500.00 – 1,700.00

Mold 9531, painted hair, open/closed mouth, glass eyes

Toddler

18" ....$1,900.00 – 2,000.00

All Bisque: See All-Bisque section.

E.I. HORSMAN

1878 – 1980s, New York City. Founded by Edward Imeson Horsman as company importing, assembling, wholesaling, and distributing various dolls and doll lines. From 1909 to 1919 they distributed Aetna Doll & Toy company's dolls, in 1919 the two companies merged. Eventually Horsman made their own dolls as well as distributing other lines. They took out their first patent for a complete doll in 1909 for a Billiken doll. They made dolls of composition, rubber, hard plastic, and vinyl.

Early Composition on Cloth Body, composition head, sometimes lower arms, cloth body. Dolls listed are in good condition with original clothing, add more for exceptional doll.

Baby Bumps, 1910 – 1917, composition head, cloth cork stuffed body, blue and white cloth label on romper, copy of K*R #100 Baby mold

11"................................ $250.00

Black .... $300.00 – 350.00

Baby Butterfly, 1914 on, composition head, hands, cloth body, painted hair and features

13"................. $250.00 – 300.00

15"................. $350.00 – 400.00

Billiken, 1909, composition head, molded hair, slanted eyes, smiling closed mouth, on stuffed mohair or velvet body, cloth label on body, "Billiken" on right foot

12"................. $200.00 – 400.00

Campbell Kids, 1910 on, designed by Helen Trowbridge, based on Grace Drayton's drawings, composition head, painted and molded hair, side-glancing painted eyes, closed smiling mouth, composition arms, cloth body and feet, mark: "EIH © 1910"; cloth label on sleeve, "The Campbell Kids// Trademark by //Joseph Campbell// Mfg. by E.I. Horsman Co."

    10" – 11"........ $325.00 – 350.00
    15" – 16"........ $375.00 – 400.00

Can't Break "Em Characters, 1911 on
Child, boy or girl
    11" – 13"........ $200.00 – 275.00
Cotton Joe, black
    13".................. $350.00 – 400.00
Little Mary Mix-up
    15".................. $350.00 – 375.00
Master & Miss Sam, in patriotic outfits
    15".................. $350.00 – 375.00
Polly Pru
    13".................. $325.00 – 350.00

Fairy, 1911, composition head and hands, molded hair, painted side-glancing eyes, cloth body, designed by Helen Trowbridge, based on Little Fairy Soap advertising by N.K. Fairbanks Co., mark "EIH © 1911"
    13".................. $325.00 – 400.00

Gene Carr Kids, 1915 – 1916, composition head, molded and painted hair, painted eyes, open/closed smiling mouth with teeth, big ears, cloth body, composition hands, original outfit, cloth tag reads: "MADE GENE CARR KIDS U.S.A.//FROM NEW YORK WORLD'S//LADY BOUNTIFUL COMIC SERIES//By E.I. HORSMAN CO. NY"
Blink, Lizzie, Mike, Skinney
    14".................. $300.00 – 350.00
Snowball, black .... $450.00 – 500.00

Gold Medal Baby, 1911 on, line of baby dolls with composition head and limbs, upper and lower teeth, included Baby Suck-a-Thumb, Baby Blossom, Baby Premier, and others
    10".................. $200.00 – 250.00

13" Gene Carr Kid by Horsman. $325.00.
Photo courtesy of McMasters Harris Auction Co.

    12".................. $250.00 – 300.00
    19".................. $325.00 – 375.00
Early All-Composition Dolls
Peek-a-Boo, 1913, designed by Grace Drayton
    8".................... $100.00 – 125.00
Peterkin, 1914 – 1930
    11".................. $250.00 – 300.00
Puppy & Pussy Pippin, 1911, designed by Grace Drayton, composition head, plush body .... $450.00 – 550.00
Composition Dolls on Cloth Body, 1920 on
Brother & Sister, 1937, marked: "Brother//1937//Horsman//©"& "Sister//1937//Horsman//©"
Brother 21" and Sister 23"
            $300.00 – 350.00 each
Ella Cinders, 1928 – 1929, based on a cartoon character, composition head, black painted hair or wig, round painted eyes, freckles under eyes, open/closed mouth, also came as all-cloth, mark: "1925//MNS"
    14".................. $400.00 – 450.00
    18".................. $650.00 – 700.00
Jackie Coogan, "The Kid," 1921 – 1922, composition head, hands, molded hair, painted eyes, turtleneck sweater, long gray pants, checked cap, button

13" Fairy, based on advertising for
Little Fairy Soap, c. 1911. $225.00.
**Photo courtesy of Joan & Lynette Antique
Dolls and Accessories.**

reads: "HORSMAN DOLL// JACKIE//
COOGAN// KID// PATENTED"

    13½"............. $450.00 – 475.00
    15½"............. $500.00 – 550.00

Jeanie Horsman, 1937, composition head
and limbs, painted molded brown hair, sleep
eyes, mark: "Jeanie© Horsman"

    14"................ $225.00 – 250.00

All-Composition Dolls, 1930 on

Body Twist, 1930, with jointed waist

    11"................ $175.00 – 200.00

Bright Star, 1937 – 1946,

    14"................ $225.00 – 250.00
    20"................ $375.00 – 425.00

Campbell Kids, 1930 – 1940s, all-
composition

    13"................ $250.00 – 300.00

Child, including Gold Metal child

    13" – 14"........ $175.00 – 200.00
    16" – 18"........ $200.00 – 225.00
    21"................ $225.00 – 250.00

HEbee-SHEbees, 1925 – 1927, based on
drawings by Charles Twelvetrees, painted
features, molded undershirt and booties or
various costumes

    10½"............. $400.00 – 475.00

**All-bisque HEbee & SHEbee: See All-Bisque
section.**

Jo Jo, 1937, blue sleep eyes, wigged,
over molded hair, toddler body, mark:
"HORSMAN JO JO//©1937"

    13".................. $325.00 – 375.00

Naughty Sue, 1937, jointed body

    16".................. $400.00 – 450.00

Patsy-Type, names such as Sue, Babs, Joan
were given to the various sizes

    12".................. $200.00 – 225.00
    14".................. $250.00 – 275.00

Roberta, 1937, all-composition

    16".................. $375.00 – 450.00

Composition Baby, 1920s – 1940s

Dimples, 1927 – 1937 on, composition head,
arms, cloth body, bent-leg body or bent-limb
baby body, molded dimples, open mouth,
sleep or painted eyes, marked "E.I. H."

    13" – 14"........ $200.00 – 225.00
    16" – 18"........ $275.00 – 375.00
    20" – 22"........ $350.00 – 400.00

Toddler

    20".................. $300.00 – 350.00

13" composition
Campbell Kid,
1940s. $275.00.
**Photo courtesy of The
Museum Doll Shop.**

24".............. $425.00 – 475.00

Tynie Baby, ca. 1924 – 1929, bisque or composition head, sleep or painted eyes, cloth body, some all-bisque, marks: "©1924//E.I. HORSMAN//CO. INC." or "E.I.H. Co. 1924" on composition or "©1924 by//E I Horsman Co. Inc//Germany//37" incised on bisque head

All-bisque, with wardrobe, cradle

6".............................$1,785.00*

9"................................$2,500.00

Bisque, head circumference

9" $600.00

12" $200.00

15"................................$300.00

Composition, heads and arms, cloth body

18"................. $150.00 – 175.00

21"................. $200.00 – 225.00

Vinyl, 1950s, boxed

15"................... $90.00 – 110.00

Mama Dolls, 1920 on, composition head, arms, and lower legs, cloth body with crier and stitched hip joints so lower legs will swing, painted or sleep eyes, mohair or molded hair, models including Peggy Ann, Rosebud, and others

14" – 15"........ $225.00 – 250.00

19" – 21"........ $300.00 – 350.00

23" – 24"........ $300.00 – 375.00

Hard Plastic and Vinyl, dolls listed are in excellent condition with original clothing and tags, allow more for mint-in-box doll, add more for accessories or wardrobe

Angelove, 1974, plastic/vinyl made for Hallmark

12"..................... $20.00 – 25.00

Answer Doll, 1966, button in back moves head

10"..................... $10.00 – 15.00

Baby Dimples, vinyl re-issue

19" – 21"............ $45.00 – 55.00

Baby First Tooth, 1966, vinyl head, limbs,

12" Mary Poppins, MIB. $125.00. **Photo courtesy of The Museum Doll Shop.**

cloth body, open/closed mouth with tongue and one tooth, molded tears on cheeks, rooted blond hair, painted blue eyes, mark: "©Horsman Dolls Inc. //10141"

16"..................... $30.00 – 40.00

Baby Sofskin, 1972 on, vinyl

12" – 15" .... $20.00 – 30.00

Baby Tweaks, 1967, vinyl head, cloth body, inset eyes, rooted saran hair, mark: "54//HORSMAN DOLLS INC.//Copyright 1967/67191" on head

20"..................... $20.00 – 30.00

Ballerina, 1957, vinyl, one-piece body and legs, jointed elbows

18"................................$50.00

Betty, 1951, all-vinyl, one-piece body and limbs

14"..................... $50.00 – 60.00

Vinyl head, hard plastic body

16"..................... $20.00 – 25.00

Betty Ann, vinyl head, hard plastic body

19"..................... $50.00 – 60.00

Betty Jane, vinyl head, hard plastic body

25"..................... $65.00 – 75.00

Betty Jo, vinyl head, hard plastic body

16"..................... $20.00 – 30.00

Bright Star, ca. 1952 on, all hard plastic

11" Poor Pitiful Pearl, c. 1963, MIB. $225.00. **Photo courtesy of The Museum Doll Shop.**

15".............. $175.00 – 250.00
Bye-Lo Baby, 1972, reissue, molded vinyl head, limbs, cloth body, white nylon organdy bonnet dress, mark: "3 (in square)// HORSMAN DOLLS INC.//©1972"
14"..................... $25.00 – 30.00
1980 – 1990s
14"..................... $15.00 – 20.00
Celeste, portrait doll, in frame, eyes painted to side
12"..................... $30.00 – 35.00
Cinderella, 1965, vinyl head, hard plastic body, painted eyes to side
11½"................. $25.00 – 30.00
Cindy, 1950s, all hard plastic child, "170"
15"................ $125.00 – 175.00
17"................ $175.00 – 200.00
19"................ $200.00 – 225.00
Cindy Fashion-type doll, vinyl head, soft vinyl stuffed high-heel body
15"..................... $65.00 – 90.00
18"................ $100.00 – 125.00
Vinyl head, solid vinyl body jointed at shoulders and hips, high-heel foot
10"..................... $25.00 – 30.00
Cindy Kay, 1950s+, all-vinyl child with long legs

15"..................... $70.00 – 80.00
20"................ $110.00 – 125.00
27"................ $200.00 – 225.00
Crawling Baby, 1967, vinyl, rooted hair
14"..................... $20.00 – 25.00
Disney Exclusives, 1981, Cinderella, Snow White, Mary Poppins, Alice in Wonderland
8"....................... $35.00 – 40.00
Elizabeth Taylor, 1976
11½"................. $45.00 – 50.00
Floppy, 1958, vinyl head, foam body and legs
18"..................... $20.00 – 25.00
Flying Nun, 1965, TV character portrayed by Sally Field
12"................. $100.00 – 125.00
Gold Medal Doll, 1953, vinyl head, soft vinyl foam stuffed body, molded hair
26"................. $150.00 – 175.00
1954, vinyl, boy
12"..................... $35.00 – 40.00
15"..................... $65.00 – 75.00
Hansel & Gretel, 1963, vinyl head, hard plastic body, rooted synthetic hair, closed mouth, sleep eyes, marks: "MADE IN USA" on body, on tag, "HORSMAN, Michael Meyerberg, Inc.," "Reproduction of the

famous Kinemins in Michael Myerberg's marvelous Technicolor production of Hansel and Gretel"

15"................. $200.00 – 225.00

HEbee-SHEbees, 1987, vinyl re-issues

$12.00 – 18.00

Jackie, 1961, vinyl doll, rooted hair, blue sleep eyes, long lashes, closed mouth, high-heeled feet, small waist, nicely dressed, designed by Irene Szor who says this doll named Jackie was not meant to portray Jackie Kennedy, mark: "HORSMAN//19©61//BC"

18" – 25"....... $120.00 – 155.00

Joey Stivic, Archie Bunker's grandson, 1976, vinyl, rooted hair

14"...................... $15.00 – 20.00

Lil' David & Lil' Ruth, 1970s, all vinyl, anatomically correct babies

12"...................... $20.00 – 25.00

Lullabye Baby, 1967 – 1968, vinyl bent-leg body, rooted hair, inset blue eyes, drink and wet feature, musical mechanism, Sears 1968 catalog, came on suedette pillow, in terry-cloth p.j.s, mark: "2580//B144 8 // HORSMAN DOLLS INC//19©67"

12"...................... $10.00 – 15.00

Mary Poppins, 1965, all in good condition with original clothing, mint-in-box can bring double the value listed

12"...................... $50.00 – 75.00

16"...................... $65.00 – 85.00

26", 1966......... $75.00 – 100.00

36"................. $150.00 – 200.00

Mary Poppins with Michael and Jane, 1966

12" and 8"...... $150.00 – 160.00

1970s version Mary Poppins

12" .... $10.00 – 20.00

Police Woman, ca. 1976, vinyl, plastic fully articulated body, rooted hair

9"...................... $35.00 – 40.00

Poor Pitiful Pearl, 1963, from cartoon by William Steig, marked on neck: "Horsman 1963"

11"................. $100.00 – 120.00

17"................. $175.00 – 200.00

Ruthie, 1962

15"..................... $25.00 – 30.00

19"..................... $35.00 – 40.00

Softee, 1959, vinyl baby

15"..................... $20.00 – 25.00

Tessie Talk, 1974, ventriloquist doll

16"..................... $40.00 – 50.00

Thirsty Walker, 1962

26"..................... $20.00 – 25.00

MARY HOYER DOLL MFG. CO.

1937 – 1968, 1990 – present, Reading, Pennsylvania. Designed by Bernard Lipfert, all-composition, later hard plastic, then vinyl, swivel neck, jointed body, mohair or human hair wig, sleep eyes, closed mouth, original clothes, or knitted from Mary Hoyer patterns, company re-opened by Hoyer's granddaughter in 1990. Dolls listed are in good condition with appropriate clothing.

Composition, less for painted eyes

14" composition Mary Hoyer doll with the painted eyes of the WWII years. $295.00. **Photo courtesy of The Museum Doll Shop.**

14".................. $325.00 – 400.00
Hard Plastic
In knit outfit
14".................. $475.00 – 500.00
In tagged Hoyer outfit
14".................. $650.00 – 800.00
Boy in original wig
14".................. $575.00 – 600.00
Modern, values are for secondary market dolls, dolls are still available at retail
14"........... $100.00 – 120.00 MIB
Gigi, circa 1950, with round Mary Hoyer mark found on 14" dolls, only 2,000 made by the Frisch Doll Company
18".............. $750.00 – 1,200.00
Wearing gown, carrying parasol
$1,425.00*
Vinyl, circa 1957 on
Vicky, all-vinyl, high-heeled doll, body bends at waist, rooted saran hair, two larger sizes 12" and 14" were discontinued
10½".............. $90.00 – 100.00
Margie, circa 1958, toddler, rooted hair, made by Unique Doll Co.
10"..................... $70.00 – 75.00
Cathy, circa 1961, infant, made by Unique Doll Co.
10"..................... $20.00 – 25.00
Janie, circa 1962, baby
8"..................... $20.00 – 25.00

18" Gigi, hard plastic. $900.00. **Photo courtesy of My Dolly Dearest.**

ADOLPH HÜLSS

1915 – 1930+, Waltershausen, Germany. Made dolls with bisque heads, jointed composition bodies. Trademark: "Nesthakchen," "h" in mold mark often resembles a "b." Heads made by Simon & Halbig.

Baby, bisque socket head, sleep eyes, open mouth, teeth, wig, bent-leg baby, composition body, add more for flirty eyes
Mold 156
14" – 15"........ $550.00 – 575.00
17" – 19"........ $625.00 – 675.00
23"................. $800.00 – 825.00
Toddler
9" – 10".......... $850.00 – 900.00
16"................. $775.00 – 800.00
20"................. $900.00 – 925.00
Painted bisque
22"................. $200.00 – 225.00
Child, bisque socket-head, wig, sleep eyes, open mouth, teeth, tongue, jointed composition body
Mold 176
15"................. $650.00 – 675.00
18"................. $650.00 – 750.00
22"................. $950.00 – 975.00

MAISON HURET

1812 – 1930 on, France. May have pressed, molded bisque, or china heads, painted or glass eyes, closed mouths, bodies of cloth, composition, gutta-percha, kid, or wood, sometimes metal hands. Used fur or mohair for wigs, had fashion-type body with defined waist. Look for dolls with beautiful painting on eyes and face; painted eyes are more common than glass, but the beauty of the painted features and/or wooden bodies increases the price.

Poupée
Bisque shoulder head, kid body with bisque lower arms, glass eyes

   15".......$13,000.00 – 14,000.00
   17" – 18"..$16,000.00 – 20,000.00
With trunk & wardrobe
   17" $41,000.00*
Gutta-percha body
   17".......$12,000.00 – 13,000.00
Round face, painted blue eyes, cloth body
   16" – 18"..$11,000.00 – 14,000.00
Wood body
   17" ......$20,000.00 – 24,000.00
China shoulder head, kid body, china lower arms
   17".......$15,000.00 – 20,000.00
Wood body
   17".......$25,000.00 – 30,000.00
Gutta percha body
   17".......$20,000.00 – 25,000.00
Huret Bébé, 1878, bisque head, glass eyes, closed mouth
Composition body
   13"..........$7,000.00 – 11,000.00
Gutta percha body
   18".......$70,000.00 – 80,000.00
Wooden body
   18".......$34,000.00 – 36,000.00
Prevost Era Lady or Gentleman, 1914 – 1918, elongated face on composition body
   17" – 18"..$15,000.00 – 20,000.00

IDEAL NOVELTY AND TOY CO.

1906 – 1980s, Brooklyn, New York. Produced their own composition dolls in early years. Later made dolls of rubber, hard plastic, vinyl, and cloth. Up to 1950 dolls listed are in good condition with appropriate clothing, after 1950 dolls listed are in excellent condition with original clothing and tags for values listed.

Cloth
Dennis the Menace, 1976, all-cloth, printed doll, comic strip character by Hank Ketcham, blond hair, freckles, wearing overalls, striped shirt

   7"........................$10.00 – 15.00
   14".....................$15.00 – 20.00
Internationals, 1920s on, cloth mask faces, cloth bodies...............$75.00 – 100.00
Peanuts Gang, 1976 – 1978, all-cloth, stuffed printed dolls from Peanuts cartoon strip by Charles Schulz, Charlie Brown, Lucy, Linus, Peppermint Patty, and Snoopy

   7"........................$20.00 – 35.00
   14".....................$30.00 – 40.00
Snow White and the Seven Dwarves, 1939 on, cloth mask face dolls, cloth body
Snow White, black mohair wig, dress with dwarves printed on skirt

   16".................$550.00 – 600.00
Dwarves
   10"..........$200.00 – 250.00 each
Strawman, 1939, all-cloth, scarecrow character played by Ray Bolger in Wizard of

16" cloth mask faced Snow White. $250.00.
Photo courtesy of The Museum Doll Shop.

Oz movie, yarn hair, all original, wearing dark jacket and hat, tan pants, round paper hang tag

    17"............. $900.00 – 1,200.00
    21".......... $1,400.00 – 1,500.00

Composition

Early Composition Character Children, composition heads, lower arms and sometimes shoes on cloth body, excelsior stuffed

Cracker Jack Boy, 1917, sailor suit, carries package of Cracker Jacks

    14"................. $350.00 – 375.00

Happy Hooligan, 1910

    21"................. $475.00 – 525.00

Liberty Boy, 1917, molded uniform

    12"................. $225.00 – 275.00

Naughty Marietta (Coquette-type), 1912

    14"................................ $150.00

Snookums, 1910, plush body

    14"................. $500.00 – 600.00

Uneeda Kid, 1914 – 1919, original clothing including rain slicker and biscuit box

    16"................. $475.00 – 500.00

Zu Zu Kid, 1916 – 1917

    16"................. $350.00 – 375.00

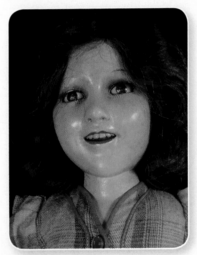

24" Deanna Durbin doll by Ideal. $1,200.00.
Photo courtesy of Richard Withington, Inc.

Child or Toddler, 1913 on, composition head, molded hair, or wigged, painted or sleep eyes, cloth or composition body, may have Ideal diamond mark or hang tag, original clothes

    13"................. $175.00 – 250.00
    15" – 16"........ $250.00 – 275.00
    18"................. $275.00 – 300.00

Baby Doll, 1913 on, composition head, molded hair or wigged, painted or sleep eyes, cloth or composition body, models such as Baby Mine, Our Pet, Prize baby, and others

    15" – 16"........ $175.00 – 250.00

Mama Doll, 1921 on, composition head and arms, molded hair or wigged, painted or sleep eyes, cloth body with crier and stitched swing leg, lower part composition

    16"................. $225.00 – 275.00
    20"................. $275.00 – 325.00
    24"................. $350.00 – 375.00

Babies, mid 1920s – 1940s, composition head, arms and legs, cloth body

Flossie Flirt, 1924 – 1931, composition head, limbs, cloth body, crier, tin flirty eyes, open mouth, upper teeth, original outfit, dress, bonnet, socks, and shoes, mark: "IDEAL" in diamond with "U.S. of A"

    14"................. $225.00 – 250.00
    18"................. $250.00 – 275.00
    20"................. $300.00 – 350.00
    22"................. $350.00 – 375.00
    24"................. $375.00 – 400.00
    28"................. $400.00 – 525.00

Tickletoes, 1928 – 1939, composition head, rubber arms, legs, cloth body, squeaker in each leg, flirty sleep eyes, open mouth, two painted teeth, original organdy dress, bonnet, paper hang tag, marks: "IDEAL" in diamond with "U.S. of A." on head

    14"................. $275.00 – 300.00
    17"................. $300.00 – 325.00

20".................. $325.00 – 350.00

Snoozie, 1933 on, composition head, painted hair, hard rubber hands and feet, cloth body, open yawning mouth, molded tongue, sleep eyes, designed by Bernard Lipfert, marks: "©B. Lipfert//Made for Ideal Doll & Toy Corp. 1933" or "©by B. Lipfert" or "IDEAL SNOOZIE//B. LIPFERT" on head

12" composition Dopey, foot damaged. $125.00. **Photo courtesy of The Museum Doll Shop.**

    14".................. $175.00 – 200.00
    16".................. $275.00 – 325.00
    18".................. $325.00 – 350.00
    20".................. $350.00 – 375.00

Princess Beatrix, 1938 – 1943, represents Princess Beatrix of the Netherlands, composition head, arms, legs, cloth body, flirty sleep eyes, fingers molded into fists, original organdy dress and bonnet

    14".................. $200.00 – 250.00
    16".................. $300.00 – 350.00
    22".................. $375.00 – 425.00
    26".................. $400.00 – 425.00

Soozie Smiles, 1923, two-faced composition doll with smiling face, sleep or painted eyes, and crying face with tears, molded and painted hair, cloth body and legs, composition arms, original clothes, tag, also in gingham check romper

    15" – 17"........ $375.00 – 425.00

Composition Child, 1920s – 1940s

Buster Brown, 1929, composition head, hands, legs, cloth body, tin eyes, red outfit. mark: "IDEAL" (in a diamond)

    17" .... $325.00 – 375.00

Charlie McCarthy, 1938 – 1939, hand puppet, composition head, felt hands, molded hat, molded features, wire monocle, cloth body, painted tuxedo, mark: "Edgar Bergen's//©CHARLIE MCCARTHY//MADE IN U.S.A."

    8"...................... 450.00 – 60.00

Cinderella, 1938 – 1939, all-composition, brown, blond, or red human hair wig, flirty brown sleep eyes, open mouth, six teeth, same head mold as Ginger, Snow White, Mary Jane with dimple in chin, some wore formal evening gowns of organdy and taffeta, velvet cape, had rhinestone tiara, silver snap shoes, Sears catalog version has Celanese rayon gown, marks: none on head; "SHIRLEY TEMPLE//13" on body

    13".................. $300.00 – 325.00
    16".................. $325.00 – 350.00
    20".................. $350.00 – 375.00
    22".................. $375.00 – 400.00
    25".................. $400.00 – 425.00
    27".................. $425.00 – 450.00

Deanna Durbin, 1938 – 1941, all-composition, fully jointed, dark brown human hair wig, brown sleep eyes, open mouth, six teeth, felt tongue, original clothes, pin reads: "DEANNA DURBIN//A UNIVERSAL STAR," more for fancy outfits, marks: "DEANNA DURBIN//IDEAL DOLL" on head; "IDEAL DOLL//21" on body

    15".................. $600.00 – 700.00
    18".................. $700.00 – 800.00
    21".............. $900.00 – 1,000.00
    24".......... $1,400.00 – 1,500.00

Flexy, 1938 – 1942, composition head,

gauntlet hands, molded and painted hair, painted eyes, wooden torso and feet, flexible wire tubing for arms and legs, original clothes, paper tag, marks: "IDEAL DOLL// Made in U.S. A." or just "IDEAL DOLL" on head

Black Flexy, closed smiling mouth, tweed patched pants, felt suspenders

 13½"............... $275.00 – 300.00

Baby Snooks, (Fannie Brice), open/closed mouth with teeth

 13½"............... $225.00 – 250.00

Clown Flexy, looks like Mortimer Snerd, painted white as clown

 13½"............... $175.00 – 200.00

Mortimer Snerd, Edgar Bergen's dummy, smiling closed mouth, showing two teeth

 13½"............... $225.00 – 250.00

Soldier, closed smiling mouth, in khaki uniform

 13½"............... $200.00 – 225.00

Sunny Sam and Sunny Sue, girl bobbed hair, pouty mouth, boy as smiling mouth

 13½"............... $200.00 – 225.00

Judy Garland

1939 – 1940, as Dorothy from The Wizard of Oz, all-composition, jointed, wig with braids, brown sleep eyes, open mouth, six

18" Beautiful Crissy, grow-hair doll. $60.00. **Photo courtesy of The Museum Doll Shop.**

teeth, designed by Bernard Lipfert, blue or red checked rayon jumper, white blouse, marks: "IDEAL" on head plus size number, and "USA" on body

 13"........... $1,000.00 – 1,100.00
 15½"........ $1,400.00 – 1,500.00
 18"........... $1,600.00 – 1,700.00

1940 – 1942, teen, all-composition, wig, sleep eyes, open mouth, four teeth, original long dress, hang tag reads: "Judy Garland// A Metro Goldwyn Mayer//Star//in//'Little Nellie//Kelly," original pin reads "JUDY GARLAND METRO GOLDWYN MAYER STAR," marks: "IN U.S.A." on head, "IDEAL DOLLS," a backwards "21" on body

 15"................. $700.00 – 800.00
 21"........... $1,000.00 – 1,100.00

Seven Dwarfs, 1938 on, composition head and cloth body, head turns, removable clothes, each dwarf has name on cap, pick, and lantern

 12"................. $175.00 – 200.00

Dopey, 1938, one of Seven Dwarfs, a ventriloquist doll, composition head and hands, cloth body, arms, and legs, hinged mouth with drawstring, molded tongue, painted eyes, large ears, long coat, cotton pants, felt shoes sewn to leg, felt cap with name, can stand alone, mark: "IDEAL DOLL" on neck

 20"................. $700.00 – 800.00

Snow White, 1938 on, all-composition, jointed body, black mohair wig, flirty glass eyes, open mouth, four teeth, dimple in chin, used Shirley Temple body, red velvet bodice, rayon taffeta skirt pictures seven Dwarfs, velvet cape, some unmarked, marks: "Shirley Temple/18" or other size number on back

 11½"............... $350.00 – 400.00
 13" – 14"........ $400.00 – 450.00
 19" – 21"........ $550.00 – 650.00

Snow White, 1938 – 1939, as above, but with molded and painted bow and black hair, painted side-glancing eyes, add 50 percent more for black version, mark: "IDEAL DOLL" on head

14½".............. $200.00 – 250.00
17½" – 19½".. $450.00 – 550.00

Shirley Temple, 1934 on: See Shirley Temple section.

Composition and Wood Dolls, 1940 on, segmented wooden body, strung with elastic

Gabby
10½".............. $250.00 – 275.00

Jiminy Cricket
9"................... $225.00 – 275.00

Ferdinand the Bull
9"................... $200.00 – 250.00

Pinocchio, 1939
8"................... $200.00 – 250.00
11"................. $300.00 – 400.00
20"................. $575.00 – 650.00

Magic Skin Dolls, 1940 on, latex body, stuffed, original clothing. These doll bodies are prone to disintegration.

Baby Coos, 1948 – 1953, also Brother and Sister Coos, designed by Bernard Lipfert, hard plastic head, jointed arms, sleep eyes, molded and painted hair, closed mouth, squeeze box voice, later on cloth and vinyl body, marks on head, "16 IDEAL DOLL// MADE IN U.S. A." or unmarked

14"................... $90.00 – 100.00
16" – 18"........ $125.00 – 135.00
20" – 22"........ $145.00 – 165.00
27" – 30"........ $195.00 – 215.00

Bonnie Braids, 1951 – 1953, comic strip character, daughter of Dick Tracy and Tess Trueheart, vinyl head, jointed arms, one-piece body, open mouth, one tooth, painted yellow hair, two yellow saran pigtails, painted blue eyes, coos when squeezed, long white gown, bed jacket, toothbrush, Ipana toothpaste, mark: "©1951//Chi. Tribune//IDEAL DOLL//U.S.A." on neck

14" Harriet Hubbard Ayer make-up doll, MIB. $250.00. **Photo courtesy of McMasters Harris Auction Co.**

Baby
11½".............. $230.00 – 255.00
14"................. $305.00 – 330.00

Toddler, 1953, vinyl head, jointed hard plastic body, open-closed mouth with two painted teeth, walker

11½".............. $100.00 – 125.00
13½".............. $125.00 – 175.00

Magic Skin Baby, 1940, 1946 – 1949, hard plastic head, one-piece body and legs, jointed arms, sleep eyes, molded and painted hair, some with fancy layettes or trunks, latex usually darkened

13" – 14"............ $40.00 – 65.00
15" – 16"............ $65.00 – 80.00
17" – 18"........ $190.00 – 110.00
20"................. $110.00 – 125.00

Joan Palooka, 1953, daughter of comic strip character, Joe Palooka, vinyl, head, "Magic Skin" body, jointed arms and legs, yellow molded hair, topknot of yellow saran, blue painted eyes, open/closed mouth, smells like baby powder, original pink dress with blue ribbons, came with Johnson's baby powder and soap, mark: "©1952//HAM FISHER//

IDEAL DOLL" on head

    14"................. $175.00 – 200.00

Snoozie, 1951, open/closed mouth, vinyl head

    11"................. $100.00 – 125.00

    16"................. $125.00 – 150.00

    20"................. $150.00 – 175.00

Sparkle Plenty, 1947 – 1950, hard plastic head, "Magic Skin" body may be dark, yarn hair, character from Dick Tracy comics

    14"................. $175.00 – 200.00

    MIB........$689.00 at online auction

Hard Plastic and Vinyl Dolls, all in good condition with original clothing, mint-in-box can bring double the value listed

Baby

    11"..................... $35.00 – 45.00

    14"..................... $55.00 – 65.00

Child

    14"..................... $25.00 – 35.00

April Shower, 1969, vinyl, battery operated, splashes hands, head turns

    14"..................... $35.00 – 40.00

15" Honeybunch, MIB. $200.00. **Photo courtesy of Emmie's Antique Doll Castle.**

Baby Pebbles, 1963 – 1964, character from the Flintstone cartoons, Hanna Barbera Productions, vinyl head, arms, legs, soft body, side-glancing blue painted eyes, rooted hair with topknot and bone, leopard print nightie and trim on flannel blanket, also as an all-vinyl toddler, jointed body, outfit with leopard print

    14"................. $110.00 – 140.00

Tiny Pebbles, 1964 – 1966, hard vinyl body, came with plastic log cradle in 1965

    8"....................... $65.00 – 75.00

    12".................... $90.00 – 100.00

    16"................. $110.00 – 130.00

Bamm-Bamm, 1964, character from Flintstone cartoon, Hanna Barbera Productions, all-vinyl head, jointed body, rooted blond saran hair, painted blue side-glancing eyes, leopard skin suit, cap, club

    12"..................... $60.00 – 70.00

    16".................... $85.00 – 100.00

Belly Button Babies, 1971, Me So Glad, Me So Silly, Me So Happy, vinyl head, rooted hair, painted eyes, press button in belly to move arms, head, and bent legs, both boy and girl versions

White

    9½" .... $30.00 – 40.00

Black

    9½"..................... $40.00 – 45.00

Betsy McCall, 1952 – 1953: See Betsy McCall section.

Betsy Wetsy, 1937 – 1938, 1954 – 1956, 1959 – 1962, 1982 – 1985, open mouth for bottle, drinks, wets, came with bottle, some in layettes, marks: "IDEAL" on head, "IDEAL" on body

Hard rubber head, soft rubber body, sleep or painted eyes

    11".................... $75.00 – 100.00

    13½".............. $100.00 – 125.00

    15"................. $125.00 – 150.00

17"................. $150.00 – 175.00
19"................. $175.00 – 200.00
Hard plastic head, vinyl body
11½"............... $250.00 – 300.00
13½"............... $275.00 – 325.00
16"................. $300.00 – 350.00
20"................. $325.00 – 275.00
All-vinyl
11½"................... $70.00 – 80.00
13½"................ $90.00 – 100.00
16"................. $110.00 – 120.00
Bizzie-Lizzie, 1971 – 1972, vinyl head, jointed body, rooted blond hair, sleep eyes, plugged into power pack, she irons, vacuums, uses feather duster, two D-cell batteries
White
18"...................... $50.00 – 60.00
Black
18"...................... $55.00 – 65.00
Blessed Event, crying baby, vinyl head, squinting eyes
21"................... $80.00 – 100.00
Butterick Sew Easy Designing Set, 1953, hard vinyl mannequin of adult woman, molded blond hair, came with Butterick patterns and sewing accessories
14"................. $100.00 – 125.00
Captain Action® Superhero, 1966 – 1968, represents a fictional character who changes disguises to become a new identity, vinyl articulated figure, dark hair and eyes
Captain Action
12"................. $250.00 – 300.00
Batman disguise $150.00
Silver Streak box only $400.00
Too few in database for a reliable range.
Capt. Flash Gordon accessories . $150.00
Phantom disguise only $200.00
Steve Canyon disguise $200.00
Superman set w/dog $175.00
Lone Ranger outfit only $150.00
Spiderman disguise only $150.00

25" Miss Ideal, c. 1961. $175.00. **Photo courtesy of The Museum Doll Shop.**

Tonto outfit only $150.00
Action Boy
9"................................... $250.00
Robin Accessories $150.00
Special Edition $300.00
Dr. Evil $250.00
Dr. Evil Lab Set $2,000.00
Super Girl
11½"............................. $300.00
Clarabelle, 1954, clown from Howdy Doody TV show, mask face, cloth body, dressed in satin Clarabelle outfit with noise box and horn, later vinyl face
16"................. $200.00 – 225.00
20"................. $225.00 – 250.00
Crissy® Family of Dolls, 1969 – 1974, 1982, vinyl grow-hair dolls, all in good condition with original clothing, mint-in-box can bring double the value listed
Baby Crissy, 1973 – 1976, all-vinyl, jointed body, legs and arms foam filled, rooted auburn grow hair, two painted teeth, brown sleep eyes, mark: "©1972//IDEAL TOY COPR.//2M 5511//B OR GHB-H-225" on back
White
24"....................... 65.00 – 75.00

18" Miss Revlon, MIB. $600.00. **Photo courtesy of American Beauty Dolls.**

Black

24".................. $95.00 – 105.00

Beautiful Crissy, 1969 – 1974, all-vinyl, dark brown eyes, long hair, turn knob in back to make hair grow, some with swivel waist (1971), pull string to turn head (1972), pull string to talk (1971), reissued ca. 1982 – 1983, first year hair grew to floor length

White

18"..................... $60.00 – 70.00

Black

17½".................. $80.00 – 90.00

1982 doll ....$35.00 – 40.00

Crissy's Friends, Brandi, 1972 – 1973; Kerry, 1971; Tressy, 1970 (Sears Exclusive), vinyl head, painted eyes, rooted growing hair, swivel waist

White

18"..................... $75.00 – 85.00

Black

18"..................... $70.00 – 80.00

Cinnamon, Velvet's Little Sister, 1972 – 1974, vinyl head, painted eyes, rooted auburn growing hair, orange polka dotted outfit, additional outfits sold separately, marks: "©1971//IDEAL TOY CORP.//G-H-

12-H18//HONG KONG//IDEAL 1069-4 b" head; "©1972//IDEAL TOY CORP.//U.S. PAT-3-162-976//OTHER PAT. PEND.// HONG KONG" on back

White

13½".................. $50.00 – 60.00

Black

13½".................. $60.00 – 70.00

Cricket, 1971 – 1972 (Sears Exclusive); Dina, 1972 – 1973; Mia, 1971, vinyl, members of the Crissy® family, growing hair dolls, painted teeth, swivel waist

15"..................... $45.00 – 50.00

Tara, 1976, all-vinyl black doll, long black rooted hair that "grows," sleep eyes, marked "©1975//IDEAL TOY CORP//H-250// HONG KONG" on head and "©1970// IDEAL TOY CORP//GH-15//M5169-01// MADE IN HONG KONG" on buttock

15½".................. $75.00 – 85.00

Velvet

1971 – 1973, Crissy's younger cousin, talker

15"..................... $50.00 – 65.00

1974, non-talker, other accessories, grow hair

White

15".................. $55.00 – 60.00

Black

15".................. $60.00 – 65.00

Movin' Groovin Velvet..$30.00 – 40.00

Dina.................. $45.00 – 50.00

Kerri................ $100.00 – 125.00

Mia.................. $75.00 – 95.00

Daddy's Girl, 1961, vinyl head and arms, plastic body, swivel waist, jointed ankles, rooted saran hair, blue sleep eyes, closed smiling mouth, preteen girl, label on dress reads "Daddy's Girl," marks: "IDEAL TOY CORP.//g-42-1" on head, "IDEAL TOY CORP.//G-42" on body

38".......... $1,200.00 – 1,300.00

42".......... $1,400.00 – 1,500.00

Davy Crockett and his horse, 1955 – 1956, all-plastic, can be removed from horse, fur cap, buckskin clothes

4¾".................. $40.00 – 50.00

Diana Ross, 1969, from the Supremes (singing group), all-vinyl, rooted black bouffant hairdo, gold sheath, feathers, gold shoes, or chartreuse mini-dress, print scarf, and black shoes

17½".............. $295.00 – 310.00

Dorothy Hamill, 1978, Olympic skating star, vinyl head, plastic posable body, rooted short brown hair, comes on ice rink stand with skates; also extra outfits available

11½".................. $30.00 – 40.00

Eddy Munster, 1965, vinyl, molded hair

8¼".................. $65.00 – 75.00

Evel Knievel, 1974 – 1977, all-plastic stunt figure, helmet, more with stunt cycle

7"...................... $35.00 – 45.00

Flatsy, 1969, flat vinyl doll with wire armature, rooted hair

6"...................... $20.00 – 30.00

Giggles, 1960, vinyl head, giggling doll

18".................. $200.00 – 250.00

Harmony, 1972, vinyl, battery operated, makes music with guitar

21".................. $75.00 – 100.00

Harriet Hubbard Ayer, 1953, cosmetic doll, vinyl stuffed head, hard plastic (Toni) body, wigged or rooted hair, came with eight-piece H. H. Ayer cosmetic kit, beauty table and booklet, marks: "MK 16//IDEAL DOLL" on head "IDEAL DOLL//P-91" on body

14".................. $100.00 – 125.00

16".................. $125.00 – 150.00

19".................. $150.00 – 175.00

21".................. $175.00 – 200.00

Honeybunch, 1956 – 1957, soft vinyl head, vinyl body and limbs are stuffed with cotton, curlable hair

15" – 23"........ $100.00 – 125.00

Hopalong Cassidy, 1949 – 1950, vinyl stuffed head, vinyl hands, molded and painted gray hair, painted blue eyes, one-piece body, dressed in black cowboy outfit, leatherette boots, guns, holster, black felt hat, marks: "Hopalong Cassidy" on buckle

20".................. $185.00 – 200.00

16" Plassie, c. 1942, hard plastic head, composition breastplate and limbs, oilcloth body. $145.00. **Photo courtesy of McMasters Harris Auction Co.**

16" Saucy Walker. $275.00. Photo courtesy of McMasters Harris Auction Co.

24"................. $200.00 – 225.00

Plastic, with horse, Topper

4½"..................... $40.00 – 50.00

Howdy Doody, 1950 – 1953, television personality, hard plastic head, red molded and painted hair, freckles, ventriloquist doll, mouth operated by pull string, cloth body and limbs, dressed in cowboy outfit, scarf reads "HOWDY DOODY," mark: "IDEAL" on head

18"................. $500.00 – 525.00

20"................. $525.00 – 550.00

24"................. $550.00 – 575.00

1954, with vinyl hands, wears boots, jeans

20½".............. $250.00 – 275.00

25"................. $300.00 – 350.00

Jet Set Dolls, 1967, vinyl head, posable body, rooted straight hair, mod fashions, earrings, strap shoes, Chelsea, Stephanie, and Petula

24"..................... $45.00 – 55.00

Judy Splinters, 1949 – 1950, vinylite, TV character ventriloquist doll, open/closed mouth

18"................. $200.00 – 225.00

22"................. $250.00 – 275.00

36"................. $325.00 – 350.00

Baby

15"................. $275.00 – 300.00

Kissy, 1961 – 1964, vinyl head, rigid vinyl toddler body, rooted saran hair, sleep eyes, jointed wrists, press hands together and mouth puckers, makes kissing sound, original dress, panties, t-strap sandals, marks: "©IDEAL CORP.//K-21-L" on head "IDEAL TOY CORP.// K22//PAT. PEND." on body

White

22½".............. $110.00 – 145.00

Black

22½".............. $150.00 – 175.00

Kissy Baby, 1963 – 1964, all-vinyl, bent legs

22"..................... $50.00 – 75.00

Tiny Kissy, 1963 – 1968, smaller toddler, red outfit, white pinafore with hearts, marks: "IDEAL CORP.//K-16-1" on head "IDEAL TOY CORP./K-16-2" on body

White

16"..................... $70.00 – 80.00

Black

16"..................... $80.00 – 90.00

Lori Martin, 1961, character from *National Velvet* TV show, all-vinyl, swivel waist, jointed body, including ankles, blue sleep eyes, rooted dark hair, individual fingers, dressed shirt, jeans, black vinyl boots, felt hat, marks: "Metro Goldwyn Mayer Inc.//Mfg. by// IDEAL TOY CORP//38" on head, "©IDEAL TOY CORP.//38" on back

30"................. $725.00 – 750.00

38"................. $775.00 – 800.00

42"......... $2,000.00 store display

Little Lost Baby, 1968, three faced doll

22"................... $75.00 – 100.00

Mary Hartline, 1952, from TV personality on *Super Circus* show, hard plastic, fully jointed, blond nylon wig, blue sleep eyes, lashes, black eye shadow over and under eye, red, white, or green drum majorette costume and baton, red heart paper hang tag, with original box, marks: "P-91//IDEAL DOLL//MADE IN U.S.A." on head, "IDEAL DOLL//P-91 or IDEAL//16" on body

7½" .... $100.00 – 125.00
16" .... $550.00 – 600.00
22½" .... $1,100.00 – 1,300.00

Miss Clairol, Glamour Misty, 1965 – 1966, vinyl head and arms, rigid plastic legs, body, rooted platinum blond saran hair, side-glancing eyes, high-heeled feet, teen doll had cosmetics to change her hair, all original, marks: "©1965//IDEAL TOY CORP//W-12-3" on neck, "©1965 IDEAL" in oval on lower rear torso

12" .... $50.00 – 60.00

Miss Curity, 1953, hard plastic, saran wig, sleep eyes, black eye shadow, nurse's outfit, navy cape, white cap, Bauer & Black first aid kit and book, curlers, uses Toni body, mark: "P-90 IDEAL DOLL, MADE IN U.S.A." on head

14½" .... $300.00 – 350.00

Miss Ideal, 1961, all-vinyl, rooted nylon hair, jointed ankles, wrists, waist, arms, legs, closed smiling mouth, sleep eyes, original dress, with beauty kit and comb, marks: "©IDEAL TOY CORP.//SP-30-S" head, "©IDEAL TOY CORP.//G-30-S" back

25" .... $180.00 – 210.00
30" .... $300.00 – 350.00

Miss Revlon, 1956 – 1959, vinyl, hard plastic teenage body, jointed shoulders, waist, hips, and knees, high-heeled feet, rooted saran hair, sleep eyes, lashes, pierced ears, hang tag, original dress, some came with trunks, mark: "VT 20//IDEAL DOLL." Dolls listed are in good condition with original clothing, mint-in-box examples can bring double the values listed

15" .... $200.00 – 300.00
18" .... $275.00 – 350.00
20" .... $300.00 – 350.00
23" .... $375.00 – 400.00
26", 1957 only .. $300.00 – 350.00

Little Miss Revlon, 1958 – 1960, vinyl head

9" Pepper, Tammy's little sister. $45.00.
Photo courtesy of The Museum Doll Shop.

and body, jointed head, arms, legs, swivel waist, high-heeled feet, rooted hair, sleep eyes, pierced ears with earrings, original clothes, with box, many extra boxed outfits available

10½" .... $175.00 – 250.00

Mysterious Yokum, Li'l Honest Abe, 1953, son of comic strip character, Li'l Abner, hard plastic head, body, "Magic Skin" arms and legs, painted eyes, molded hair, forelock, wears overalls, one suspender, knit cap, and sock

$125.00 – 150.00

Plassie, 1942, hard plastic head, molded and painted hair, composition shoulder plate, composition limbs, stuffed pink oilcloth body, blue sleep eyes, original dress, bonnet, mark: "IDEAL DOLL//MADE IN USA//PAT.NO. 225 2077" on head

16" .... $120.00 – 145.00
19" .... $145.00 – 155.00
22" .... $155.00 – 180.00
24" .... $180.00 – 200.00

Play Pal family of Dolls, 1959 – 1962

Patty, all-vinyl, jointed wrists, sleep eyes, curly or straight saran hair, bangs, closed mouth, blue or red and white check dress

9" Toddler Thumbelina, c. 1969, MIB.
$120.00. **Photo courtesy of The Museum Doll Shop.**

with pinafore, three-year-old size, reissued in 1981 and 1982 from old molds, more for redheads, mark: "IDEAL TOY CORP.//G 35 OR B-19-1" on head

35" .... $300.00 – 350.00

Carrot red hair .. $700.00 – 800.00

Bonnie Play Pal, 1959, Patti's three-month-old sister, made only one year, rooted blond hair, blue sleep eyes, blue and white check outfit, white shoes and socks

24" .... $375.00 – 400.00

Johnny Play Pal, 1959, blue sleep eyes, molded hair, Patti's three-month-old brother

24" .... $375.00 – 400.00

Pattite, 1960, rooted saran hair, sleep eyes, red and white check dress, white pinafore with her name on it, looks like Patti Playpal

18" .... $750.00 – 800.00

18" .... $1,060.00* MIB

Penny Play Pal, 1959, rooted blond or brown curly hair, blue sleep eyes, wears organdy dress, vinyl shoes, socks, Patti's two-year-old sister, made only one year, marks: "IDEAL DOLL//32-E-L" or "B-32-B PAT. PEND." on head, "IDEAL" on back

32" .... $400.00 – 450.00

Peter Play Pal, 1960 – 1961, gold sleep eyes, freckles, pug nose, rooted blond or brunette

hair, original clothes, black plastic shoes, marks: "©IDEAL TOY CORP.// BE-35-38" on head, "©IDEAL TOY CORP.//W-38//PAT. PEND." on body

38" .... $700.00 – 750.00

Walker

38" .... $850.00 – 875.00

Suzy Play Pal, 1959, rooted curly short blond saran hair, blue sleep eyes, wears purple dotted dress, Patti's one-year-old sister

28" .... $375.00 – 400.00

Reissue Patty .... $200.00 – 225.00

Posie Walker, 1954 – 1956

17" .... $40.00 – 45.00

23" .... $100.00 – 125.00

25" .... $125.00 – 150.00

Samantha, 1965 – 1966, from TV show *Bewitched,* vinyl head, body, rooted saran hair, posable arms and legs, wearing red witch's costume, with broom, painted side-glancing eyes, other costume included negligee, mark: "IDEAL DOLL//M-12-E-2" on head

12" .... $255.00 – 275.00

All original, with broom .. $550.00 – 600.00

Tabitha, 1966, baby from TV show *Bewitched,* vinyl head, body, rooted platinum hair, painted blue side-glancing eyes, closed mouth, came in pajamas, mark: "©1965// Screen Gems, Inc.//Ideal Toy Corp.//T.A. 18-6//H-25" on head

    12½".............. $250.00 – 300.00

    Mint-in-box.................. $1,500.00

Saucy Walker, 1951 – 1955, all hard plastic, walks, turns head from side to side, flirty blue eyes, crier, open/closed mouth, teeth, holes in body for crier, saran wig, plastic curlers, came as toddler, boy, and "Big Sister"

    14"................. $150.00 – 175.00

    16"................. $175.00 – 200.00

    22"................. $250.00 – 250.00

Black

    16"................. $250.00 – 275.00

Big Sister, 1954

    25"................. $425.00 – 475.00

Snoozie

1958 – 1965, all-vinyl, rooted saran hair, blue sleep eyes, open/closed mouth, cry voice, knob makes doll wiggle, close eyes, crier, in flannel pajamas

    14"................. $175.00 – 200.00

1964 – 1965, vinyl head, arms, legs, soft body, rooted saran hair, sleep eyes, turn knob, she squirms, opens and closes eyes, and cries

    20"..................... $70.00 – 80.00

Storybook dolls, 1985, all-vinyl, rooted hair

    8"....................... $10.00 – 15.00

Tammy Family Dolls, dolls listed are in good condition wearing original clothing, mint-in-box examples can bring double the values listed.

Tammy, 1962+, vinyl head, arms, plastic legs and torso, head joined at neck base, marks: "©IDEAL TOY CORP.//BS12" on head, "©IDEAL TOY CORP.//BS-12//1" on back

    White

    12"..................... $45.00 – 55.00

    Black

    12"..................... $55.00 – 65.00

    Pos'n

    12"..................... $40.00 – 50.00

Mom

    12½"................. $40.00 – 45.00

Dad

    13"..................... $40.00 – 45.00

Ted

    12½"................. $35.00 – 40.00

Pepper

    9"....................... $45.00 – 50.00

Pos'n Pepper

    9"....................... $40.00 – 50.00

    Clothing (MIP)....... $70.00 – 80.00

Tearie Dearie, 1964

    9"....................... $45.00 – 55.00

Thumbelina

1961 – 1962, vinyl head and limbs, soft cloth body, painted eyes, rooted saran hair, open/closed mouth, wind knob on back moves body, crier in 1962

    16"................. $200.00 – 250.00

    20"................. $250.00 – 275.00

1982 – 1983, all-vinyl one-piece body, rooted hair, non-moving, comes in quilted carrier, also black

    7"....................... $20.00 – 30.00

1982, 1985, reissue from 1960s mold, vinyl head, arms, legs, cloth body, painted eyes, crier, open mouth, molded or rooted hair, original with box

16" Toni, marked P91. $400.00. **Photo courtesy of McMasters Harris Auction Co.**

18".................... $30.00 – 40.00

Thumbelina, Ltd. Production Collector's Doll, 1983 – 1985, porcelain, painted eyes, molded and painted hair, beige crocheted outfit with pillow booties, limited edition 1,000

18".................... $65.00 – 75.00

Tiny Thumbelina, 1962 – 1968, vinyl head, limbs, cloth body, painted eyes, rooted saran hair, wind key in back makes body head move, original tagged clothes, marks: "IDEAL TOY CORP.//OTT 14" on head, "U.S. PAT. #3029552" on body

14"................. $100.00 – 125.00

Newborn Thumbelina, 1968, vinyl head and arms, foam stuffed body, rooted hair, painted eyes, pull-string to squirm

9"........................ $70.00 – 80.00

Toddler Thumbelina, 1969 – 1971, vinyl head and arms, cloth body, rooted hair, painted eyes

9"........................ $55.00 – 65.00

Tiffany Taylor, 1974 – 1976, all-vinyl, rooted hair, top of head turns to change color, painted eyes, teenage body, high-heeled, extra outfits available

19".................... $40.00 – 50.00

Black

19".................... $60.00 – 70.00

Tuesday Taylor, 1976 – 1977, vinyl, posable body, turn head to change color of hair, clothing tagged "IDEAL Tuesday Taylor"

11½".................. $20.00 – 25.00

Tippy Tumbles, 1977

17".................... $25.00 – 30.00

Toni, 1949, designed by Bernard Lipfert, all hard plastic, jointed body, DuPont nylon wig, usually blue eyes, rosy cheeks, closed mouth, came with Toni wave set and curlers in original dress, with hang tag, marks: "IDEAL DOLL//MADE IN U.S.A." on head, "IDEAL DOLL" and

P-series number on body

P-90

14"................. $325.00 – 375.00

P-91

16"................. $375.00 – 400.00

P-92

19"................. $425.00 – 475.00

P-93

21"................. $450.00 – 500.00

P-94

22½".............. $900.00 – 950.00

Whoopsie, 1978 – 1981, vinyl, reissued in 1981, marked: "22//©IDEAL TOY CORP// HONG KONG//1978//H298"

13"...................... $25.00 – 35.00

Wizard of Oz Series, 1984 – 1985, Tin Man, Lion, Scarecrow, Dorothy, and Toto, all-vinyl, six-piece posable bodies

9"................$15.00 – 20.00 each

Batgirl, Mera Queen of Atlantis, Wonder Woman, and Super Girl, 1967 – 1968, all-vinyl, posable body, rooted hair, painted side-glancing eyes, dressed in costume

11½"................ 800.00 – 900.00

Mint-in-box.. $1,200.00 – 1,500.00

JULLIEN

1827 – 1904, Paris, France. After 1904 became a part of S.F.B.J. Had a porcelain factory, won some awards, purchased bisque heads from Francois Gaultier. Dolls listed are in good condition, appropriately dressed.

Child, bisque socket head, wig, glass eyes, pierced ears, open mouth with teeth or closed mouth, on jointed composition body

Closed mouth

17" – 19".. $4,000.00 – 4,500.00

24" – 26".. $5,000.00 – 5,200.00

Open mouth

18" – 20".. $1,700.00 – 1,800.00

29" – 30".. $2,300.00 – 2,500.00

JUMEAU

1842 – 1899, Paris and Montreuil-sous-Bois; in 1899 joined in S.F.B.J. which continued to make dolls marked Jumeau through 1958. Founder Pierre Francois Jumeau made fashion dolls with kid or wood bodies, head marked with size number, bodies stamped "JUMEAU//MEDAILLE D'OR//PARIS." Early Jumeau heads were pressed pre-1890. By 1878, son Emile Jumeau was head of the company and made Bébé Jumeau, marked on back of head, on chemise, band on arm of dress. Tête Jumeaux have poured heads. Bébé Protige and Bébé Jumeau registered trademarks in 1886, Bee mark in 1891, Bébé Marcheur in 1895, Bébé Francaise in 1896. Mold numbers of marked EJs and Têtes approximate the following heights: 1 – 10", 2 – 11", 3 – 12", 4 – 13", 5 – 14", 6 – 16", 7 – 17", 8 – 18", 9 – 20", 10 – 21", 11 – 24", 12 – 26", 13 – 30". Dolls listed are in good condition, nicely wigged, and with appropriate clothing. Exceptional dolls may be much more.

Poupée Jumeau (so-called French Fashion-type), 1860s on, marked with size number on swivel head, closed mouth, paperweight eyes, pierced ears, stamped kid body, add more for original clothes

Poupée Peau (kid body)
11" – 13".. $2,500.00 – 3,000.00
15" – 16".. $4,000.00 – 5,000.00
17" – 18".. $4,000.00 – 5,000.00
20".......... $6,000.00 – 6,100.00

Poupée Bois (wood body), bisque lower arms
10" – 11". $5,000.00 – 5,500.00
14" – 16". $6,200.00 – 6,500.00

So-called Portrait face
17" – 19". $6,500.00 – 7,000.00
21" – 23". $7,000.00 – 9,000.00

17" Jumeau Portrait Poupée Peau. $6,500.00. **Photo courtesy of Richard Withington, Inc.**

Wood body
19" – 21"..$10,000.00 – 12,000.00
Mature face with wooden body
18" $18,000.00*
Child Doll
Portrait, 1877 – 1883, closed mouth, paperweight eyes, pierced ears, wigged (sometimes skin wig), straight wristed composition body with separate balls at joints, head marked with size number only.
First Series, almond eye
12" – 14½"
$16,000.00 – 20,000.00
16" – 18½"
$23,500.00 – 25,500.00

15" Portrait Jumeau, second series. $7,595.00. **Photo courtesy of Sharing My Dolls & Stuff.**

179

18" EJ bébé. $16,000.00. **Photo courtesy of Richard Withington, Inc.**

19" – 20"..$27,000.00 – 32,000.00
23"....... $35,000.00 – 37,000.00
25"....... $54,000.00 – 64,000.00
Second Series
  11" – 12".. $6,000.00 – 6,500.00
  13" – 15".. $7,000.00 – 9,000.00
  18" – 20"..$13,000.00 – 15,000.00
  22"....... $15,000.00 – 16,000.00
  25"....... $18,000.00 – 19,000.00
Long Face Triste Bébé, 1879 – 1886, head marked with number only, pierced applied ears, closed mouth, paperweight eyes, straight wrists on Jumeau marked body
  21" – 23"..$26,000.00 – 28,000.00
  26" – 27"..$26,000.00 – 30,000.00
  31" – 33"..$33,000.00 – 35,000.00
Premiere, 1880, unmarked bébé, allow more for exceptional couturier outfit
  9" – 12" ... $7,400.00 – 8,000.00
  15" – 16"..$12,000.00 – 13,000.00
  17"....... $15,000.00 – 17,000.00
E.J. Bébé, 1881 – 1886, earliest "EJ" mark above with number over initials, pressed bisque socket head, wig, paperweight eyes, pierced ears, closed mouth, jointed body with straight wrists
  12" – 16"..$7,000.00 – 11,000.00

17" – 18"..$12,000.00 – 16,000.00
19" – 21"..$16,000.00 – 23,000.00
23" – 24"..$23,000.00 – 25,000.00
EJ/A marked Bébé
  25"....... $30,000.00 – 32,000.00
Mid "EJ," mark has size number centered between E and J (E 8 J), later with Déposé above
  11" – 14".. $7,500.00 – 9,500.00
  16" – 20"..$12,000.00 – 14,000.00
  23" – 26"..$15,000.00 – 16,000.00
Déposé Jumeau, 1886 – 1889, poured bisque head marked, "Déposé Jumeau," and size number, pierced ears, closed mouth, paperweight eyes, composition and wood body with straight wrists marked "Medaille d'Or Paris"
  12" – 14" ..$5,500.00 – 6,500.00
  16" – 18" .. $8,000.00 – 10,000.00
  20" – 23" ..$10,000.00 – 12,000.00
  25" – 26"..$14,000.00 – 15,000.00
Tête Jumeau, 1885 on, poured bisque socket head, red stamp on head, stamp or sticker on body, wig, glass eyes, pierced ears, closed mouth, jointed composition body with straight wrists, may also be marked E.D. with size number when Douillet ran factory, uses

18" EJ Depose mark. $12,000.00. **Photo courtesy of Richard Withington, Inc.**

22" open mouth Tête Jumeau. $2,000.00. **Photo courtesy of The Museum Doll Shop.**

tête face. The following sizes were used for Têtes: 0 – 9", 1 – 10", 2 – 11", 3 – 12", 4 – 13", 5 – 14 ½", 6 – 16", 7 – 17", 8 – 19", 10–21 ½", 11 – 24", 12 – 26", 13 – 29", 14 – 31", 15 – 33", 16 – 34" – 35"

Bébé (Child), closed mouth

9" .... $18,000.00 – 19,000.00
10"....... $11,000.00 – 12,000.00
12" – 13"..$8,000.00 – 12,000.00
16" – 17".. $7,000.00 – 8,000.00
19" – 21½" .. $7,200.00 – 8,000.00
24" – 26".. $8,000.00 – 9,000.00
29" – 31"..$11,000.00 – 12,000.00

Lady body

14" – 16".. $3,700.00 – 4,500.00
18" – 22".. $5,000.00 – 7,800.00

Open mouth, child

12"........... $2,500.00 – 3,000.00
17" – 22".. $1,700.00 – 2,000.00
24" – 25".. $2,200.00 – 2,400.00
27" – 29".. $2,600.00 – 2,800.00
32" – 35".. $3,100.00 – 4,000.00

B. L. Bébé, 1892 on, marked "B. L." for the Louvre department store, socket head, wig, pierced ears, paperweight eyes, closed mouth, jointed composition body

15" – 16".. $3,500.00 – 4,500.00
18" – 23".. $4,700.00 – 5,100.00

Phonographe Jumeau, 1894 – 1899, bisque head, open mouth, phonograph in torso, working condition

24" – 25".. $7,000.00 – 8,000.00

R.R. Bébé, 1892 on, wig, pierced ears, paperweight eyes, closed mouth, jointed composition body with straight wrists

21" – 23".. $4,400.00 – 4,800.00

Child, 1907 on, some with Tété Jumeau stamp, sleep or set eyes, open mouth, jointed French body

14" – 16".. $2,600.00 – 2,900.00
19" – 20".. $3,200.00 – 3,400.00
23" – 26".. $3,700.00 – 4,200.00
29" – 32".. $4,500.00 – 4,700.00
35"........... $4,000.00 – 4,200.00

Character Child

Mold 203, 208, and other 200 series, 1882 – 1899, glass eyes

20" $70,000.00

Too few in database for reliable range.

Mold 217, crier

20"........................... $88,000.00
21"......................... $110,000.00

Too few in database for reliable range.

Mold 230 child, 1910 on, open mouth socket-

10" mold 221 Marie Antoinette. $700.00. **Photo courtesy of The Museum Doll Shop.**

head, glass eyes, wig, composition body

12".............. $950.00 – 1,100.00

16"........... $1,600.00 – 1,800.00

21" – 23".... $2,00.00 – 2,600.00

Two-Faced Jumeau, crying and smiling

18"....... $11,000.00 – 14,000.00

Too few in database for reliable range.

Princess Elizabeth, made after Jumeau joined SFBJ and adopted Unis label, mark will be "71 Unis//France 149//306// Jumeau//1938//Paris," bisque socket head with high color, closed mouth, flirty eyes, jointed composition body

Mold 306

15"........... $1,300.00 – 1,500.00

18" – 19".. $1,800.00 – 1,900.00

32" – 33".. $3,400.00 – 3,900.00

Great Ladies of Fashion, Mold 221, 1940s – 1950s, bisque head, five-piece composition body with hole in one foot for stand, elaborate costumes and wigs representing Queen Victoria, Marie Antoinette, etc.

10"................. $600.00 – 800.00

Accessories

Marked Jumeau shoes

5" – 6"............. $300.00 – 400.00

7" – 10" .... $600.00 – 700.00

KAMKINS

1919 – 1928, Philadelphia, Pennsylvania, and Atlantic City, New Jersey. Cloth doll made by Louise R. Kampes Studio. Clothes made by cottage industry workers at home. All-cloth, molded mask face, painted features, swivel head, jointed shoulders and hips, mohair wig. Dolls listed are in good, clean, un-faded condition, allow 50% less for soiled or faded examples.

18" – 20".. $2,600.00 – 3,000.00

Boy with additional clothing

18"........................... $9,500.00*

18" Kamkins girl. $2,600.00.
Photo courtesy of McMasters Harris Auction Co.

KÄMMER & REINHARDT

1885 – 1933, Waltershausen, Germany. Registered trademark K☆R, Majestic Doll, Mein Liebling, Die Kokette, Charakterpuppen (character dolls). Designed doll heads, most bisque were made by Simon & Halbig; in 1918, Schuetzmeister & Quendt also supplied heads; Rheinische Gummi und Celluloid Fabrik Co. made celluloid heads for Kämmer & Reinhardt. Kämmer & Reinhardt dolls were distributed by Bing, Borgfeldt, B. Illfelder, L. Rees & Co., Strobel & Wilken, and Louis Wolfe & Co. Also made heads of wood and composition, later cloth and rubber dolls. Mold numbers identify heads starting with 1) bisque socket heads, 2) shoulder heads, as well as socket heads of black or mulatto babies, 3) bisque socket heads or celluloid shoulder heads, 4) heads having eyelashes, 5) googlies, black heads, pincushion heads, 6) mulatto heads, 7) celluloid heads, bisque head walking dolls, 8) rubber heads, 9) composition heads, some rubber heads. Other letters refer to style or material of wig or clothing. All dolls listed are in good condition with appropriate clothing.

Child

Bisque Socket head child

Mold 192 (possibly as early as 1892), jointed composition body, sleep eyes

Closed mouth

6" – 7"........... $600.00 – 700.00
10" – 11" .... $900.00 – 1,000.00
16" – 18".. $2,000.00 – 2,200.00
22" – 24".. $2,400.00 – 2,600.00

Open mouth

7" – 8"........... $550.00 – 600.00
12" – 14"........ $700.00 – 750.00
16" – 18"........ $750.00 – 850.00
20" – 22"........ $875.00 – 975.00
26" – 28".. $1,100.00 – 1,300.00

Child, Dolly Face, 1910 to 1930s, bisque head with open mouth, jointed composition body, sleep eyes

No Mold Number or Molds 191, 401, 402, 403

On five-piece body

5" – 6"........... $450.00 – 475.00
7" – 8"........... $475.00 – 500.00
10"................. $650.00 – 700.00

Jointed composition body

8" – 10" on flapper body
　　　　　$500.00 – 650.00

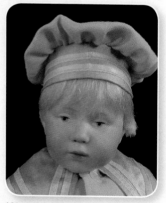

12" mold 101 Peter by Kämmer & Reinhardt. $4,000.00. **Photo courtesy of Richard Withington, Inc.**

12" – 14"..... $850.00 – 1,000.00
16" – 18"........ $650.00 – 700.00
19" – 21"........ $700.00 – 800.00
25" – 26"........ $600.00 – 700.00
28" – 30"..... $800.00 – 1,000.00

Child Shoulder Head Doll, kid body

14".................. $350.00 – 400.00
19" – 22" .... $450.00 – 475.00

Character Dolls, 1909 on

Mold 100, Baby often referred to by collectors as "Kaiser Baby," solid dome head, intaglio eyes, open-closed mouth, composition bent-limb body

11" – 12"........ $425.00 – 475.00
14" – 15"........ $550.00 – 635.00
18" – 20"........ $800.00 – 900.00

Mold 101, Peter or Marie, painted eyes, closed mouth, jointed body

7 – 8" .... $1,800.00 – 2,100.00
10" – 12".. $3,000.00 – 4,000.00
14" – 15".. $4,200.00 – 4,500.00
17" – 18".. $4,700.00 – 5,100.00
19" – 20".. $5,500.00 – 6,000.00

Glass eyes

18" – 20"..$9,000.00 – 12,500.00

Mold 102, Elsa or Walter, painted eyes, molded hair, closed mouth, very rare

14"......................... $32,000.00

Too few in database for reliable range.

22" $65,000.00

Too few in database for reliable range.

Mold 103, painted eyes, closed mouth

19"......................... $80,000.00+

Too few in database for reliable range.

Mold 104, ca. 1909, painted eyes, laughing closed mouth, very rare

18"......................... $80,000.00+

Too few in database for reliable range.

Mold 105, painted eyes, open-closed mouth, very rare

21" $170,956.00

Too few in database to give reliable range.

22" mold 117N My New Darling, flirty eyes. $2,100.00. Photo courtesy of The Museum Doll Shop.

Mold 106, painted intaglio eyes to side, closed mouth, very rare

22"..........................$145,000.00

Too few in database for reliable range.

Mold 107, Karl, painted intaglio eyes, closed mouth

21"........ $46,000.00 – 56,000.00

Too few in database for reliable range.

Mold 108, one example reported

$275,000.00+

Too few in database for reliable range.

Mold 109, Elise, painted eyes, closed mouth

9" – 10".... $9,000.00 – 8,000.00

12" – 14"..$10,000.00 – 12,000.00

20" – 24"..$18,000.00 – 21,000.00

Mold 112, painted open-closed mouth

13" – 15".. $8,000.00 – 9,000.00

17" – 18"..$10,000.00 – 12,000.00

Glass eyes

16" $18,000.00

Too few in database for reliable range.

Mold 112X, flocked hair

17"........ $14,000.00 – 16,000.00

Mold 114, Hans or Gretchen, painted eyes, closed mouth

8" – 9"...... $2,100.00 – 2,500.00

12" – 13".. $2,500.00 – 3,000.00

18" – 20".. $5,000.00 – 6,900.00

23" – 25".. $7,000.00 – 9,000.00

Glass eyes

9"............. $5,900.00 – 6,200.00

15".......... $9,250.00 – 9,350.00

Mold 115, solid dome, painted hair, sleeping eyes, closed mouth, toddler

15"........... $4,250.00 – 5,750.00

Mold 115A, sleep eyes, closed mouth, wig

Baby, bent-leg body

10" – 12".. $2,000.00 – 2,200.00

14" – 16".. $2,600.00 – 2,900.00

19" – 22".. $3,000.00 – 3,300.00

Toddler, composition, jointed body

11"...........................$4,300.00*

15" – 16".. $3,750.00 – 4,300.00

18" – 20".. $4,900.00 – 5,300.00

Mold 116, dome head, sleep eyes, open-closed mouth

17"........... $3,200.00 – 3,400.00

Mold 116A, sleep eyes, open-closed mouth or open mouth, wigged, bent-leg

Baby

10" – 12".. $1,000.00 – 1,200.00

15" – 18".. $1,100.00 – 1,400.00

21" – 23".. $1,600.00 – 2,000.00

Toddler body

16" – 18".. $3,000.00 – 3,400.00

12" mold 121 on a ball-jointed composition child body. $900.00. Photo courtesy of William Jenack Estate Appraisers and Auctioneers.

12" mold 126 character baby.
$400.00. Photo courtesy of William Jenack
Estate Appraisers and Auctioneers.

Mold 117, 117A Mein Liebling (My Darling),
glass eyes, closed mouth

    8" – 11".... $3,000.00 – 3,400.00
    14" – 16".. $3,800.00 – 4,200.00
    18" – 20".. $4,600.00 – 4,800.00
    22" – 24".. $5,000.00 – 5,600.00
    28" – 30".. $5,500.00 – 6,000.00

Flapper body

    8"............................... $3,500.00

Too few in database for reliable range.

Mold 117N, Mein Neuer Liebling (My New Darling), flirty eyes, open mouth

    14" – 16" ..$1,400.00 – 1,600.00
    20" – 22".. $2,000.00 – 2,100.00
    28" – 30".. $2,100.00 – 2,400.00

Mold 117X, socket head, sleep eyes, open mouth

    14" – 16"........ $850.00 – 950.00

    22" – 24"....$1,300.00 – 1,400.00
    30" – 32"....$1,600.00 – 1,800.00

Molds 118, 118A, sleep eyes, open mouth, baby body

    11"........... $1,100.00 – 1,200.00
    15"........... $1,300.00 – 1,500.00
    18"........... $1,900.00 – 2,200.00

Mold 119, sleep eyes, open-closed mouth, marked "Baby," five-piece baby body

    24" – 25"................. $16,000.00

Too few in database for reliable range.

Molds 121, 122, sleep eyes, open mouth

Baby

    10" – 11"........ $525.00 – 575.00
    15" – 16"........ $750.00 – 850.00
    20".............. $900.00 – 1,000.00
    22" – 24".. $1,150.00 – 1,250.00

7" mold 126 on a toddler body.
$700.00. Photo courtesy of William Jenack
Estate Appraisers and Auctioneers.

10½" K * R cloth doll, c. 1927. $400.00. **Photo courtesy of The Museum Doll Shop.**

Toddler body

10"............. $900.00 – 1,000.00

13" – 14".. $1,150.00 – 1,250.00

18" – 20".. $1,400.00 – 1,600.00

Mold 123 Max and Mold 124 Moritz, flirty sleep eyes, laughing/closed mouth, special body with molded shoes

16"..$48,000.00 – 55,000.00 pair

Mold 126 Mein Liebling Baby (My Darling Baby), sleep or flirty eyes, bent-leg

Baby

10" – 12"........ $375.00 – 400.00

14" – 16"........ $450.00 – 500.00

18" – 20"........ $400.00 – 450.00

22" – 24"........ $500.00 – 600.00

Toddler body

Five-piece body, with "starfish" hands

6" – 8"............ $700.00 – 800.00

9" – 10".......... $900.00 – 950.00

22" with flirty eyes

$1,200.00 – 1,300.00

Jointed composition body

15" – 17"........ $850.00 – 950.00

22" – 24".. $1,100.00 – 1,400.00

Mold 127, 127N, domed head-like mold 126, bent-leg body, add more for flirty eyes

Baby

10" – 11"........ $650.00 – 750.00

14" – 15"........ $600.00 – 700.00

18" – 22"..... $900.00 – 1,000.00

Toddler body

15" – 16".. $1,100.00 – 1,300.00

20" – 22".. $1,600.00 – 1,700.00

26".......... $1,900.00 – 2,000.00

Mold 128, sleep eyes, open mouth, baby body

10"................. $550.00 – 600.00

13" – 15"........ $700.00 – 800.00

20" – 24".. $1,200.00 – 1,600.00

Mold 131: See Googly category.

Mold 135, sleep eyes, open mouth, baby body

13" – 16"..... $950.00 – 1,100.00

Mold 171 Klein Mammi (Little Mammy), dome, open mouth

14" – 15".. $3,000.00 – 3,500.00

Too few in database for reliable range.

Mold 214, shoulder head, painted eyes, closed mouth, similar to mold 114, muslin body

15"........... $3,100.00 – 3,400.00

Too few in database for reliable range.

Mold 314, socket head, composition body, painted eyes, flocked hair

14" $6,250.00*

Puz, composition head, cloth body

16" – 17"........ $450.00 – 500.00

25"................. $750.00 – 800.00

17½" celluloid headed mold 717. $650.00. **Photo courtesy of McMasters Harris Auction Co.**

Cloth Character Dolls, 1927, wire armature body, needle-sculpted stockinette heads, painted features, wooden feet, all in good clean, unfaded condition

12" – 13"........ $400.00 – 450.00

Composition, 1930s on, sleep eyes, wigged
Baby, Mold 926

22"................ $150.00 – 200.00

Adult

Fat Character Man & Woman pair

8".................. $600.00 – 800.00

Too few in database for reliable range.

Celluloid: See Celluloid section.

KENNER

1947 to 2000, Cincinnati, Ohio. Purchased by Tonka Toys in 1987 and then by Hasbro in 1991, run as a separate division by both. Dolls listed are in very good condition with all original clothing and accessories.

Baby Bundles
White

16"..................... $10.00 – 15.00

Baby Yawnie, 1974, vinyl head, cloth body

15"..................... $15.00 – 20.00

Blythe, 1972, pull string to change color of eyes, "mod" clothes

11½"........... $900.00 – 1,200.00

Bob Scout, 1974

9"...................... $50.00 – 60.00

Butch Cassidy or Sundance Kid

4"....................... $10.00 – 15.00

Charlie Chaplin, 1973, all-cloth, walking mechanism

14"..................... $80.00 – 90.00

Cover Girls, 1978, posable elbows and knees, jointed hands
Dana, black

12½".................. $40.00 – 50.00

Darci, 1979

11½" Blythe by Kenner, c. 1972. $1,100.00. **Doll courtesy of Yasuko Swaim.**

12½".................. $35.00 – 45.00

Erica, redhead

12½"................ $90.00 – 100.00

Crumpet, 1970, vinyl and plastic

18".................. $90.00 – 100.00

Dusty, 1974, vinyl teenage doll

11"...................... $15.00 – 20.00

Skye, black, teenage friend of Dusty

11"...................... $20.00 – 25.00

Gabbigale, 1972
White

18"..................... $15.00 – 20.00

Black

18"..................... $30.00 – 35.00

Garden Gals, 1972, hand bent to hold watering can

6½"....................... $4.00 – 6.00

Hardy Boys, 1978, Shaun Cassidy, Parker Stevenson

12"..................... $35.00 – 45.00

Indiana Jones, 1981

12"................. $130.00 – 150.00

International Velvet, 1976, Tatum O'Neill

11½".................. $20.00 – 25.00

Jenny Jones and baby, 1973, all-vinyl, Jenny, 9", Baby, 2½"

Set..................... $20.00 – 25.00

13" Steve Astin, The Bionic Man. $75.00. Photo courtesy of The Museum Doll Shop.

Nancy Nonsense, 1975, pull string taker
    17"..................... $50.00 – 60.00
Rose Petal, 1984, scented
    7"...................... $15.00 – 20.00
Six Million Dollar Man Figures, 1975 – 1977, TV show starring Lee Majors
Bionic Man, Big Foot
    13"..................... $20.00 – 25.00
Bionic Man, Masketron Robot
    13"..................... $25.00 – 30.00
Bionic Woman, Robot
    13"..................... $75.00 – 85.00
Jaime Sommers, Bionic Woman
    13"..................... $75.00 – 95.00
Oscar Goldman, 1975 – 1977, with exploding briefcase
    13"..................... $40.00 – 50.00
Steve Austin, The Bionic Man
    13" .... $75.00 – 95.00
Steve Austin, Bionic Grip, 1977
    13"..................... $75.00 – 95.00
Star Wars Figures, 1974 – 1978, large size action figures. Dolls listed are complete dolls in excellent condition. Never-removed-from-box would bring double the price or more.
Ben-Obi-Wan Kenobi
    12"..................... $75.00 – 95.00

Boba Fett
    13"............... $155.00 – 175.00
    16"................ $175.00 – 200.00
C-3PO
    12"................ $160.00 – 180.00
Chewbacca
    12".................. $95.00 – 115.00
Darth Vader
    12"................ $205.00 – 220.00
Han Solo
    12"................ $400.00 – 500.00
IG-88
    15"................ $450.00 – 550.00
Jawa
    8½"................ $80.00 – 100.00
Leia Organa
    11½"............. $225.00 – 275.00
Luke Skywalker
    12"................ $225.00 – 275.00
R2-D2, robot
    7½"............... $125.00 – 175.00
Stormtrooper
    12"................ $200.00 – 235.00
Steve Scout, 1974, black
    9"...................... $60.00 – 70.00

5" Orange Blossom from the World of Strawberry Shortcake, MIB. $65.00. Photo courtesy of Sharing My Dolls & Stuff.

Strawberry Shortcake, ca. 1980 – 1986
   5"...................... $35.00 – 40.00
Sweet Cookie, 1972
   18"...................... $25.00 – 30.00
Terminator, Arnold Schwarzenegger, 1991, talks
   13½"................... $20.00 – 25.00

J.D. KESTNER

13" early socket head child, no mold number, closed mouth. $2,100.00. **Photo courtesy of Joan & Lynette Antique Dolls and Accessories.**

1805 – 1938, Waltershausen, Thüringia, Germany. Kestner was making dolls by the 1820s and was one of the first firms to make dressed dolls. Besides wooden dolls, papier-mâché, wax over composition, and Frozen Charlottes, Kestner made bisque dolls with leather or composition bodies, chinas, all-bisque dolls, and celluloid dolls. Supplied bisque heads to Catterfelder Puppenfabrik. Borgfeldt, Butler Bros., Century Doll Co., Horsman, R.H. Macy, Sears, Siegel Cooper, F.A.O. Schwarz, and others were distributors for Kestner. Early bisque heads with closed mouths marked X or XI, turned shoulder head, and swivel heads on shoulder plates are thought to be Kestners. After 1892, dolls were marked "made in Germany" with mold numbers.

Bisque heads with early mold numbers are stamped "Excelsior DRP No. 70 685," heads of 100 number series are marked "dep." Some early characters are unmarked or only marked with the mold number. After "211" on, it is believed all dolls were marked "JDK" or "JDK, Jr." Registered the "Crown Doll" (Kronen Puppe) in 1915, used crown on label on bodies and dolls.

The Kestner Alphabet was registered in 1897 as a design patent. It is possible to identify the sizes of doll heads by this key. Letter and number always go together: B/6, C/7, D/8, E/9, F/10, G/11, H/12, H ¾ /12 ¾ , J/13, J ¾ /13 ¾ , K/14, K ½ /14 ½ , L/15, L ½ /15 ½ , M/16, N/17.

Dolls listed are in good condition with original clothes or appropriately dressed. Exceptional dolls may be more.

Early Socket-head Child, bisque socket head, 1880 on. Closed or open-closed mouth, plaster pate, may be marked with size numbers only, glass eyes, may sleep, composition ball-jointed body, sometimes with straight wrists, appropriate wig and dress, in good condition, more for original clothes.

Mold 128, 169, or no mold number, closed mouth

   7" on five-piece body in original presentation box with wardrobe.... $2,523.00*

24" 154 shoulder head doll. $500.00. **Doll courtesy of Lucy DiTerlizzi.**

22" turned shoulder head, marked J. $1,200.00.
Doll courtesy of Lucy DiTerlizzi.

10" – 12".. $1,700.00 – 1,900.00
12" on jointed ankle body
$2,800.00*
14" – 16".. $2,800.00 – 3,100.00
19" – 21".. $2,200.00 – 2,900.00
24" – 25".. $3,000.00 – 3,400.00
Square face, closed mouth, some with white space between lips, no mold number
14" – 16".. $1,800.00 – 2,400.00
18" on jointed ankle body
$6,200.00*
19" – 21".. $2,600.00 – 2,700.00
24" – 25".. $2,800.00 – 2,900.00
A.T. look, closed mouth, glass eyes, marked only with size number such as 15 for 24"
12" – 13".. $7,500.00 – 8,000.00
21" ...... $10,000.00 – 13,000.00
26" .... $15,000.00 – 16,000.00
Mold X
15" .... $3,900.00 – 4,200.00
Mold XI
16" .... $4,000.00 – 4,200.00
Mold XII
17" .... $4,400.00 – 4,600.00
Mold 102, open mouth with square-cut teeth
9" .... $2,200.00 – 2,400.00
12" – 14".. $2,200.00 – 2,600.00
16" – 18".. $2,800.00 – 3,000.00

24" – 25".. $3,400.00 – 3,500.00
30" $4,400.00*
Mold 103, pouty closed mouth
20" .... $2,200.00 – 2,500.00
23" .... $3,300.00 – 3,400.00
Early Shoulder Head Child, 1880 on, bisque shoulder head, glass eyes, plaster pate, wig, kid body with bisque lower arms, marked with size numbers or letter only
Closed mouth
12" .... $450.00 – 475.00
14" – 16" .... $550.00 – 650.00
20" – 22" .... $700.00 – 750.00
26" .... $900.00 – 950.00
AT look, closed mouth
11" .... $1,400.00 – 1,500.00
21" – 25".. $4,000.00 – 4,800.00
Open mouth
16" – 18" .... $350.00 – 400.00
22" – 24" .... $500.00 – 550.00
Turned shoulder head, closed mouth
16" – 18" ..... $800.00 – 1,200.00
22" – 25".. $1,200.00 – 1,500.00
28" .... $1,700.00 – 1,900.00

15½" Baby Jean by Kestner. $1,000.00.
Photo courtesy of McMasters Harris Auction Co.

26" mold 257 character baby. $1,000.00. Photo courtesy of William Jenack Estate Appraisers and Auctioneers.

Shoulder Head Child, 1892 on, bisque shoulder head with sleep eyes, open mouth, plaster pate, wigged, kid body
Molds 145, 147, 148, 154, 166, 195
  10" – 14"........ $250.00 – 300.00
  15" – 18"........ $375.00 – 475.00
  20" – 22"........ $400.00 – 450.00
  26" – 29"........ $550.00 – 600.00
Bisque Socket Head Child, open mouth, glass eyes, Kestner ball-jointed body
Mold 142, 144, 146, 164, 167, 171, 214
  8" – 12".......... $675.00 – 800.00
  14" – 16".. $1,000.00 – 1,200.00
  18" – 22"........ $800.00 – 900.00
  24" – 26"........ $800.00 – 900.00
  28" – 32"..... $900.00 – 1,000.00
  40" – 42".. $2,900.00 – 3,800.00
Mold 171, 18" size only called "Daisy"
  18"........... $1,300.00 – 1,500.00
Mold 129, 130, 149, 152, 160, 161, 168, 173, 174
  10" – 12"........ $775.00 – 825.00
  14" – 16".. $1,000.00 – 1,200.00
  18" – 22"..... $900.00 – 1,100.00
  24" – 26"..... $800.00 – 1,000.00
  28"................ $700.00 – 900.00
Mold 155, open mouth, glass eyes, five-piece or fully jointed body
  11"................. $750.00 – 850.00
Molds 196, 215

  18" – 20"........ $550.00 – 650.00
  26" – 28"........ $700.00 – 750.00
  32"................. $800.00 – 900.00
Character Baby, 1910 on, socket head with wig or solid dome with painted hair, glass eyes, open mouth with bent-leg baby body, more for toddler body
Marked "JDK," solid dome bisque socket head, glass sleep eyes, molded and/or painted hair, composition bent-leg baby body, add more for body with crown label and/or original clothes
  12" – 14"........ $475.00 – 600.00
  16" – 18"........ $700.00 – 900.00
  21" – 25"........ $850.00 – 950.00
So-called Baby Jean, solid dome, fat cheeks, marked JDK
  12" – 13".. $1,000.00 – 1,100.00
  13"........................... $2,400.00*
  15" – 18".. $1,000.00 – 1,300.00
  22" – 24".. $1,600.00 – 1,800.00
Molds 211, 226, 236, 257, 260, allow 25% more for toddler body
  8" – 13".......... $500.00 – 675.00
  16" – 18"........ $750.00 – 900.00
  20" – 22"........ $800.00 – 900.00
  24" – 26"..... $950.00 – 1,000.00
Molds 210, 234, 235, 238, shoulder head, solid dome, sleep eyes, open-closed mouth or open mouth

22" mold 168. $1,100.00. **Photo courtesy of Dolls & Lace.**

12" – 14"........ $750.00 – 900.00
Mold 220, sleep eyes, open-closed mouth
14"........... $3,800.00 – 4,200.00
Toddler
19" – 20".. $5,000.00 – 5,500.00
26½"........ $8,000.00 – 9,000.00
Hilda, molds 237, 245, 1070 (bald solid dome), sleep eyes, open mouth
11" – 13".. $2,000.00 – 2,400.00
16" – 18".. $2,700.00 – 3,000.00
20" – 22" ..$3,400.00 – 4,000.00
25" – 26" .. $4,800.00 – 5,000.00
Mold 243, Oriental baby, sleep eyes, open mouth
13" – 14" ..$4,300.00 – 4,800.00
16" – 18".. $5,000.00 – 5,500.00
Mold 247, socket-head, open mouth, sleep eyes
14" – 16".. $1,700.00 – 2,000.00
20"........................... $2,800.00*
Toddler
16" – 21".. $2,000.00 – 3,100.00
26"........................... $6,000.00*
Mold 255, marked "O.I.C. made in Germany," solid dome flange neck, glass eyes, large open-closed screamer mouth, cloth body

11" – 13".. $2,300.00 – 2,500.00
Character Child, 1910 on, socket head, wig, glass eyes, composition and wood jointed body
Mold 143 (1897 on, precursor to character dolls), open mouth, glass eyes, jointed body
8"................ $950.00 – 1,000.00
9" – 10".... $1,200.00 – 1,400.00
12" – 14".. $1,400.00 – 1,600.00
16" – 20".. $1,600.00 – 2,000.00
Mold 178, 179, 180, 181, 182, 184, 185, 186, 187, 189, 190, 191
Painted eyes
9" – 12".... $2,400.00 – 3,400.00
15"........... $3,900.00 – 4,200.00
18"........... $7,500.00 – 9,000.00
Glass eyes
12"........... $3,200.00 – 3,500.00
15"........... $4,800.00 – 5,200.00
18"........... $6,000.00 – 6,500.00
Mold 206, fat cheeks, closed mouth, glass eyes child or toddler
12" – 15" ..$9,000.00 – 10,000.00
Too few in database for a reliable range.

11" mold 178 character child. $3,000.00. **Photo courtesy of Atlanta Antique Gallery.**

8" mold 143. $1,000.00. **Photo courtesy of The Museum Doll Shop.**

19"....... $22,000.00 – 25,000.00
Too few in database for a reliable range.
Mold 208, for all-bisque, see that category
Painted eyes
12"......... $9,500.00 – 10,500.00
Too few in database for a reliable range.
Glass eyes
16"........... $6,750.00 – 9,000.00
Too few in database for reliable range.
Mold 239, socket head, open mouth, sleep eyes
Toddler, also comes as baby
15" – 17".. $3,600.00 – 4,000.00

20" mold 162 on lady style composition body. $2,200.00. **Photo courtesy of The Museum Doll Shop.**

Mold 241, socket head, open mouth, sleep eyes
17" – 18".. $4,800.00 – 5,100.00
21" – 22".. $5,800.00 – 6,100.00
25"........... $4,300.00 – 5,500.00
28" – 30".. $7,200.00 – 7,800.00
Other Character dolls
Mold 243, man with molded mustache and helmet
16".......................... $5,800.00*
Max & Moritz, socket head on composition body
13" pair $17,000.00*

19" Gibson girl. $2,400.00. **Photo courtesy of Dolls & Lace.**

Lady Doll, 1998 on, bisque socket head, open mouth, glass eyes, composition body, slender waist and molded breasts
Mold 162
16" – 22".. $1,800.00 – 2,500.00
"Gibson Girl" Mold 172, shoulder head, closed mouth, glass eyes, kid body, bisque forearms
10"............. $950.00 – 1,000.00
15"........... $1,500.00 – 1,600.00
18" – 21".. $1,900.00 – 2,200.00
Wunderkind, set includes doll body with four interchangeable heads, some with extra apparel

With heads 174, 178, 184, and 185
11".......... $9,000.00 – 9,500.00
With heads, 171, 179, 182, and 183
14½".......................... $12,650.00
Too few in database for reliable range.
Celluloid shoulder head doll, sleep eyes, kid body, wigged
Molds 200, 201
16" – 20"........ $275.00 – 400.00

KEWPIE

1913 on, designed by Rose O'Neill. Manufactured by Borgfeldt, later Joseph Kallus, and then Jesco in 1984, and various companies with special license, as well as unlicensed companies. They were made of all–bisque, celluloid, cloth, composition, rubber, vinyl, zylonite, and other materials. Kewpie figurines (action Kewpies) have mold numbers 4843 through 4883. Kewpies were also marked with a round paper sticker on back, "KEWPIES DES. PAT. III, R. 1913; Germany; REG. US. PAT. OFF." On the front, was a heart–shaped sticker marked "KEWPIE//REG. US.// PAT. OFF." May also be incised on the soles of the feet, "O'Neill."

5½" all-bisque Kewpie. $300.00.
Photo courtesy of The Museum Doll Shop.

Dolls listed are in good condition, add more for label, accessories, original box, or exceptional doll.
All-Bisque
Immobiles, standing, legs together, immobile, no joints, blue wings, molded and painted hair, painted side-glancing eyes
2" – 2½"........... $90.00 – 110.00
4".................. $110.00 – 125.00
5".................. $135.00 – 145.00
6".................. $200.00 – 225.00
Jointed shoulders
2" – 2½"......... $125.00 – 150.00
4".................. $225.00 – 250.00
5".................. $250.00 – 300.00
6".................. $300.00 – 350.00
7".................. $400.00 – 450.00
8".................. $475.00 – 525.00
10"................. $775.00 – 800.00
12"............. $900.00 – 1,000.00
Jointed hips and shoulders
4".................. $600.00 – 650.00
5" – 6"............ $700.00 – 850.00
7" – 8"......... $950.00 – 1,050.00
10"........... $1,150.00 – 1,250.00
12½"...... $1,300.00 – 1,350.000
Jointed shoulders with any article of molded clothing
2½"............... $500.00 – 550.00
4½"......... $1,000.00 – 2,000.00
6"............. $1,500.00 – 2,500.00
8"............. $1,800.00 – 2,800.00
With Mary Jane shoes
6½"............... $500.00 – 575.00
Bisque Action Figures
Arms folded
6".................. $525.00 – 600.00
Aviator
8½"............... $775.00 – 850.00
Back, laying down, kicking one foot
4".................. $250.00 – 300.00
Basket and ladybug, Kewpie seated

4".......... $1,400.00 – 1,700.00

"Blunderboo," Kewpie falling down

4½"............... $400.00 – 425.00

Bottle, green beverage, Kewpie standing, kicking out

2½"............... $525.00 – 575.00

Bottle stopper

2"................... $100.00 – 150.00

Box, heart shaped, with Kewpie kicker atop

4"................... $775.00 – 850.00

Bride and Groom

3½"............... $300.00 – 350.00

Boutonnière

1½"................. $85.00 – 110.00

2"................... $115.00 – 135.00

Bunny in lap of seated Kewpie

2"................... $425.00 – 475.00

Candy container

4"................... $400.00 – 500.00

Carpenter, wearing tool apron

8½"............ $975.00 – 1,100.00

Cat, on lap of seated Kewpie

3" – 3½"......... $525.00 – 575.00

Chick with seated Kewpie

2"................... $525.00 – 575.00

Cowboy

10"................. $700.00 – 800.00

Dog, with Kewpie on stomach

3" $3,400.00*

Dog, with Red Cross Kewpie

4"................... $250.00 – 300.00

Doodle Dog alone

1½"............ $900.00 – 1,000.00

3"............ $1,400.00 – 2,000.00

Doodle Dog with Kewpie

2½"......... $1,000.00 – 1,500.00

Drum on brown stool, with Kewpie

3½"......... $2,000.00 – 2,200.00

Farmer

6½"............... $800.00 – 900.00

Flowers, Kewpie with bouquet in right hand

5"................... $825.00 – 925.00

10" cloth Kuddle Kewpie by Krueger. $400.00. **Photo courtesy of The Museum Doll Shop.**

Gardener

4"................... $475.00 – 525.00

Governor

2½"............... $325.00 – 375.00

3¼"............... $400.00 – 475.00

Hatbox (turquoise), held by seated Kewpie

3"............ $1,500.00 – 1,600.00

Hottentot, black Kewpie

3½"............... $425.00 – 500.00

5"................... $575.00 – 675.00

9"................... $925.00 – 975.00

Huggers

2½"............... $125.00 – 150.00

3½"............... $175.00 – 225.00

4½"............... $250.00 – 300.00

Inkwell, with writer Kewpie

4½"............... $500.00 – 575.00

Jack-O-Lantern between legs of Kewpie

2"................... $450.00 – 500.00

Jester, with white hat on head

4½"............... $500.00 – 575.00

Kneeling

4"................... $475.00 – 550.00

Lying on Tummy with Doodle Dog on back

3" long......... $950.00 – 1,000.00

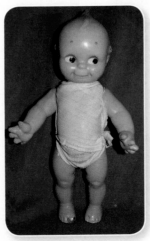

13" composition Kewpie.
$250.00. **Photo courtesy of The Museum Doll Shop.**

Mailing label in hand
2¼" .... $550.00 – 650.00
Mandolin, green basket and seated Kewpie
2" .... $300.00 – 350.00
Mandolin, with Kewpie on nut dish
2½" .... $475.00 – 500.00
Mayor, seated Kewpie in green wicker chair
4½" .... $775.00 – 875.00
Minister
5" .... $200.00 – 250.00
Reader Kewpie seated with book
2" .... $200.00 – 250.00
3½" .... $275.00 – 325.00
4" .... $450.00 – 500.00
Rose in hand Kewpie on place card holder
2" .... $60.00 – 75.00
Sack held by Kewpie with both hands
4½" $1,430.00*
Salt Shaker
2" .... $150.00 – 175.00
Seated in Adirondack chair
4" $1,600.00*
Soldier "Hero" with mold hat, belt with saber and supply sack at feet

4" $850.00*
Soldier, Confederate
4" .... $250.00 – 275.00
Soldier in Prussian helmet
5½" .... $775.00 – 800.00
Soldier lying on stomach aiming rifle
3" .... $400.00 – 450.00
Soldier lying on stomach aiming rifle on pin dish
4" .... $650.00 – 700.00
Soldier vase
6½" .... $575.00 – 650.00
Soldier
2¾" .... $450.00 – 500.00
4½" .... $500.00 – 550.00
Stomach, Kewpie laying flat, arms and legs out
4" .... $375.00 – 450.00
Sweeper with dust bin by leg
4" .... $325.00 – 350.00
Teddy Bear held in arm of Kewpie
3¾" .... $625.00 – 650.00
Thinker
4" – 5" .... $275.00 – 325.00
7" $1,050.00*
Traveler with dog and umbrella
3½" .... $1,300.00 – 1,550.00
Traveler with umbrella and bag
4" .... $350.00 – 400.00
5" .... $500.00 – 550.00
Traveler with Doodle Dog
3½" $1,800.00*
Vase with card holder and Kewpie
2½" .... $275.00 – 325.00
Vase with huggers
3¾" .... $575.00 – 650.00
Writer, seated Kewpie with pen in hand
2" .... $425.00 – 475.00
4" .... $500.00 – 550.00
Carnival chalk Kewpie with jointed shoulders
13" .... $75.00 – 125.00
Bisque Shoulder Head, on cloth body

Painted eyes
7".............. $875.00 – 1,000.00
Glass eyes
12".......... $2,500.00 – 2,800.00
Celluloid
Bride and Groom
4"...................... $15.00 – 40.00
Jointed arms, heart label on chest
5".................. $80.00 – 100.00
8".................. $165.00 – 185.00
12"................ $275.00 – 325.00
China
Perfume holder, one-piece with opening at back of head
4½" .... $550.00 – 1,100.00
Salt Shaker
1¼".................. $85.00 – 165.00
Dishes
Service for 4 .... $850.00 – 900.00
Service for 6 ...... $1,000.00 – 1,200.00
Cloth
Richard Krueger "Kuddle Kewpie," silk screened face, stockinette or sateen body, tagged
8" – 10".......... $300.00 – 400.00
13" – 14"........ $325.00 – 400.00
18" – 23"........ $625.00 – 700.00
Plush, with stockinette face, tagged
8".................. $195.00 – 225.00
Composition, made by Cameo Doll Co., Mutual Doll Co., and Rex Doll Co.
Hottentot, all-composition, heart decal to chest, jointed arms, red wings, ca. 1946
11" – 13"........ $400.00 – 450.00
All-composition, jointed body, blue wings
8".................. $160.00 – 180.00
11"................. $200.00 – 250.00
13"................. $275.00 – 325.00
Composition head, cloth body, flange neck, composition forearms, tagged floral dress
11"................. $250.00 – 300.00
Talcum container

One-piece composition talcum shaker with heart label on chest
7"...................... $175.00 – 25.00
Hard Plastic
Original box, 1950s, Kewpie design
8½"............... $275.00 – 300.00
Sleep eyes, five-piece body with starfish hands
14"................. $400.00 – 475.00
Metal
Figurine, cast steel on square base, excellent condition
5½"................... $40.00 – 55.00
Sitting on a stamp box
4".................. $300.00 – 400.00
Soap
Kewpie soap figure with cotton batting, colored label with rhyme, marked "R.O. Wilson, 1917"
4"..................... $90.00 – 110.00
Vinyl
Knickerbocker, late 1950s on, vinyl mask face on plush body
8" – 10" seated ... $60.00 – 70.00
Bunny Kuddles, Kewpie mask faced bunny wearing vinyl hat
11" seated.......... $30.00 – 35.00
Cameo Dolls, 1960s, in very good condition with original clothing
12"..................... $55.00 – 65.00
14" – 16"............ $70.00 – 90.00
27"................. $125.00 – 175.00
Jesco Dolls, 1980s, mint, all-original condition
8"....................... $50.00 – 60.00
12"..................... $55.00 – 65.00
18"..................... $70.00 – 80.00
24"................. $140.00 – 160.00
R. John Wright, 1999 on, molded felt, jointed shoulders, values listed are for secondary market dolls, dolls also available at retail
6"................... $450.00 – 500.00

KLEY & HAHN

1902 – 1930s, Ohrdruf, Thüringia, Germany. Bisque heads, jointed composition or leather bodies, composition and celluloid head dolls. Was an assembler and exporter; bought heads from Bähr & Pröschild, Kestner (Walkure), Hertel Schwab & Co, and Rheinische Gummi. Dolls listed are in good condition, appropriately dressed.

Character Baby, bisque socket head, bent limb composition body, molds such as 133, 135, 138, 158, 160, 161, 167, 176, 525, 571, 680, and others

11" – 13"........	$725.00 – 775.00
16" – 18"........	$775.00 – 825.00
20" – 22"........	$825.00 – 875.00
24" – 26"........	$850.00 – 900.00

Toddler body

14" – 16"..	$1,200.00 – 1,500.00
18" – 21"..	$1,700.00 – 2,000.00
26"..........	$2,200.00 – 2,300.00

Mold 567 (made by Bähr & Pröschild) character multi-face, laughing face, glass eyes, open mouth; crying face, painted eyes, open-closed mouth

11"..........	$1,000.00 – 1,400.00
15"..........	$1,950.00 – 2,100.00
17"..........	$2,200.00 – 2,400.00
19"..........	$2,400.00 – 2,600.00

Child, 1920, dolly face, sleep eyes, open mouth, molds 250, 282, or Walkure

12" – 13"........	$475.00 – 550.00
16" – 18"........	$550.00 – 750.00
22" – 24"........	$575.00 – 700.00
28" – 30"........	$525.00 – 600.00
33" – 34"........	$700.00 – 800.00
39" – 40"..	$1,400.00 – 1,600.00

Mold 325, "Dollar Princess," open mouth

18"– 20".........	$425.00 – 475.00
23" – 25"........	$400.00 – 450.00

Character Child, 1912, bisque socket head, jointed composition body

Mold numbers 154, 166, 169

Closed mouth

14" – 16" .	$1,700.00 – 2,100.00
19" – 20"..	$2,400.00 – 2,700.00
27"..........	$3,000.00 – 3,300.00

Open mouth

17" – 20"..	$1,000.00 – 1,200.00

Painted eye character, molds 520, 525, 526, 531

14" – 16"..	$2,100.00 – 2,700.00
17" – 19"..	$3,000.00 – 3,500.00
21"..........	$4,000.00 – 4,500.00

Mold 336, open/closed mouth, intaglio eyes

11" – 16"..	$4,000.00 – 5,000.00

Mold 546, 549, ca. 1912, character face

15" – 16"..	$4,100.00 – 4,700.00
18" – 21"..	$5,000.00 – 5,500.00

Mold 554, 568, ca. 1912, character face

21".............................	$1,400.00

Too few in database for reliable range.

14" Kley & Hahn baby. $775.00. **Photo courtesy of Dollhappy.**

C.F. KLING & CO.

1834 – 1940s, Ohrdruf, Thüringia, Germany. Porcelain factory that began

23" Kling mold 189 china head doll. $650.00. **Doll courtesy of Elaine Holda.**

making doll heads in 1879, made china, bisque, and all-bisque dolls, and snow babies. Often mold number marks are followed by size number. Dolls listed are in good condition, appropriately dressed, more for exceptional doll with elaborate molded hair or bodice.

Bisque Shoulder Head, 1880 on

Painted eyes, molded hair, cloth or kid body, molds such as123, 124, 131, 167, 178, 182, 186, 189, and others

7" – 8"............	$275.00 – 325.00
12" – 14"........	$325.00 – 500.00
15" – 16"........	$650.00 – 900.00
18" – 20".....	$800.00 – 1,100.00
23" – 25"........	$850.00 – 950.00

Glass eyes, molded hair, cloth or kid body, molds such as 190, 203, 204, 214, 217, 247, 254, and others

15" – 16".....	$800.00 – 1,100.00
22" – 23"..	$1,000.00 – 1,300.00

Bisque Lady, molded bodices, fancy hair, molds such as 135,144, 170, and others

15"...........	$1,000.00 – 1,100.00
19" – 21"..	$1,300.00 – 1,600.00

China Shoulder Head, 1880 on, molded hair, painted eyes, closed mouth, molds such as 131, 188, 189, 202, 220, 285, and others

13" – 15"........ $300.00 – 350.00

18" – 20"........	$600.00 – 700.00
24" – 25"........	$700.00 – 775.00

Mold 188, glass eyes

18" – 20"........ $450.00 – 500.00

Bisque socket head, 1900 on, open mouth, sleep eyes, jointed body, molds such as 182, 370, 372, 373, 377

13" – 15"........	$250.00 – 375.00
17" – 22"........	$375.00 – 500.00

All-Bisque: See All-Bisque section.

KLUMPE

1952 – 1970s, Barcelona, Spain. Caricature figures made of felt over wire armature with painted mask faces. Figures represent professionals, hobbyists, Spanish dancers, historical characters, and contemporary males and females performing a wide variety of tasks. Of the 200 or more different figures, the most common are Spanish dancers, bull fighters, and doctors. Some Klumpes were imported by Effanbee in the early 1950s. Originally the figures had two sewn-on identifying cardboard tags. Dolls listed are in good condition.

Average figure

10½".............. $100.00 – 120.00

Elaborate figure, with tags & accessories

10½"... $250.00 – 275.00 and up

10½" Violinist. $120.00. **Photo courtesy of The Museum Doll Shop.**

KNICKERBOCKER DOLL & TOY CO.

1927 – 1980s, New York, New York. Made dolls of cloth, composition, hard plastic, and vinyl.

Cloth

Clown

17" .... $18.00 – 25.00

Disney characters

Donald Duck, Mickey Mouse, etc., all-cloth

10½" .... $475.00 – 525.00

Flintstone characters

6" .... $8.00 – 10.00

Mickey Mouse, ca. 1930s, oil-cloth eyes

15" $3,100.00*

Pinocchio, cloth and plush

13" .... $200.00 – 250.00

Seven Dwarfs, 1939 on, mask face, mohair beard, up-turned toes

14" ....$225.00 – 260.00 each

Snow White, all-cloth, mask face

16" .... $375.00 – 425.00

11" Dopey by Knickerbocker, cloth mask face. $220.00. **Photo courtesy of The Museum Doll Shop.**

Flintstones

6½" .... $12.00 – 16.00

Holly Hobby, 1970s, cloth, later vinyl

Cloth

7" – 9" .... $8.00 – 20.00

14" – 16" .... $20.00 – 25.00

26" .... $35.00 – 40.00

Vinyl

11" – 16" .... $10.00 – 25.00

Levi's Big E Jeans dolls, 1973

10" – 16" .... $20.00 – 30.00

Little Orphan Annie, 1977

16" .... $25.00 – 35.00

Composition

"Blondie" comic strip characters, composition, painted features, hair

Alexander Bumstead, molded hair

9" .... $375.00 – 425.00

Blondie Bumstead, mohair wig

11" .... $725.00 – 800.00

Dagwood Bumstead, molded hair

14" .... $950.00 – 1,050.00

Child, 1938 on, mohair wig, sleep eyes

15" .... $220.00 – 265.00

18" .... $275.00 – 300.00

Mickey Mouse, 1930s – 1940s, composition, cloth body

18" .... $900.00 – 1,100.00

Jiminy Cricket, all-composition

10" .... $500.00 – 550.00

Pinocchio, all-composition

14" .... $500.00 – 550.00

14" $1,500.00*

in original labeled box

17" .... $775.00 – 825.00

Seven Dwarfs, 1939+

9" ....$225.00 – 250.00 each

Sleeping Beauty, 1939+, bent right arm

15" .... $375.00 – 425.00

18" .... $450.00 – 495.00

Snow White, 1937+, all-composition, bent right arm, black wig

15".................. $395.00 – 425.00
20".................. $425.00 – 475.00
Molded hair and ribbon, mark: "WALT DISNEY//1937//KNICKERBOCKER"
13".................. $250.00 – 275.00
15".................. $250.00 – 300.00
Plastic and Vinyl Mask Face Dolls, 1950s – 1960s
Plush Body
Pinocchio
13"..................... $40.00 – 60.00
Sleepy Head
23"..................... $30.00 – 35.00
Cloth Body
Lovely Lori
15"..................... $65.00 – 75.00
Hard Plastic and Vinyl
Bozo Clown
14"..................... $18.00 – 25.00
17" – 24"............ $40.00 – 60.00
Cinderella, two faces, one sad, one with tiara
16"..................... $15.00 – 20.00
Flintstone characters
17"..................... $36.00 – 43.00
Kewpies: See Kewpie section.
Little House on the Prairie, 1978
12"..................... $25.00 – 35.00
Little Orphan Annie comic strip characters, 1982
Little Orphan Annie, vinyl
6"..................... $10.00 – 12.00
11"..................... $20.00 – 30.00
Daddy Warbucks
7"..................... $12.00 – 17.50
Punjab
7" .... $12.00 – 15.00
Miss Hannigan
7"..................... $12.00 – 17.50
Molly
5½"..................... $8.00 – 12.00
Rattle Dolls, hard plastic, jointed shoulders,

6½" Fred Flintstone. $10.00. Photo courtesy of The Museum Doll Shop.

painted side-glancing eyes
6"..................... $12.00 – 18.00
Snoopy, Charles Schultz character, 1965
8"..................... $35.00 – 45.00
Outfits MOC............... $10.00 – 30.00
Two-faced dolls, 1960s, vinyl face masks, one crying, one smiling
12"..................... $14.00 – 18.00
Dolly Pops, 1979 on, molded vinyl with synthetic hair, molded changeable vinyl clothing
2½"..................... $15.00 – 20.00
Dolly Pops playhouse
1982 .... $40.00 – 60.00

GEBRUDER KNOCH

1887 – 1919, Neustadt, Thüringia, Germany. Porcelain factory that made bisque doll heads with cloth or kid body.
Shoulder Head
Mold 203, 205, ca. 1910
Mold 203, character face, painted eyes, closed mouth, stuffed cloth body
Mold 205, "GKN" character face, intaglio eyes, open-closed mouth, molded tongue
12" – 13"........ $500.00 – 600.00
14" – 15"........ $675.00 – 725.00
Too few in database for reliable range.
Socket Head
Mold 179, 181, 190, 192, 193, 201, ca. 1900, mold 201 also came as black, dolly

face, glass eyes, open mouth
  7" on five-piece body
    $225.00 – 275.00
  13"................ $250.00 – 350.00
  18" – 25"........ $500.00 – 900.00
Mold 204, 205, ca. 1910, character face
  15"............. $865.00 – 1,150.00
Mold 206, ca. 1910, "DRGM" solid dome, intaglio eyes, open-closed mouth
  11"............................. $750.00*
Mold 216, ca. 1912, "GKN" solid dome, intaglio eyes, laughing, open-closed mouth
  12"................................. $315.00
Too few in database for reliable range.
Mold 229: See All-Bisque category.
Mold 230, ca. 1912, molded bonnet, character shoulder head, painted eyes, open-closed mouth laughing, mold 232, ca. 1912, molded bonnet, character shoulder head, laughing
  13"................ $675.00 – 900.00
  15"........... $1,200.00 – 1,600.00

KÖNIG & WERNICKE GMBH

1912 – 1930s, Waltershausen, Germany. Had doll factory, made bisque or celluloid dolls with composition bodies, later dolls with hard rubber heads. Bought bisque heads from Bähr & Pröschild, Hertel & Schwab and Armand Marseille. Made "My Playmate" for Borgfeldt. Dolls listed are in good condition, appropriately dressed.
Bisque Baby
Mold 98, 99, ca. 1910, **Mold 1070,** ca. 1915 "made in Germany" (made by Hertel Schwab & Co.), character, socket head, sleep eyes, open mouth, teeth, tremble tongue, wigged, composition bent-leg baby body

  9" – 12"......... $325.00 – 450.00
  15" – 16"........ $475.00 – 650.00
  18" – 22"........ $600.00 – 900.00
  24" – 27"....... $975.00 – 1,100.0
Toddler
  11" –13" .... $825.00 – 875.00
  15" – 17"........ $750.00 – 850.00
  19" – 20".. $1,000.00 – 1,200.00
Child, socket head, composition body
Dolly face
  15"................ $475.00 – 525.00
  26" – 29"..... $950.00 – 1,000.00
Mold 1070, character child, sleep eyes
  15" .... $1,100.00 – 1,300.00
Painted bisque child, regional dress
  18"................. $125.00 – 175.00
Composition Child, composition head on five-piece or fully jointed body, open mouth, sleep eyes, add more for flirty eyes
  14"................. $225.00 – 300.00
  16"................. $350.00 – 450.00
Celluloid Child, celluloid socket head, glass eyes, wigged
  13" – 15"........ $175.00 – 200.00

19" Konig & Wernicke mold 179. $700.00. **Photo courtesy of McMasters Harris Auction Co.**

RICHARD KRUEGER

1907 – 1950s, New York City. Made cloth mask faced dolls.

8" cloth angel by Richard Krueger. $75.00. **Photo courtesy of The Museum Doll Shop.**

Child, 1930 on
Cloth body
10"..................	$85.00 – 100.00
12".................	$115.00 – 135.00
16".................	$155.00 – 185.00
20".................	$225.00 – 250.00

Oilcloth body
10".....................	$65.00 – 80.00
14" – 16"..........	$85.00 – 100.00

Walt Disney and other characters
Dwarf, plush beard
12½"..............	$200.00 – 250.00

Snow White
18".................	$350.00 – 400.00

Three Little Pigs
7"................$50.00 – 65.00 each

Pinocchio
16".................	$425.00 – 475.00

Kuddle Kewpie: See Kewpie section.
Scootles, 1935, designed by Rose O'Neill, yarn hair
10".................	$425.00 – 475.00

18"................. $825.00 – 875.00

KÄTHE KRUSE

1910 to present, Prussia, after W.W.II, Bavaria. Made cloth dolls with molded stockinette heads and waterproof muslin bodies, heads, hair, and hands oil painted. Early dolls are stuffed with deer hair. Early thumbs are part of the hand; after 1914 they are attached separately, later they're again part of the hand. Marked on the bottom of the left foot with number and name "Käthe Kruse," in black, red, or purple ink. After 1929, dolls had wigs, but some still had painted hair. Later dolls have plastic and vinyl heads. Original doll modeled after bust sculpture "Fiamingo" by Francois Duquesnois. Dolls listed are in good condition, appropriately dressed, allow significantly less for dirty or faded examples.

Cloth
Miniatures, dollhouse-size character dolls
6"...........$6,100.00* set of three*

Doll I Series, 1910 – 1929, all-cloth, jointed shoulders, wide hips, painted eyes and hair, three vertical seams in back of head, marked on left foot
16"...........	$6,000.00 – 7,000.00

16" Käthe Kruse model I doll with wide hips. $6,500.00. **Photo courtesy of McMasters Harris Auction Co.**

18" model VIII. $2,000.00. Photo courtesy of Dollsantique.

Ball-jointed knees, 1911 variant produced by Kämmer & Reinhardt

17"....... $12,000.00 – 14,000.00

Later model, 1929+, now with slim hips

17"........... $3,000.00 – 3,500.00

Doll IH Series, wigged version, 1930+

17"........... $3,200.00 – 3,500.00

Bambino, a doll for a doll, circa 1915 – 1925

8".................................. $500.00

Too few in database for reliable range.

Doll II Series, "Schlenkerchen," ca. 1922 – 1936, smiling baby, open-closed mouth, stockinette covered body and limbs, one seam head

13"........... $8,000.00 – 9,000.00

Doll V, VI, Sandbabies Series, 1920s+, "Traumerchen" (closed eyes) and "Du Mein" (open eyes) were cloth dolls with painted hair, weighted with sand or unweighted, with or without belly buttons, in 19⅝" and 23⅝" sizes, one- or three-seam heads or cloth over cardboard, later heads were made in the 1930s from a heavy composition called magnesit

19⅝" – 23½"

$6,000.00 – 8,000.00

Magnesit head, circa 1930s+

20"........... $1,500.00 – 1,600.00

Doll VII Series, circa 1927 – 1952, two versions were offered

Smaller 14" Du Mein open eye baby, painted hair or wigged, three-seam head, wide hips, sewn on thumbs, 1927 – 1930

14"........... $3,000.00 – 3,200.00

Doll I version, with wide hips, separately sewn on thumbs, painted hair or wigged, after 1930 – 1950s slimmer hips and with thumbs formed with hand

14"........... $2,200.00 – 2,500.00

Doll VIII Series

Deutsche Kind, the "German child," 1929 on, modeled after Kruse's son, Friedebald, hollow head, swivels, one vertical seam in back of head, wigged, disk-jointed legs, later made in plastic during the 1950s

20"........... $2,000.00 – 2,200.00

Doll IX Series

"The Little German Child," 1929 on, wigged, one seam head, a smaller version of Doll VIII

14"........... $1,400.00 – 1,600.00

16" pair of celluloid Käthe Kruse dolls. $400.00 each. Photo courtesy of McMasters Harris Auction Co.

20" doll from the 1980s. $325.00. **Photo courtesy of The Museum Doll Shop.**

Doll X Series, 1935 on, smaller Doll I with one-seam head that turns

14".......... $2,500.00 – 2,800.00

Doll XII Series, 1930s, Hampelchen with loose legs, three vertical seams on back of head, painted hair, button and band on back to make legs stand. The 14" variation has head of Doll I; the 16" variation also has the head of Doll I, and is known after 1940s as Hempelschatz, Doll XIIB

14".......... $1,600.00 – 2,000.00

18".......... $2,600.00 – 3,000.00

Hard Plastic, 1948 – 1975, celluloid and other synthetics

US Zone mark

14"................ $500.00 – 600.00

Turtle Mark Dolls, 1955 – 1961, synthetic bodies

14"................ $275.00 – 325.00

16"................ $350.00 – 400.00

18"................ $450.00 – 500.00

1975 to date, marked with size number in centimeters, B for baby, H for hair, and G for painted hair

10"................ $150.00 – 200.00

13"................ $175.00 – 225.00

GEBRUDER KUHNLENZ

1884 – 1935, Kronach, Bavaria, Germany. Porcelain factory made dolls, doll heads, movable children, and swimmers. Butler Bros. and Marshall Field distributed their dolls.

Closed Mouth Child

Mold 28, 31, 32, 39, ca. 1890, bisque socket head, closed mouth, glass eyes, pierced ears, wig, wood and composition jointed body

8" – 10".......... $700.00 – 900.00

15" – 16".. $1,400.00 – 1,500.00

21" – 23".. $2,200.00 – 2,500.00

Mold 34, Bru type, paperweight eyes, closed mouth, pierced ears, composition jointed body

12½" – 15".. $2,900.00 – 4,000.00

18" – 20".. $4,500.00 – 6,300.00

Mold 38, solid dome turned shoulder head, closed mouth, pierced ears, kid body

12" – 15"........ $500.00 – 575.00

17" – 20"........ $800.00 – 900.00

Mold 39, socket head

14"........................ $2,500.00*

Mold 46, socket head

17"........................ $1,000.00*

Open Mouth Child

Mold 41, 44, socket head, glass eyes, open mouth, composition body

9" – 10" .... $575.00 – 675.00

15" – 19"........ $750.00 – 850.00

24" – 26" . $1,050.00 – 1,200.00

30".......... $1,400.00 – 1,600.00

Mold 165, ca. 1900, socket head, sleep eyes, open mouth, teeth

16" – 18"........ $400.00 – 450.00

22" – 24"........ $550.00 – 700.00

30" – 33"........ $725.00 – 775.00

Mold 47, 61, shoulder head

    14"................. $350.00 – 400.00

    18"................. $400.00 – 425.00

Character dolls

Mold 205, shoulder head, open/closed mouth, intaglio eyes, molded painted hair

    20"................. $550.00 – 600.00

No mold #, open/closed laughing mouth, glass eyes

    15"........... $1,000.00 – 1,200.00

Small Dolls, 44 marked "Gbr. K" in sunburst, socket head, glass eyes, open mouth, five-piece body composition body

    7" – 8"........... $250.00 – 325.00

All-Bisque, swivel neck, molds 31, 41, 44, 56, others, glass eyes

    5" – 7"......... $650.00 – 1,000.00

Adult, ca. 1915

Marked "Caprice," "Lorraine," "Favorite," bisque socket head, open-closed mouth with teeth, composition adult body

    13"................. $750.00 – 800.00

    16" – 18"........ $800.00 – 900.00

    22"........... $1,000.00 – 1,200.00

Painted eyes

    12½"........ $1,000.00 – 1,975.00

Child, no mold name or "Cherie," "Favorite," "La Georgienne," or "Toto," bisque socket head, open mouth with teeth, wig, composition jointed body

    12" – 14"........ $500.00 – 650.00

    16" – 20"........ $650.00 – 850.00

    22" – 24"..... $900.00 – 1,000.00

    25" – 26".. $1,100.00 – 1,200.00

A. LANTERNIER & CIE.

1915 – 1924, Limoges, France. Porcelain factory, made dolls and heads. Lady dolls were dressed in French provincial costumes, bodies by Ortyz; dolls were produced for Association to Aid War Widows.

21" marked "Depose// Fabrication// Francaise//Favorite// No. 6//JE Masson// SC//Al & Cie.// Limoges." $1,200.00. **Photo courtesy of McMasters Harris Auction Co.**

17½" open mouth child by Lanternier & Cie. $700.00. **Doll courtesy of Elaine Holda.**

LAWTON DOLL CO.

1979 to present, Turlock, California. Founded by Wendy Lawton. Dolls listed are mint-in-box; dolls missing accessories or with flaws would be priced less.

Connoisseur Collections
Best Friends
Bianca & Bratwurst, 2003
$250.00 – 300.00
Cherished Customs
The Blessing, 1990
13½" .... $165.00 – 195.00
Childhood Classics
Bobbsey Twins, 1991
$135.00 – 175.00 each
Hans Brinker, 1985
14" .... $300.00 – 350.00
Heidi, 1984
14" .... $150.00 – 200.00
Li'l Princess, 1989
14" .... $400.00 – 450.00
Marcella & Raggedy Ann, 1988
$350.00 – 400.00
Pollyanna,1986
14" .... $350.00 – 400.00
Christmas Collection
Christmas Joy, 1988
$650.00 – 700.00
Christmas Angel, 1990
$100.00 – 150.00
Yuletide Carole, 1991
$150.00 – 200.00
Victorian Christmas, 1997
$175.00 – 200.00
Music of Christmas, 2001
$215.00 – 265.00
Classic Playthings
Patricia & Her Patsy, 1993
$250.00 – 300.00
Bessie & Her Bye-Lo Baby, 1995
$250.00 – 300.00
Henriette and her Hilda, 1996
$400.00 – 450.00
Madison and her Madame Alexander® Doll,
2001 .... $350.00 – 400.00
Daughters of Faith
Ransom's Mark, 2003 ..$350.00 – 400.00

14" Bessie from the Classics Playthings Collection by Lawton. $300.00 (with her Bye-Lo baby).
Photo courtesy of René Walden.

Hallelujah Lass, 2004
$350.00 – 400.00
Little Women
Set of four, 1994 – 1995
15" $1,525.00
Too few in database for a reliable range.
Tribute to June Amos Grammer
June Amos & Mary Anne, 1996
16" $1,305.00*
Gallery Editions
Toy's N' Treasures collection
Sarah's Sock Monkey, porcelain doll
12" .... $55.00 – 65.00
Ashton Drake Collection
Lawton's Nursery Rhymes
Little Bo Peep, Miss Muffet, Mary Mary, Mary Had A little Lamb .... $25.00 – 35.00
Little Women Collection, 1994
Set of 4 .... $275.00 – 300.00
Walt Disney Collection

Main Street, 1989 (250)
$200.00 – 300.00
Liberty Square, 1990 (250)
$250.00 – 350.00
Tish, 1991 (250)...... $250.00 – 350.00
Karen, 1992 (50)..... $650.00 – 750.00
Melissa & Her Mickey, 1994 (100)
$600.00 – 700.00
Snow White, 1997 (200)
$100.00 – 150.00

Guild Doll Collection
Ba Ba Black Sheep, 1989, porcelain
14"................. $200.00 – 300.00
Lavender Blue, 1990.. $300.00 – 400.00
Uniquely Yours, 1995, porcelain
14"................. $120.00 – 170.00
Travel Doll, 1997, with trunk and accessories
$900.00 – 1,000.00
Bon Voyage, 2003 ... $350.00 – 400.00
Exclusive Editions Collection
Convention/Event dolls
1ˢᵗ **WL Convention, Lotta Crabtree**, 1992
$1,300.00
Too few in database for a reliable range.
Beatrice Louise, UFDC, 1998 Luncheon
$890.00 – 975.00
Josephine, UFDC Regional
12"................. $700.00 – 750.00
Katrena, UFDC Convention, 2002
9½"................ $200.00 – 225.00
Store Specials
Little Colonel, Dolly Dears, Birmingham,
Alabama................. $375.00 – 425.00

LEATHER

Leather was an available resource for Native Americans to use for making doll heads, bodies, or entire dolls. It was also used by American doll makers such as Darrow and by French and Moroccan doll makers, as well as others. Some

10½" leather doll made in England by M. Todhunter. $140.00. **Photo courtesy of The Museum Doll Shop.**

examples of Gussie Decker's dolls were advertised as "impossible for child to hurt itself" and leather was fine for teething babies.

Darrow, American, molded rawhide. These dolls are almost always found with very little original paint remaining, value listed reflects this condition
18" – 22"........ $550.00 – 650.00
French all-leather baby, molded head, jointed body, painted eyes
4" – 4½"... $2,200.00 – 2,800.00
Moroccan leather dolls, 1900 – 1940s, souvenir type dolls depicting regional characters
9" – 11".............. $25.00 – 45.00
Native American Dolls
Plains tribes, various, 1900 on
12" – 14"........ $150.00 – 250.00
Eskimo, ca. 1940
10"............................$110.00
12"............................$125.00
Sioux, ca. 1900
11½", buckskin.............. $800.00
Sioux, ca. 2005
14" buckskin..................... $50.00
Todhunter, M. 1926 on, England, leather

over molded clay face, wire armature body wrapped with suede

10" – 12"........ $120.00 – 150.00

LENCI

1919 to 2003, Turino, Italy. Lenci was the trademark and name of firm started by Enrico and Elena di Scavini that made felt dolls with pressed faces, also made composition head dolls, wooden dolls, and porcelain figurines and dolls. Early Lenci dolls have tiny metal button, hang tags with "Lenci//Torino//Made in Italy." Ribbon strips marked "Lenci//Made in Italy" were found in the clothes ca. 1925 – 1950. Some, but not all dolls have Lenci marked in purple or black ink on the sole of the foot. Some with original paper tags may be marked with a model number in pencil. Dolls have felt swivel heads, oil–painted features, often side-glancing eyes, jointed shoulders and hips, third and fourth fingers are often sewn together, sewn-on

18" & 16" Lenci girls. $1,800.00 and $2,200.00. **Dolls courtesy of Carol Barboza.**

double felt ears, often dressed in felt and organdy original clothes, excellent condition. May have scalloped socks.

The most sought after are the well constructed early dolls from the 1920s and 1930s, when Madame Lenci had control of the design and they were more elaborate with fanciful, well made accessories. They carried animals of wood or felt, baskets, felt vegetables, purses, or bouquets of felt flowers. This era of dolls had eye shadow, dots in corner of eye, two-tone lips, with lower lip highlighted and, depending on condition, will command higher prices.

After WWII the company was purchased by the Garella Brothers. The later dolls of the 1940s and 1950s have hard cardboard-like felt faces, with less intricate details, like less elaborate appliqués, fewer accessories, and other types of fabrics such as taffeta, cotton, and rayon, all showing a decline in quality and should not be priced as earlier dolls. The later dolls may have fabric covered cardboard torsos. Model numbers changed over the years, so what was a certain model number early, later became another letter or number.

Lenci characteristics include double layer ears, scalloped cotton socks. Early dolls may have rooted mohair wig, 1930s dolls may have "frizzed" played-with wigs. Later dolls are less elaborate with hard cardboard-type felt faces. Dolls listed are in clean condition and wearing original clothing. Soiled, faded examples will bring significantly less. Add more for tags, boxes, or accessories. Exceptional dolls and rare examples may go much higher.

Baby

13" – 15".. $1,700.00 – 1,900.00

18" – 22".. $2,700.00 – 3,000.00

27" long-limbed Lenci lady doll. $3,600.00.
Photo courtesy of Joan & Lynette Antique Dolls and Accessories.

Child
1920s – 1930s, softer face, more elaborate costume, face model numbers 300, 109, 149, 159, 111

12" – 14"..	$1,300.00 – 1,500.00
16" – 18"..	$1,900.00 – 2,400.00

Model 1500, scowling face

17" – 19".. $2,200.00 – 2,700.00

Model 500

21"........... $1,600.00 – 1,800.00

1940s – 1950s+, hard face, less intricate costume

13".................	$300.00 – 400.00
15".................	$400.00 – 500.00
17".................	$500.00 – 600.00

Small Dolls

Mascottes and Miniatures, 9"

Child .... $450.00 – 675.00
Regional costume...... $500.00 – 650.00
Long Limbed Lady Dolls, with adult face, flapper or boudoir body with long slim limbs

17" – 20".. $2,000.00 – 2,800.00
24" – 28".. $3,100.00 – 3,600.00
32".......... $3,200.00 – 3,400.00

Rarities
Celebrities
Bach

17".......... $2,500.00 – 2,850.00

Tom Mix

18".......... $3,000.00 – 3,500.00

Mendel

22".......... $3,400.00 – 3,700.00

Mozart

11".......... $2,300.00 – 2,400.00
14".......... $3,000.00 – 3,200.00

Pastorelle

14".......... $2,900.00 – 3,100.00

Valentino

30"...$15,099.00 at online auction

Characters
Aladdin

14".......... $7,000.00 – 7,750.00

Aviator, girl with felt helmet

18".......... $2,900.00 – 3,200.00

Becassine

11"................. $925.00 – 975.00
20" glass eyes
$2,900.00 – 3,100.00

Benedetta

19".......... $1,000.00 – 1,100.00

18" series 300 boy in regional costume. $2,600.00.
Doll from private collection.

Black Child, in native garb

15".......... $2,600.00 – 3,000.00

Cowboy

14".......... $1,000.00 – 1,100.00

Cupid

17".......... $4,900.00 – 5,200.00

Elf, ca. 1926, black

7"............................ $3,000.00*

Fascist Boy, rare

14".......... $1,200.00 – 1,500.00

Flower Girl, ca. 1930

20".......... $1,200.00 – 1,400.00

Henriette

26".......... $1,800.00 – 2,100.00

Indian

17".......... $3,200.00 – 3,600.00

Laura

16".............. $950.00 – 1,100.00

Pierrot

21".......... $2,100.00 – 2,900.00

Pinocchio

11"...................... $1,100.00 MIB

Salome, ca. 1920, brown felt, ball at waist allows doll to swivel

17".......... $3,000.00 – 3,500.00

Smoker

Painted eyes

28".......... $2,500.00 – 3,000.00

Glass eyes

24".......... $4,000.00 – 4,200.00

Solider, in Italian uniform

17".......... $2,500.00 – 3,000.00

Sport Series

16" – 18".. $3,000.00 – 7,000.00

Polo player

16" – 17"..$9,000.00 – 12,000.00

Val Gardena

19"................. $800.00 – 900.00

Winking Boy

11".............. $950.00 – 1,050.00

Puppet

13"............................ $700.00*

18" surprise eyed Lenci. $2,100.00.
Photo courtesy of Richard Withington, Inc.

Ethnic or Regional Costume

Asian, Lia Tia Guai

16"........................ $4,600.00*

Bali dancer

15".............. $950.00 – 1,500.00

Cossack Man

27".............. $950.00 – 1,200.00

Eugenia

25".............. $900.00 – 1,100.00

Madame Butterfly, ca. 1926

17".......... $3,000.00 – 3,200.00

25".......... $4,300.00 – 4,800.00

Marenka, Russian girl, ca. 1930

19".......... $3,000.00 – 3,500.00

Scottish girl, ca. 1930

14"................. $600.00 – 700.00

Spanish girl, ca. 1930

14".......... $1,200.00 – 1,400.00

19".......... $2,200.00 – 2,500.00

Tyrol boy or girl, ca. 1935

14"................. $700.00 – 800.00

Eye Variations

Glass eyes

16".......... $1,400.00 – 1,600.00

22".......... $2,800.00 – 3,000.00

Flirty glass eyes

15".......... $2,000.00 – 2,200.00

20".......... $2,600.00 – 2,800.00
Surprise eye, widow, "O" shaped eyes and mouth
19" – 20".. $2,200.00 – 2,700.00
Modern, 1979 on
12" – 14"........ $100.00 – 150.00
21" – 26"........ $200.00 – 400.00
Pinocchio, 1981
18"................. $100.00 – 120.00
Accessories
Lenci Dog .... $100.00 – 150.00
Purse .... $175.00 – 225.00

LENCI-TYPE

1920 – 1950. These were made by many English, French, or Italian firms like Anili, Gre-Poir, or Raynal from felt with painted features, mohair wig, original clothes. These must be in very good condition, tagged or unmarked. Usually Lenci-types have single felt ears or no ears.
Child
Low quality
15" – 17"........ $145.00 – 165.00
High quality
15" – 17"........ $450.00 – 650.00
Regional costume, makers such as Alma, Vecchiotti, and others
8" – 9"............ $125.00 – 145.00

17" Poir. $450.00.
Photo courtesy of Dollsantique.

10" pair of felt dolls by Alma. $400.00 pair.
Photo courtesy of Joan & Lynette Antique Dolls and Accessories.

11" – 15"........ $200.00 – 275.00
Smoker
16"................. $350.00 – 400.00
Anili, founded by the daughter of Elena Di Scavini (Lenci), molded felt dolls
Child
16" – 21" .... $175.00 – 200.00
Gre Poir, France, New York City, 1927 – 1930s, Eugenie Poir made felt or cloth mask face dolls, unmarked on body, no ears, white socks with three stripes, hang tag
16" – 18"
Cloth face .... $375.00 – 425.00
Felt face .... $800.00 – 900.00
Messina-Vat, 1923 on, Turin, Italy
20" .... $375.00 – 450.00

LIBERTY OF LONDON

1906 to 1950s, London, England. Liberty of London was founded in 1873. In 1920 they registered the name "Liberty" for their line of needle-sculpted cloth art dolls.

British Characters and Historical Figures, such as Shakespeare, John Bull, Queen Victoria and others

9" – 10".......... $200.00 – 300.00
Beefeater................. $125.00 – 200.00
Coronation dolls
9" – 10".......... $200.00 – 225.00
Princess Elizabeth or Margaret
7" .... $325.00 – 350.00

King George VI and Princess Elizabeth by Liberty of London. $225.00 and $350.00.
Photo courtesy of Richard Withington, Inc.

A.G. LIMBACH

1772 – 1927 on, Limbach, Thüringia, Germany. This porcelain factory made bisque head dolls, china dolls, bathing dolls, and all-bisque dolls beginning in 1872. Usually marked with three leaf clover.

All-Bisque

Child, small doll, molded hair or wigged, painted eyes, molded and painted shoes and socks, may have mark "8661," and cloverleaf, more for exceptional dolls

3½".................... $75.00 – 85.00
4" – 5"........... $110.00 – 125.00

6" – 7"........... $175.00 – 225.00
11" – 12"........ $350.00 – 450.00
Paper sticker marked "Our Mary," all-bisque, glass sleep eyes, wigged

6" – 8"........... $225.00 – 275.00
Baby, mold 8682, character face, bisque socket head, glass eyes, clover mark, bent-leg baby body, wig, open-closed mouth

8½"................ $325.00 – 400.00
Child
Bisque Socket Head, may have name above mold mark, such as Norma, Rita, Wally, glass eyes, clover mark, wig, open mouth

18" – 20"........ $400.00 – 500.00
Bisque Shoulder Head, open mouth, glass eyes, kid body

10" – 11".......... $75.00 – 100.00
Lady
"The Irish Queen": See Parian-type, Untinted Bisque.

MAROTTES

1860 on and earlier. Doll's head on wooden or ivory stick, sometimes with whistle, when twirled some play music. Bisque head on stick made by various French and German companies.

12" marotte with a French head and an ivory handle. $900.00. **Photo courtesy of The Museum Doll Shop.**

Bisque

German head, open mouth dolly face mold, various German makers such as Armand Marseille, Gebruder Heubach, etc.
9" – 14".......... $600.00 – 900.00
Character mold
9" – 14"....... $900.00 – 1,100.00
French head
14" – 16".. $1,000.00 – 1,400.00
Celluloid
11"................. $200.00 – 250.00

ARMAND MARSEILLE

1884 – 1950s, Sonneberg, Köppelsdorf, Thüringia, Germany. One of the largest suppliers of bisque doll heads, ca. 1900 – 1930, to such companies as Amberg, Arranbee, Bergmann, Borgfeldt, Butler Bros., Dressel, Montgomery Ward, Sears, Steiner, Wiegand, Louis Wolfe, and others. Made some doll heads with no mold numbers, but names, such as Alma, Baby Betty, Baby Gloria, Baby Florence, Baby

22" AM 390 on oilcloth body with composition arms, 1920s. $375.00.
Doll courtesy of Ruth Cayton.

Phyllis, Beauty, Columbia, Duchess, Ellar, Florodora, Jubilee, Mabel, Majestic, Melitta, My Playmate, Nobbi Kid, Our Pet, Princess, Queen Louise, Rosebud, Superb, Sunshine, and Tiny Tot. Some Indian dolls had no mold numbers. Often used Superb kid bodies, with bisque hands. After WWII and into the 1950s the East German government continued to produce dolls marked AM. Dolls listed are in good condition, appropriately dressed.

Child Doll, 1890 on, mo mold number, or just marked "A.M.," and molds 390, Floradora, 1894, bisque socket head, open mouth, glass eyes, wig, composition fully jointed body. Dolls listed are in good condition, appropriately dressed, allow more for flirty eyes.

Composition Body
9" – 10".......... $175.00 – 200.00
12" – 14"........ $220.00 – 300.00
16" – 18"........ $300.00 – 450.00
20" – 24"........ $300.00 – 450.00
28" – 30"........ $450.00 – 550.00
32" – 36"........ $600.00 – 650.00
42"................. $800.00 – 900.00
Five-piece flapper body, high quality
6" – 7"............ $275.00 – 300.00
10" – 13"........ $350.00 – 400.00
Five-piece body, low quality
10" – 12"........ $125.00 – 135.00
14" – 16"........ $150.00 – 175.00
Molds Queen Louise, Rosebud
12" – 13"........ $225.00 – 275.00
15" – 17"........ $250.00 – 300.00
22" – 24"........ $350.00 – 400.00
28"................. $350.00 – 400.00
31" – 34"........ $700.00 – 750.00
Mold Baby Betty
14" – 16"........ $375.00 – 425.00
18" – 20"........ $300.00 – 350.00
Kid Body

Shoulder heads mold 370, 1894, 3200, Alma, Beauty, Floradora, Lily, Mabel, My Playmate, Princess, Rosebud

    10" – 12"........ $125.00 – 150.00
    14" – 16"........ $250.00 – 300.00
    18" – 20"........ $325.00 – 375.00
    22" – 24"........ $250.00 – 300.00

Molds 1890, 1892, 1895, 1897, 1899, 1901, 1902, 1903, 1909

    10" – 12"........ $175.00 – 225.00
    14" – 16"........ $275.00 – 300.00
    18" – 20"........ $300.00 – 375.00
    22" – 24"........ $375.00 – 425.00

Character Baby

Baby Betty, usually found on child composition body, some on bent-leg baby body

    16"................................. $500.00

Too few in database for reliable range.

Molds Kiddiejoy, 256, 259, 326, 327, 328, 329, 360a, 750, 790, 900, 927, 970, 971, 975, 990, 991, 992 Our Pet, 995, 996, 1330, bisque solid-dome or wigged socket head, open mouth, glass eyes, composition bent-leg baby body, add more for toddler body or flirty eyes or exceptional doll

    8".................... $350.00 – 375.00
    12"................. $225.00 – 300.00
    15"................. $425.00 – 450.00
    17"................. $475.00 – 500.00
    21"................. $500.00 – 550.00
    24"................. $600.00 – 625.00

Mold 233

    12" – 13"........ $400.00 – 425.00
    15"................. $500.00 – 550.00

Mold 251/248

Open/closed mouth

    10" – 12"........ $500.00 – 600.00

Closed mouth

    12"................. $425.00 – 450.00

Mold 410, two rows of teeth

    12"................. $600.00 – 700.00

12" mold 500. $1,000.00. **Photo courtesy of Richard Withington, Inc.**

Mold 500, intaglio eye, bent-limb composition body

    13" – 15"........ $575.00 – 700.00

Mold 518

    16" – 18"........ $430.00 – 450.00

Mold 560A

    8" – 9"............ $180.00 – 200.00
    15" – 16"........ $475.00 – 500.00

Mold 580, 590

    15" – 16"........ $750.00 – 900.00
    19"........... $1,000.00 – 1,100.00

Mold 920

    21"................................. $650.00

Too few in database for reliable range.

Melitta, toddler

    16"................. $800.00 – 900.00

Character Child

Mold 225, ca. 1920, bisque socket head, glass eyes, open mouth, two rows of teeth, composition jointed body

    14"........... $3,000.00 – 3,600.00
    19"........... $4,000.00 – 4,650.00

Fany, ca. 1912, can be child, toddler, or baby

230, molded hair

    15" – 16" . $6,000.00 – 7,000.00
    17" – 18".. $8,500.00 – 9,500.00

231 (wigged)

    13" – 14".. $4,500.00 – 5,000.00

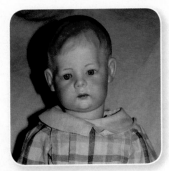

18" Fany. $9,500.00. **Doll courtesy of Jean Grout.**

16"........... $5,800.00 – 6,100.00
Mold 250, ca. 1912, domed
    9" – 13".......... $575.00 – 600.00
    15"................. $600.00 – 650.00
    18"................. $750.00 – 875.00
Mold 251, ca. 1912, socket head, open-closed mouth
    12" – 13".. $1,100.00 – 1,250.00
    17" – 18".. $2,000.00 – 2,200.00
Mold 253: See Googly section.
Mold 310, Just Me, ca. 1929, bisque socket head, wig, flirty eyes, closed mouth, composition body
    5" $1,300.00*
    7½" – 8"... $1,700.00 – 1,900.00
    9" – 10".... $1,800.00 – 2,100.00
    11"........... $2,200.00 – 2,500.00
    13"........... $2,400.00 – 2,800.00
Painted bisque, with Vogue labeled outfits
    7" – 8"......... $850.00 – 1,100.00
    10"........... $1,000.00 – 1,100.00
Mold 345, pouty
Painted intaglio eyes
    10" – 11".. $3,700.00 – 4,200.00
Glass eyes
    10"................. $825.00 – 900.00
Mold 350, ca. 1926, glass eyes, closed mouth
    16"........... $1,950.00 – 2,250.00
    20"........... $2,500.00 – 2,850.00

Mold 360a, ca. 1913, open mouth
    12"................. $350.00 – 400.00
Mold 400, 401, ca. 1926, glass eyes, closed mouth
    13"........... $1,400.00 – 1,600.00
    24".............................$1,800.00
Mold 449, ca. 1930, painted eyes, closed mouth
    13"................. $575.00 – 625.00
    18".............. $900.00 – 1,000.00
Painted bisque
    11"................. $200.00 – 250.00
    15"................. $375.00 – 450.00
Mold 450, glass eyes, closed mouth
    14"................. $575.00 – 700.00
Mold 500, 600, ca. 1910, domed shoulder head, molded/painted hair, painted intaglio eyes, closed mouth
    10" – 12" .... $800.00 – 1,000.00
    17"................. $800.00 – 950.00
Painted bisque
    21"................. $175.00 – 200.00
Mold 520, ca. 1910, domed head, glass eyes, open mouth
Composition body
    12"................. $675.00 – 750.00
    19"........... $1,800.00 – 2,000.00

9" painted bisque Just Me. $1,100.00. **Doll courtesy of Ruth Cayton.**

Kid body

16".................. $800.00 – 900.00

20".......... $1,200.00 – 1,400.00

Mold 550, ca. 1926, domed, glass eyes, closed mouth

14" – 15".. $1,600.00 – 1,900.00

Mold 560, ca. 1910, character, domed, painted eyes, open-closed mouth or 560A, ca. 1926, wigged, glass eyes, open mouth

14".................. $850.00 – 900.00

22".......... $1,200.00 – 1,300.00

Mold 570, ca. 1910, domed, closed mouth

12".......... $1,600.00 – 1,750.00

Mold 590, ca. 1926, sleep eyes, open-closed mouth

9".................... $450.00 – 500.00

16".............. $900.00 – 1,000.00

18" – 20".. $1,000.00 – 1,100.00

Mold 600, shoulder head, solid dome with molded hair, closed mouth, intaglio eyes

14".................. $575.00 – 600.00

Mold 690, socket head, open mouth

18".................. $800.00 – 850.00

Mold 700, ca. 1920, closed mouth

Painted eyes

12½"........ $1,800.00 – 2,000.00

Glass eyes

14".......... $3,800.00 – 4,200.00

Mold 701, 711, ca. 1920, socket or shoulder head, sleep eyes, closed mouth

16".......... $2,000.00 – 2,250.00

Mold 800, ca. 1910, socket head, 840 shoulder head

18".......... $2,000.00 – 2,200.00

Lady, 1910 on, bisque head, wigged, sleep eyes, open or closed mouth, composition lady body

Molds 400, 401, 14"

Open mouth ..... $1,100 .00 – 1,300.00

Closed mouth ..... $2,100.00 – 2,400.00

Painted Bisque ...... $900.00 – 1,000.00

Newborn Baby, 1924 on, newborn, bisque

12" Dream Baby by Armand Marseille. $225.00. **Photo courtesy of The Museum Doll Shop.**

solid-dome socket head or flange neck, may have wig, glass eyes, closed mouth, cloth body with celluloid or composition hands

Mold 341, My Dream Baby, 351, 345, Kiddiejoy, 352, Rock-A-Bye Baby, marked "AM."

6" in original playpen $255.00

at online auction

10" – 13"........ $200.00 – 225.00

14" – 16"........ $250.00 – 300.00

22" – 24"........ $375.00 – 425.00

On bent-limb composition body

11" – 12"........ $275.00 – 325.00

16"................. $350.00 – 375.00

With toddler body

28".............. $900.00 – 1,200.00

Pillow puppet

10"................. $150.00 – 200.00

Baby Gloria, solid dome, open mouth, painted hair

12"................. $325.00 – 350.00

15"................. $475.00 – 525.00

Baby Phyllis, head circumference:

9" – 10"......... $325.00 – 400.00

13" – 15"........ $425.00 – 500.00

Composition Child, 1940s – 1950s, mold 2966 and others. sleep eyes, synthetic wig, five-piece composition body (very thin cardboard like composition)

22".............. $165.00 – 175.00

MARX TOY CORP.

1919 to present, Sebring, Ohio. Founded in 1919 as Louis Marx & Co. in New York City. Dolls listed are in perfect condition with original clothing.

Archie and Friends, characters from comics, vinyl, molded hair or wigged, painted eyes, in package

Archie, Betty, Jughead, Veronica

8½"................... $12.00 – 18.00

Freddy Krueger, 1989, vinyl, pull string talker horror movie Nightmare on Elm Street character played by Robert England

18"..................... $40.00 – 50.00

Johnny Apollo Double Agent, vinyl, trench coat, circa 1970s

12".................... $40.00 – 50.00

Johnny West Family of Action Figures, 1965 – 1976, adventure or Best of the West Series, rigid vinyl, articulated figures, molded clothes, came in box with vinyl accessories and extra

11½" Jane West, by Marx, one hand missing. $20.00. **Photo courtesy of The Museum Doll Shop.**

clothes, had horses, dogs, and other accessories available, dolls listed are complete with box and all accessories, allow more if never removed from box or special sets

Bill Buck, brown molded-on clothing, 13 pieces, coonskin cap

11½"............. $100.00 – 125.00

Captain Tom Maddox, blue molded-on clothing, brown hair, 23 pieces

11½".................. $75.00 – 90.00

Chief Cherokee, tan or light color molded-on clothing, 37 pieces

11½"................ $80.00 – 100.00

Daniel Boone, tan molded-on clothing, coonskin cap

11½"................ $95.00 – 115.00

Fighting Eagle, tan molded-on clothes, with Mohawk hair, 37 pieces

11½"............. $115.00 – 135.00

General Custer, dark blue molded-on clothing, yellow hair, 23 pieces

11½".................. $70.00 – 85.00

Geronimo, light color molded-on clothing

11½".................. $55.00 – 75.00

Orange body

11½"................ $90.00 – 110.00

Jamie West, dark hair, molded-on tan clothing, 13 accessories

9"...................... $35.00 – 45.00

Jane West, blond hair, turquoise molded-on clothing, 37 pieces

11½".................. $60.00 – 75.00

Orange body .... $35.00 – 45.00

Janice West, dark hair, turquoise molded-on clothing, 14 pieces

9"...................... $35.00 – 45.00

Jay West, blond hair, tan molded-on clothing, 13 accessories, later brighter body colors

9".................... $80.00 – 100.00

Jed Gibson, c. 1973, black figure, molded-on green clothing

12"................ $220.00 – 260.00

Johnny West, brown hair, molded-on brown clothing, 25 pieces
    12".................... $80.00 – 100.00
Johnny West, with quick draw arm, blue clothing
    12".................... $90.00 – 115.00
Josie West, blond, turquoise molded-on clothing, later with bright green body
    9"........................ $35.00 – 45.00
Princess Wildflower, off-white molded-on clothing, with papoose in vinyl cradle, 22 pieces of accessories
    11½".............. $110.00 – 130.00
Sam Cobra, outlaw, with 26 accessories
    11½"................. $80.00 – 100.00
Sheriff Pat Garrett (Sheriff Goode in Canada), molded-on blue clothing, 25 pieces of accessories
    11½".............. $100.00 – 125.00
Zeb Zachary, dark hair, blue molded-on clothing, 23 pieces
    11½"................. $90.00 – 110.00
Knight and Viking Series, ca. 1960s, action figures with accessories
Gordon, the Gold Knight, molded-on gold clothing, brown hair, beard, mustache
    11½".............. $100.00 – 125.00
Sir Stuart, Silver Knight, molded-on silver clothing, black hair, mustache, goatee
    11½".............. $100.00 – 125.00
Brave Erik, Viking with horse, ca. 1967, molded-on green clothing, blond hair, blue eyes
    11½".............. $125.00 – 150.00
Odin, the Viking, ca. 1967, brown molded-on clothing, brown eyes, brown hair, beard
    11½".............. $125.00 – 150.00
Miss Seventeen, 1961, hard plastic, high heeled, fashion-type doll, modeled like the German Bild Lilli (Barbie doll's predecessor), came in black swimsuit, black box, fashion brochure pictures 12 costumes, she was advertised as "A Beauty Queen"
    18"................. $150.00 – 200.00
Miss Marlene, hard plastic, high heeled, Barbie-type, ca. 1960s, blond rooted wig
    11"................. $125.00 – 150.00
Miss Toddler, also know as Miss Marx, vinyl, molded hair, ribbons, battery operated walker, molded clothing
    18"................. $125.00 – 155.00
PeeWee Herman, 1987 TV character, vinyl and cloth, ventriloquist doll in gray suit, red bow tie
    18"..................... $18.00 – 25.00
Pull string talker, 18"..... $20.00 – 30.00
Sindy, ca. 1963+, in England by Pedigree, a fashion-type doll, rooted hair, painted eyes, wires in limbs allow her to pose, distributed in U.S. by Marx c. 1978 – 1982
    11" .... $60.00 – 80.00
Pedigree................... $90.00 – 110.00
Gayle, Sindy's friend, black vinyl
    11"................. $120.00 – 140.00
Outfits......................... $75.00 – 95.00
Soldiers, ca. 1960s, articulated action figures with accessories
Buddy Charlie, Montgomery Wards, exclusive, a buddy for GI Joe, molded-on military uniform, brown hair
    11½".............. $80.00 – 100.00
Stony "Stonewall" Smith, molded-on Army fatigues, blond hair, 36-piece accessories
    11½"................ $80.00 – 100.00
Twinkie, doll with vinyl clothing and wigs
    4½".................... $70.00 – 80.00

MATTEL

1959 to present, founded by Ruth and Elliot Handler. Many dolls of the 1960s and 1970s designed by Martha Armstrong Hand. Dolls listed are in excellent condition with all

18" Bozo, pull string talker. $70.00.
Photo courtesy of Atlanta Antique Gallery.

original clothing and accessories. Allow double for mint-in-box examples.

Baby Beans, 1971 – 1975, vinyl head, bean bag dolls, terry cloth or tricot bodies filled with plastic and foam
12".................... $50.00 – 60.00
Talking
12".................... $30.00 – 40.00
Baby First Step, 1965 – 1967, battery operated walker, rooted hair, sleep eyes, pink dress
18".................. $80.00 – 100.00
Talking
18"................ $110.00 – 120.00
Longer hair, pink outfit... $70.00 – 90.00
Baby Go Bye-Bye and Her Bumpety Buggy, 1970, doll sits in car, battery operated, 12 maneuvers
11"................ $120.00 – 140.00
Baby's Hungry, 1967 – 1968, battery operated, eyes move and lips chew when magic bottle or spoon is put to mouth, wets, plastic bib
17".................... $20.00 – 25.00
Baby Love Light, battery operated
16".................... $14.00 – 18.00

Baby Pattaburp, 1964 – 1966, vinyl, drinks milk, burps when patted, pink jacket, lace trim
16"..................... $70.00 – 85.00
Baby Play-A-Lot, 1972 – 1973, posable arms, fingers can hold things, comes with 20 toys, moves arm to brush teeth, moves head, no batteries, has pull string and switch
16"..................... $18.00 – 22.00
Baby Say 'N See, 1967 – 1968, eyes and lips move while talking, white dress, pink yoke
17".................. $95.00 – 125.00
Baby Secret, 1966 – 1967, vinyl face and hands, stuffed body, limbs, red hair, blue eyes, whispers 11 phrases, moves lips
18"..................... $75.00 – 85.00
Baby Small Talk, 1968 – 1969, says eight phrases, infant voice, additional outfits available
10¾".................. $40.00 – 50.00
Black
10¾".................. $50.00 – 60.00
In Nursery Rhyme outfit
10¾".................. $55.00 – 65.00
Baby Tender Love, 1970 – 1973, baby doll, realistic skin, wets, can be bathed
Newborn
13".................... $50.00 – 60.00
Talking
16".................... $25.00 – 35.00
Molded hairpiece, 1972
11½".................. $9.00 – 30.00
Brother, sexed
11½".................. $50.00 – 60.00
Baby Walk 'n Play, 1968
11"...................... $8.00 – 12.00
Baby Walk 'n See
18".................... $12.00 – 18.00
Barbie: See that section.
Big Jim Series, vinyl action figures, many boxed accessory sets available
Big Jim, black hair, muscular torso

9½".............. $80.00 – 100.00
Big Josh, dark hair, beard
9½"................... $25.00 – 35.00
Dr. Steele, bald head, silver tips on right hand
9½"................... $40.00 – 50.00
Beanie, From Beanie & Cecile TV show, 1962, vinyl head, hands, feet, cloth body, pull string talker .... $75.00 – 100.00
Bozo, 1964
18"..................... $75.00 – 85.00
Buffy and Mrs. Beasley, 1967 & 1974, characters from TV sitcom, *Family Affair*
Buffy, vinyl, rooted hair, painted features, holds small Mrs. Beasley, vinyl head, on cloth body
6½".................. $75.00 – 100.00
Talking Buffy, vinyl, 1969 – 1971, holds tiny 6" rag Mrs. Beasley
10¾".............. $150.00 – 200.00
Mrs. Beasley
1965, vinyl head, cloth body
16"................. $200.00 – 250.00
1973, non-talker
15½".............. $175.00 – 200.00
Captain Kangaroo, 1967, Sears only, talking character, host for TV kids program
19"................... $80.00 – 100.00
Captain Laser, 1967, vinyl, painted features, blue uniform, silver accessories, batteries operate laser gun, light-up eyes
12"................. $150.00 – 200.00
Casper, the Friendly Ghost
ca. 1964
16"................. $100.00 – 120.00
1971
5"..................... $50.00 – 60.00
Chatty Cathy Series
Chatty Cathy, 1960 – 1963, vinyl head, hard plastic body, pull string activates voice, dressed in pink and white checked or blue party dresses, 1963 – 1965, says 18 new

20" Chatty Cathy. $275.00. **Photo courtesy of The Museum Doll Shop.**

phrases, red velvet and white lace dress, extra outfits available
Blond
20"................. $300.00 – 400.00
Canadian version ..... $450.00 – 550.00
Black
20"......... $1,000.00 – 1,400.00*
1995 Re-issue doll ...... $75.00 – 100.00
Charmin' Chatty, 1963 – 1964, talking doll, soft vinyl head, closed smiling mouth, hard vinyl body, long rooted hair, long legs, five records placed in left side slot, one-piece navy skirt, white middy blouse, with red sailor collar, red socks and saddle shoes, glasses, five disks; extra outfits and 14 more disks available
24"................. $175.00 – 225.00
Chatty Baby, 1962 – 1964, red pinafore over rompers
18"................... $80.00 – 110.00
Tiny Chatty Baby, 1963 – 1964, smaller version of Chatty Baby, blue rompers, blue, white striped panties, bib with name, talks, other outfits available
15½"................. $60.00 – 80.00
Black
15½".............. $100.00 – 125.00
Tiny Chatty Brother, 1963 – 1964, boy version of Tiny Chatty Baby, blue and white suit

and cap, hair parted on side

15½"................. $85.00 – 95.00

Cheerful Tearful, 1966 – 1967, vinyl, blond hair, face changes from smile to pout as arm is lowered, feed her bottle, wets and cries real tears

7"...................... $75.00 – 85.00

13"..................... $40.00 – 50.00

Dancerina, 1969 – 1971, battery operated, posable arms, legs, turns, dances with control knob on head, pink ballet outfit

24"................. $175.00 – 200.00

Baby Dancerina, 1970, smaller version, no batteries, turn-knob on head, white ballet outfit

16"..................... $85.00 – 95.00

Black

16"................ $125.00 – 150.00

Teeny Dancerina

12"..................... $25.00 – 35.00

Debbie Boone, 1978

11½"................. $45.00 – 55.00

Dick Van Dyke, 1969, as Mr. Potts in movie, Chitty Chitty Bang Bang, all-cloth, flat features, talks in actor's voice, mark: "© Mattel 1969" on cloth tag

2" Liz from the Lucy Locket Kiddle series, MOC. $80.00. **Photo courtesy of McMasters Harris Auction Co.**

23" Scooba Doo, c. 1964. $150.00. Photo courtesy of The Museum Doll Shop.

24"................. $100.00 – 120.00

Drowsy, 1965 – 1974, vinyl head, stuffed body, sleepers, pull-string talker

15½"................ $50.00 – 100.00

Dr. Dolittle, 1968, character patterned after Rex Harrison in movie version, talker, vinyl with cloth body

24"..................... $40.00 – 50.00

All vinyl

6"....................... $15.00 – 20.00

Gramma Doll, 1970 – 1973, Sears only, cloth, painted face, gray yarn hair, says ten phrases, talker, foam-filled cotton

11"..................... $15.00 – 20.00

Grizzly Adams, 1971

10"..................... $40.00 – 50.00

Guardian Goddesses, 1979

11½"................. $40.00 – 50.00

Herman Munster, 1965, cloth doll, talking TV character, The Munsters

21"................. $150.00 – 175.00

Liddle Kiddles, 1966 on, small dolls of vinyl over wire frame, posable, painted features, rooted hair and came with bright costumes and accessories, packaged on 8½" x 9½" cards, mark: "1965//Mattel Inc.//Japan"

11½" Tiny Swingy MIB. $175.00. **Photo courtesy of Emmie's Antique Doll Castle.**

on back, dolls listed are in excellent condition with all accessories, add double for mint in package (or card) and never removed from package, less for worn dolls with missing accessories

1966, First Series

3501 Bunson Bernie
3".......................... $60.00 – 80.00
3502 Howard "Biff" Boodle
3½".................... $85.00 – 115.00
3503 Liddle Diddle
2¾".................. $125.00 – 150.00
3504 Lola Liddle
3½".................... $80.00 – 90.00
3505 Babe Biddle
3½".................... $75.00 – 100.00
3506 Calamity Jiddle
3".......................... $50.00 – 75.00
3507 Florence Niddle
2¾".................... $85.00 – 100.00
3508 Greta Griddle
3".......................... $70.00 – 80.00
3509 Millie Middle
2¾".................... $45.00 – 55.00
3510 Beat A Diddle
3½".................... $75.00 – 100.00

1967, Second Series

3513 Sizzly Friddle
3".......................... $90.00 – 110.00
3514 Windy Fiddle
2½".................... $125.00 – 150.00
3515 Trikey Triddle
2¾".................... $125.00 – 150.00
3516 Freezy Sliddle
3½".................... $90.00 – 110.00
3517 Surfy Skiddle
3".......................... $60.00 – 70.00
3518 Soapy Siddle
3½".................... $55.00 – 75.00
3519 Rolly Twiddle
3½".................... $90.00 – 100.00
3548 Beddy Bye Biddle (with robe)
$70.00 – 90.00
3549 Pretty Priddle
3½".................... $50.00 – 65.00

1968, Third Series

3587 Baby Liddle
2¾".................... $100.00 – 120.00
3551 Telly Viddle
3½".................... $115.00 – 125.00
3552 Lemons Stiddle
3½".................... $60.00 – 75.00

6" Rock Flower doll, c. 1970. $30.00. **Photo courtesy of The Museum Doll Shop.**

3553 Kampy Kiddle
     3½"................. $80.00 – 100.00
3554 Slipsy Sliddle
     3½"................. $75.00 – 100.00
Storybook Kiddles, 1967 – 1968
               $100.00 – 175.00
Skediddle Kiddles, 1968 – 1970
     4"..................... $90.00 – 130.00
Kiddles 'N Kars, 1969 – 1970
     2¾"............................ $177.50*
Tea Party Kiddles, 1970 – 1971
     3½".................... $60.00 – 80.00
Lucky Locket Kiddles, 1967 – 1970
     2"........................ $35.00 – 40.00
Kiddle Kolognes, 1968 – 1970
     2"........................ $50.00 – 80.00
Kiddle Kones, 1968 – 1969
     2"........................ $65.00 – 85.00
Kola Kiddles, 1968 – 1969
     2"........................ $60.00 – 75.00
Kosmic Kiddle, 1968 – 1969
     2½"............... $100.00 – 125.00
Sweet Treat Kiddles, 1969 – 1970
     2"..................... $80.00 – 100.00
Liddle Kiddle Playhouses, 1966 – 1968
               $65.00 – 75.00

Matty Mattel
     16"..................... $55.00 – 65.00
Mork & Mindy, 1979

     9"...............$20.00 – 30.00 each
My Child, 1986, cloth over vinyl head, cloth body, synthetic wig
     13"................. $100.00 – 160.00
Osmond Family
Donny or Marie Osmond, 1978
     12"................... $$25.00 – 35.00
Jimmy Osmond, 1979
     10".................... $40.00 – 50.00
Rainbow Brite, 1983 vinyl head, cloth body, orange yarn hair
     18½"................. $60.00 – 70.00
Rock Flowers, 1970, vinyl mod dolls
     6"....................... $30.00 – 35.00
Scooba Doo, 1964, vinyl head, rooted hair, cloth body, talks in Beatnik phrases, blond or black hair, striped dress
     23"................. $125.00 – 150.00
Shogun Warrior, all plastic, battery operated
     23½".............. $100.00 – 225.00
Shrinkin' Violette, 1964 – 1965, cloth, yarn hair, pull-string talker, eyes close, mouth moves
     16"................. $175.00 – 200.00
Sister Belle, 1961 – 1963, vinyl, pull string talker, cloth body
     16"..................... $55.00 – 65.00
Star Spangled dolls, uses Sunshine Family adults, marked "1973"
Pioneer Daughter.......... $30.00 – 40.00
Sunshine Family, vinyl, posable, come with Idea Book, Father, Mother, Baby
Steve
     9"....................... $20.00 – 30.00
Stephie
     7½"................... $20.00 – 30.00
Sweets
     3½"................... $20.00 – 30.00
Swingy, 1968, mechanical dancing doll
     18"................. $100.00 – 125.00
Tatters, 1965 – 1967, talking cloth doll, wears rag clothes

13" My Child doll by Mattel. $140.00. **Photo courtesy of The Museum Doll Shop.**

19".................... $95.00 – 110.00
Teachy Keen, 1966 – 1970, Sears only, vinyl head, cloth body, ponytail, talker, tells child to use accessories included, buttons, zippers, comb
16"...................... $20.00 – 30.00
Tinkerbelle, 1969, talking, patter pillows
18"...................... $18.00 – 22.00
Tippee Toes, 1968 – 1970, battery operated, legs move, rides accessory horse, tricycle, knit sweater, pants
17".................... $85.00 – 100.00
Truly Scrumptious, character from movie Chitty Chitty Bang Bang
11½".............. $150.00 – 175.00
Talking.................... $300.00 – 350.00
Welcome Back Kotter, 1973, characters from TV sitcom
Freddie "Boom Boom" Washington, Arnold Horshack
9"...................... $30.00 – 40.00
Vinnie Barbarino (John Travolta)
9"...................... $70.00 – 80.00
Gabe Kotter
9"...................... $15.00 – 25.00

Zython, 1977, has glow-in-the-dark head, Enemy in Space 1999 series
$80.00 – 90.00

MAWAPHIL

1920 – 1942, Atlanta, Georgia. Dolls designed by Mary Waterman Philips, manufactured by the Rushton Co. Stockinette crib dolls and cloth mask face dolls.
Crib doll, all cloth, stockinette or velveteen
8" – 12".............. $60.00 – 90.00
Cloth mask face doll, cloth body, appropriately dressed
15"................. $200.00 – 250.00

16" Mawaphil boy, cloth mask face. $250.00. **Photo courtesy of The Museum Doll Shop.**

MEGO CORPORATION

1954 to 1982. Made many vinyl "action figure" dolls during the 1970s. Prices shown are for excellent condition dolls with

12" Sonny Bono, MIB. $70.00. **Photo courtesy of The Museum Doll Shop.**

all appropriate clothes and accessories, allow double values listed for mint in box examples.

Action Jackson, 1971 – 1972, vinyl head, plastic body, molded hair, painted black eyes, action figure, many accessory outfits, mark: "©Mego Corp//Reg. U.S. Pat. Off.// Pat. Pend.//Hong Kong//MCMLXXI"

8".................... $20.00 – 30.00
Black
8".................... $45.00 – 55.00
Dinah-mite, Black .... $30.00 – 40.00
Batman, 1979
8".................... $125.00 – 175.00
Arch enemies
8".................... $65.00 – 75.00
Mobile Bat Lab, 1975 .... $350.00*
*original box
Candy, 1979, fashion doll
18".................... $65.00 – 75.00
Captain and Tennille, Daryl Dragon and Toni Tennille, 1977, recording and TV personalities, Toni Tennille doll has no molded ears
12½".................... $40.00 – 55.00
Charlie's Angels, 1977, TV show dolls based

on characters played by Farrah Fawcett, Jaclyn Smith, Kate Jackson, and Cheryl Ladd, vinyl dolls, rooted hair
9".................... $10.00 – 15.00
12½".................... $50.00 – 100.00
Cher, 1976, TV and recording personality, husband Sonny Bono, all-vinyl, fully jointed, rooted long black hair, also as grow-hair doll
Cher
12".................... $40.00 – 50.00
Growing Hair Cher, 1976
12".................... $85.00 – 100.00
Sonny Bono
12".................... $25.00 – 35.00
CHiPs, 1977, California Highway Patrol TV show, Jon Baker (Larry Wilcox), Frank "Ponch" Poncherello (Erik Estrada)
8".................... $30.00 – 40.00
Diana Ross, 1977, recording and movie personality, all-vinyl, fully jointed, rooted black hair, long lashes
12½".................... $75.00 – 100.00
Dukes of Hazzard, 1982, from TV show, Bo, Luke, Boss Hogg, Cletus, Rosco
8" – 9".................... $35.00 – 80.00
Flash Gordon Series, ca. 1976, vinyl head, hard plastic articulated body
Dale Arden
9".................... $100.00 – 125.00
Dr. Zarkov
9½".................... $75.00 – 100.00
Flash Gordon
9½".................... $75.00 – 100.00
Ming, the Merciless
9½".................... $55.00 – 65.00
Happy Days Series, 1976, characters from *Happy Days* TV sitcom, Henry Winkler starred as Fonzie, Ronnie Howard as Richie, Anson Williams as Potsie, and Donny Most as Ralph Malph
Fonzie
8".................... $65.00 – 75.00

Fonzie with motorcycle $125.00*
Richie, Potsie, Ralph, each
    8" .... $50.00 – 60.00
Joe Namath, 1970, football player, actor, soft vinyl head, rigid vinyl body, painted hair and features
    12" .... $75.00 – 100.00
Outfit, MIP $32.50
KISS, 1978, rock group, with Gene Simmons, Ace Frehley, Peter Cris, and Paul Stanley, all-vinyl, fully jointed, rooted hair, painted features and makeup
    12½" .... $120.00 – 140.00 each
Kristy McNichol, 1978, actress, starred in TV show, *Family,* all-vinyl, rooted brown hair, painted eyes, marked on head: "©MEGO CORP.//MADE IN HONG KONG," marked on back: "©1977 MEGO CORP.//MADE IN HONG KONG"
    9" .... $25.00 – 35.00
Laverne and Shirley, 1977, TV sitcom; Penny Marshall played Laverne, Cindy Williams played Shirley, also, from the same show, David Lander as Squiggy, and Michael McKean as Lenny, all-vinyl, rooted hair, painted eyes
    11½" .... $60.00 – 75.00
Marvel Super Heros, 1974 on, vinyl head, rooted black hair, painted eyes, plastic body
    8"
Aquaman .... $80.00 – 100.00
Batgirl .... $200.00 – 250.00
Batman .... $150.00 – 200.00
Catwoman .... $100.00 – 125.00
Flash .... $100.00 – 125.00
Green Arrow .... $80.00 – 100.00
Joker .... $45.00 – 55.00
Mr. Fantastic .... $80.00 – 100.00
Mr. Mxyzptlk .... $75.00 – 90.00
Riddler .... $70.00 – 80.00
Robin .... $80.00 – 100.00
Supergirl .... $150.00 – 200.00

Wonderwoman .... $80.00 – 90.00
Our Gang, 1975, from *Our Gang* movie shorts, that replayed on TV, included characters Alfalpha, Buckwheat, Darla, Mickey, Porky, and Spanky
    6" .... $15.00 – 25.00
Planet of the Apes
Planet of the Apes Movie Series, ca. 1970s
Astronaut
    8" .... $95.00 – 120.00
Ape Soldier
    8", Palitoy, MOC $800.00*
Cornelius
    8" .... $80.00 – 100.00
Dr. Zaius
    8" .... $80.00 – 100.00
Zira
    8" .... $80.00 – 100.00
Planet of the Apes TV Series, ca. 1974
Alan Verdon
    8" .... $65.00 – 75.00
Galen
    8", Palitoy $140.00*
General Urko
    8" .... $125.00 – 150.00
General Urko
    8", MOC $950.00*
General Ursus
    8" .... $400.00 – 450.00
Peter Burke
    8" .... $125.00 – 150.00
Star Trek
Star TV Series, ca. 1973 – 1975
Captain Kirk
    8" .... $55.00 – 65.00
Dr. McCoy
    8" .... $60.00 – 70.00
Klingon
    8" .... $45.00 – 60.00
Lt. Uhura
    8" .... $50.00 – 60.00
Mr. Scott

8" Captain Kirk. $25.00.
Photo courtesy of The
Museum Doll Shop.

8" .... $60.00 – 80.00
Mr. Spock
8" .... $35.00 – 45.00
Star Trek Aliens, ca. 1975 – 1976
Andorian
8" .... $130.00 – 170.00
Cheron
8" .... $50.00 – 75.00
Mugato
8" .... $125.00 – 150.00
Talos
8" .... $100.00 – 125.00
The Gorn
8" .... $50.00 – 75.00
The Romulan
8" .... $250.00 – 300.00
Star Trek Movie Series, ca. 1979, 12½" dolls
Acturian .... $80.00 – 100.00
Captain Kirk .... $45.00 – 60.00
Commander Decker ...... $45.00 – 60.00
Ilia .... $50.00 – 60.00
Klingon .... $75.00 – 85.00
Mr. Spock .... $80.00 – 100.00
Starsky and Hutch, 1976, police TV series,
Paul Michael Glaser as Starsky, David Soul
as Hutch, Bernie Hamilton as Captain Dobey,
Antonio Fargas as Huggy Bear, also included
a villain, Chopper, all-vinyl, jointed waists

7½" .... $25.00 – 50.00
Suzanne Somers, 1978, actress, TV person-
ality, starred as Chrissy in *Three's Company,*
all-vinyl, fully jointed, rooted blond hair,
painted blue eyes, long lashes
12½" .... $45.00 – 55.00
Waltons, The, 1975, from TV drama series,
set of two 8" dolls per package, all-vinyl
John Boy and Mary Ellen set
$20.00 – 25.00
Mom and Pop set .... $20.00 – 25.00
Grandma and Grandpa
set .... $30.00 – 40.00
Wizard of Oz, 1974
Dorothy, Glinda, Cowardly Lion, Scarecrow,
Tin Man .... $25.00 – 30.00
Munchkins .... $55.00 – 60.00
Wonder Woman Series, ca. 1976 – 1977,
vinyl head, rooted black hair, painted eyes,
plastic body
Lt. Diana Prince
12½" .... $125.00 – 150.00
Nubia
12½" .... $65.00 – 75.00
Nurse
12½" .... $30.00 – 40.00
Queen Hippolyte
12½" .... $75.00 – 100.00
Steve Trevor
12½" .... $75.00 – 100.00
Wonder Woman
12½" .... $125.00 – 150.00

METAL HEADS

1850 – 1930 on. Made in
Germany, Britain and America, by various
manufactures, including Buschow & Beck
(Minerva), Alfred Heller (Diana), Karl
Standfuss (Juno), and Art Metal Works.
Various metals used were aluminum, brass,
and others, and they might be marked

14" German metal shoulder head doll with sleep eyes. $150.00. Photo courtesy of The Museum Doll Shop.

with just a size and country of origin or unmarked. Dolls listed are in good condition with original or appropriate dolls. Dolls with chipped paint will bring significantly less.

Metal shoulder head, cloth or kid body, molded and painted hair, glass eyes, more for wigged

12" – 14"	$150.00 – 175.00
16" – 18"	$175.00 – 225.00
20" – 22"	$250.00 – 275.00

Painted eyes

12" –14"	$135.00 – 150.00
20" – 22"	$200.00 – 225.00

All metal or with composition body, metal limbs

Baby

20" metal head Mama style doll. $200.00. Doll courtesy of Elaine Holda.

11" – 15"	$125.00 – 150.00
16" – 20"	$150.00 – 200.00

Child

15"	$250.00 – 300.00
20"	$350.00 – 400.00

Mama doll, metal shoulder head, cloth body

18"	$200.00 – 250.00

Swiss: See Bucherer section.

MISSIONARY RAG BABY (BEECHER BABY)

22" Missionary Rag Doll. $4,000.00. Private collection.

1893 – 1910, Elmira, New York. Julia Jones Beecher, wife of Congregational Church pastor Thomas K. Beecher, sister-in-law of Harriet Beecher Stowe. Made Missionary Ragbabies with the help of the sewing circle of her church. The dolls were made from old silk or cotton jersey underwear, with hand-painted and needle-sculpted features. All proceeds used for missionary work. Sizes 16" to 23" and larger. Dolls listed are in good condition, appropriately dressed. Exceptional examples will bring more.

16"........... $2,500.00 – 2,800.00

21" – 23".. $3,900.00 – 4,500.00

Black Beecher, same construction and appearance as the white babies but from brown fabric with black yarn hair. Please note, this is not the black stockinette doll often erroneously referred to as "a black Beecher," which is quite different in construction from a true Black Beecher.

21" – 23".. $6,000.00 – 6,500.00

MOLLY-'ES

1920 to 1970s, Philadelphia, Pennsylvania. International Doll Co. was founded by Mollye Goldman. Molly-'es made cloth mask faced dolls, doll clothing, briefly Raggedy Ann, as well as composition and vinyl dolls. Her mask faced dolls had yarn or mohair hair, painted features, sewn joints at the shoulders and hips.

Cloth, fine line painted lashes, pouty mouth

14" Maraquita of Spain, cloth mask faced doll by Molly-es. $175.00.
Photo courtesy of The Museum Doll Shop.

Child

15"................. $100.00 – 125.00

18"................. $130.00 – 140.00

24"................. $165.00 – 190.00

29"................. $230.00 – 270.00

Internationals

13".................... $90.00 – 100.00

15"................. $125.00 – 175.00

27"................. $175.00 – 225.00

Lady

16"................. $150.00 – 175.00

21"................. $200.00 – 275.00

Princess, Thief of Baghdad

Prince, cloth

23"................. $700.00 – 750.00

Princess

   Composition

   15"................. $575.00 – 625.00

   Cloth

   18"................. $600.00 – 650.00

Sabu, composition

15"................. $550.00 – 650.00

Sultan, cloth

19"................. $650.00 – 750.00

Composition

Baby

15"................. $140.00 – 190.00

21"................. $210.00 – 225.00

Cloth body

18".................... $90.00 – 110.00

Toddler

15"................. $240.00 – 280.00

21"................. $250.00 – 300.00

Child

15"................. $160.00 – 190.00

18"................. $210.00 – 260.00

Lady, add more for ball gown

16"................. $275.00 – 325.00

21"................. $400.00 – 500.00

Hard Plastic

Baby

14"..................... $65.00 – 85.00

20"..................	$100.00 – 135.00

Cloth body

17"....................	$55.00 – 75.00
25".................	$100.00 – 125.00

Child

14".................	$150.00 – 175.00
18".................	$325.00 – 375.00
25".................	$400.00 – 425.00

Lady

17".................	$250.00 – 300.00
20".................	$325.00 – 375.00
25".................	$375.00 – 425.00

Vinyl

Baby

8½"....................	$12.00 – 20.00
12"....................	$18.00 – 25.00
15"....................	$28.00 – 40.00

Child

8"......................	$12.00 – 20.00
10"....................	$18.00 – 25.00
15"....................	$28.00 – 40.00

Little Women

9"......................	$45.00 – 55.00

MONICA DOLLS

1941 – 1951. Monica Dolls from Hollywood, designed by Mrs. Hansi Share, made composition and later hard plastic with long face and painted or sleep eyes, eye shadow, unique feature is very durable rooted human hair, did not have high-heeled feet and unmarked, but wore paper wrist tag reading "Monica Doll, Hollywood," composition dolls had pronounced widow's peak in center of forehead.

Composition, 1941 – 1949, painted eyes, Veronica, Jean, and Rosalind were names of 17" dolls produced in 1942

15".................	$300.00 – 375.00
17"	$400.00 – 450.00
20"..................	$575.00 – 625.00

20" Monica doll. $600.00. **Photo courtesy of The Museum Doll Shop.**

Hard plastic, 1949 – 1951, sleep eyes, Elizabeth, Marion, or Linda

14".................	$400.00 – 500.00
18".................	$500.00 – 600.00

MORAVIAN

1872 – present, Bethelhem, Pennsylvaia. Cloth dolls made by the Ladies Sewing Society of the Moravian Church Guild. Fund raiser to support church work. Flat faced rag

18" Moravian rag doll. $2,000.00. **Photo courtesy of The Museum Doll Shop.**

doll with sewn joints at shoulders, elbows, hips, and knees, hand painted faces, dressed in pink or blue gingham with apron and double bonnet, 18".

19th – early 20th century doll
$2,500.00 – 3,000.00

1920s – 1940s doll
$1,100.00 – 1,500.00

1950s to present....... $150.00 – 250.00

MULTI-FACE, MULTI-HEAD DOLLS

1866 – 1930 on. Various firms made dolls with two or more faces, or more than one head.

Bisque

French

Bru, Surprise poupée, awake/asleep faces
12"............................. $9,500.00
Too few in database for reliable range.

Jumeau, crying, laughing faces, cap hides knob
18"........................... $15,950.00
Too few in database for reliable range.

German

Bartenstein, bisque socket head, papier-mâché hood and molded blouse shoulder plate, cloth over carton body with composition limbs, awake face with open mouth and glass eyes, crying face with open-closed mouth and glass eyes
20"............................. $2,750.00

Bergner, Carl, bisque socket head, two or three faces, sleeping, laughing, crying, molded tears, glass eyes, on composition jointed body may have molded bonnet or hood, marked "C.B." or "Designed by Carl Bergner"
12"........... $1,200.00 – 1,400.00
15"........... $1,300.00 – 1,600.00

Black face/white face doll
13"............................. $3,650.00
Too few in database for reliable range

Kämmer and Reinhardt, set of four bisque character heads, composition body
12"......................... $13,000.00*

Kestner, J. D., ca. 1900+, Wunderkind, bisque doll with set of several different mold number heads that could be attached to body, set of one doll and body with additional three heads and wardrobe
With heads 174, 178, 184 & 185

12" three-faced doll by Carl Bergner. $1,400.00. **Photo courtesy of McMasters Harris Auction Co.**

11".......... $9,000.00 – 9,400.00

With heads, 171, 179, 182 & 183

14½"......................$12,650.00

Too few in database for reliable range.

Kley & Hahn, solid-dome bisque socket head, painted hair, smiling baby and frowning baby, closed mouth, tongue, glass eyes, baby body

13".......... $1,500.00 – 1,700.00

Simon & Halbig, smiling, sleeping, crying, turn ring at top of head to change faces, glass/painted eyes, closed mouth

14½"........ $3,000.00 – 3,200.00

Awake, asleep faces

11".......................... $3,000.00*

SFBJ, mold 200 character faces, laughing, crying

18"........................... $4,200.00*

Hermann Steiner topsy turvy baby

8".................... $500.00 – 600.00

Cloth

Topsy-Turvy: one black, one white head

Babyland

   Painted face

   13"................. $800.00 – 900.00

   Lithographed face

   13"................. $650.00 – 750.00

Bruckner

   13"................. $600.00 – 700.00

China

Topsy Turvy, white head and black head, mid nineteeth century

12".......... $1,200.00 – 1,600.00

Too few in database for reliable range.

Composition

Berwick Doll Co., Famlee Dolls, 1926 on, composition head and limbs, cloth body with crier, neck with screw joint, allowing different heads to be screwed into the body, painted features, mohair wigs and/or molded and painted hair, came in sets of two to 12 heads, with different costumes for each head

Four-head set including baby, girl in fancy dress, girl in sports dress, Indian, and clown

16"................. $600.00 – 650.00

Effanbee, Johnny Tu Face

16"................. $375.00 – 425.00

Too few in database for reliable range.

Ideal, 1923, Soozie Smiles, composition, sleep or painted eyes on happy face, two faces, smiling, crying, cloth body, composition hands, cloth legs, original romper and hat

15½".............. $300.00 – 400.00

Three-in-One Doll Corp., 1946 on, Trudy, composition head with turning knob on top, cloth body and limbs, three faces, "Sleepy, Weepy, Smiley," dressed in felt or fleece snowsuit, or sheer dresses, more for exceptional doll

15½".............. $225.00 – 300.00

Papier-mâché

Smiling/crying faces, glass eyes, cloth body, composition lower limbs

19"................. $650.00 – 700.00

Wax

Bartenstein, glass eyes, carton body, crier

Black face, white face

12".......... $1,100.00 – 1,200.00

Smiling/crying faces

15"................. $550.00 – 600.00

MUNICH ART DOLLS

1908 – 1920s. Marion Kaulitz hand painted heads designed by Marc-Schnur, Vogelsanger, and Wackerle, dressed in German or French regional costumes. Usually composition heads and bodies distributed by Cuno & Otto Dressell and Arnoldt Doll Co.

Composition, painted features, wig, composition body, unmarked

17" – 18"..$12,000.00 – 17,000.00

NANCY ANN STORYBOOK

1936 on, San Francisco, California. Started by Nancy Ann Abbott. Made small painted bisque and hard plastic dolls with elaborate costumes. Also made an 8" toddler doll to compete with Vogue's Ginny, 10" fashion dolls and larger size "style show" dolls. Painted bisque, mohair wig, painted eyes, head molded to torso, jointed limbs, either sticker on outfit or hang tag, in box, later made in hard plastic.

Dolls listed are in good condition with original clothing and wrist tags. Allow more for mint-in-box, add 30 percent or more for black dolls. Selected auction prices reflect once-only extreme high prices and should be noted accordingly. Painted bisque baby prices vary with outfits.

Painted Bisque

1936 – 1937, pink/blue mottled or sunburst box with gold label, gold foil sticker on clothes "Nancy Ann Dressed Dolls," marked "87," "88," or "93," "Made in Japan," no brochure

Baby

3½" – 4½"...... $500.00 – 600.00

5" Judy Ann doll in Swedish costume. $1,200.00. Photo courtesy of Turn of the Century Antiques.

Child

5"............. $1,300.00 – 1,400.00

1938, early, marked "America" (baby marked "87," "88," or "93" "Made in Japan"), colored box, sunburst pattern with gold label, gold foil sticker on clothes: "Judy Ann," no brochure

Baby

3½" – 4½"...... $475.00 – 525.00

Child

5"................ $800.00 – 1,000.00

1938, late, marked "Judy Ann USA" and "Story Book USA" (baby marked "Made in USA" and "88, 89, and 93 Made in Japan"), colored box, sunburst pattern with gold or silver label, gold foil sticker on clothes: "Storybook Dolls," no brochure

Judy Ann mold...... $900.00 – 1,200.00

Storybook mold........ $550.00 – 750.00

1939, child, Story Book Doll USA, molded socks and molded bangs (baby has star-shaped hands), colored box with small silver dots, silver label, gold foil sticker on clothes, "Storybook Dolls," no brochure

Baby

3½" – 4½"...... $200.00 – 225.00

Child

5"................... $250.00 – 350.00

1940, child has molded socks only (baby has star-shaped bisque hands), colored box with white polka dots, silver label, gold foil sticker on clothes, "Storybook Dolls," has brochure

Baby

3½" – 4½"...... $100.00 – 135.00

Child

5"................... $225.00 – 325.00

1941 – 1942, child has pudgy tummy or slim tummy, baby has star-shaped hands or fist, white box with colored polka dots, with silver label, gold foil bracelet with name of doll and brochure

Baby

4" Nancy Ann Storybook baby, painted bisque with starfish shaped hands. $225.00. **Photo courtesy of McMasters Harris Auction Co.**

3½" – 4½"...... $100.00 – 125.00
Child
5"................... $225.00 – 275.00
1943 – 1947, child has one-piece head, body, and legs ("stiff" legs), baby has fist hands, white box with colored polka dots, silver label, ribbon tie or pin fastener, gold foil bracelet with name of doll and brochure
Baby
3½" – 4½"........... $50.00 – 65.00
Child
5"....................... $35.00 – 55.00
Hard Plastic
1947 – 1949, child has hard plastic body, painted eyes, baby has bisque body, plastic arms and legs, white box with colored polka dots with "Nancy Ann Storybook Dolls" between dots, silver label, brass snap, gold foil bracelet with name of doll and brochure, more for special outfit
Baby
3½" – 4½"........... $55.00 – 70.00
Child
5½"..................... $65.00 – 75.00
1949 on, hard plastic, both have black sleep

eyes, white box with colored polka dots and "Nancy Ann Storybook Dolls" between dots, silver label, brass or painted snaps, gold foil bracelet with name of doll and brochure
Baby
3½" – 4½"......... $40.00 – 55.00
Child
5"....................... $40.00 – 50.00
Special Dolls
Mammy and Baby, marked "Japan 1146" or America mold
5"............. $1,000.00 – 1,200.00
Storybook USA
5".................... $400.00 – 500.00
Topsy, bisque black doll, jointed leg
All-bisque .... $450.00 – 500.00
Plastic arms .... $150.00 – 200.00
All-plastic, painted or sleep eye
$125.00 – 150.00
White boots, bisque jointed leg dolls
5".............................. Add $50.00
Series Dolls, depending on mold mark
All-Bisque
American Girl Series
Jointed legs ...... $125.00 – 200.00
Stiff legs.............. $45.00 – 65.00

4" hard plastic Nancy Ann baby. $55.00. **Photo courtesy of McMasters Harris Auction Co.**

5" Nancy Ann Storybook hard plastic bride. $75.00. **Photo courtesy of McMasters Harris Auction Co.**

Around the World Series
$600.00 – 1,000.00
Masquerade Series
Ballet Dancer, Cowboy, Pirate
$750.00 – 900.00
Sports Series
$1,000.00 – 1,300.00
Margie Ann Series
Margie Ann...... $150.00 – 250.00
Powder & Crinoline Series
$75.00 – 100.00
Bisque or Plastic
Operetta or Hit Parade Series
$140.00 – 175.00
Hard Plastic
Big and Little Sister Series, or Commencement Series (except baby) ... $75.00 – 100.00
Bridal, Dolls of the Day, Dolls of the Month, Fairytale, Mother Goose, Nursery Rhyme, Religious, and Seasons Series, painted or sleep eye .... $60.00 – 75.00
Other Dolls
Audrey Ann, toddler, marked "Nancy Ann Storybook 12"
6"................... $900.00 – 975.00

Nancy Ann Style Show, ca. 1954
Hard plastic, sleep eyes, long dress, unmarked
18".......... $1,000.00 – 1,200.00
Long black lace gown costume
18".......... $1,800.00 – 2,000.00
Vinyl head, plastic body, all original, complete
18"................. $400.00 – 500.00
Muffie
1953, hard plastic, wig, sleep eyes, strung straight leg, non-walker, painted lashes
8".................... $375.00 – 450.00
1954, hard plastic walker, molded eyelashes, brows
8"................... $200.00 – 250.00
1955 – 1956, vinyl head, molded or painted upper lashes, rooted saran wig, walker or bent-knee walker
8"..................... $150.00 – 175.00
1968+, reissued, hard plastic
8"..................... $90.00 – 105.00
Lori Ann
Vinyl
7½"................ $100.00 – 140.00
Debbie
Hard plastic in school dress, name on wrist tag/box
10"................. $200.00 – 250.00
Vinyl head, hard plastic body
10"................... $75.00 – 100.00
Hard plastic walker
10½"............. $125.00 – 150.00
Vinyl head, hard plastic walker
10½"................. $65.00 – 75.00
Little Miss Nancy Ann, 1959, high-heel fashion doll
8½"................ $125.00 – 175.00
Miss Nancy Ann, 1959, marked "Nancy Ann," vinyl head, rooted hair, rigid vinyl body, high-heeled feetln undergarments or in day dress

10½" .... $175.00 – 225.00
Baby Sue Sue, 1960s, vinyl
Doll only.................. $125.00 – 150.00

8" Nancy Ann Storybook Muffie, straight leg, strung. $450.00. **Photo courtesy of McMasters Harris Auction Co.**

NESBIT

House of Nesbit, 1956 on, England. Historical costume and character dolls designed by Peggy Nesbit. Hard plastic heads on vinyl bodies.

8" King Henry VIII by Peggy Nesbit. $110.00. **Photo Courtesy of Hatton's Gallery of Dolls.**

7" – 10"
Simple costumes .... $25.00 – 40.00
Elaborate costumes ..... $75.00 – 150.00

GEBRUDER OHLHAVER

10½" Coquette marked Revalo for Gebruder Olhaver. $800.00. **Photo courtesy of Emmie's Antique Doll Castle.**

1913 – 1930, Sonneberg, Germany. Had Revalo (Ohlhaver spelled backwards omitting the two H's) line; made bisque socket and shoulder head and composition dolls. Bought heads from Ernst Heubach, Gebrüder Heubach, and others. Dolls listed are in good condition with original or appropriate clothing.

Baby or Toddler, character face, bisque socket head, glass eyes, open mouth, teeth, wig, composition and wood ball-jointed body (bent-leg for baby)

Baby

    15" – 17"........ $375.00 – 425.00
    21"................. $600.00 – 650.00

Toddler

14".............. $650.00 – 750.00
22".............. $850.00 – 950.00
Child, Mold 150, or no mold number, bisque socket head, open mouth, sleep eyes, composition body
    14" – 16"........ $375.00 – 475.00
    18" – 20"........ $600.00 – 675.00
    24" – 28"........ $700.00 – 800.00
Character, bisque solid dome with molded and painted hair, intaglio eyes, composition body
Molded curl with bow, on five-piece body
    9".................. $300.00 – 350.00
Coquette-type, molded hair ribbon with bows
High quality bisque
    11" – 12"........ $750.00 – 800.00
Low quality bisque
    11" – 12"........ $375.00 – 450.00

OLD COTTAGE DOLLS

Late 1948 on, England. Dolls were designed by Greta and Susi Fleischmann. Made with hard rubber or plastic heads, felt body, some with wire armature, oval hang tag has trademark "Old Cottage Dolls," special characters may be more
    8" – 9"............ $115.00 – 150.00
    12" – 13"........ $235.00 – 285.00

ORIENTAL DOLLS

1850 to present. Dolls depicting Asian peoples. Made by companies in Germany, America, Japan, and others.
All-Bisque
Heubach, Gebrüder, Chin-Chin
    4".................. $250.00 – 325.00
Kestner
    6"............ $1,400.00 – 1,700.00

16" Kestner 243. $5,000.00. **Photo courtesy of The Museum Doll Shop.**

    8"............. $1,600.00 – 1,900.00
Simon & Halbig, mold 852, ca. 1880, all-bisque, Oriental, swivel head, yellow tint bisque, glass eyes, closed mouth, wig, painted socks and curled pointed toe shoes
    4½"................ $650.00 – 700.00
    5½ "............. $875.00 – 950.00
    7"................ $975.00 – 1,025.00
Unmarked or unknown maker, presumed German or French
    6".................. $450.00 – 550.00
European Bisque
Bisque head, jointed body
Barrois Poupée, swivel neck, glass eyes, kid body
    15"..........................$10,000.00
Too few in database for reliable range.
Belton-type, mold 193, 206
    10"........... $1,900.00 – 2,075.00
    14"........... $2,500.00 – 2,700.00
Bru, pressed bisque swivel head, glass eyes, closed mouth
    17"..........................$20,000.00
    20"..........................$26,000,00

Kestner, J. D., 1899 – 1930+, mold 243, bisque socket head, open mouth, wig, bent-leg baby body, add more for original clothing

    13" – 14" . $4,300.00 – 4,800.00
    16" – 18".. $5,000.00 – 5,500.00
    Solid dome, painted hair
    15"........... $4,500.00 – 5,000.00

Armand Marseille, 1925, mold 353, solid-dome bisque socket head, glass eyes, closed mouth

    Baby body
    7½".......... $1,000.00 – 1,200.00
    9" – 12".......... $850.00 – 950.00
    14" – 16".. $1,200.00 – 1,500.00
    Toddler
    16"........... $1,200.00 – 1,500.00
    Painted bisque
    7"...................................$350.00

Too few in database for reliable range.

Schmidt, Bruno, marked "BSW," mold 500, ca. 1905, glass eyes, open mouth

    13" – 14".. $1,600.00 – 2,000.00

Schoenau & Hoffmeister, mold 4900, bisque socket head, glass eyes, open mouth, tinted composition wood jointed body

    10"................. $500.00 – 600.00

Simon & Halbig, mold 1079, 1099, 1129, 1159, 1199,1329, bisque socket head, glass eyes, open mouth, pierced ears, composition wood jointed body

    8" – 10".... $1,200.00 – 1,400.00
    12" – 13".. $1,500.00 – 2,000.00
    16" – 18".. $2,400.00 – 2,800.00
    20" – 24".. $3,000.00 – 3,800.00

Unknown maker, socket head, jointed body, closed mouth, glass eyes

    4½"................ $500.00 – 600.00
    8" – 10".......... $650.00 – 850.00
    12" – 14".. $1,000.00 – 1,200.00
    20"........... $2,600.00 – 2,800.00

Cloth

8" Schoenau Hoffmeister mold 4900. $400.00. Photo courtesy of The Museum Doll Shop.

Ada Lum dolls, 1940s on, Shanghai, cloth dolls depicting Chinese people, embroidered features, black yarn hair

    8" – 10"............. $20.00 – 30.00
    14" – 18"............ $45.00 – 65.00

Composition

Amusco, 1925, composition

    17".......... $1,000.00 – 1,200.00

Effanbee

Butin-nose, in basket with wardrobe, painted Oriental features including black bobbed hair, bangs, side-glancing eyes, excellent color and condition

    8".................... $400.00 – 500.00

15" Simon Halbig mold 1329. $2,200.00. Photo courtesy of Turn of the Century Antiques.

10" Ellar baby by Armand Marseille.
$900.00. **Doll courtesy of Ruth Cayton.**

Patsy, painted Oriental features, including black bangs, straight across the forehead, brown side-glancing eyes, dressed in silk Chinese pajamas and matching shoes, excellent condition

14"................. $700.00 – 800.00

Horsman

Molded Turban head child, 1910 on, composition head and lower arms, cloth body, molded turban on head, painted eyes

11"................. $375.00 – 425.00

Jap Rose Kids, 1911 on, composition head, arms, cloth body, molded painted hair, painted eyes, made as an advertising tie-in to Jap Rose soap

13" boy or 14" girl

$350.00 – 375.00

Baby Butterfly, 1914+, composition head, hands, cloth body, painted hair, features

13"................. $250.00 – 300.00

15"................. $350.00 – 400.00

Quan-Quan Co., California, Ming Ming Baby, all-composition jointed baby, painted features, original costume, yarn queue, painted shoes

9"................... $150.00 – 175.00

11"................. $225.00 – 250.00

Traditional Chinese

Man or woman, composition type head, cloth-wound bodies, may have carved arms and feet, in traditional costume

11"................. $200.00 – 275.00

14"................. $400.00 – 475.00

Traditional Japanese

Ichimatsu, 1870s on, a play doll made of papier-mâché-type material with gofun finish of crushed oyster shells, swivel head, shoulder plate, cloth midsection, upper arms, and legs, limbs and torso are papier-mâché, glass eyes, pierced nostrils. Early dolls may have jointed wrists and ankles, in original dress. Later 1950s+ dolls imported by Kimport

Meiji era, ca. 1870s – 1912

10" – 12"........ $600.00 – 700.00

16" – 18"........ $850.00 – 900.00

22" – 24".. $1,500.00 – 1,800.00

Child

Painted hair, 1920s

12" – 15"........ $450.00 – 550.00

17" – 18"........ $575.00 – 625.00

24"................. $825.00 – 875.00

1930s

12" – 15"........ $350.00 – 425.00

17" – 18"........ $550.00 – 600.00

1940s on

12" Ichimatsu, 1940s type. $100.00. **Photo courtesy of The Museum Doll Shop.**

10" – 12"......... $90.00 – 100.00
14" – 16"........ $125.00 – 150.00
Lady
1920s – 1930s
12" – 14"........ $200.00 – 250.00
16"................. $250.00 – 275.00
1940s – 1950s
12" – 14"............ $70.00 – 95.00
16"................. $100.00 – 135.00
Hina Matsuri, Emperor or Empress, seated,
Ca. 1890s
8"................... $500.00 – 575.00
Ca. 1920s
4" – 6"............ $150.00 – 175.00
10" – 12"........ $250.00 – 300.00
Warrior
1880 – 1890s
16"................. $750.00 – 850.00
Too few in database for reliable range.
On horse
15"........... $1,000.00 – 1,100.00
Too few in database for reliable range.
1920s
15"................. $350.00 – 400.00
Too few in database for reliable range.
On horse
13"................. $800.00 – 850.00
Japanese baby, ca. 1920s, bisque head,
sleep eyes, closed mouth, papier-mâché
body
8"...................... $50.00 – 70.00
14"...................... $65.00 – 90.00
Glass eyes
8"................... $95.00 – 125.00
14"................. $200.00 – 265.00
Gofun finish of crushed oyster-shell head,
painted flesh color, papier-mâché body, glass
eyes and original clothes
8" – 10"............. $55.00 – 75.00
14" – 18"......... $95.00 – 185.00
Wooden dolls
Door of Hope: See Door of Hope section.

PAPIER-MACHÉ

Pre-1600 on. Papier-mâché is an elastic substance made of paper pulp and a variety of additives. Dolls of papier-mâché were being made in France as early as the sixteenth century. In Germany and France papier-mâché dolls were being mass produced in molds for heads after 1810. It reached heights of popularity by mid-1850s and was also used for bodies. Papier-mâché shoulder head, glass or painted eyes, molded and painted hair, sometimes in fancy hairdos. Usually no marks. Dolls listed are in good condition, nicely dressed. More for exceptional examples, considerably less for dolls which have been repainted.

Molded Hair Papier-mâché, so-called Milliner's Models, German, 1820 – 1860s, molded hair, a shapely waist, kid body, and wooden limbs

Apollo top knot, side curls
8" – 10" .... $800.00 – 950.00
12" – 14".. $1,200.00 – 1,600.00
16" – 18".. $1,900.00 – 2,125.00
Braided bun, side curls or long puffy side curls with simple bun
8" – 11".... $1,000.00 – 1,400.00
15" – 18".. $1,600.00 – 1,800.00
with braided bun, original clothing
18" $6,200.00*
Center part, molded bun
7" – 10".......... $550.00 – 750.00
7" all original in original box
$2,900.00*
13" – 15".. $1,200.00 – 1,700.00
18" – 24".. $1,600.00 – 2,200.00
Center part, sausage curls
14"................. $575.00 – 675.00
21"............. $950.00 – 1,050.00
Coiled braids over ears, braided bun
9" – 11".... $1,000.00 – 1,100.00

11" molded hair papier-mâché so-called milliner's model with bun. $550.00.
Photo courtesy of The Museum Doll Shop.

20" – 21".. $2,100.00 – 2,300.00
Covered Wagon or Flat Top hair style
6" – 10".......... $350.00 – 500.00
14" – 16"........ $550.00 – 675.00
Empire style short curls
14" – 20".. $1,200.00 – 1,700.00
Long curls on shoulders
7" – 14".... $1,200.00 – 2,000.00
Molded comb, side curls, braided coronet
25".......... $1,300.00 – 2,000.00
Too few in database for reliable range.
Early Type Shoulder Head, German, 1840s – 1860s, cloth body; wooden limbs, with top-knots, buns, puff curls, or braids, dressed in original clothing or excellent copy, may have some wear; more for painted pate
Painted eyes
9" – 14"....... $550.00 – 1,000.00
16" – 18".. $1,100.00 – 1,300.00
21" – 24".. $1,400.00 – 1,800.00
26" – 30".. $2,200.00 – 3,100.00
Glass eyes
16" – 18" ..$1,400.00 – 1,700.00
20" – 24".. $2,100.00 – 2,600.00
29" – 33".. $1,700.00 – 3,000.00
Long curls
14"................. $850.00 – 950.00

16".......... $1,350.00 – 1,550.00
24".......... $2,500.00 – 2,700.00
Pre-Greiner Type, 1850s, German or American made shoulder head, molded painted black hair, black glass eyes, cloth body
16" – 18" . $1,400.00 – 2,000.00
20" – 25" . $1,000.00 – 1,200.00
29" – 31".. $1,100.00 – 1,200.00
French Type, 1835 – 1850, made by German companies for the French trade, painted black hair, brush marks, solid-dome, shoulder head, some have nailed on wigs, open mouth, bamboo teeth, kid or leather body, appropriately dressed
Glass eyes
13" – 14"..... $900.00 – 1,200.00
18" – 20".. $1,400.00 – 1,800.00
24"............................ $2,400.00
28" – 34".. $3,400.00 – 3,800.00
Painted eyes
8" – 12".......... $600.00 – 800.00
14" – 16".. $1,100.00 – 1,500.00
17" – 20".. $1,500.00 – 2,500.00
Fine quality on poupée peau body, wigged
16"............................ $1,400.00*
Papier-mâché, American, Greiner 1858 – 1883: See Greiner section.
Poupard, French and German, all papier-mâché to represent a swaddled baby
12"................. $300.00 – 400.00
Sonneberg Taufling (so-called Motschmann): See Sonneberg Taufling section.
Patent Washable, 1879 – 1910s, shoulder head with mohair wig, open or closed mouth, glass eyes, cloth body, composition limbs, made by companies such as F. M. Schilling and others
Better quality
12" – 15"..... $800.00 – 1,000.00
18"................. $675.00 – 700.00
22" – 24"....... $825.00 – 925.00

18½" patent washable type attributed to Schilling. $700.00. **Doll courtesy of Elaine Holda.**

Lesser quality

    10" – 12"........ $125.00 – 175.00

    14" – 16"........ $225.00 – 250.00

    23" – 25"........ $300.00 – 400.00

Sonneberg-Type, 1880 – 1910, "M & S Superior," Muller & Strasburger, Cunno & Otto Dressel, and others shoulder head, with blond or molded hair, painted blue or brown eyes, cloth body, with kid or leather arms and boots

    13" – 15"........ $350.00 – 400.00

    18" – 20"........ $450.00 – 525.00

    24" – 29"........ $575.00 – 650.00

Glass eyes

    12"................ $400.00 – 500.00

    16" – 18"........ $550.00 – 650.00

Wigged

    18"................ $650.00 – 750.00

Papier-mâché Child, 1920 on, head has brighter coloring, wigged, child often in ethnic costume, stuffed cloth body and limbs, or papier-mâché arms

French

    9" – 13".......... $100.00 – 125.00

    13" – 15"........ $200.00 – 275.00

German

    10"..................... $70.00 – 80.00

    15"................ $150.00 – 165.00

Unknown maker

    8"....................... $50.00 – 60.00

    12".................. $90.00 – 115.00

    16"................ $150.00 – 175.00

Clowns, papier-mâché head, with painted clown features, open or closed mouth, molded hair or wigged, cloth body, composition or papier-mâché arms, or five-piece jointed body

High quality child body

    16".............. $800.00 – 1,000.00

    20".......... $1,200.00 – 1,300.00

Lower quality crude body type

    8".................. $200.00 – 235.00

    14"................ $450.00 – 485.00

16½" Sonneberg type papier-mâché doll. $450.00. **Photo courtesy of Joan & Lynette Antique Dolls and Accessories.**

PARIAN-TYPE, UNTINTED BISQUE

1850 – 1900 on, Germany. The term "parian" as used in doll collecting refers to dolls of untinted bisque, in other words the doll's skin tone is white rather than tinted. These dolls were at the height of their popularity from 1860 through the 1870s.

They are often found with molded blond hair, some with fancy hair arrangements and ornaments or bonnets, can have glass or painted eyes, pierced ears, may have molded jewelry or clothing, occasionally solid dome with wig, cloth body, nicely dressed in good condition. Dolls listed are in good condition, appropriately dressed. Exceptional examples may be much higher.

Lady

Common hair style

Painted eyes

   Undecorated, simple molded hair

     8" – 10" .... $145.00 – 185.00

     14" – 16"........ $375.00 – 450.00

     18" – 25"........ $625.00 – 700.00

   Molded bodice, fancy trim

     17"................. $700.00 – 900.00

   Glass eyes

     10".............. $900.00 – 1,000.00

     12" – 14".. $1,500.00 – 2,100.00

     16" – 18".. $2,300.00 – 2,600.00

Fancy hair style, with molded combs, ribbons, flowers, bands, or snoods, cloth body, untinted bisque limbs, more for very elaborate hairstyle

17" with snood and molded collar with gold trim and luster tie. $2,000.00. **Photo courtesy of Richard Withington, Inc.**

12" Countess Dagmar style. $550.00.
Photo courtesy of The Museum Doll Shop.

Painted eyes, pierced ears

     10" – 13"..... $900.00 – 1,000.00

     14" – 16"..... $900.00 – 1,000.00

     18" – 22".. $1,300.00 – 1,600.00

     24" .... $1,500.00 – 1,600.00

Decorated shoulder-plate

   Simple bodice or tie

     8½"................ $275.00 – 300.00

     13" – 15"........ $400.00 – 500.00

   More elaborate bodice and hair

     14" – 16".. $1,600.00 – 2,400.00

     17" – 21".. $2,800.00 – 3,000.00

Glass eyes, pierced ears

     14" – 15".. $1,400.00 – 1,600.00

     18" – 20".. $2,500.00 – 3,000.00

   Swivel neck

     14" – 15".. $2,400.00 – 2,700.00

Alice in Wonderland, molded head band or comb

     14" – 16"........ $475.00 – 600.00

     19" – 21"........ $625.00 – 700.00

Countess Dagmar, no mark, head band, cluster curls on forehead

     12"................. $550.00 – 600.00

     18" – 21"..... $900.00 – 1,000.00

Dolly Madison
18" – 22"..... $750.00 – 1,200.00
Empress Eugenie, headpiece snood
15"........... $1,000.00 – 1,100.00
25"........... $1,100.00 – 1,300.00
Irish Queen, Limbach, clover mark, #8552
14" – 16"........ $775.00 – 800.00
Molded hat, blond or black painted hair
Painted eyes
16"........... $2,000.00 – 2,300.00
19"........... $2,500.00 – 2,900.00
Glass eyes
14"........... $2,100.00 – 2,400.00
17"........... $2,800.00 – 3,000.00
Necklace, jewels, or standing ruffles
17"........................... $9,700.00+
Too few in database for reliable range.
Princess Augusta Victoria, molded shoulder plate with cross necklace, glass eyes
13"........... $2,200.00 – 2,500.00
Men or Boys, center or side-part hair style, cloth body, decorated shirt and tie
Painted eyes
13"................. $700.00 – 800.00
16" – 17".. $1,000.00 – 1,100.00
Glass eyes
16"........... $2,400.00 – 2,825.00

15" Irish Queen by Limbach. $750.00.
Photo courtesy of The Museum Doll Shop.

RONNAUG PETTERSEN

1901 – 1980, Norway. Made cloth dolls, pressed felt head, usually painted side-glancing eyes, cloth bodies, intricate costumes, paper tags
7" – 8"........... $150.00 – 200.00
14½" .... $400.00 – 500.00

8" Ronnaug Pettersen doll. $125.00. **Doll courtesy of Armory Antiques.**

DORA PETZOLD

Germany, 1919 – 1930+. Made and dressed dolls, molded composition head, painted features, wig, stockinette body, sawdust filled, short torso, free-formed thumbs, stitched fingers, shaped legs
18"........... $1,000.00 – 1,500.00
20" – 22".. $1,600.00 – 2,000.00

18" Dora Petzold doll. $1,500.00. **Doll courtesy of Jean Grout.**

PHILADELPHIA BABY (SHEPPARD BABY)

1900, Philadelphia, Pennsylvania. Rag baby sold be the J.B. Sheppard & Co. store. Molded stockinette, painted features, sewn joints at shoulders, hips, and knees. Dolls listed are in good condition, appropriately dressed. Allow more for exceptional condition.

18" – 22" .. $4,100.00 – 4,500.00
Doll in somewhat worn condition
18" – 22".. $1,600.00 – 2,200.00

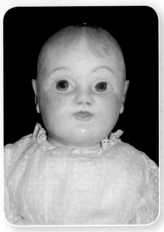

21" Philadelphia Baby in excellent condition. $5,000.00. **Doll courtesy of Dominique Perrin.**

PLEASANT COMPANY

1985 – present. Middleton, Wisconsin, founded by Pleasant T. Rowland. In 1998 the company was purchased by Mattel, Inc. Values listed are for good condition secondary market dolls in appropriate clothing, many dolls are still available at retail as well.

American Girl®, vinyl doll with wig
18"...................... $6.00 – 85.00
Marisol, limited edition from 2005
$225.00 – 250.00

Julie the girl of the 1970s. $75.00. **Doll courtesy of Emily Spinner.**

POLISH RELIEF DOLLS

1914 on, Paris, France. Polish Relief dolls were created in the workshop of Madame Lazarski during and shortly after WWI. This project provided work for war refugees and the money raised from the sale of the dolls aided Polish widows and orphans. Cloth dolls with embroidered features and floss hair.

Adult
19"................. $200.00 – 250.00
Child
11" – 17" .... $275.00 – 350.00

17" Polish Relief girl. $325.00. **Doll courtesy of Elaine Holda.**

PRESBYTERIAN RAG DOLL

1885 on, Bucyrus, Ohio. The First Presbyterian Church made cloth dolls as a fund raiser, cloth doll with "pie-shaped gusseted" piece across top of head, flat face, painted hair and features, mitten hands, 17".
1880s – 1930s .. $4,500.00 – 5,500.00
1950s – 1980s .... $250.00 – 350.00

17" Presbyterian Rag Doll, 1950s. $350.00. **Photo courtesy of The Museum Doll Shop.**

RABERY & DELPHIEU

1856 – 1930 and later, Paris. Became part of S.F.B.J. in 1899. Some heads pressed (pre-1890) and some poured, purchased some heads from Francois Gaultier. Dolls listed are in good condition, appropriately dressed. Exceptional dolls may be more.

23" closed mouth child. $4,800.00. **Photo courtesy of Trish's Treasures Antique Dolls.**

Child
Closed mouth, bisque socket head, paperweight eyes, pierced ears, mohair wig, cork pate, French composition and wood jointed body
9" – 10".... $2,400.00 – 2,600.00
13" – 15" . $3,500.00 – 4,000.00
20" – 24".. $4,000.00 – 5,000.00
Open mouth, row of upper teeth
18" – 21".. $1,600.00 – 1,800.00
24" – 26".. $1,850.00 – 2,300.00

RAGGEDY ANN & ANDY

1915 to present. Rag doll designed by

15" Beloved Belindy by Georgene Novelties. $1,600.00. **Photo courtesy of McMasters Harris Auction Co.**

Johnny Gruelle in 1915, made by various companies. Ann wears dress with apron, Andy, shirt and pants with matching hat

P.J. Volland, 1918 – 1934, early dolls marked "Patented Sept. 7, 1915," all-cloth, tin or wooden button eyes, painted features, some have sewn knee or arm joints, sparse brown or auburn yarn hair, oversize hands, feet turned outward. Dolls listed are in clean un-faded condition, appropriately dressed.

Raggedy Ann and Andy, 15" – 18"

Painted face....... $2,800.00 – 3,000.00

Printed face .... $1,700.00 – 2,100.00

Beloved Belindy, 1926 – 1930 painted face, 1931 – 1934 print face

    15"........... $3,000.00 – 3,500.00

Pirate Chieftain and other characters

    18"........... $2,200.00 – 2,400.00

Exposition, 1935

Raggedy Ann, no eyelashes, no eyebrows, outline nose, no heart, satin label on hem of dress

    18"........... $5,000.00 – 6,000.00

Too few in database for reliable range.

Mollye Goldman, 1935 – 1937, marked on chest "Raggedy Ann and Andy Dolls Manufactured by Molly'es Doll Outfitters," nose outlined in black, red heart on chest,

reddish-orange hair, multicolored legs, blue feet, some have oilcloth faces

    15"................. $850.00 – 900.00

    17" – 21".. $1,000.00 – 1,350.00

Baby Ann

    14"................. $700.00 – 800.00

Georgene Novelties, 1938 – 1962, Ann has orange hair and a top knot, six different mouth styles, early ones had tin eyes, later ones had plastic, six different noses, seams in middle of legs and arms to represent knees and elbows, feet turn forward, red and white striped legs, all have hearts that say "I love you" printed on chest, tag sewn to left side seam, several variations, all say "Georgene Novelties, Inc."

Raggedy Ann or Andy, 1930s – 1960s

Nose outlined with black, 1938 – 1944

    15" – 17"........ $650.00 – 800.00

    19" – 21"..... $900.00 – 1,100.00

Awake/Asleep, 1940s

    Nose outlined black,

    14"................. $650.00 – 850.00

    Plain nose, pair

    14"................. $800.00 – 900.00

14" Georgene Novelties Awake/Asleep Raggedy Ann. $700.00. **Photo courtesy of The Museum Doll Shop.**

Asleep side of Georgene Ann, outlined nose. **Photo courtesy of The Museum Doll Shop.**

Long nose face, 1944 – 1946
19".......... $1,000.00 – 1,200.00
Curved nose edges, 1946 on
15" – 19"........ $225.00 – 325.00
23" .... $500.00 – 600.00
Beloved Belindy, 1940 – 1944
14" – 18".. $1,400.00 – 1,900.00
Knickerbocker, 1962 – 1982, printed features, hair color change from orange to red, there were five mouth and five eyelash variations, tags were located on clothing back or pants seam
Raggedy Ann or Andy
1964, cloud box
15"................. $200.00 – 275.00
Later examples
6"....................... $25.00 – 40.00
15".................. $85.00 – 110.00
19"................ $120.00 – 195.00
30" – 36"........ $200.00 – 275.00
Musical Ann
15"................. $100.00 – 150.00
Raggedy Ann Talking, 1972
19"................. $200.00 – 250.00
Beloved Belindy, ca. 1965
15".............. $900.00 – 1,000.00

Camel with Wrinkled Knees
15"................ $275.00 – 350.00
Nasco/Bobbs-Merrill, 1972, cloth head, hard plastic doll body, printed features, apron marked "Raggedy Ann"
24"................ $125.00 – 150.00
Bobbs-Merrill Co., 1974, ventriloquist dummy, hard plastic head, hands, foam body, printed face
30"................ $125.00 – 175.00
Applause Toy Company, 1981 – present, owned by Hasbro which also markets Raggedy Ann through its Playskool line
8"...................... $10.00 – 15.00
17"..................... $30.00 – 35.00
48"................ $100.00 – 125.00
Limited Editions, Applause marketed as part of their Dakin line
75th anniversary Ann or Andy, 1992
19"..................... $75.00 – 85.00
Molly-E Raggedy Ann, 1993
18"..................... $40.00 – 50.00

17" Knickerbocker Raggedy Andy. $100.00. **Photo courtesy of The Museum Doll Shop.**

Georgene re-issues, 1996

15".................... $30.00 – 40.00

Ann or Andy, 1994

13".................... $80.00 – 90.00

US Patent Ann, 1995

17".................... $65.00 – 85.00

Stamp Ann, 1997

17".................... $45.00 – 55.00

R. John Wright, present, molded felt doll, secondary market values, dolls still available retail

Ann or Andy

17".............. $650.00 – $900.00

Ann, Andy, and the Camel with the Wrinkled Knees .... $1,800.00 – 2,000.00

JESSIE MCCUTCHEON RALEIGH

1916 – 1920, Chicago, Illinois. McCutcheon was a businesswoman who developed a line of dolls. These were distributed by Butler Brothers and perhaps others. She produced dolls of cloth and composition.

Shoebutton Sue, flat face, painted spit curls, mitten hands, sewn on red shoes, shown in 1921 Sears catalog

15"..............................$1,900.00

Too few in database for reliable range.

Baby, composition head on composition body

12"................. $350.00 – 450.00

18"................. $475.00 – 600.00

Child

Composition head on composition body, wigged

11"................. $425.00 – 500.00

13"................. $525.00 – 575.00

18"................. $775.00 – 975.00

Molded hair

11" – 13"........ $600.00 – 650.00

Composition head on cloth body with composition lower arms and legs

22" – 24" .... $325.00 – 400.00

RAYNAL

1922 – 1930 on, Paris. Edouard Raynal made dolls of felt, cloth, or with celluloid heads with widely spaced eyebrows. Dressed, some resemble Lenci, except fingers were together or their hands were of celluloid, marked "Raynal" on soles of shoes and/or pendant

Cloth, 1922, molded head, cloth body, sometimes celluloid hands

14" – 16"........ $600.00 – 800.00

17" – 22".. $1,600.00 – 2,200.00

Celluloid, 1936, then Rhodoid

Baby

18" – 24"........ $575.00 – 675.00

Vinyl, 1960s – 1970s

Margareth

14" .... $50.00 – 60.00

THEODOR RECKNAGEL

1886 – 1930, Alexandrienthal, Coburg, Germany. Made bisque and composition doll heads of varying quality, incised or raised mark, wigged or molded hair, glass or painted eyes, open or closed mouth, flange neck or socket head. Dolls listed are in good condition, appropriately dressed.

Baby

Mold 121, 126, 1924, bent-limb baby body, painted or glass eyes

6" – 7"............ $200.00 – 250.00

9½" mold 57 by Theodor Recknagel. $925.00. **Photo courtesy of McMasters Harris Auction Co.**

8" – 9"............ $275.00 – 300.00

Bonnet head baby, Mold 22, 23, 28, 44: See bonnet head section.

Oriental baby, solid-dome bisque socket head, sleep eyes, closed mouth five-piece yellow tinted body

11".......................... $2,300.00*

Mold 137, Newborn, ca. 1925, flange neck, sleep eyes, closed mouth, cloth body, boxed

13".............................. $545.00*

Child

Dolly face, 1890s – 1914

Mold 1907, 1909, 1914, open mouth, glass eyes

7" – 9".............. $75.00 – 100.00
10" – 12"........ $100.00 – 150.00
15" – 18"........ $175.00 – 225.00
22" – 24" .... $275.00 – 350.00

Character face, ca. 1910+, may have crossed hammer mark

7" – 8"............ $300.00 – 350.00
12" – 14"........ $675.00 – 750.00

Mold 57, open/closed mouth with teeth, molded hair

9" – 10".......... $875.00 – 975.00

Mold 58, open/closed mouth with teeth, molded hair with molded ribbon and three flowers

7"................... $300.00 – 325.00

Mold 31, 32, Max and Moritz

8"............$625.00 – 675.00 each

Googly molds 43, 45, 46, 50, no mold number: See googly section.

REGIONAL DRESS DOLLS

7" mold 58. $300.00. **Photo courtesy of The Museum Doll Shop.**

9" German bisque doll in Scottish costume. $175.00. **Photo courtesy of The Museum Doll Shop.**

5" Irish man by Jay. $20.00. **Doll courtesy of Elaine Holda.**

Bisque, German
 10" – 13"....... $200.00 – 340.00
Painted bisque
 4"........................ $45.00 – 65.00
 10" .... $95.00 – 150.00
Celluloid
 8"........................ $40.00 – 50.00
 15"................. $100.00 – 125.00
Cloth
 8".................. $100.00 – 155.00
 13"................. $125.00 – 175.00

9" Skookum dolls with plastic feet. $70.00. **Doll courtesy of Elaine Holda.**

This category describes dolls costumed in regional dress to show different nationalities, facial characteristics, or cultural background. Examples are dolls in regional costumes that are commonly sold as souvenirs to tourists. These dolls became popular about 1875 and continue to be made today. A well-made beautiful doll with accessories or wardrobe may be more.

Russian, 1920 on, all-cloth, molded and painted stockinette head, hands, in regional costumes
 7"........................ $55.00 – 70.00
 15"................. $125.00 – 150.00
 18"................. $160.00 – 180.00
Composition Child
 8"................... $150.00 – 185.00
 13"................. $200.00 – 250.00
Walker in Dutch costume, post-WWII era
 22" .... $150.00 – 175.00
Jay Dolls, Dublin, Ireland, molded heads, cloth wrapped bodies
 5"........................ $14.00 – 28.00
 11"...................... $40.00 – 65.00

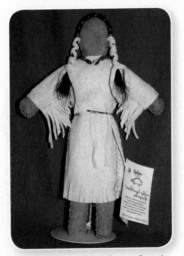

9" Metis Nation doll, Alberta, Canada, late twentieth century. $100.00. **Doll courtesy of Elaine Holda.**

7¼" Polish wooden doll.
$5.00. Photo courtesy of The
Museum Doll Shop.

Native American Indian, cloth, leather, natural fibers, etc, nineteenth and early twentieth centuries

8".................. $175.00 – 225.00
13"................. $225.00 – 300.00
23"................. $300.00 – 350.00

Seminole, woven fiber

4½" – 6"............. $28.00 – 35.00

Skookum, 1913 on, designed by Mary McAboy, painted features, with side-glancing eyes, mohair wigs, cloth figure wrapped in Indian blanket, with folds representing arms, wooden feet, later plastic, label on bottom of foot, box marked "Skookum Bully Good"

6" – 9"................ $65.00 – 90.00
10 – 12"......... $200.00 – 300.00
14" – 16"........ $325.00 – 425.00
18" – 20"........ $550.00 – 700.00
27" – 33".. $1,000.00 – 1,350.00

Hard Plastic, regional dress, unmarked or unknown maker

7"......................... $8.00 – 15.00
12"..................... $20.00 – 30.00

Baitz, Austria, 1970s, painted hard plastic, painted side-glancing eyes, open "o" mouth, excellent quality, tagged and dressed in regional dress

8½" – 9½".......... $45.00 – 55.00

Vinyl

6"........................ $20.00 – 25.00
12"..................... $40.00 – 45.00

Wood

Polish, painted features, 1930s on

7"........................... $4.00 – 6.00

RELIABLE TOY CO.

1920 on, Toronto, Canada. Made composition, hard plastic and vinyl dolls.

Composition, all-composition or composition shoulder head and arms on cloth body, some with composition legs. Dolls listed are in good condition, appropriately dressed.

Baby, 1930s

20"................. $200.00 – 250.00

Baby Precious, 1947, Mama-style doll, sleep eyes, mohair wig

20"................. $175.00 – 225.00

Barbara Scott Ice Skating Doll

15" .... $400.00 – 475.00

Her Highness

15"................. $275.00 – 325.00

Hiawatha or Indian child

10½"................. $45.00 – 60.00
13"................. $100.00 – 135.00
16"................. $155.00 – 185.00

Military Man

14"................. $175.00 – 225.00

Mountie

17"................. $300.00 – 350.00

Scottish child

14".................. $75.00 – 100.00
17"................. $150.00 – 165.00

Shirley Temple

18" – 22".. $1,000.00 – 1,200.00

Toddler

13"................. $150.00 – 200.00

Hard Plastic

Baby, 1958, sleep eyes, open mouth
    8" .... $40.00 – 50.00
Indian child, all hard plastic
    8" .... $20.00 – 30.00
Suzy Steps, walker, 1950, Canadian version of Ideal's Saucy Walker
    19" .... $40.00 – 50.00
Toni, P-90
    14" .... $300.00 – 350.00

Vinyl

Margaret, 1955, vinyl head, vinyl-flex body, rooted hair
    19" .... $30.00 – 40.00
Suzie, walker
    9" .... $15.00 – 20.00
Tammy, Canadian version of Ideal's Tammy
    12" .... $65.00 – 80.00

REMCO INDUSTRIES

1959 – 1974, Harrison, New Jersey. One of the first companies to market with television ads. Dolls listed are in good condition with original clothing and accessories, allow more for MIB.

Addams Family, 1964
Lurch
    5½" .... $45.00 – 55.00
Morticia
    4¾" .... $100.00 – 128.00
Uncle Fester
    4½" .... $40.00 – 50.00
Baby Crawl-Along, 1967
    20" .... $15.00 – 20.00
Baby Glad 'N Sad, 1967, vinyl and hard plastic, rooted blond hair, painted blue eyes
    14" .... $12.00 – 18.00
Baby Grow a Tooth, 1968, vinyl and hard plastic, rooted hair, blue sleep eyes, open/closed mouth, one tooth, grows her own tooth, battery operated

    15" .... $18.00 – 22.00
Black
    14" .... $20.00 – 25.00
Baby Know It All, 1969
    17" .... $15.00 – 20.00
Baby Laugh A Lot, 1970, rooted long hair, painted eyes, open/closed mouth, teeth, vinyl head, hands, plush body, push button, she laughs, battery operated
    16" .... $18.00 – 22.00
Baby Stroll A Long, 1966
    15" .... $10.00 – 15.00
Beatles, 1964, vinyl and plastic, Paul McCartney, Ringo Starr, George Harrison, and John Lennon, Paul 4⅞", all others 4½" with guitars bearing their names
Set of 4 .... $600.00 – 700.00
Individual Beatles ..... $100.00 – 120.00
Dave Clark Five, 1964, set of five musical group, vinyl heads, rigid plastic bodies
Set .... $60.00 – 65.00
Dave Clark
    5" .... $10.00 – 15.00
Other band members have name attached to leg
    3" .... $6.00 – 10.00
Finger Dings, 1969 on, finger puppets, vinyl head
    6" .... $15.00 – 20.00
Growing Sally, 1968, doll "grows" ¾", has extra clothes and additional wig
    6" .... $20.00 – 30.00
Black .... $30.00 – 40.00
Heidi and friends, 1967, in plastic case, rooted hair, painted side-glancing eyes, open/closed mouth, all-vinyl, press button and dolls wave
Heidi
    5½" .... $40.00 – 50.00
Herby
    4½" .... $25.00 – 35.00
Jan, Oriental

5½".................... $35.00 – 45.00
Pip
5½".................... $35.00 – 45.00
Winking Heidi, 1968
5½".................... $20.00 – 30.00
Hildy
4½"................... $30.00 – 40.00
Jeannie, I Dream of
6"...................... $45.00 – 55.00
Plastic Bottle Playset, 6", Jeannie doll and
accessories............. $115.00 – 130.00
Jumpsy, 1970, vinyl and hard plastic, jumps
rope, rooted blond hair, painted blue eyes,
closed mouth, molded-on shoes and socks
14".................... $30.00 – 35.00
Black
14".................... $35.00 – 40.00
Laurie Partridge, 1973
19"................. $120.00 – 140.00
L.B.J., 1964
5½".................... $20.00 – 25.00
Littlechap Family, 1963+, vinyl head, arms,
jointed hips, shoulders, neck, black molded
and painted hair, black eyes, box
Set of four boxed together
$400.00 – 450.00
Dr. John Littlechap
14½"................. $60.00 – 75.00
Judy Littlechap
12"..................... $50.00 – 65.00
Libby Littlechap
10½"................. $50.00 – 60.00
Lisa Littlechap
13½"................. $40.00 – 50.00
Littlechap Accessories
Dr. John's Office .... $275.00 – 325.00
Bedroom .... $75.00 – 110.00
Family room................ $45.00 – 75.00
Dr. John Littlechap's outfits
Golf outfit ....$30.00 MIP
Medical ....$65.00 MIP
Suit ....$50.00 MIP

10½" Libby Littlechap by Remco.
$50.00. **Photo courtesy of The Museum
Doll Shop.**

Tuxedo ....$70.00 MIP
Lisa's outfits
Evening dress.....................$90.00 MIP
Coat, fur trim ....$50.00 MIP
Libby's, Judy's outfits
Jeans/sweater....................$30.00 MIP
Dance dress.......................$45.00 MIP
Mimi, 1973, vinyl and hard plastic, battery
operated singer, rooted long blond hair,
painted blue eyes, open/closed mouth,
record player in body, sings I'd Like to Teach
the World to Sing, song used for Coca-Cola®
commercial, sings in different languages
19"..................... $50.00 – 60.00
Black
19" .... $75.00 – 85.00
The Monkees, musical group
$25.00 – 35.00 each
Munsters
Herman, pull string talker
20"................. $200.00 – 275.00
Lily #1822, 1964, vinyl, one-piece body,
played by Yvonne DeCarl
4¾"................. $90.00 – 105.00
Grandpa, #1821, 1964, vinyl head, one-
piece plastic body
4¾"................. $95.00 – 110.00
Orphan Annie, 1967

15".................. $95.00 – 120.00
Polly Puff, 1970, vinyl, came with inflatable furniture
12"..................... $30.00 – 35.00
Sweet April, 1971, vinyl
5½"................... $40.00 – 45.00
Black
5½"................... $45.00 – 50.00
Tippy Tumbles, 1968, vinyl, rooted red hair, stationary blue eyes, does somersaults, batteries in pocketbook
16"..................... $65.00 – 75.00
Tumbling Tomboy, 1969, rooted blond braids, closed smiling mouth, vinyl and hard plastic, battery operated
17"..................... $30.00 – 45.00

RICHWOOD TOYS INC.

1950s – 1960s, Annapolis, Maryland. Produced hard plastic dolls.
Sandra Sue, 1940s, 1950s, hard plastic, walker, head does not turn, slim body, saran wigs, sleep eyes, some with high-heeled feet, only marks are number under arm or leg, all prices reflect outfits with original socks, shoes, panties, and accessories, 8". Dolls listed are in good condition with appropriate clothing and tags, naked, played with dolls will bring one-fourth to one-third the value listed.
Flat feet
In camisole, slip, panties, shoes, and socks
$150.00 – 175.00
In school dress.......... $150.00 – 200.00
In party/Sunday dress
$175.00 – 225.00
Special coat, hat, and dress, limited editions, Brides, Heidi, Little Women, Majorette
$200.00 – 250.00

8" hard plastic Sandra Sue by Richwood Toy Co. $150.00. **Photo courtesy of American Beauty Dolls.**

Sport or play clothes .. $100.00 – 150.00
Twin Sandra Sues, MIB $395.00
Too few in database for reliable range.
High-heeled feet
Camisole, slip, panties, shoes, socks
$95.00 – 125.00
In school dress.......... $100.00 – 150.00
In party/Sunday dress ..$125.00 – 175.00
Special coat, hat and dress, limited editions, Brides, Heidi, Little Women, Majorette
$125.00 – 175.00
Sport or play clothes ... $95.00 – 125.00
Twin Sandra Sues, MIB $350.00
Too few in database for reliable range.
Sandra Sue Outfits, mint, including all accessories
School dress .... $10.00 – 15.00
Party dress.................. $20.00 – 25.00
Specials .... $35.00 – 50.00
Sport sets .... $20.00 – 25.00
Cindy Lou, 14", hard plastic, jointed dolls were purchased in bulk from New York distributor, fitted with double-stitched wigs by Richwood
In camisole, slip, panties, shoes, and socks
$200.00 – 250.00
In school dress.......... $200.00 – 250.00

In party dress .... $225.00 – 250.00
In special outfits .... $225.00 – 275.00
In sports outfits .... $200.00 – 250.00
Cindy Lou Outfits, mint, including all accessories
School dress .... $35.00 – 45.00
Party dress .... $45.00 – 50.00
Special outfit .... $50.00 – 60.00
Sports clothes .... $35.00 – 45.00

GRACE CORRY ROCKWELL

1926 – 1928, USA. Artist who designed dolls. Her bisque doll heads were made in Germany and were distributed by Borgfeldt. Her composition headed dolls were made by Averill.

Pretty Peggy, bisque socket head, open mouth
   12" – 14" ..$3,000.00 – 5,000.00
   16" – 19" .. $4,900.00 – 5,600.00
Little Sister & Brother, composition, smiling mouth, molded hair
   14" .... $350.00 – 450.00

ROHMER

1857 – 1880, Paris, France. Mme. Rohmer held patents for doll bodies, made dolls of various materials. Dolls listed are in good condition, appropriately dressed, may be much more for exceptional dolls.

Poupée (so-called Fashion-type), bisque or china glazed shoulder or swivel head on shoulder plate, closed mouth, kid body with green oval stamp, bisque or wood lower arms

Glass eyes
   13" – 16".. $6,000.00 – 6,500.00
   17" – 19" ..$8,000.00 – 12,000.00
Painted eyes
   13" – 18".. $4,000.00 – 5,000.00

ROLDAN

1960s – 1970s, Barcelona. Spain. Roldan characters are similar to Klumpe figures in many respects. They are made of felt over a wire armature with painted mask faces. Like Klumpe, Roldan figures represent professionals, hobbyists, dancers, historical characters, and contemporary males and females performing a wide variety of tasks. Some, but not all Roldans, were imported by Rosenfeld Imports and Leora Dolores of Hollywood. Figures originally came with two sewn-on identifying cardboard tags. Roldan characters most commonly found are doctors, Spanish dancers, and bull fighters. Roldan characters tend to have somewhat smaller heads, longer necks, and more defined facial features than Klumpe. Dolls listed are all in good, clean, un-faded condition, allow more for elaborate figure with many accessories.
   9" – 11" .... $95.00 – 150.00

10" can-can dancer by Roldan. $160.00.
Photo courtesy of My Dolly Dearest.

GERTRUDE F. ROLLINSON

1916 – 1929, Holyoke, Massachusetts.

Designed and made cloth dolls with molded faces, painted over the cloth on head and limbs, treated to be washable. Painted hair or wigged, some closed mouth, others had open/closed mouths with painted teeth. Some dolls closely resemble the dolls of the Chase Company while others are heavily sanded between coats of paint giving them a look of composition. Rollinson had her dolls made by the Utley Co. (later called New England Doll Company), and distributed by G. Borgfeldt, L. Wolfe, and Strobel & Wilken.

Chase-look doll with painted hair or wig
13" – 17"..... $900.00 – 1,400.00
22" – 26".. $1,300.00 – 1,500.00
Composition look doll with painted hair or wig
22" – 24".. $1,500.00 – 2,000.00

17" painted hair Rollinson doll. $1,100.00. **Photo courtesy of The Museum Doll Shop.**

RUBBER

1860s on, various European and American makers produced rubber dolls.
Goodyear Doll, molded shoulder head doll in the style of the china and papier-mâché dolls of the era.
10" – 18"..... $600.00 – 1,000.00
20" – 28".. $1,100.00 – 1,600.00
American rubber doll, 1920s on
Baby
12" – 15"............ $65.00 – 75.00

SANTONS

Santons (little Saints) France, 1930 on. Character figures depicting elderly peasants. Earthenware heads, hand, and legs on wire armature bodies. Dressed in regional or occupational costume.
7" – 8"................ $30.00 – 45.00
10" – 12" .... $50.00 – 100.00

SASHA

1945 – 2001. Sasha dolls were created by Swiss artist, Sasha Morgenthaler, who handcrafted 20" children and 13" babies in Zurich, Switzerland, from the 1940s until her death in 1975. Her handmade studio dolls had cloth or molded bodies, five different head molds, and were hand painted by Sasha Morgenthaler. To make her dolls affordable as children's playthings, she licensed Götz Puppenfabric (1964 – 1970 and 1995 – 2001) in Germany and Frido Trendon Ltd. (1965 – 1986) in England to manufacture 16" Sasha dolls in series. The manufactured dolls were made of rigid vinyl with painted features.

Price range reflects rarity, condition, and completeness of doll, outfit, and packaging, and varies with geographic location. Dolls listed are in good condition, with original clothing. Allow more for mint-in-box.
Original Studio Sasha Doll, ca. 1940s – 1974, made by Sasha Morgenthaler in Switzerland, some are signed on soles of feet, have wrist tags, or wear labeled clothing
20"......... $9,000.00 – 13,000.00
Götz Sasha Doll, 1964 – 1970, Germany, girls or boys, two face molds, marked "Sasha Series" in circle on neck and in three-circle logo on back, three different boxes were

Gregor by Frido-Trendon Ltd., 1972 – 1975. $250.00. **Doll courtesy of Pat Buckley.**

used, identified by wrist tag and/or booklet

16".......... $1,000.00 – 1,500.00

Frido-Trendon Ltd., 1965 – 1986, England, unmarked on body, wore wrist tags and current catalogs were packed with doll

Child

1965 – 1968, packaged in wide box

16"................ $500.00 – 600.00

1969 – 1972, packaged in crayon tubes

16"................ $650.00 – 800.00

Sexed Baby, 1970 – 1978, cradle, styrofoam cradles package or straw box and box, white or black.......... $160.00 – 300.00

Unsexed Baby, 1978 – 1986, packaged in styrofoam wide or narrow cradles or straw basket and box........ $100.00 – 150.00

Child

1973 – 1975, packaged in shoe box style box

16"................ $200.00 – 300.00

Black child........ $300.00 – 325.00

1975 – 1980, white, shoe box style box

16"................ $175.00 – 225.00

Black child........ $200.00 – 225.00

1980 – 1986, white, packaged in photo box with flaps................ $150.00 – 200.00

#1 Sasha Anniversary doll

16"................ $175.00 – 300.00

1986, Sasha "Sari" 117S, black hair, estimated only 400 produced before English factory closed January 1986

16"................ $700.00 – 800.00

130E Sasha "Wintersport," 1986, blond hair

16"................ $400.00 – 600.00

Limited Editions

Made by Trendon Sasha Ltd. in England, packaged in box with outer sleeve picturing individual doll, limited edition Sasha dolls marked on neck with date and number, number on certificate matches number on doll's neck

1981 "Velvet," girl, light brown wig, 5,000 production planned .. $400.00 – 450.00

1982 "Pintucks" girl, blond wig, 6,000 production planned....... $450.00 – 600.00

1983 "Kiltie" girl, red wig, 4,000 production planned.................. $400.00 – 500.00

1984 "Harlequin" girl, rooted blond hair, 4,000 production planned

$300.00 – 375.00

1985 "Prince Gregor" boy, light brown wig, 4,000 production planned

$275.00 – 325.00

1986 "Princess Sasha" girl, blond wig, 3,500

Sasha Kiltie, 1983. $450.00. **Photo courtesy of McMasters Harris Auction Co.**

production planned, but only 350 were made............... $1,000.00 – 1,500.00

Götz Dolls Inc., 1995+, Germany, they received the license in September 1994; dolls introduced in 1995

Child, 1995 – 1996, marked "Götz Sasha" on neck and "Sasha Series" in three circle logo on back, about 1,500 of the dolls produced in 1995 did not have mold mark on back, earliest dolls packaged in generic Götz box, currently in tube, wear wrist tag, Götz tag, and have mini-catalog.

16½"............... $175.00 – 300.00

Baby, 1996, uunmarked on neck, marked "Sasha Series" in three circle logo on back, first babies were packaged in generic Götz box or large tube, currently packaged in small "Baby" tube, wears Sasha wrist tag, Götz booklet and current catalog.

12"................. $125.00 – 150.00

BRUNO SCHMIDT

1898 – 1930, Waltershausen, Germany. Made bisque, composition, and wooden head dolls, after 1913 also celluloid.

12" Bruno Schmidt mold 2095. $395.00. **Photo courtesy of McMasters Harris Auction Co.**

Acquired Bähr & Pröschild in 1918. Often used a heart-shaped tag. Dolls listed are in good condition, appropriately dressed.

Character Baby, bisque socket head, glass eyes, composition bent leg body

Mold 2092, 2094, 2095, 2097 ca. 1920, Mold 2097, ca. 1911

13" – 15"........ $425.00 – 525.00

18" – 20"........ $675.00 – 800.00

33"................. $800.00 – 900.00

Mold 2097, toddler

15"................. $850.00 – 900.00

21"........... $1,200.00 – 1,400.00

34"........... $1,700.00 – 1,800.00

Child, BSW, no mold numbers, bisque socket head, jointed body, sleep eyes, open mouth, add $50.00 more for flirty eyes

14"................. $350.00 – 450.00

18" – 20"........ $525.00 – 600.00

22" – 24"........ $425.00 – 525.00

Character

Oriental, mold 500, ca. 1905, yellow tint bisque socket head, glass eyes, open mouth, teeth, pierced ears, wig, yellow tint composition jointed body

11" – 14".. $1,375.00 – 1,600.00

18"........... $1,800.00 – 2,000.00

Mold 529, "2052," ca. 1912, painted eyes, closed mouth

20"........... $2,800.00 – 4,000.00

Mold 539, "2023," ca. 1912, solid dome or with wig, painted eyes, closed mouth

24"........... $3,000.00 – 3,200.00

Mold 537, "2033" (Wendy), ca. 1912, sleep eyes, closed mouth

11" – 13"..$15,000.00 – 18,000.00

15" – 17"..$23,000.00 – 25,000.00

20"....... $32,000.00 – 34,000.00

Mold 2048, ca. 1912, Tommy Tucker, 2094, 2096, ca. 1920, solid dome, molded and painted hair or wig, sleep eyes, open or closed mouth, composition jointed body

Open mouth

12" – 14"..	$1,000.00 – 1,300.00
18" – 20"..	$1,600.00 – 1,900.00
26" – 28"..	$1,800.00 – 2,100.00

Mold 2072, ca. 1920, sleep eyes, closed mouth

16"..........	$2,200.00 – 2,450.00
19"..........	$2,500.00 – 2,900.00

FRANZ SCHMIDT

1890 – 1937, Georgenthal, Thüringia, Germany. Made, produced, and exported dolls with bisque, composition, wood, and celluloid heads. Used bisque heads made by Simon & Halbig. Heads marked "S & C," mold 269, 293, 927, 1180, 1310. Heads marked "F.S. & C," mold 1250, 1253, 1259, 1262, 1263, 1266, 1267, 1270, 1271, 1272, 1274, 1293, 1295, 1296, 1297, 1298, 1310. Walkers: mold 1071, 1310. Dolls listed are in good condition, appropriately dressed.

Baby, bisque head, solid dome or cut out for wig, bent-leg body, sleep or set eyes, open mouth, some pierced

16" mold 1295 on toddler body.
$975.00. **Photo courtesy of McMasters Harris Auction Co.**

16" 1286 character.
$12,000.00. **Photo courtesy of Turn of the Century Antiques.**

nostrils, add more for flirty eyes
Mold 1271, 1272, 1295, 1296, 1297, 1310

10" – 12"........	$625.00 – 700.00
13" – 14"........	$525.00 – 575.00
18" – 20"........	$600.00 – 700.00
22" – 24"........	$750.00 – 825.00

Toddler

10" – 12".........	$850.00 – 97500
16" – 20".....	$975.00 – 1,100.00
22" – 24"..	$1,600.00 – 2,000.00

Character Face

Mold 1237, baby, open mouth, molded hair, breather, glass eyes

13"..........	$1,200.00 – 1,300.00

Mold 1266, 1267, ca. 1912, marked "F.S. & Co.," solid dome, painted eyes, closed mouth

14"..........	$2,750.00 – 2,850.00
19" – 23"..	$3,700.00 – 4,000.00

Mold 1270, ca. 1910, solid dome, painted eyes, open-closed mouth

9"...................	$575.00 – 650.00
13"..........	$1,500.00 – 1,800.00

With two faces

16"..........	$1,275.00 – 1,450.00

Child

Dolly face, five-piece body, Mold 269, ca. 1890s, Mold 293, ca. 1900, marked "S & C," open mouth, glass eyes

    5" – 7"............ $300.00 – 375.00
    10" – 12"........ $475.00 – 550.00
    19" – 23"........ $550.00 – 650.00
    27" – 29".. $1,000.00 – 1,100.00

Character

Mold 1259, ca. 1912, marked "F.S. & Co." character, sleep eyes, pierced nostrils, open mouth

    15"................ $400.00 – 500.00

Mold 1262, 1263, ca. 1910, marked "F.S. & Co.," painted eyes, closed mouth

    14"........... $5,400.00 – 5,800.00

Too few in database for reliable range.

Mold 1272, ca. 1910, marked "F.S. & Co.," solid dome or wig, sleep eyes, pierced nostrils, open mouth

    9½".............. $850.00 – 950.00

Mold 1286, ca. 1915, marked "F.S. & Co. 1286/40 Germany," molded hair side-glancing glass eyes

    14" – 16"..$8,000.00 – 12,000.00

SCHMITT & FILS

1854 – 1891, Noget-sur-Marne & Paris, France. Made bisque and wax-over-bisque or wax-over-composition dolls. Heads were pressed. Used neck socket like on later composition Patsy dolls. Dolls listed are in good condition, appropriately dressed; more for exceptional doll with wardrobe or other attributes.

Child, pressed bisque head, closed mouth, glass eyes, pierced ears, mohair or human hair wig, French composition and wood eight ball-jointed body with straight wrists

Early round face

    12" – 14"..$14,000.00 – 16,000.00
    15" – 16"..$16,000.00 – 22,000.00
    18" – 24"..$24,500.00 – 28,000.00

Long face modeling

    16" – 18"..$23,000.00 – 29,000.00
    24" – 26"..$32,000.00 – 38,000.00

Wax over papier mâché, swivel head, cup and saucer type neck, glass eyes, closed mouth, eight ball-jointed body

    16" – 17".. $3,000.00 – 3,500.00

16" round face Schmitt. $22,000.00. **Photo courtesy of Richard Withington, Inc.**

23" marked with Schmitt shield. $30,000.00. **Photo courtesy of Richard Withington, Inc.**

SCHOENAU & HOFFMEISTER

11½" Schoenau & Hoffmeister Hanna on toddler body. $475.00. **Photo courtesy of McMasters Harris Auction Co.**

1901 – 1939, Burggrub, Bavaria. Had a porcelain factory, produced bisque heads for dolls, also supplied other manufacturers, including Bruckner, Dressel, Eckhardt, E. Knoch, and others. Dolls listed are in good condition, appropriately dressed. More for exceptional dolls.

Baby, bisque solid-dome or wigged socket head, sleep eyes, teeth, composition bent-leg body, closed mouth, newborn, solid dome, painted hair, cloth body, may have celluloid hands, add more for original outfit
Solid dome infant
    10" – 12"........ $400.00 – 500.00
    13" – 15"........ $600.00 – 700.00
Mold 169, 170 (Porzellanfabrik Burggrub), bent-limb body
    13" – 15"........ $250.00 – 300.00
    18" – 20"........ $375.00 – 450.00
    23" – 25"........ $475.00 – 550.00
Hanna, sleep eyes, open-closed mouth, bent-leg baby body, $100.00 more for toddler
    13" – 15"........ $450.00 – 500.00
    18" – 20"........ $675.00 – 775.00
    22" – 24"..... $850.00 – 1,150.00
Princess Elizabeth, 1929, socket head, sleep eyes, smiling open mouth, chubby leg toddler body
    16" – 17".. $2,000.00 – 2,200.00
    20" – 22".. $2,500.00 – 3,000.00
    25"........... $3,500.00 – 4,000.00
Child, dolly face, bisque socket head, open mouth with teeth, sleep eyes, composition ball-jointed body

24" mold 1909 dolly face doll. $575.00. **Photo courtesy of William Jenack Estate Appraisers and Auctioneers.**

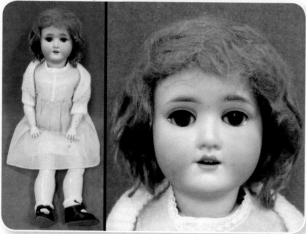

Mold 1906, 1909, 2500, 4000, 4600, 4700, 5500, 5700, 5800
  14" – 16"........ $300.00 – 400.00
  18" – 24"........ $400.00 – 600.00
  26" – 28"........ $400.00 – 650.00
Mold 914, ca. 1925, character
  24" – 25"........ $250.00 – 350.00
  27" – 28"........ $350.00 – 400.00
Mold 4900, ca. 1905, Oriental, dolly-face
  10"................. $400.00 – 475.00
Shoulder head dolly, open mouth with teeth, sleep eyes, kid body
Mold 1800
  14"................. $225.00 – 275.00

A. SCHOENHUT & CO.

1872 – 1930 on, Philadelphia, Pennsylvania. Made all-wood dolls, using spring joints, had holes in bottoms of feet to fit into stands. Later made elastic strung with cloth bodies. Carved or molded and painted hair or wigged, intaglio or sleep eyes, open or closed

19" Schoenhut girl. $900.00. **Photo courtesy of The Museum Doll Shop.**

mouth. Later made composition dolls. Dolls listed are in good condition, appropriately dressed; more for exceptional doll.

Babies
Graziano Infants, circa May 1911 – 1912
Schnickel-Fritz, carved hair, open-closed grinning mouth, four teeth, large ears, toddler
  15"........... $3,600.00 – 4,000.00
Tootsie Wootsie, carved hair, open-closed mouth, two upper teeth, large ears on child body
  15"........... $3,800.00 – 4,200.00
Too few in database for reliable range.
Model 107, 107W (walker), 108, 108W (walker), 1913 – 1926, 109W, 110W, 1921 – 1923
Baby, nature (bent) limb
  13" – 15"........ $400.00 – 550.00
Toddler
  11" – 14"........ $600.00 – 675.00
  17"................. $400.00 – 600.00
  Elastic strung, 1924 – 1926
  14"................. $675.00 – 750.00
  Cloth body with crier
  14"................. $750.00 – 825.00
Bye-Lo Baby, "Grace S. Putnam" stamp, cloth body, closed mouth, sleep eyes
  13"............................. $2,400.00
Too few in database for reliable range.
Child
Salesman's cut-away sample child
  $3,400.00*
Graziano Period, 1911 – 1912, dolls may have heavily carved hair or wigs, painted intaglio eyes, outlined iris, all with wooden spring-jointed bodies and are 16" tall, designated with 16 before the model number, like "16/100"
Model 100, girl, carved hair, solemn face
Model 101, girl, carved hair, grinning, squinting eyes
Model 102, girl, carved hair, bun on top

Model 103, girl, carved hair, loose ringlets

Model 200, boy, carved hair, short curls

Model 201, boy, carved hair, based on K*R 114

Model 202, boy, carved hair, forelock

Model 203, boy, carved hair, grinning, some with comb marks

Model 300, girl, long curl wig, face of 102

Model 301, girl, bobbed wig with bangs, face of 300

Model 302, girl, wig, bases on K*R 101

Model 303, girl, short bob, no bangs, grinning, squinting eyes

Model 304, girl, wig in braids, ears stick out

Model 305, girl, snail braids, grinning, face of 303

Model 306, girl, wig, long curls, face of 304

Model 307, girl, short bob, no bangs, "dolly-type" smooth eye

Model 400, boy, short bob, K*R 101 face

Model 401, boy, side part bob, face of 300/301

Model 402, boy, side part bob, grin of 303

Model 403, boy, dimple in chin

Transition Period, 1911 – 1912, designs by Graziano and Leslie, dolls may no longer have outlined iris, some models have changed, dolls measure 16" – 17", now have a groove above knee for stockings

Model 100, girl, same, no iris outline

Model 101, girl, short carved hair, bob/bow, round eyes/smile

Model 102, girl, braids carved around head

Model 103, girl, heavy carved hair in front/fine braids in back

Model 104, girl, fine carved hair in front/fine braids in back

Model 200, boy, carved hair, same, no iris outline

Model 201, boy, carved hair, same, iris outline, stocking groove

Model 202, boy, carved hair, same, smoother

13" composition doll, c. 1924. $1,000.00. Photo courtesy of McMasters Harris Auction Co.

Model 203, boy, smiling boy, round eyes, no iris outline

Model 204, boy, carved hair brushed forward, serious face

Model 300, girl, long curl wig, dimple in chin

Model 301, girl, bob wig, face of 102

Model 302, girl, wig, same like K*R 101

Model 303, girl, wig, similar to 303G, smiling, short bob, no bangs

Model 304, girl, wig, braids, based on K*R

Model 305, girl, wig, braids, face of 303

Model 306, girl, long curl wig, same face as 304

Model 307, girl, smooth eyeball

Model 400, boy, same (like K*R 101)

Model 401, boy, like K*R 114 (304)

Model 402, boy, smiling, round eyes

Model 403, boy, same as 300 with side part bob

Model 404, boy, same as 301, side part bob

Classic Period, 1912 – 1923, some models discontinued, some sizes added, those marked with * were reissued in 1930

Model 101, girl, short carved hair bob, no iris outline

19" Manikin. $3,300.00. **Doll** from private collection.

1912 – 1923*, 14"
1911 – 1916, 16"
Model 102, girl, heavy carved hair in front, fine braids in back
1912 – 1923, 14"
1911 – 1923, 16"
1912 – 1916, 19" – 21"
Model 105, girl, short carved hair bob, carved ribbon around head
1912 – 1923, 14" – 16"
1912 – 1916, 19" – 21"
Model 106, girl, carved molded bonnet on short hair,
1912 – 1916, 14", 16", 19"
Model 203, 16" boy, same as transition
Model 204, 16" boy, same as transition*
Model 205, carved hair boy, covered ears
1912 – 1923, 14" – 16"
1912 – 1916, 19" – 21"
Model 206, 19" carved hair boy, covered ears
1912 – 1916
Model 207, 14" carved short curly hair boy
1912 – 1916
Model 300, 16" wigged girl, same as transition period

1911 – 1923
Model 301, 16" wigged girl, same as transition
1911 – 1924
Model 303, 16" wigged girl, same as transition 305
1911 – 1916
Model 307, 16" long curl wigged girl, smooth eye
1911 – 1916
Model 308, 14" girl, braided wig
1912 – 1916
1912 – 1924
19", bobbed hair
1917 – 1924
19" – 21", bob or curls
Model 309, 16", wigged girl, two teeth, long curls, bobbed hair, 1912 – 1913
19" – 21"
Model 310, wigged girl, same as 105 face, long curls, 1912 – 1916
14" – 16"
19" – 21"
Model 311, wigged girl, heart shape 106 face, bobbed wig, no bangs, 1912 – 1916
14" – 16"
1912 – 1913
19"
Model 312, 14", wigged girl, bobbed, 1912 – 1924, bobbed wig or curls, 1917 – 1924
Model 313, wigged girl, long curls, smooth eyeball, receding chin, 1912 – 1916
14" – 16"
19" – 21"
Model 314, 19", wigged girl, long curls, wide face, smooth eyeball, 1912 – 1916
19"
Model 315, 21", wigged girl, long curls, four teeth, triangular mouth, 1912 – 1916
Model 403, 16", wigged boy, same as transition, bobbed hair, bangs, 1911 – 1924

Model 404, 16", wigged boy, same as transition, 1911 – 1916

Model 405, boy, face of 308, bobbed wig, 1912 – 1924
    14"
    19"

Model 407, 19" – 21", wigged boy, face of 310 girl, 1912 – 1916

Carved hair, allow more for earlier examples and those in all original condition
    14" – 16".. $2,600.00 – 3,200.00
    19" – 21".. $2,400.00 – 2,900.00

Wigged, allow more for earlier examples and those in all original condition
    14"............. $750.00 – 1,000.00
    16"............. $800.00 – 1,000.00
    19" – 21".. $1,200.00 – 1,700.00

Miss Dolly

Model 316, open mouth, teeth, wigged girl, curls or bobbed wig, painted or decal eyes, all four sizes, circa 1915 – 1925
    15" – 21"........ $800.00 – 900.00

Model 317, sleep eyes, open mouth, teeth, wigged girl, long curls or bob, sleep eyes, four sizes, 1921 – 1928
    15" – 21"..... $900.00 – 1,100.00

Composition doll, 1924, molded curly hair, painted eyes, closed moth
    13"............. $900.00 – 1,000.00

Manikin

Model 175, man with slim body, ball-jointed waist, circa 1914 – 1918
    19" .... $3,000.00 – 3,500.00

Small dolls, such as circus figures, storybook and comic characters

Circus performers, rare figures may be much higher

Bisque head
    Bareback Lady Rider or Ringmaster, all original
    9".................. $600.00 – 650.00

Wood heads

8" comic character Moritz. $475.00. **Photo courtesy of Richard Withington, Inc.**

Clowns
    8".................. $250.00 – 300.00
    Lion Tamer
    8½"............... $350.00 – 450.00
    Ringmaster, Acrobat Gent, Lady Bareback Rider
    8".................. $250.00 – 325.00
    Animals, *some rare animals may be much higher
    Camel
    8"................................. $200.00
    Giraffe
    11"............................... $350.00
    Horse
    7"................................. $350.00
    Tiger
    7½"............................. $200.00

Cartoon Characters

Barney Google & Sparkplug, comic strip characters created by Billy De Beck
    7½" & 8" ..$850.00 – 950.00 pair

Maggie and Jiggs, from cartoon strip "Bringing up Father"
    7" – 9".....$425.00 – 475.00 each

Max and Moritz, carved figures, painted hair, carved shoes

    8"...........$500.00 – 550.00 each

Mary and her lamb............. $1,500.00*

Pinn Family, all wood, egg-shaped head, original costumes, names such as Bobby Pinn, Hattie Pinn, Ty Pinn, etc.

Mother, and four children

                $650.00 – 700.00

Individual Pinn dolls

    5" – 9" .... $75.00 – 150.00

Rolly-Dolly figures

    9" – 12"........... $350.00 – 850.00

Teddy Roosevelt

    8"................ $800.00 – 1,600.00

SCHUETZMEISTER & QUENDT

1889 – 1930 on, Boilstadt, Gotha, Thüringia. A porcelain factory that made and exported bisque doll heads, all-bisque dolls, and Nankeen dolls. Used initials "S & Q," mold 301 was sometimes incised "Jeannette." Dolls listed are in good condition, appropriately dressed.

Baby, character face, bisque socket head, sleep eyes, open mouth, bent-leg body

Mold 201, 204, 300, 301, ca. 1920

    10" – 12"........ $350.00 – 400.00

    14" – 17"........ $475.00 – 550.00

    19" – 22"........ $700.00 – 800.00

Mold 252, ca. 1920, character face, black baby

    15"................. $550.00 – 600.00

Child

Mold 101, 102, ca. 1900, dolly face

    16" – 17"........ $375.00 – 450.00

    19" – 22"........ $550.00 – 625.00

Mold 1376, ca. 1900, character face

    19"................. $475.00 – 550.00

S.F.B.J.

Société Francaise de Fabrication de Bébés & Jouets, 1899 – 1930+, Paris and Montreuil-sous-Bois. Competition with German manufacturers forced many French companies to join together including Bouchet, Fleischmann & Bloedel, Gaultier, Rabery & Delphieu, Bru, Jumeau, Pintel & Godchaux, Remignard and Wertheimer, and others. This alliance lasted until the 1950s. Fleischman owned controlling interest. See also Unis France. Dolls listed are in good condition, appropriately dressed; more for exceptional dolls.

Child, bisque head, glass eyes, open mouth, pierced ears, wig, composition jointed French body

Jumeau type, no mold number, open mouth

    13" – 15"..... $950.00 – 1,000.00

    20" – 22".. $1,250.00 – 1,450.00

    24" – 26".. $1,900.00 – 2,000.00

    28"........... $2,200.00 – 2,300.00

Mold 301

    6" – 8" on five-piece body

                $250.00 – 300.00

    8" – 10" .... $625.00 – 725.00

    12" – 14" .... $625.00 – 700.00

    18" – 20"........ $850.00 – 900.00

    22" – 24"........ $850.00 – 900.00

    26" – 28".. $1,100.00 – 1,500.00

Bleuette: See Bleuette section.

Kiss Thrower

    24"........... $1,650.00 – 1,750.00

Mold 60

    6" – 8"............ $325.00 – 400.00

    12" – 14"........ $450.00 – 500.00

    18" – 21"....... $650.00. – 750.00

    25" – 28"........ $600.00 – 800.00

Mold 301 or 60, papier-mâché head

    8" – 10".......... $150.00 – 200.00

    13" –16" .... $275.00 – 300.00

    18" – 22"........ $325.00 – 450.00

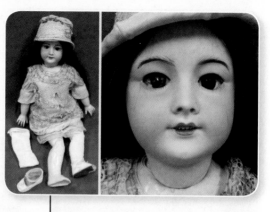

24" S.F.B.J mold 301. $900.00. Photo courtesy of William Jenack Estate Appraisers and Auctioneers.

Character Faces, bisque socket head, wigged or molded hair, set or sleep eyes, composition body, some with bent baby limb, toddler or child body, mold number 227, 235, and 236 may have flocked hair, add $100.00 for toddler body

Mold 226, glass eyes, closed mouth
 18" – 20".. $1,900.00 – 2,200.00
Mold 227, open mouth, teeth, glass eyes
 14"........... $1,900.00 – 2,000.00
 17"........... $2,500.00 – 2,800.00
 19" – 21".. $2,900.00 – 3,300.00
Mold 230, glass eyes, open mouth, teeth
 12" – 14"........ $650.00 – 700.00

 20" – 23"... $1,100.00 – 1,300.00
Mold 233, ca. 1912, crying mouth, glass eyes
 14" – 16".. $3,600.00 – 4,000.00
Mold 234
 18"........... $2,800.00 – 3,050.00
Mold 235, glass eyes, open-closed mouth
 14" – 15".. $1,400.00 – 1,600.00
 18" .... $1,700.00 – 1,800.00
Mold 236, glass eyes, laughing open/closed mouth
Baby
 12" – 13"........ $700.00 – 800.00
 15" – 17"..... $875.00 – 1,000.00
 20" – 22".. $1,100.00 – 1,200.00

18" mold 60. $575.00. Doll courtesy of Lucy DiTerlizzi.

11" mold 236. $900.00. Photo courtesy of The Museum Doll Shop.

26" mold 230. $2,200.00. **Photo courtesy of Aunt Mary's Antique Dolls.**

Toddler

13"..........	$1,000.00 – 1,200.00
15" – 18"..	$1,300.00 – 1,400.00

Mold 237, glass eyes, open-closed mouth
13" – 14"..	$2,700.00 – 2,900.00
16" – 17"...	$3600.00 – 3,900.00

Mold 238, small open mouth
18"..........	$2,200.00 – 2,400.00

Mold 239, ca. 1913, designed by Poulbot
13".......	$11,000.00 – 16,500.00

Mold 242, ca. 1910, nursing baby
13" – 15"..	$2,900.00 – 3,000.00

Mold 247, glass eyes, open-closed mouth
13"..........	$1,900.00 – 2,100.00
16"..........	$2,000.00 – 2,200.00
20"..........	$2,700.00 – 2,900.00

Mold 248, ca. 1912, glass eyes, lowered eyebrows, very pouty closed mouth
10" – 12"..	$7,500.00 – 8,000.00*

Mold 250, open mouth with teeth
12".......	$3,300.00* trousseau box
18" – 20"..	$3,250.00 – 3,400.00

Mold 251, open-closed mouth, teeth, tongue
15" – 16"..	$1,800.00 – 2,100.00
27"..........	$3,100.00 – 3,300.00

Mold 252, closed pouty mouth, glass eyes

Baby
8"	$2,000.00 – 2,200.00
10"	$3,200.00 – 3,500.00
15"	$3,800.00 – 4,000.00
19"	$8,000.00 – 9,000.00
26"	$10,750.00*

22" mold 227. $3,400.00. **Photo courtesy of Cybermogul Dolls.**

SHIRLEY TEMPLE

1934 on, Ideal Novelty Toy Corp., New York. Designed by Bernard Lipfert. Dolls listed are in very good condition, all original. Add more for exceptional dolls or special outfits like Ranger or Wee Willie Winkie.

Composition, 1934 – 1940s, composition head and jointed body, dimples in cheeks, green sleep eyes, open mouth, teeth, mohair wig, tagged original dress, center-snap shoes, prototype dolls may have paper sticker inside head and bias trimmed wig

Shirley Temple
11".................	$850.00 – 950.00
13"..............	$900.00 – 1,000.00
16"..........	$1,000.00 – 1,100.00
17".................	$850.00 – 875.00

13" composition Shirley Temple in original trunk with extra tagged outfits. $1,400.00.
Photo courtesy of The Museum Doll Shop.

18"	$800.00 – 900.00
20"	$900.00 – 1,000.00
22"	$1,000.00 – 1,100.00
27"	$1,200.00 – 1,300.00

Baby Shirley

15"	$1,100.00 – 1,300.00
18"	$1,000.00 – 1,100.00
21"	$1,200.00 – 1,300.00

Hawaiian, "Marama," Ideal used the composition Shirley Temple mold for this doll representing a character from the movie Hurricane, black yarn hair, wears grass skirt, Hawaiian costume

18"	$875.00 – 950.00

Accessories:

Button, three types	$125.00
Buggy, wicker or wood	$500.00 – 575.00
Dress, tagged	$125.00 – 575.00
Satin pajamas, tagged	$670.00
Trunk	$175.00 – 225.00

Reliable Shirley Temple, composition, made in Canada

18" – 22"	$1,000.00 – 1,200.00

Japanese, unlicensed Shirley dolls
All-bisque

6"	$195.00 – 225.00

Celluloid

5"	$125.00 – 175.00
8"	$200.00 – 225.00

Celluloid

Dutch Shirley Temple, ca. 1937+, all-celluloid, open crown, metal pate, sleep eyes, dimples in cheeks, marked: "Shirley Temple" on head, may have additional marks, dressed in Dutch costume

13"	$295.00 – 320.00
15"	$295.00 – 320.00

Cloth

Wacker Manufacturing Co. Chicago, painted features, side-glancing, molded face, mohair wig

17"	$300.00 – 400.00

Composition Japanese, heavily molded brown curls, painted eyes, open-closed mouth with teeth, body stamped "Japan"

7½"	$250.00 – 275.00

Vinyl, dolls listed are in excellent condition, original clothes, accessories, the newer the doll the more perfect it must be to command higher prices

16" 1973 Stand Up & Cheer. $75.00.
Photo courtesy of The Museum Doll Shop.

1957, all-vinyl, sleep eyes, synthetic rooted wig, open-closed mouth, teeth, came in two-piece slip and undies, tagged Shirley Temple, came with gold plastic script pin reading "Shirley Temple," marked on back of head: "ST//12"

    12"................. $350.00 – 375.00

1958 – 1961, marked on back of head: "S.T.//15," "S.T.//17," or "S.T.//19," some had flirty ("Twinkle") eyes; add more for flirty eyes or 1961 Cinderella, Bo Peep, Heidi, and Red Riding Hood

    15"................. $300.00 – 350.00
    17"................. $350.00 – 400.00
    19"................. $500.00 – 600.00

1960, jointed wrists, marked "ST–35–38–2"
    35" – 36".. $1,200.00 – 1,900.00

1972, Montgomery Wards reissue, plain box
    17"................. $175.00 – 200.00

1973, red dot "Stand Up and Cheer" outfit
    16".................... $75.00 – 150.00

1982 – 1983
    8"........................ $25.00 – 35.00
    12".................... $30.00 – 35.00

1984, by Hank Garfinkle, marked "Doll Dreams & Love"
    36"................. $200.00 – 225.00

Danbury Mint, re-issue
    36"................. $300.00 – 350.00

Porcelain
1987 on, Danbury Mint, various outfits
    18".................... $50.00 – 100.00

SIMON & HALBIG

1869 – 1930 on, Hildburghausen and Grafenhain, Germany. Porcelain factory, made heads for Jumeau (200 series), bathing dolls (300 series), porcelain figures (400 series), perhaps doll house or small dolls (500 – 600 series), bisque head dolls (700 series), bathing and small dolls (800 series), more bisque head dolls (900 – 1000 series). The earliest models of a series had the last digit of their model number ending with an 8, socket heads ended with 9, shoulder heads ended with 0, and models using a shoulder plate for swivel heads ended in 1.

Dolls listed are in good condition, appropriately dressed. All original or exceptional dolls may be more.

Shoulder Head child, 1870s, molded hair, painted or glass eyes, closed

10½" shoulder head lady doll with partially molded hair and partial wig, attributed to Simon & Halbig. $2,000.00. **Photo courtesy of Turn of the Century Antiques.**

mouth, cloth body with bisque lower arms, appropriately dressed, marked "S&H," no mold number

    13" – 15".. $1,100.00 – 1,200.00
    17" – 19".. $1,375.00 – 1,700.00
    21" – 23".. $2,200.00 – 2,400.00
Swivel neck
    9" – 10"...................... $1,250.00
    12" $1,500.00

Poupée (fashion-type doll), 1870s, bisque socket head with bisque shoulder plate on kid or twill over wood body, closed mouth, glass eyes, wigged

Kid body
    15" – 18" ..$2,200.00 – 2,700.00
Twill covered wood body
    10" – 11".. $5,000.00 – 6,000.00
    15" – 16"..$9,000.00 – 10,500.00

Closed-mouth Child, 1879, socket head, most on composition and wood body, glass eyes, wigged, pierced ears, appropriately dressed

Mold 719
    16"........... $5,900.00 – 6,100.00
    18" – 22" . $7,500.00 – 8,000.00

Edison phonograph mechanism in torso
    23"........... $4,900.00 – 5,400.00

Mold 739
    15" – 20".. $1,700.00 – 2,600.00

Mold 749
    8" – 11"....... $700.00 – 1,200.00

Mold 905, 908
    15" – 17".. $3,300.00 – 4,300.00

Mold 919
    15"........... $5,300.00 – 7,200.00
    19"........... $6,000.00 – 8,150.00

Mold 929
    14"........... $1,725.00 – 2,300.00
    23"........... $2,450.00 – 3,400.00
    25"........................ $6,600.00*

Mold 939
    14" – 16".. $2,300.00 – 2,500.00
    18" – 20".. $2,600.00 – 3,000.00

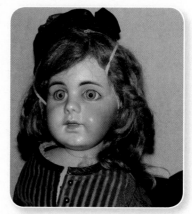

18" 929 closed mouth child. $3,000.00.
Doll courtesy of Jean Grout.

    27"........................... $2,700.00
Mold 949
    10" – 12".. $2,000.00 – 2,400.00
    14" – 16".. $2,800.00 – 3,200.00
    21" – 23".. $4,200.00 – 4,600.00
    31"........... $4,250.00 – 4,500.00

Mold 720, 740, 940, 950, dome shoulder head, kid body
    8" – 10".......... $700.00 – 900.00
    14" – 18".. $1,400.00 – 1,700.00
    20" – 22".. $1,700.00 – 1,800.00

All-bisque child: See All-Bisque, German section.

Open-mouth child, 1889 – 1930s, socket head on composition body (sometimes French), wigged, glass eyes may be stationary or sleep, appropriately dressed

Mold 530, 540, 550, 570, Baby Blanche
Walker body
    17"................. $800.00 – 850.00
    19"................. $425.00 – 475.00
    22"................. $500.00 – 575.00

Mold 719, 739, 749, 759, 769, 939, 979
    5½"................ $375.00 – 550.00
    9" – 13".... $1,200.00 – 1,700.00
    15" – 17".. $1,800.00 – 1,900.00
    20" – 22".. $2,100.00 – 2,400.00

22" mold 719 open mouth child.
$2,400.00. **Photo courtesy of Joan & Lynette Antique Dolls and Accessories.**

Mold 905, 908
18".......... $1,750.00 – 2,200.00
22".......... $1,425.00 – 2,600.00
Mold 949
15" – 17".. $1,150.00 – 1,450.00
22" – 24".. $1,550.00 – 1,700.00
29".......... $2,350.00 – 2,500.00
Mold 1009
15" – 16"........ $675.00 – 775.00
19" – 21"........ $800.00 – 900.00
24" – 25".. $1,125.00 – 1,400.00
Mold 1029
16" – 18"........ $475.00 – 575.00
24" – 25"........ $700.00 – 800.00
28"................ $825.00 – 900.00
Mold 1039, 1049, 1059, 1069, 1078, 1079
Flapper body
8" – 9"............ $350.00 – 450.00
12" – 13" .... $675.00 – 725.00
16" – 18"..... $900.00 – 1,200.00
21" – 25"........ $850.00 – 950.00
27" – 28"........ $800.00 – 900.00
33".......... $1,000.00 – 1,100.00
Mold 1109
13"................ $750.00 – 800.00
18".......... $1,000.00 – 1,000.00
Mold 1248, 1249, Santa

6"................... $500.00 – 650.00
10" – 13"........ $825.00 – 900.00
15" – 18"..... $900.00 – 1,000.00
20" – 24".... $1,10.00 – 1,800.00
26" – 28".. $1,900.00 – 2,000.00
38".......... $2,200.00 – 2.600.00
Open-mouth shoulder head child, 1889 – 1930s, kid body
Mold 1009, 1039
12" – 13" .... $950.00 – 1,100.00
19"................ $350.00 – 525.00
23".............. $750.00 – 1,000.00
Mold 1010, 1040, 1070, 1080
18"................ $425.00 – 575.00
23" – 25"........ $600.00 – 800.00
28"................ $675.00 – 900.00
Mold 1250, 1260
16"................ $500.00 – 625.00
18" – 19"........ $700.00 – 800.00
23" – 26"........ $750.00 – 900.00
Character Face, 1909 on, bisque socket head, composition body, wig or molded hair, glass or painted eyes, open or closed mouth, appropriately dressed
Mold 111
18" – 22"..$16,000.00 – 18,000.00
Mold 150, ca. 1912, intaglio eyes, closed mouth
21"........................$15,500.00
Too few in database for reliable range.
Mold 151, ca. 1912, painted eyes, closed laughing mouth
13" – 15".... $6,20.00 – 7,000.00
Too few in database for reliable range.
Mold 152, lady, intaglio eyes
19" – 22"..$25,000.00 – 29,000.00
Mold 153, ca. 1912, molded hair, painted eyes, closed mouth
17"........................$32,000.00
Too few in database for reliable range.
Mold 163, closed mouth
14"........................$17,000.00*

18" mold 1249. $1,000.00. **Photo courtesy of William Jenack Estate Appraisers and Auctioneers.**

Mold 600, ca. 1912, sleep eyes, open mouth
17"............................... $900.00
Too few in database for reliable range.
Mold 611, solid dome
16"........... $4,000.00 – 5,000.00
Mold 729, ca. 1888, laughing face, glass eyes, open-closed mouth
16"........... $1,900.00 – 2,550.00
Mold 969, ca. 1887, open smiling mouth
19"........... $5,700.00 – 7,600.00
Too few in database for reliable range.
Mold 1019, ca. 1890, laughing, open mouth
14"........... $4,275.00 – 5,700.00
Too few in database for reliable range.
Mold 1269, 1279, sleep eyes, open mouth
14"........... $1,100.00 – 1,500.00
16"............................. $3,500.00
25"............................. $2,550.00
Mold 1299, ca. 1912, marked "S&H"
13"........... $1,200.00 – 1,600.00
Mold 1448, ca. 1914, bisque socket head, sleep eyes, closed mouth, pierced ears, composition/wood ball-jointed body
16"............................. $17,500.00
Too few in database for reliable range.
Little Women (so-called), 1909, mold 1160 shoulder head lady, fancy hairdo wig, closed mouth, glass eyes, cloth body with bisque lower limbs, appropriately dressed
6" – 7"............ $425.00 – 475.00

10" – 11"........ $725.00 – 800.00
14" .... $750.00 – 800.00
Baby, character face, 1910 on, molded hair or wig, painted or glass eyes, open or closed mouth, bent-leg baby body, appropriately dressed, add more for flirty eyes or toddler body
Mold 1294, ca. 1912, glass eyes, open mouth
16"................. $550.00 – 750.00
19".............. $800.00 – 1,100.00
Mold 1294, clockwork mechanism moves eyes
26"........................... $1,575.00*
Mold 1428, ca. 1914, glass eyes, open-closed mouth
13"........... $1,200.00 – 1,600.00
Toddler
12"........... $2,600.00 – 2,700.00
16"........... $2,100.00 – 2,300.00
Mold 1488, ca. 1920, glass eyes, open-closed or open mouth
19" – 20".. $4,500.00 – 5,000.00
Mold 1489, "Baby Erika," ca. 1925, glass eyes, open mouth, tongue
20" – 23".. $4,200.00 – 6,000.00
Mold 1498, ca. 1920, solid dome, painted or sleep eyes, open-closed mouth
24"............................. $3,700.00
Too few in database for reliable range.

20" mold 1079 in original bobbed wig, c. 1920. $800.00. **Doll courtesy Ruth Cayton.**

Lady doll, 1910 on, bisque socket head, composition lady body, sleep eyes, wigged, appropriately dressed

Mold 1079, open mouth, glass eyes

24"........... $1,500.00 – 2,000.00

Mold 1159, ca.1894, glass eyes, open mouth, Gibson Girl

Flapper body

13" – 15" . $1,600.00 – 1,700.00

18" – 20". $2,000.00 – 2,500.00

22" – 24".. $2,200.00 – 3,000.00

28"........... $3,800.00 – 4,000.00

Mold 1199, open mouth

34"....... $17,500.00 – 18,000.00

Too few in database for reliable range.

8" dolly on flapper body. $450.00. **Doll courtesy of Jean Grout.**

Mold 1303, ca. 1902, lady face, glass eyes, closed mouth

14"............................ $5,815.00

Too few in database for reliable range.

25"......................... $25,300.00*

Mold 1305, ca. 1902, old woman, glass eyes, open-closed laughing mouth

18"........................... $10,035.00

Too few in database for reliable range.

Mold 1308, ca. 1902, old man, molded mustache/dirty face, may be solid dome

18"........... $4,200.00 – 5,600.00

Too few in database for reliable range.

Mold 1329

18"........... $1,300.00 – 1,500.00

Too few in database for reliable range.

Mold 1388, ca. 1910, glass eyes, closed smiling mouth, teeth, wig

18" – 22".. $19,000.00 – 24,000.00*

Mold 1468, 1469, ca. 1920, flapper, glass eyes, closed mouth

15"........... $3,000.00 – 3,200.00

17" mold 1159 on lady body. $1,900.00. **Photo courtesy of The Museum Doll Shop.**

SNOW BABIES

1901 – 1930 on. All-bisque dolls covered with ground porcelain slip to resemble snow, made by Bähr & Pröschild, Hertwig, C.F. Kling, Kley & Hahn, and others, Germany. Mostly unjointed, some jointed at shoulders and hips. The Eskimos named Peary's daughter Marie, born in 1893, Snow Baby, and her mother published a book in which she called her daughter Snow Baby and showed a picture of a little girl in white snowsuit. These little figures have painted features, various poses.

Figure listed are in good condition, allow more for exceptional figures.

New Snow Babies are being made today. Department 56 makes a line of larger scale figures (see below) and reproductions of earlier Snow Babies are being produced in Germany and by individual artisans.

1½" Snow Baby on sled, stamped "made in Germany." $125.00. **Photo courtesy of The Museum Doll Shop.**

Single Snow Baby, standing or sitting

1½"..................... $45.00 – 55.00

3" – 4"............. $80.00 – 100.00

Snow Baby child with wire jointed limbs

3½"............... $150.00 – 175.00

Action Babies

Baby with umbrella

2¾" .... $75.00 – 125.00

Bear on sled

3".................. $175.00 – 200.00

Child on skis

4½"............... $350.00 – 375.00

Riding on bear .... $300.00 – 350.00

Riding on sled

2".................. $150.00 – 200.00

Riding on reindeer

2½"............... $300.00 – 325.00

With broom

4½"............... $500.00 – 550.00

Melting snowman

1½"..................... $75.00 – 95.00

Skiing child on snow ball

4½"............... $350.00 – 375.00

Snow kid teddy bear on skis

2".................. $150.00 – 200.00

Two Snow Babies, molded together

1½"................ $100.00 – 125.00

3".................. $200.00 – 250.00

Two climbing an igloo

2½"................ $250.00 – 350.00

Mold 3200, Armand Marseille, candy container, two Snow Babies on sled

11"........................... $3,100.00*

Three Snow Babies, molded together

3".................. $300.00 – 350.00

Three on sled

2½"................ $200.00 – 250.00

Snow Baby doll, jointed hips, shoulders

4".................. $300.00 – 400.00

5".................. $400.00 – 500.00

New Snow Babies, today's commercial reproductions are by Dept. 56 and are larger and the coloring is more like cream. Dept. 56 Snow Babies and their Village Collections are collectible on the secondary market. As with all newer collectibles, items must be mint to command higher prices. Values listed are for secondary market pieces, many are still available at retail.

Snow Baby winged clip ornament

1986 .... $45.00 – 60.00

Snow Baby Adrift
    1987 .... $90.00 – 125.00
Pony Express
    1988 .... $70.00 – 90.00
All Fall Down, set 4
    1989 .... $65.00 – 85.00
Penguin Parade
    1989 .... $50.00 – 70.00
1990 on, pieces, various
                $15.00 – 30.00
Disney pieces, various ... $65.00 – 85.00
Eloise on the Polar Express
    2002 .... $35.00 – 40.00

SONNEBERG TAUFLING

1851 – 1900 on, Sonneberg, Germany. Various companies made an infant doll with special separated body with bellows and voice mechanism. Motchmann is erroneously credited with the body style; but he did patent the voice mechanism. Some bodies stamped "Motchmann" refer to the voice mechanism. The Sonneberg Taufling was made with head, shoulder plate, pelvis, lower arms and lower legs of papier-mâché/composition, wax over papier-mâché, china, and bisque. Body parts put together with twill cloth in what are called "floating" joints. These dolls have glass eyes, closed mouth or open mouth, painted hair, or wigged. Dolls listed are in good condition.

Bisque: See also Jules Steiner.
    7" .... $2,100.00 – 2,300.00
    14" – 19" .. $3,700.00 – 4,500.00
China
    6" – 7" ...... $4,500.00 – 5,500.00
    10" – 12" .. $3,300.00 – 3,700.00
    14" – 16" .. $3,900.00 – 4,200.00

Papier-mâché/composition or wax over papier-mâché
    10" – 12" ..... $750.00 – 1,000.00
    13" – 15" .. $1,200.00 – 1,400.00
    18" – 20" .. $1,500.00 – 2,000.00
    22" – 24" .. $2,200.00 – 2,400.00
Wood
Bébé tout en Bois, carved wooden socket head, closed mouth, painted hair, glass eyes, twill and wood torso, nude
    9" $1,000.00
Too few in database for reliable range.

24" wax-over-composition Sonneberg Taufling. $2,000.00. **Photo courtesy of The Museum Doll Shop.**

MARGARETE STEIFF

1877 to present, Giengen, Wurtemburg, Germany. Known today for their plush stuffed animals, Steiff made clothes for children, dolls with mask faces in 1889, clown dolls by 1898. Most Steiff dolls of felt, velvet, or plush have seam down the center of the face, but not all. Registered trademark button in ear in 1905. Button type eyes, painted features, sewn-on ears, big feet/shoes enable them to stand alone, all in excellent condition.

Values given are for dolls in good

10" Steiff felt girl with center seam. $1,200.00. **Photo courtesy of Richard Withington, Inc.**

13" Steiff Sheppard with rubber face. $135.00. **Photo courtesy of Sharing My Dolls & Stuff.**

condition, for soiled, ragged, or worn dolls, use 35% of this price.

Adults

14½" – 18" .. $1,800.00 – 2,500.00

Characters, center seam face, military men in uniform and conductors, firemen, English bobby, bellhop, etc.

10½" – 12" .. $1,200.00 – 1,700.00

18" .... $3,200.00 – 4,275.00

Children

Center seam face

12" – 14" .. $1,500.00 – 1,900.00

16" – 18" .. $2,500.00 – 3,000.00

Molded felt face

13" .... $475.00 – 550.00

Made in U.S. Zone Germany, 1947 – 1953, glass eyes

12" .... $550.00 – 650.00

Rubber head doll, cloth body

12" – 13" .... $125.00 – 150.00

Vinyl characters, wire armature in body

Max or Moritz

4" .... $125.00 – 175.00

Limited Edition Dolls, 1986 – 1987, felt, characters such as Tennis lady, Gentleman in morning coat, Peasant lady, Peasant Jorg

MIB .... $125.00 – 175.00

HERMANN STEINER

1909 – 1930 on, near Coburg, Germany. Porcelain and doll factory. First made plush animals, then made bisque, composition, and celluloid head dolls. Patented the Steiner eye with moving pupils.

Baby

Mold 240, circa 1925, newborn, solid dome, closed mouth, sleep eyes

6" – 8½" .... $75.00 – 100.00

12" – 16" .... $300.00 – 350.00

Mold 246, circa 1926, character, solid dome, glass eyes, open-closed mouth, laughing baby, teeth, cloth or composition body

15" .... $475.00 – 600.00

Topsy Turvy baby doll

8" .... $500.00 – 600.00

Child

Dolly face, no mold number, open mouth, glass eyes, jointed composition body

7" – 10" .... $100.00 – 200.00

14" – 16" .... $500.00 – 600.00

18" – 20" .... $300.00 – 350.00

Shoulder Head child, no mold number, open mouth, glass eyes, kid body

9" character mold 401 with open/closed mouth with tongue. $175.00.
Photo courtesy of The Museum Doll Shop.

18".................. $150.00 – 175.00
Living Steiner-eye doll, character with molded hair and Steiner patented eye
10".................. $675.00 – 750.00
Mold 128, character bisque socket head, sleep eyes, open mouth, teeth, wig, composition/wood jointed body
8" – 9"............ $175.00 – 225.00
14".................. $650.00 – 700.00
Mold 401, shoulder head, solid dome, painted eyes, open-closed laughing mouth, teeth, molded tongue
15".................. $350.00 – 475.00

JULES STEINER

1855 – 1891 on, Paris. Made dolls with pressed heads, wigs, glass eyes, pierced ears on jointed composition bodies. Advertised talking, mechanical jointed dolls and bébés. Some sleep eyes were operated by a wire behind the ear, marked "J. Steiner." May also carry the Bourgoin mark.

Dolls listed are in good condition, appropriately dressed. Add more for original clothes, rare mold numbers.

Baby with Taufling (Motchmann type) body, solid dome bisque shoulder head, hips, lower arms and legs, with twill body in-between, closed mouth, glass eyes, wig
13" – 14" .. $9,000.00 – 10,000.00
20" – 22".. $6,300.00 – 8,000.00
Gigoteur, crying, kicking child, key-wound mechanism, solid dome head, glass eyes, open mouth, two rows tiny teeth, pierced ears, mohair wig, papier-mâché torso
Earlier, paler doll head
17" – 20" ..$3,500.00 – 4,500.00
Later, more highly colored head
17" – 20".. $1,900.00 – 2,500.00
Round face Bébé, 1870s, early unmarked, pale pressed bisque socket head, rounded face, pierced ears, bulgy paperweight eyes, open mouth, two rows teeth, pierced ears, wig, composition/wood jointed body
16" – 18".. $5,500.00 – 6,800.00
Closed mouth, round face, dimples in chin
16" – 18".. $10,000.00 – $11,500.00
Bébé with Series marks, 1880 on, bourgoin red ink, Caduceus stamp on body, pressed bisque socket head, cardboard pate, wig,

12" Steiner Taufling. $9,000.00. **Photo courtesy of Richard Withington, Inc.**

18½" Gigoteur, crying kicking doll. $3,000.00. **Doll courtesy of Alfred Edward.**

pierced ears, closed mouth, glass paperweight eyes, French composition/papier-mâché (purple) body with straight wrists or bisque hands, Series C and A more common, marked with series mark: Sie and letter and number, rare Series B, E, F, and G models may be valued much higher

Series A or C
  8" – 10" ..$9,000.00 – 15,000.00
  14" – 16"..$13,000.00 – 15,000.00
  21" – 23"..$14,000.00 – 17,000.00
  27" – 28"..$19,000.00 – 22,000.00
Series E
  24"...........................$18,000.00
Too few in database for reliable range.
Series F
  24"...........................$48,000.00
Too few in database for reliable range.
Series G
  19"....... $26,000.00 – 29,000.00
Too few in database for reliable range.

Bébé with Figure marks, 1887 on, bisque socket head, pierced ears, closed mouth, glass eyes, wig, composition/wood jointed French body, may use body marked "Le Parisien" or "Le Petit Parisien," head marked "Fire" and letter and number, and "J. Steiner," figure marks included A, B, C, D,

and E, A and C are the most often found
Closed mouth
A or C
  8" – 10".... $4,500.00 – 5,500.00
  12" – 16"..$4,500.00 – 9,000.00
  18" – 24" ..$7,000.00 – 8,500.00
  28" – 29"..$9,000.00 – 10,000.00
  34" – 35"..$18,000.00 – 19,000.00
Open mouth
Figure A
  18" – 23" ..$3,600.00 – 4,500.00
Figure B
  33"............................$9,000.00*
Figure E
  26 – 27" ..$33,000.00 – 36,000.00

28" Series A mold, 1880 on. $17,000.00. **Photo courtesy of Richard Withington, Inc.**

SUN RUBBER

1919 – 1950s, Barberton, Ohio. Made rubber and later vinyl dolls. Dolls listed are in excellent condition, allow less for faded, cracked dolls or missing paint.

Psyllium, 1937, molded painted hard rubber, moving head, blue pants, white suspenders, black shoes and hat
  10"..................... $10.00 – 15.00

One-piece Squeeze dolls, 1940s, designed by

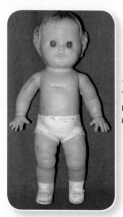

10½" girl marked Tod-L-Dee. $12.00. Photo courtesy of The Museum Doll Shop.

Ruth E. Newton, molded clothes, squeaker, names such as Bonnie Bear, Happy Kappy, Rompy, and others

8"....................... $45.00 – 65.00

So-Wee, 1941, molded hair, painted or sleep eyes

10" – 12" .... $35.00 – 45.00

Black .... $55.00 – 65.00

Sunbabe, 1950, drink and wet baby, painted eyes, molded hair

11" – 13" .... $80.00 – 100.00

Black.................. $65.00 – 75.00

Betty Bows, 1953, molded hair with loop for ribbon, drink and wet baby, jointed body

11".................... $75.00 – 100.00

Constance Bannister Baby, 1954, molded hair, drink and wet, sleep eyes

18".................... $85.00 – 105.00

Tod L Dee, 1950s, all vinyl soft stuffed one-piece body, molded underclothes and shoes, molded painted hair, sleep eyes, open mouth, there is also a Tod L Tee & Tod L Tim

10"..................... $25.00 – 35.00

Peter Pan, 1950s, all vinyl soft stuffed one-piece body, molded outfit, molded painted hair, sleep eyes

10"..................... $25.00 – 30.00

Amosandra: See Black Dolls.

Gerber Baby: See Advertising Dolls.

SWAINE & CO.

1910 – 1927, Huttensteinach, Thüringia, Germany. Made porcelain doll heads. Marked "S & Co.," with green stamp. May also be incised "DIP" or "Lori."

Baby

Baby Lori, marked "Lori," solid dome, open-closed mouth molded hair, sleep eyes

16" – 18".. $1,200.00 – 1,400.00

23"........... $1,600.00 – 2,000.00

Mold 232, Lori variation, open mouth

12" – 14" .... $750.00 – 1,000.00

20" – 23".. $1,300.00 – 1,600.00

DI, solid dome, intaglio eyes, closed mouth

11" – 13"........ $500.00 – 700.00

16"................ $1,100.00* toddler

DV, solid dome, sleep eyes, closed mouth

13"........... $1,000.00 – 1,200.00

15"........... $1,300.00 – 1,450.00

FP, S&C, socket head, sleep eyes, closed mouth

8".................... $750.00 – 850.00

Too few in database for reliable range.

Child

AP, socket head, intaglio eyes, closed mouth

15"........................... $5,200.00*

14" DIP by Swaine. $1,100.00. Photo courtesy of Dollsantique.

BP, socket head, open-closed smiling mouth, teeth, painted eyes

14½".......... $4,500.00 – 5,500.00

Too few in database for reliable range.

DIP, S&C, socket head, sleep eyes, closed mouth

8" – 9"......... $800.00 – 1,000.00

Toddler body

8"............. $1,000.00 – 1,300.00

13" – 14".. $1,100.00 – 1,400.00

TERRI LEE

16" Terri Lee. $400.00.
Doll courtesy of Ruth Cayton.

1946 – 1962, Lincoln, Nebraska, and Apple Valley, California. Company was founded by Violet Lee Gradwohl, the company went out of business in 1962. In 1997, Fritz Duda, Violet's nephew, was instrumental in founding Terri Lee Associates which is making Terri Lee dolls now. First dolls composition, then hard plastic and vinyl, the modern dolls are now being produced of a newer type of hard plastic. Closed pouty mouth, hand-painted features, wigged, jointed body. Values listed are for dolls in good condition and wearing original clothing. Allow significantly less for undressed, played-with dolls. Dolls in mint condition, with fancy costume, or additional wardrobe will bring more.

Terri Lee

Composition, 1946 – 1947

16".............. $300.00 – 400.00

Painted hard plastic, 1947 – 1949

16" .... $1,200.00 – 1,600.00

Flesh colored hard plastic, 1949 – 1952

16"............... $550.00 – 650.00

Hard plastic, 1952 – 1962

16"............... $375.00 – 475.00

16", MIB .... $650.00 – 750.00

Vinyl, less if sticky, 1950 – 1951

16"............... $500.00 – 600.00

Talking

16"............... $300.00 – 400.00

Hard plastic, 1997 – 2005, values listed are secondary market values, dolls are available at retail as well

16" .... $50.00 – 100.00

Benji, painted plastic, brown, 1946 – 1962, black lamb's wool wig

16"........... $1,800.00 – 2,000.00

Connie Lynn, 1955, hard plastic, sleep eyes, fur wig, bent-limb baby body

19"............... $350.00 – 400.00

Gene Autry, 1949 – 1950, painted plastic

16"........... $1,600.00 – 1,800.00

Jerri Lee, hard plastic, caracul wig

16"............... $375.00 – 425.00

Vinyl, 16"......... $1,200.00 – 1,500.00

Linda Lee, 1950 – 1951, vinyl

12"..................... $60.00 – 75.00

1952 – 1958, vinyl baby

10"............... $175.00 – 225.00

Mary Jane, Terri Lee look-alike, hard plastic walker

16"............... $225.00 – 275.00

Patty Jo, 1947 – 1949

16"............. 1,200.00 – 1,500.00

10" Tiny Terri Lee. $250.00. **Photo courtesy of Usefulcollectibles.**

Bonnie Lou, black
    16"........... $1,200.00 – 1,800.00
Tiny Terri Lee, 1955 – 1958
    10"................. $200.00 – 250.00
Accessories
Terri Lee Outfits:
Girl Scout/Brownie uniform......... $50.00
Heart Fund $325.00
School dress $150.00
Shoes...................................... $35.00
Tiny Terri Lee dresses ..... $20.00 – 50.00
Jerri Lee Outfits:
Gene Autrey $865.00*

A. THUILLIER

1875 – 1893, Paris. Made bisque head dolls with composition, kid, or wooden bodies. Some of the heads were reported made by Francoise Gaultier. Bisque socket head or swivel on shoulder plate, glass eyes, closed mouth with white space, pierced ears, cork pate, wig, nicely dressed, in good condition. Dolls listed are in good condition, appropriately dressed. Exceptionally beautiful dolls may run more.
Child
Closed mouth

12" – 13"
    $70,000.00 – 75,000.00
12", all original $100,000.00*
16" – 18"
    $78,000.00 – 85,000.00

12" size 3 AT Bébé. $75,000.00. **Photo courtesy of Taecker House Antique Dolls.**

ROBERT TONNER

1991 to present, Hurley, New York. Robert Tonner is a fashion designer and sculptor who has created numerous dolls in porcelain and vinyl. Tonner Company also owns Effanbee Dolls.
Values listed are for secondary market dolls, many of these dolls are still available retail as well.
American Models, 1993 on, vinyl, basic dolls at low end of value, dolls in elaborate costume at high end of value
    16".................... $75.00 – 100.00
    19"................. $200.00 – 300.00
    22"................. $150.00 – 300.00
Ann Estelle, 1999, a Mary Engelbreit character, hard plastic, blond wig, glasses
    10"...................... $55.00 – 65.00
Sophie, 10"............... $75.00 – 100.00
    18"................. $275.00 – 325.00

Betsy McCall, see Betsy McCall section.

Kripplebush Kids, 1997, hard plastic, Marni, Eliza, Hannah

8".................... $40.00 – 60.00

Tiny Kitty Collier, vinyl, basic dolls at low end of value, dolls in elaborate costume at high end of value

10".................... $45.00 – 85.00

Tyler Wentworth, 1999, fashion-type, long, straight, brunette, blond, or red hair

16".................... $65.00 – 75.00

11" Tiny Kitty, Wedding Hat Box set by Robert Tonner Doll Co. $85.00. **Doll courtesy of Elaine Holda.**

TROLLS

Trolls portray supernatural beings from Scandinavian folklore. They have been manufactured by various companies including Helena and Martii Kuuslkoski who made Fauni Trolls, ca. 1952+ (sawdust filled cloth dolls); Thomas Dam, 1960+; and Scandia House, later Norfin®; Uneeda Doll and Toy Wishniks®; Russ Berrie; Ace Novelty; Treasure Trolls; Applause Toys; Magical Trolls; and many other companies who made lesser quality vinyl look-alikes, mostly unmarked, to take advantage of the fad. Most are all-vinyl or vinyl with stuffed cloth bodies.

Troll Figures

1960s

2½".................... $35.00 – 60.00

5".................... $45.00 – 60.00

7".................... $60.00 – 75.00

Bank, 8" .... $18.00 – 22.00

10".................... $55.00 – 60.00

12".................... $65.00 – 80.00

15".................... $75.00 – 85.00

1977

9".................... $30.00 – 40.00

12".................... $35.00 – 45.00

Thumb sucker, 18" $55.00

Too few in database for reliable range.

Wishnik trolls, by Uneeda

3".................... $20.00 – 25.00

Troll Animals, Thomas Dam, 1964

Cow

6".................... $100.00 – 150.00

3" Wishnik by Uneeda Doll Co, MIB. $50.00. **Photo Courtesy of Hatton's Gallery of Dolls.**

Elephant

2½" .... $15.00 – 20.00

Giraffe

12" .... $60.00 – 75.00

Horse

6" .... $70.00 – 75.00

UNEEDA

1917 on, New York City. Made composition head dolls, including Mama dolls and made the transition to plastics and vinyl.

Composition

Rita Hayworth, as "Carmen," 1939, from The Loves of Carmen movie, all-composition, red mohair wig, unmarked, cardboard tag

14" .... $425.00 – 500.00

Hard Plastic and Vinyl

Baby Dollikins, 1960, vinyl head, hard plastic jointed body with jointed elbows, wrists, and knees, drink and wet

21" .... $150.00 – 200.00

21" Dollikin with pink hair. $495.00. **Doll courtesy Suzanne Vlach.**

Baby Trix, 1965

19" .... $18.00 – 25.00

Bareskin Baby, 1968

12½" .... $15.00 – 20.00

Blabby, 1962+

14" .... $20.00 – 28.00

Coquette, 1963+

16" .... $15.00 – 20.00

Black

16" .... $25.00 – 35.00

Dollikin, 1957 on, multi-joints, marked "Uneeda//2S," special costumes or outstanding condition will bring more

19" .... $250.00 – 300.00

Pink hair

19" .... $350.00 – 450.00

Fairy Princess, 1961

32" .... $75.00 – 100.00

Freckles, 1960, vinyl head, rigid plastic body, marked "22" on head

32" .... $65.00 – 75.00

1973, ventriloquist doll, vinyl head, hands, rooted hair, cotton stuffed cloth body

30" .... $45.00 – 60.00

Granny & Me, 1978

11½" & 5½" ...$28.00 – 32.00 set

Jennifer, 1973, rooted side-parted hair, painted features, teen body, mod clothing

18" .... $15.00 – 20.00

Magic Meg, w/Hair That Grows, vinyl and plastic, rooted hair, sleep eyes

16" .... $30.00 – 45.00

Miss Dollikin, also called Action Girl, 1957 on, fashion doll

11½" .... $40.00 – 50.00

Pir-thilla, 1958, blows up balloons, vinyl, rooted hair, sleep eyes

12½" .... $8.00 – 12.00

Priscilla, 1960s

12½" .... $15.00 – 18.00

Purty, 1973, long rooted hair, vinyl, plastic, painted features

5" Tinyteens doll wearing Fun Time. $27.00. **Photo courtesy of The Museum Doll Shop.**

Child

Mold 60, 301, bisque head, fully jointed composition/wood body, wig, sleep eyes, open mouth

5" – 6"	$75.00 – 120.00
8" – 10"	$375.00 – 475.00
13" – 16"	$550.00 – 650.00
21" – 23"	$525.00 – 600.00

Five-piece composition body, glass eyes

5" – 8"	$250.00 – 300.00
10" – 14"	$300.00 – 350.00

Mold 247, 251, toddler body

15"	$1,10.00 – 1,450.00
27"	$1,700.00 – 2,300.00

11" .... $20.00 – $25.00

Pollyanna, 1960, for Disney

11" .... $25.00 – 35.00
17" .... $50.00 – 70.00
31" .... $100.00 – 125.00

Saranade, 1962, vinyl head, hard plastic body, rooted blond hair, blue sleep eyes, red and white dress, speaker in tummy, phonograph and records came with doll, used battery

21" .... $75.00 – 100.00

Suzette (Carol Brent)

12" .... $100.00 – 125.00

Tiny Teen, 1957 – 1959, vinyl head, rooted hair, pierced ears, six-piece hard plastic body, high-heeled feet to compete with Little Miss Revlon, wrist tag

10½" .... $45.00 – 65.00

Tinyteens, 1968 on, vinyl doll, rooted hair, posable body, rooted lashes,12 dolls in series

5" .... $19.00 – 27.00

UNIS FRANCE

1922 – 1930 on. Mark used by S.F.B.J. (Société Francaise de Fabrication de Bébés & Jouets) after 1922 is Union Nationale Inter-Syndicale.

6" Unis France mold 60. $100.00. **Photo courtesy of The Museum Doll Shop.**

VINYL

1950s on. By the mid-1950s, vinyl (polyvinylchloride) was being used for dolls. Material that was soft to the touch and processing that allowed hair to be rooted were positive attractions. Vinyl became a desirable material and the market was soon deluged with dolls manufactured from this product. Many dolls of this period are of little known manufacturers, unmarked, or marked only with a number. With little history behind them, these dolls need to be mint-in-box and complete to warrant top prices. With special accessories or wardrobe values may be more.

Unknown Maker

Baby, vinyl head, painted or sleep eyes, molded hair or wig, bent legs, cloth or vinyl body

    12".......................$8.00 – 10.00
    16".....................$10.00 – 12.00
    20".....................$16.00 – 20.00

Child, vinyl head, jointed body, painted or sleep eyes, molded hair or wig, straight legs

    14".....................$10.00 – 14.00
    22".....................$18.00 – 25.00

Adult, vinyl head, painted or sleep eyes, jointed body, molded hair or wig, smaller waist with male or female modeling for torso

    8".......................$20.00 – 25.00
    18".....................$55.00 – 75.00

Known Maker

Baby Barry

Alfred E. Newman

    20"................$135.00 – 175.00

Captain Kangaroo

    16"....................$50.00 – 60.00
    19" – 24".........$95.00 – 150.00

Christopher Robin

    18".................$100.00 – 135.00

Daisy Mae

    14".................$125.00 – 175.00

Emmett Kelly (Willie the Clown)

    15"...................$95.00 – 120.00
    21".................$140.00 – 200.00

Li'l Abner

    14".................$100.00 – 150.00
    21".................$150.00 – 200.00

Mammy Yokum, 1957

    Molded hair

20" soft vinyl fashion doll marked "AE 200." $60.00.
Photo courtesy of The Museum Doll Shop.

    14"...................$90.00 – 125.00
    21"................$195.00 – 225.00

    Yarn hair

    14"................$125.00 – 150.00
    21"................$200.00 – 250.00

    Nose lights up

    23"................$275.00 – 325.00

Pappy Yokum, 1957

    14"...................$85.00 – 100.00
    21"................$195.00 – 225.00

    Nose lights up

    23"................$275.00 – 325.00

Belle Doll & Toy Co, Brooklyn, New York, 1950s

Ballerina or Miss Revlon type

    18"....................$50.00 – 60.00

Dee & Cee, Canada

Calypso Bill, 1961, black, vinyl, marked "DEE CEE"

    16"................................$50.00

Glad Toy/BrookGlad

Poor Pitiful Pearl, 1955, vinyl, some with stuffed one-piece vinyl bodies, others jointed

    13" ....$150.00 – 200.00
    17"................$250.00 – 300.00

Libby

I Dream of Jeannie, 1966

    20"................$350.00 – 400.00

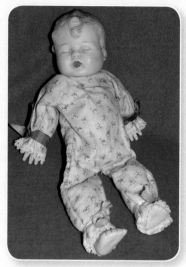

11" baby, when key wound the doll wiggles as music box plays. $15.00. **Doll courtesy of Ruth Cayton.**

Playmates, 1985 on, made animated talking dolls using a tape player in torso powered by batteries, extra costumes, tapes, and accessories available, more for black versions

Amazing Amy, 1998, vinyl, cloth body, interactive

    20"...................... $30.00 – 50.00

Cricket, 1986+ on

    25"...................... $55.00 – 75.00

Corky, 1987 on

    25"...................... $55.00 – 75.00

Jill, 1987, hard plastic, jointed body

    33".................. $225.00 – 300.00

Royal Doll Co.

Lonely Lisa

    1964, doll with large sad eyes, designed by Keane

    19".................... $80.00 – 100.00

    1965

    11½" .... $40.00 – 50.00

Sayco, 1907 – 1950s, New York City, first made composition dolls, then hard plastic and vinyl dolls

Miss America Pageant, 1950s

    11"...................... $20.00 – 45.00

    20"...................... $60.00 – 75.00

Pouty girl, soft vinyl head, rooted hair, sleep eyes, soft stuffed vinyl body

    22"...................... $40.00 – 45.00

Walker, costumed as a bride

    28"...................... $85.00 – 95.00

Shindana, 1968 – 1983, Operation Bootstrap, Los Angeles, ethnic features

    14"...................... $50.00 – 65.00

Talking Tamu, black, ethnic features

    16"................. $145.00 – 180.00

Tomy

Kimberly, 1981 – 1985, closed mouth, more for black

    17"...................... $35.00 – 55.00

Getting Fancy Kimberly, 1984, open mouth with teeth

    17"...................... $45.00 – 65.00

Tristar

Poor Pitiful Pearl, circa 1955+, vinyl jointed doll came with extra party dress

    11".................... $90.00 – 125.00

Unique

Ellie Mae Clampett, 1964

    11½" .... $20.00 – 25.00

16" Calypso Bill by Dee & Cee of Canada. $45.00. **Photo courtesy of The Museum Doll Shop.**

Worlds of Wonder, circa 1985 – 1987+, Fremont, California, made talking dolls and Teddy Ruxpin powered by batteries, had extra accessories, voice cards

Pamela, The Living Doll, 1986+

21".................. $75.00 – 100.00

Julie, 1987 on

24"..................... $75.00 – 95.00

Extra costume............... $20.00 – 30.00

Teddy Ruxpin, 1985+, animated talking bear

20"..................... $65.00 – 80.00

VOGUE DOLL CO.

1930s on, Medford, MA. Jennie Graves started the company and dressed "Just Me" and Arranbee dolls in the early years, before Bernard Lipfert designed Ginny. After several changes of ownership, Vogue dolls was purchased in 1995 by Linda and Jim Smith.

Composition dolls

Dora Lee, sleep eyes, closed mouth

11"................. $375.00 – 425.00

Jennie, 1940s, sleep eyes, open mouth, mohair wig, five-piece composition body

13"................. $300.00 – 350.00

Cynthia, 1940s, sleep eyes, open mouth, mohair wig, five-piece composition body

13"................. $300.00 – 350.00

W.A.A.C. doll in Women's Army Auxiliary Corps uniform

8" painted eye Ginny, 1948 – 1950. $375.00. **Doll courtesy of Elaine Holda.**

13"............................ $1150.00*

Ginny Family

Toddles, composition, 1937 – 1948, name stamped in ink on bottom of shoe, some early dolls which have been identified as "Toodles" (spelled with two o's) are blank dolls from various companies used by Vogue, painted eyes, mohair wig, jointed body, some had gold foil labels reading "Vogue." Dolls listed are in good condition with original clothes, more for fancy outfits such as Red Riding Hood or Cowboy/Cowgirl or with accessories

7½" – 8"........ $400.00 – 450.00

Painted Eye Ginny, 1948 – 1949, hard plastic, strung joints, marked "Vogue" on head, "Vogue Doll" on body, painted eyes, molded hair with mohair wig, clothing tagged "Vogue Dolls" or "Vogue Dolls, Inc. Medford Mass.," inkspot tag on white with blue letters

8".................. $300.00 – 375.00

Crib Crowd, 1950, baby with curved legs, sleep eyes, poodle cut (caracul) wig

8".................. $500.00 – 650.00

Strung Ginny, 1950 – 1953, hard plastic, sleep eyes, strung joints, marked "Vogue" on head, "Vogue Doll" on body, painted eyes, molded hair with mohair wig, clothing tagged "Vogue Dolls" or "Vogue Dolls, Inc. Medford Mass.," inkspot tag on white with blue letters

8".................. $300.00 – 425.00

Poodle cut, wearing Margie outfit

8" $560.00*

Painted Lash Walker Ginny, 1954, sleep eyes, strung, dynel wigs, new mark on back torso: "GINNY//VOGUE DOLLS//INC.// PAT PEND.//MADE IN U.S.A."

8".................. $225.00 – 275.00

Black Ginny, 1953 – 1954

8".................. $500.00 – 600.00

8" strung Ginny wearing Easter Sunday. $400.00. **Photo courtesy of The Museum Doll Shop.**

8"......................$2,000.00* MIB
Molded Lash Walker Ginny, 1955 – 1957, hard plastic, seven-piece body, sleep eyes, Dynel or saran wigs, marked: "VOGUE" on head, "GINNY//VOGUE DOLLS//INC.//PAT. NO. 2687594//MADE IN U.S.A." on back of torso
8".................. $160.00 – 225.00
Easter Bunny
8"............. $1,000.00 – 1,400.00
Bent-knee Molded Lash Walker Ginny, 1957 – 1962, hard plastic, jointed knees, sleep eyes, dynel or saran wigs, marked "VOGUE" on head, "GINNY//VOGUE DOLLS//INC.//PAT.NO.2687594//MADE IN U.S.A."
8".................. $150.00 – 200.00
Ginny, 1960, unmarked, big walker carried 8" doll dressed just like her
36"............................... $350.00
Too few in database for reliable range.
Vinyl Walker Ginny, 1963 – 1965, soft vinyl head, hard plastic walker body, sleep eyes, molded lashes, rooted hair, marked: "GINNY," on head, "GINNY//VOGUE DOLLS, Inc.//PAT. NO.2687594//MADE

IN U.S.A." on back
8"...................... $30.00 – 45.00
Ginny, 1965 – 1972, all-vinyl, straight legs, non-walker, rooted hair, sleep eyes, molded lashes, marked "Ginny" on head, "Ginny//VOGUE DOLLS, INC." on back
8"...................... $30.00 – 45.00
Ginny, 1972 – 1977, all-vinyl, non-walker, sleep eyes, molded lashes, rooted hair, some with painted lashes, marked "GINNY" on head, "VOGUE DOLLS©1972//MADE IN HONG KONG//3" on back, made in Hong Kong by Tonka
8"...................... $25.00 – 40.00
Ginny, 1977 – 1979, "Ginny From Far-Away Lands," made in Hong Kong by Lesney, all-vinyl, sleep eyes, jointed, non-walker, rooted hair, chubby body, same as Tonka doll overall, marked "GINNY" on head, "VOGUE DOLLS 1972//MADE IN HONG KONG//3", painted eyes, 1980 – 1981, marked "VOGUE DOLLS//©GINNYTIM//1977" on head, "VOGUE DOLLS©1977//MADE IN HONG KONG" on back
8"...................... $20.00 – 30.00
Sasson Ginny, 1981 – 1982, made in Hong Kong by Lesney, all-vinyl, fully jointed, bendable knees, rooted Dynel hair, sleep eyes in 1981, painted eyes in 1982, slimmer body, marked "GINNY" on head, "1978 VOGUE DOLLS INC//MOONACHIE N.J.//MADE IN HONG KONG" on back
8"...................... $25.00 – 35.00
Ginny, 1984 – 1986, made by Meritus® in Hong Kong, vinyl, resembling Vogue's 1963 – 1971 Ginny, marked "GINNY®" on head, "VOGUE DOLLS//(a star logo)//M.I.I. 1984//Hong Kong" on back, porcelain marked: "GW//SCD//5184" on head, "GINNNY//®VOGUE DOLLS//INC//(a star logo) MII 1984//MADE IN TAIWAN"

8" Ginny painted lash walker. $275.00.
Photo courtesy of McMasters Harris Auction Co.

8".......................... $35.00 – 55.00

Ginny, 1986 – 1995, vinyl, by Dakin, soft vinyl, marked "VOGUE®DOLLS//©1984 R. DAKIN INC.//MADE IN CHINA" on back; hard vinyl, marked "VOGUE//®//DOLLS//©1986 R. DAKIN and Co.//MADE IN CHINA"

8".......................... $15.00 – 20.00

Ginny Baby, 1959 – 1982, vinyl, jointed, sleep eyes, rooted or molded hair, a drink and wet doll, some marked "GINNY BABY//VOGUE DOLLS INC."

12"...................... $30.00 – 40.00
18"...................... $40.00 – 50.00

Ginny outfits

Talon Zipper outfit MIB $250.00
Vinyl shoes MIB.......................... $30.00

Ginnette

1955 – 1969, 1985 – 1986, vinyl, jointed, open mouth, 1955 – 1956 had painted eyes, 1956 – 1969 had sleep eyes, marked "VOGUE DOLLS INC"

8"................... $200.00 – 250.00

1962 – 1963, rooted hair Ginnette

8"................... $125.00 – 175.00

Jan, 1958 – 1960, 1963 – 1964, Jill's friend, vinyl head, six-piece rigid vinyl body, straight leg, swivel waist, rooted hair, marked "VOGUE," called Loveable Jan in 1963 and Sweetheart Jan in 1964

10½".............. $125.00 – 150.00

Jeff, 1958 – 1960, vinyl head, five-piece rigid vinyl body, molded and painted hair, marked "VOGUE DOLLS"

11"................. $100.00 – 150.00

Jill, 1957 – 1960, 1962 – 1963, 1965, seven-piece hard plastic teenage body, bent-knee walker, high-heeled doll, big sister to Ginny (made in vinyl in 1965), extra wardrobe, marked "JILL//VOGUE DOLLS//MADEI NU.S.A.//©1957"

10½".............. $175.00 – 200.00

Street dress.................. $15.00 – 25.00
Special outfits............. $50.00 – 175.00

Jimmy, 1958, Ginny's baby brother, all-vinyl, open mouth, painted eye Ginnette, marked "VOGUE DOLLS/INC."

8"...................... $45.00 – 60.00

Little Miss Ginny, 1965 – 1971, all-vinyl, promoted as a pre-teen, one-piece hard plastic body and legs, soft vinyl head and arms, sleep eyes, head marked "VOGUE DOLL//19©67" or "©VOGUE DOLL//1968" and back, "VOGUE DOLL"

12"...................... $30.00 – 40.00

Miss Ginny, 1962 – 1964, soft vinyl head could be tilted, jointed vinyl arms, two-piece hard plastic body, swivel waist, flat feet; 1965 – 1980, vinyl head and arms, one-piece plastic body

15" – 16"............ $35.00 – 45.00

Hard Plastic and Vinyl

Baby Dear, 1959 – 1964, 18" vinyl baby designed by Eloise Wilkin, vinyl limbs, cloth body, rooted topknot or rooted hair, white tag on body "Vogue Dolls, Inc."; left leg stamped

8" Sasson Ginny, 1981 – 1982. $30.00. **Photo courtesy of The Museum Doll Shop.**

"1960/E.Wilkins," 12" size made in 1961

12"................. $160.00 – 180.00

18"................. $275.00 – 300.00

Baby Dear One, 1962, a one-year-old toddler version of Baby Dear, sleep eyes, two teeth, marked "C//1961//E.Wilkin//Vogue Dolls//Inc." on neck, tag on body, mark on right leg

25"................. $200.00 – 250.00

Baby Dear Musical, 1962 – 1963, 12" metal, 18" wooden shaft winds, plays tune, doll wiggles

12"................. $100.00 – 150.00

18"................. $200.00 – 250.00

Baby Too Dear, 1963 – 1965, two-year-old toddler version of Baby Dear, all-vinyl, open mouth, two teeth

17"................. $200.00 – 250.00

23"................. $300.00 – 350.00

Brikette, 1959 – 1961, 1979 – 1980, swivel waist joint, green flirty eyes in 22" size only, freckles, rooted straight orange hair, paper hang tag reads "I'm//Brikette//the//red headed//imp," marked on head "VOGUE INC.//19©60"

22"................. $200.00 – 250.00

1960, sleep eyes only, platinum, brunette, or orange hair

16"................. $95.00 – 125.00

1980, no swivel waist, curly pink, red, purple, or blond hair

16"................. $45.00 – 60.00

Li'l Imp, 1959 – 1960, Brikette's little sister, vinyl head, bent knee walker, green sleep eyes, orange hair, freckles, marked "R and B//44" on head and "R and B Doll Co." on back

10½"................. $50.00 – 75.00

Wee Imp, 1960, hard plastic body, orange saran wig, green eyes, freckles, marked "GINNY//VOGUE DOLS//INC.//PAT.No. 2687594//MADE IN U.S.A."

8"................. $200.00 – 250.00

Littlest Angel, 1961 – 1963; 1967 – 1980

1961 – 1963, also called Saucy Littlest Angel, vinyl head, hard plastic bent knee walker, sleep eyes, same doll as Arranbee Littlest Angel, rooted hair, marked "R & B"

10½"................. $175.00 – 225.00

Gift Set with book, The Surprise Doll

$425.00*

1967 – 1980, all-vinyl, jointed limbs, rooted red, blond, or brunette hair, looks older

11"................. $150.00 – 175.00

14"................. $100.00 – 125.00

11" Jeff, 1958 – 1960. $125.00. **Photo courtesy of The Museum Doll Shop.**

Love Me Linda (Pretty as a Picture), 1965, vinyl, large painted eyes, rooted long straight hair, came with portrait, advertised as "Pretty as a Picture" in Sears and Montgomery Ward catalogs, marked "VOGUE DOLLS/©1965"

15".................. $45.00 – 65.00

Welcome Home Baby, 1978 – 1980, newborn, designed by Eloise Wilkin, vinyl head and arms, painted eyes, molded hair, cloth body, crier, marked "Lesney"

18".................. $45.00 – 65.00

Welcome Home Baby Turns Two, 1980, toddler, designed by Eloise Wilkin, vinyl head, arms, and legs, cloth body, sleep eyes, rooted hair, marked "42260 Lesney Prod. Corp.//1979//Vogue Doll"

22"................ $150.00 – 200.00

IZANNAH WALKER

1840s – 1888, Central Falls, Rhode Island. Made cloth stockinette dolls, with pressed mask face, oil-painted features, applied ears, brush-stroked or corkscrew curls, stitched hands and feet, some with painted boots. All in good condition with appropriate clothing.

Very good condition

17" – 19" ..$18,000.00 – 20,000.00

Fair condition

17" – 19" ..$9,000.00 – 12,000.00

16" Izannah Walker doll. $15,000.00.
Photo courtesy of The Museum Doll Shop.

WAX

16" English slit head wax doll. $900.00.
Photo courtesy of The Museum Doll Shop.

1850 – 1930. Made by English, German, French, and other firms, reaching heights of popularity ca. 1875. Seldom marked, wax dolls were poured, some reinforced with plaster, and less expensive, but more durable with wax over papier-mâché or composition. English makers

11½" poured wax doll. $900.00. **Photo courtesy of McMasters Harris Auction Co.**

21" wax-over-composition, wigged. $1,100.00. **Photo courtesy of Richard Withington, Inc.**

included Montanari, Pierotti, and Peck. German makers included Heinrich Stier.

Dolls listed are in good condition with original clothes, or appropriately dressed. More for exceptional dolls; much less for dolls in poor condition.

Slit-head wax, English, 1830 – 1860s, wax over composition shoulder head, hair inserted into slit on center top of head, glass eyes may use wire closure

> 14".................. $825.00 – 900.00
> 16" – 18"..... $900.00 – 1,000.00
> 23" – 25".. $1,400.00 – 1,800.00

Poured Wax, 1850s – 1900s

Baby, shoulder head, painted features, glass eyes, English Montanari type, closed mouth, cloth body, wig, or hair inserted into wax

> 13" – 18"..... $925.00 – 1,200.00
> 23" – 25".. $1,300.00 – 2,200.00

Child, shoulder head, inserted hair, glass eyes, wax limbs, cloth body

> 13" – 15".. $1,100.00 – 1,300.00
> 18" – 22".. $1,300.00 – 1,800.00
> 25" – 27".. $2,200.00 – 3,000.00

Adult

Lady

> 11" – 15".. $1,000.00 – 2,000.00

Man in uniform

> 24" .... $2,300.00 – 2,500.00

Wax over Composition or Reinforced, 1860s – 1890s

Child

ca. 1860 – 1890, early poured wax shoulder head, reinforced with plaster, inserted hair, glass eyes, cloth body

> 10" – 12"........ $600.00 – 800.00
> 14" – 16"........ $750.00 – 800.00
> 20" – 22".. $1,000.00 – 1,200.00
> 25" – 29"........ $850.00 – 600.00

25" with elaborate hairstyle with long curls coming down onto shoulders, necklace fits into holes on neck $3,500.00*

Wax over socket head, glass eyes

> 16" – 18"..... $1,3500 – 1,500.00

Later wax over composition shoulder head, open or closed mouth, glass eyes, wig, cloth body

> 10" – 12"........ $200.00 – 250.00
> 15" – 17"........ $275.00 – 350.00
> 21" – 23"........ $425.00 – 475.00

Molded hair, wax over composition, shoulder head, glass eyes, cloth body, wooden limbs, molded shoes

20" wax-over-composition with molded hair. $450.00. **Photo courtesy of Sharing My Dolls & Stuff.**

13" – 15"........ $200.00 – 275.00
19" – 23"........ $300.00 – 400.00

Alice in Wonderland style, with molded headband

16".................. $625.00 – 700.00

Lady

Wigged

15" – 22"..... $650.00 – 1,000.00

Molded hair and gloves

15" – 22".. $1,000.00 – 3,000.00

Bonnethead: See Bonnet Head section.

Wax crèche figure, 1880 – 1910, poured wax Christ Child, inset hair, glass eyes

13" – 15" .... $350.00 – 600.00

Wax fashion doll, 1910 – 1920, wax head, wire armature body, by makers such as LaFitte et Desirat and others, usually on wooden base

13" – 14" .... $600.00 – 900.00

NORAH WELLINGS

1926 to 1960, Wellington, Shropshire, England. The Victoria Toy Works was founded by Norah Wellings and her brother Leonard. Norah had previously worked as chief designer for Chad Valley. They made cloth dolls with molded heads and bodies of velvet, velveteen, plush, and felt, specializing in sailor souvenir dolls for steamship lines. The line included children, adults, blacks, ethnic, and fantasy dolls.

Baby, molded face, oil-painted features, some papier-mâché covered by stockinette, stitched hip and shoulder joints

10" .... $275.00 – 375.00
15"................. $425.00 – 600.00
22"................. $775.00 – 900.00

Child

Painted eyes

12" – 14"........ $400.00 – 500.00
16" – 18"........ $500.00 – 650.00

10½" Wellings Welsh girl. $100.00. **Doll courtesy of Elaine Holda.**

22" – 23"........ $700.00 – 800.00
28".............. $900.00 – 1,000.00

Glass eyes

15" –18"......... $700.00 – 850.00
22"........... $1,000.00 – 1,300.00

Characters in uniform, regional dress, Pixie People, floppy limbed, painted eyes, Mounties, Sailors, Policemen, Scots, others

8" – 10"............ $90.00 – 100.00

Harry the Hawk

7½" .... $360.00 – 400.00
13" – 14"........ $150.00 – 175.00

17" painted eye Wellings child. $650.00. **Photo courtesy of Richard Withington, Inc.**

Black or Asian

    8" – 13".......... $140.00 – 220.00

    16" – 18"........ $160.00 – 240.00

Black Islander, glass eyes

    13"................. $160.00 – 200.00

    16"................. $225.00 – 300.00

Too few in database for reliable range.

Jolly Toddlers

    11"................. $200.00 – 260.00

15" Georgian period wooden doll. $6,500.00. **Photo courtesy of The Museum Doll Shop.**

WOODEN

Wooden dolls have been made from the earliest recorded times. During the 1600s and 1700s they became the luxury play dolls of the era. They were made commercially in England, Germany, Switzerland, Russia, United States, and other countries. By the late 1700s and early 1800s inexpensive German wooden dolls were the affordable doll of the masses and were exported worldwide.

English

William & Mary Period, 1690s – 1700, carved wooden head, tiny multi-stroke eye-brow and eyelashes, colored cheeks, human hair or flax wig, wooden body, fork-like carved wooden hands, jointed wooden legs, cloth upper arms, medium to fair condition

    18" – 22"..$36,350.00 – 46,000.00

Too few in database for reliable range.

Queen Anne Period, early 1700s, dotted eyebrows, eyelashes, painted or glass eyes, no pupils, carved oval-shaped head, flat wooden back and hips, nicely dressed, good condition

    14"....... $10,500.00 – 11,000.00

Too few in database for reliable range.

    18"....... $14,000.00 – 18,900.00

Too few in database for reliable range.

    24"....... $22,000.00 – 26,000.00

Too few in database for reliable range.

Georgian Period, 1750s – 1800, round wooden head, gesso coated, inset glass eyes, dotted eyelashes and eyebrows, human hair or flax wig, jointed wooden body, pointed torso, medium to fair condition

    13" – 16".. $6,000.00 – 8,000.00

    18" – 24" ..$6,500.00 – 8,000.00

1800 – 1840, gesso-coated wooden head, painted eyes, human hair or flax wig, original clothing comes down below wooden legs

    12" – 15" ..$1,800.00 – 2,200.00

    18" – 22" ..$2,800.00 – 3,200.00

15" German peg wooden with wooden earrings. $2,500.00. **Photo courtesy of Richard Withington, Inc.**

24" Bébé Tout en Bois. $800.00.
Photo courtesy of Dolls & Lace.

German

1810 – 1850s, delicately carved painted hair style, spit curls, some with hair decorations such as "tuck comb," all wooden head and body, pegged or ball-jointed limbs, allow more for exceptional original costume, wooden earrings, sideburn man, etc.

4½"	$550.00 – 600.00
7"	$725.00 – 925.00
12" – 13"	$1,200.00 – 1,800.00
17" – 18"	$1,900.00 – 2,100.00

1850s – 1900

All wood with painted plain hair style, may have spit curls

1"	$100.00 – 125.00
4" – 5"	$100.00 – 125.00
6" – 8"	$150.00 – 250.00
14" – 17"	$400.00 – 550.00

Wooden shoulder head, fancy carved hair style, wood limbs, cloth body

12"	$375.00 – 500.00
16"	$1,000.00* man, carved hair
23"	$775.00 – 900.00

Bohemian, with red painted torso

8" – 10"	$175.00 – 225.00
14" – 16"	$250.00 – 300.00

1900 on, turned wooden head, carved nose, painted hair, lower legs with black shoes, peg jointed

11"	$60.00 – $80.00

Bébé Tout en Bois, 1900 – 1914, all-wooden doll made by German firms such as Rudolf Schneider, Schilling, and others, made for the French trade, child or baby, fully jointed body, glass eyes or painted, open mouth.

9" – 10"	$200.00 – 400.00
15"	$400.00 – 475.00
18"	$425.00 – 525.00
23"	$525.00 – 725.00

Kokeshi, 1900 on, Japan, traditional simple turned wooden dolls made for native and foreign tourist trade, values can be higher for unusual design or known artists.

1850s – 1900

7" – 14"	$900.00 – 1,000.00

1900 – 1930

7" – 9"	$200.00 – 400.00

1950 to present

7" – 9"	$55.00 – 125.00

Matryoskia, Russian Nesting Dolls, 1900, set of wooden canisters that separate in the middle, brightly painted with a glossy finish to represent adults, children, storybook or fairytale characters, and animals. These come in sets usually of five or more

5½" Kokeshi, second half of the twentieth century. $35.00. **Photo courtesy of The Museum Doll Shop.**

5" down Matryoskia, mid twentieth century. $100.00. **Photo courtesy of The Museum Doll Shop.**

related characters, the larger doll opening to reveal a smaller doll nesting inside, and so on, values can be much higher for unusual design or known artists.

Set pre 1930s

4"	$70.00 – 100.00
7"	$115.00 – 150.00
9"	$175.00 – 230.00

Set new

5"	$12.00 – 20.00
7"	$18.00 – 30.00

12" Swiss wooden doll. $475.00. **Photo courtesy of The Museum Doll Shop.**

Political set: Gorbachev, Yeltsin

5"	$20.00 – 35.00
7"	$50.00 – 60.00

Swiss, 1900 on, carved wooden dolls with dowel jointed bodies, joined at elbow, hips, knees, some with elaborate hair

8" – 10"	$400.00 – 600.00
12" – 16"	$475.00 – 725.00

Springfield, VT Woodens

Cooperative Manufacturing Co., 1873 – 1874, Joel Ellis manufactured wooden dolls with pressed heads and mortise and double tennon joints, with metal hands and feet painted black or blue, painted black molded hair sometimes blond, similar type wooden dolls were made by Jointed Doll Co. under patents by Martin, Sanders, Johnson, Mason & Taylor, a variety of head and jointing styles were used on these dolls.

Ellis, Joel (Cooperative Manufacturing Co.)

12"	$800.00 – 1,100.00
15"	$1,200.00 – 1,500.00

Jointed Doll Co.

11½"	$500.00 – 800.00

Tynietoy, 1917 on, Providence, Rhode Island, sold peg wooden type dolls called Peggity

11½" Jointed Doll Company doll. $750.00. **Photo courtesy of The Museum Doll Shop.**

dolls.

     5"................... $500.00 – 600.00

Hitty: See Artist Dolls.

Schoenhut: See that section

WPA, VARIOUS PROJECTS

     1935 – 1943, Works Progress Administration project to provide work for artisans and home workers. Other states also ran doll making projects under the WPA.

Milwaukee, WI project

Molded stockinette doll, cloth body, cotton yarn hair, painted features, tab hinged joint and hips

     22"........... $1,000.00 – 1,100.00

Black .... $2,500.00 – 3,500.00

Flat face cloth doll, embroidered features, cotton yarn hair

     11"................. $450.00 – 475.00

     14"................. $500.00 – 550.00

     16"................. $650.00 – 750.00

New York City project, cloth mask face

     14"................................$250.00

Too few in database for reliable range.

Papier-mâché doll, project unknown, dressed in regional or historic costume

     14" – 16".......... $300.00 – 50.00

20" W.P.A doll with molded cloth face, project unknown. $600.00.
Photo courtesy of Richard Withington, Inc.

BIBLIOGRAPHY

Johana Gast Anderton. *20th Century Dolls*. Des Moines: Wallace Homestead Book Co., 1971.

———. *More 20th Century Dolls, Vol. I & II*. Des Moines: Wallace Homestead Book Co., 1974.

———. *The Collector's Encyclopedia of Cloth Dolls*. Lombard: Wallace Homestead Book Co., 1984.

Genevieve Angione and Judith Whorton. *All Dolls Are Collectible*. New York: Crown Publishers, Inc, 1977.

Helen Bullard. *Crafts and Craftsmen of the Tennessee Mountains*. Falls Church: The Summit Press Ltd., 1976.

———. *The American Doll Artist*. Boston: the Charles T. Branford Co., 1965.

———. *The American Doll Artist*. Kansas City: Athens Publishing Co., 1975.

Jurgen and Marianne Cieslik. *German Doll Encyclopedia*. Cumberland: Hobby House Press, 1985.

Dorothy S., Elizabeth A., Evelyn J. Coleman. *The Collector's Encyclopedia of Dolls Vol. I & II*. New York: Crown Publishers, Inc., 1968 & 1986.

———. *The Collector's Book of Dolls' Clothes*. New York: Crown Publishers, Inc., 1975.

Suzanne DeMillar & Dennis Brevik. *Arranbee Dolls*. Paducah: Collector Books, 2004.

Linda Edward. *Cloth Dolls From Ancient to Modern*. Atglen: Schiffer Publishing, 1997.

Clara Hallard Fawcett. *Dolls A Guide for Collectors*. New York: H I Lindquist Publications, 1947.

———. *Dolls A New Guide for Collectors*. Boston: Charles T Branford Co., 1964.

Jan Foulke. *The Blue Book of Dolls and Values Vol. 2 through 14*. Cumberland: Hobby House Press, 1976, 1978, 1980, 1982, 1984, 1986, 1987, 1989, 1991, 1993, 1995, 1997, 1999.

Christiane Grafnitz. *German Paper-Mache Dolls 1760 – 1860*. Germany: Verlag Puppen & Spielzeug 1994.

Judith Izen. *American Character Dolls*. Paducah: Collector Books, 2004.

———. *Collector's Guide to Ideal Dolls*. Paducah: Collector Books, 2005.

Judith Izen & Carol Stover. *Collector's Encyclopedia of Vogue Dolls*. Paducah: Collector Books, 2005.

Flora Gill Jacobs. *Dolls' Houses in America*. New York: Charles Scribner's Sons, 1974.

———. *A History of Dolls' Houses*. New York: Charles Scribner's Sons, 1953.

Don Jensen. *Collector's Guide to Horsman Dolls*. Paducah: Collector Books, 2002.

Janet Pagter Johl. *The Fascinating Story of Dolls*. Watkins Glen, reissued Century House, 1970.

———. *More About Dolls*. New York: H. L. Lundquist Publications, 1946.

———. *Still More About Dolls*. New York: H. L. Lundquist Publications, 1950.

———. *Your Dolls and Mine*. New York: H. L. Lundquist Publications, 1952.

Polly Judd. *Cloth Dolls*. Cumberland: Hobby House Press, 1990.

Pam & Polly Judd. *Americas, Australia & Pacific Islands Costumed Dolls*. Grantsville: Hobby House Press, 1997.

Constance Eileen King. *The Collector's History of Dolls*. New York: Bonanza Books, 1981.

Wendy Lavitt. *American Folk Dolls*. New York: Alfred A. Knopf, Inc., 1982.

Doris Anderson Lechler. *Bleuette her Gautier-Languereau Ads and Catalogues of Fashion 1905 – 1960*. Self published.

———. *Bleuette — Her Faces, Fashions and Family*. Self published.

Sybill McFadden. *Fawn Zeller's Porcelain Dollmaking Techniques*. Cumberland: Hobby House Press, 1984.

Dorothy McGonagle. *A Celebration of American Dolls*. Grantsville: Hobby House Press, 1997.

Madeline Osborne Merrill. *The Art of Dolls*. Cumberland: Hobby House Press, 1985.

Madeline O. Merrill and Nellie O. Perkins. *Handbook of Collectible Dolls Vol. I.*,1969.

Ursula Mertz. *Collector's Encyclopedia of Composition Dolls*. Paducah: Collector Books, 1999.

———. *Collector's Encyclopedia of Composition Dolls Vol. II*. Paducah: Collector Books, 2004.

Winifred Mills & Louise Dunn. *The Story of Old Dolls and How to Make New Ones*. New York: Doubleday, Doran & Co., Inc., 1940.

Estelle Patino. *American Rag Dolls*. Paducah: Collector Books, 1988.

Elaine Pardee & Jackie Robertson. *Encyclopedia of Bisque Nancy Ann Storybook Dolls*. Paducah: Collector Books, 2003.

Julie Pelletier Robertson. *Celluloid Dolls, Toys & Playthings*. Paducah: Collector Books, 2006.

Albert Christian Revi. *Spinning Wheel's Complete Book of Dolls*. New York: Galahad Books, 1975.

Lydia Richter. *Treasury of German Dolls*. Tucson: HP Books, 1984.

———. *The Beloved Kathe Kruse Dolls*. Cumberland: Hobby House Press, 1983.

Nancy Schiffer. *Indian Dolls*. Atglen: Schiffer Publishing Ltd., 1997.

Esther Singleton. *Dolls*. New York: Payson & Clark Ltd., 1927.

Eleanor St. George. *The Dolls of Yesterday*. New York and London: Charles Scribner's Sons, 1948.

———. *Dolls of Three Centuries*. New York and London: Charles Scribner's Sons, 1951.

Patricia Smith. *Antique Collector's Dolls Vol. 2*. Paducah: Collector Books, 1976.

Lewis Sorensen. *Lewis Sorensen's Doll Scrapbook*. Alhambra: Thor Publications, 1976.

Sydney Ann Sutton. *Scouting Dolls Through the Years*. Paducah: Collector Books, 2003.

Florence Theiriault. *Catalog Reprint Series*. Annapolis: Gold Horse Publishing, 1998.

Gillian Trotter. *Norah Wellings Cloth Dolls and Soft Toys*. Grantsville: Hobby House Press, 2003.

Joan Van Patton & Linda Lau. *Nippon Dolls & Playthings*. Paducah, Collector Books, 2001.

Blair Whitton. *Bliss Toys and Dollhouses*. New York: Dover Publications.

COLLECTOR'S RESOURCES

Antique Doll Dealers

American Beauty Dolls
Nancy Stronczek
26 Bouker Street
Greenfield, MA 01301
413-774-3260
njs@crocker.com
www.rubylane.com/shops/
    americanbeautydolls

Armory Antiques
365 Thames St
Newport, RI 02840
401-848-2398

Aunt Mary's Antique Dolls
P.O. Box 198
Hawleyville, CT 06440
203-426-9557
mfurse@earthlink.net
www.rubylane.com/shops/
    auntmarysantiquedolls

Cybermogul Dolls
Marie Witherill
Statesville, NC 28677
cybermogul@roadrunner.com
www.rubylane.com/shops/cybermogul

Dollhappy
Jean Johnson
2 Meadowbrook Lane
West Memphis, AR 72301
(870) 735-8159
Fax: 870-735-8159
triplejven@aol.com
www.rubylane.com/shops/dollhappy

Dollsantique

Patricia Vaillancourt
P.O. Box 326
Adamstown, PA 19501
717-484-2443
www.dollsantique.com

Dolls and Lace
P.O. Box 743
Lehi, UT 84043
dollsandlace@hotmail.com
www.dollsandlace.com

Dollyology Vintage Dolls
Kate Gillen
15516 Sunken Bridge Rd.
Grass Valley, CA 95949
dollyology@hotmail.com
www.rubylane.com/shops/
    dollyologyvintagedolls

Emmie's Antique Doll Castle
Robbin Wilson
400 W. 32nd Court
Sand Springs, OK 74063
918-241-0269
www.rubylane.com/shops/emmiesgirl

Estate Auctions, Inc.
Norb & Marie Novocin
12221 Old Furnace Rd.
Seaford, DE 19973
1-800-573-3508
www.estateauctionsinc.com

Fine Antique Dolls & Accessories
241 Park Ridge Ct.
Kingsport, TN 37664
www.tennesseeantiquedolls.com

Glenda Antique Dolls & Collectables

Gray's Antique Market, 1–7 Davies Mews,
London W1K 5AB
Telephone 020 8367 2441
Mobile telephone 07970 722750
glenda@glenda-antiquedolls.com
www.glenda-antiquedolls.com

Hatton's Gallery of Dolls
www.hattonsgallery.com
info@hattonsgallery.com

Joan & Lynette Antique Dolls and Accessories
6551 Carrollton Avenue
Indianapolis, IN 46220
www.rubylane.com/shops/
    joanlynetteantiquedolls

Linda Kellermann
11013 Treyburn Drive
Glen Allen, VA 23059
lindasantiques@erols.com

Doris Lechler
949 E. Cooke Rd.
Columbus, OH 43224
614-261-6659
dorislechler@aol.com

Museum Doll Shop
104 Van Zandt Ave.
Newport, RI 02840
401-847-6866
www.dollmuseum.com

My Dear Dolly
PO Box 303
Sparta, NJ 07871
mydeardollypat@yahoo.com
www.mydeardolly.com

My Dolly Dearest
PO Box 909

8 S Village Circle
Adamstown, PA 19501
717-484-1137
sidneyjeffrey@mydollydearest.com

N.A.D.D.A.
National Antique Doll Dealers Association
www.nadda.org

Roberta's Doll House
475 17th Avenue
Paterson, NJ 07504
800-569-9739
robertasdollhous@aol.com
www.robertasdollhouse.com

Rosalie Whyel Museum of Doll Art
1116 108th Avenue N.E.
Bellevue, WA 98004
206-455-1116
Fax: 206-455-4793

Sharing My Dolls & Stuff
Helen Welsh
799 Bent Creek Dr.
Lititz, PA 17543
helen1005@aol.com
www.rubylane.com/shops/
    sharingmydollsnstuff

Taecker House Antique Dolls
Thela Huffman
Brawley, CA 92227
760-455-3757
www.rubylane.com/shops/
    taeckerhouseantiquedolls

Trish's Treasures Antique Dolls
www.rubylane.com/shops/antiquedolls

Turn of the Century Antiques
1475 South Broadway

Denver, CO 80210
303-702-8700
www.turnofthecenturyantiques.com

Usefulcollectibles
Marsha Anderson
Liberty, MO
816-781-5598

Auction Houses

Alderfer Auction Company, Inc.
501 Fairgrounds Rd.
Hatfield, PA 19440
215-393-3000
fax 215-368-9055
www.alderferauction.com

William J. Janack Estate Appraisals &
Auctioneers
62 Kings Highway Bypass
Chester, NY 10918
845-469-9095
www.janack.com

McMasters Harris Auction Co.
Ohio & Kansas City
800-842-3526
info@mcmastersharris.com
www.mcmastersharris.com
www.mharrislive.com

Skinner Inc.
357 Main St.
Bolton, MA 01740
978-779-6241

Richard Withington, Inc.
590 Center Rd.
Hillsboro, NH 03244
603-464-3232

Collector Clubs & Newsletters
Bleuette
Bleuette's World
Agnes J. Sura, Editor
489 Wilson Hill Rd
Hoosick Falls, NY 12090
518-686-5740
Quarterly publication

Chérie Amies de Bleuette Revue
Linda Justice, Editor
4143 Mercier
Kansas City, MO 64111
lindasruffles@yahoo.com
Quarterly publication

Celebrity Dolls
Celebrity Doll Journal
Loraine Burdick, Editor
413 10th Ave. Ct. NE
Puyallup, WA 98372
Quarterly newsletter

Chatty Cathy, Mattel
Chatty Cathy Collectors Club
Melissa Gilkey Mince, Editor
ChattynMe@aol.com
www.ttinet.com/chattycathy/

Costuming
Doll Costumer's Guild™
Pat Gosh, Editor
P O Box 247
New Harmony, IN 47631
812-682-3802
fax: 812-682-3815
patgosh@aol.com
www.edoll.org
Quarterly publication

Dionne Quintuplets
Dionne Quintuplet Collectors Too Newsletter

Leonard Belsher & Dee Dee Backus, Editors
P O Box 468
Shawville, Quebec J0X 2Y0 Canada
819-647-1965
quintly2000@yahoo.ca
Quarterly newsletter

French Fashion Gazette
Adele Leurquin, Editor
1862 Sequoia SE
Port Orchard, WA 98366

Gene-Ashton Drake Galleries
www.genemarshalldoll.com

Hitty
Friends of Hitty Newsletter
Virginia Ann Heyerdahl, Editor
2704 Belleview Ave
Cheverly, MD 20785
Four issues per subscription

Mary Hoyer
T.H.E.L.M.A
(The Hoyer Enthusiastic Ladies Mail
Association)
Thelma R. Bernard, Founder, Editor, and
    Publisher
P O Box 42604
Las Vegas, NV 89114
starrlady@webtv.net
A by-mail doll group celebrating past and
present Mary Hoyer dolls via newsletter
format.
Quarterly newsletter

Ideal
Ideal Collectors' Newsletter
Judith Izen, Editor
PO Box 623
Lexington, MA 02173
Jizen@aol.comQuarterly

Sasha Friends
Chris Kading, Editor and Publisher
P O Box 136
Cambridge, IA 50046
kading@att.net

Sharon Sams, Editor and Publisher
305 12th Avenue, N.W.
Altoona, IA 50009
sharon_sams_2000@yahoo.com
Quarterly newsletter
A newsletter for those who care for Sasha
Dolls

Shirley Temple
Australian Shirley Temple Collectors News
Quarterly Newsletter
Victoria Horne, Editor
39 How Ave.
North Dandenong
Victoria, 3175, Australia

Lollipop News
Shirley Temple Collectors by the Sea
PO Box 6203
Oxnard, CA 93031

Shirley Temple Collectors News
Rita Dubas, Editor
881 Colonial Road
Brooklyn, NY 11209
Quarterly, $20.00 year
bukowski@wazoo.com
www.ritadubasdesign.com/shirley/

United Federation of Doll Clubs, Inc.
10900 North Pomona Avenue
Kansas City, MO 64153
816-891-7040
fax 816-891-8360
ufdcinfo@ufdc.org
www.ufdc.org

Doll Manufacturers

Adora Original Doll®
300 Columbus Circle
Edison, NJ 08837
732-346-0818
fax: 732-346-1308
info@adoradoll.com
www.adoradoll.com

Alexander Doll Company, Inc
615 West 131st Street
New York, NY 10027
Gale Jarvis, President
212-939-7901; 800-229-5192
www.madamealexander.com

The Review
Manhattan Station
P O Box 2739
New York, NY 10027-9998
212-368-1047
info@madc.org
www.madc.org
Official publication of the Madame
Alexander Doll Club. Contact for club
information.

American Girl
8400 Fairway Place
P O Box 620190
Middleton, WI 53562-0190
800-845-0005
www.americangirl.com

Bella! Productions
Christina Bougas, Artistic Director
174 W. Foothill Blvd, #317
Monrovia, CA 91016
626-359-9097; 866-430-2532
www.cleabella.com

Berdine Creedy Originals, Inc.
5015 NW 71 Place
Gainesville, FL 32653
352-336-2510
fax: 352-336-7282
berdine@berdinecreedy.com
www.berdinecreedy.com

Charisma Brands, LLC
25800 Commercecentre Dr
Lake Forest, CA 92630
949-595-7900; 800-779-5335
fax: 949-595-7914
www.charimabrands.com

D.A.E. Originals
David Escobedo and Brian Schafer
1035 N. Ellsworth Rd
Suite 107, PMB 17
Mesa, AZ 85207
877-581-7056
www.daeoriginals.com

Heidi Plusczok Puppen Design
Heidi Plusczok
Erlenweg 5
D-61130 Nidderau, Germany
011-49-6187-23222
fax: 011-49-6187-24608
plusdolls@aol.com
www.heidiplusczok.com

Horsman Ltd.
Kenneth Young
17 Barstow Rd, Ste 407
Great Neck, NY 11021-2213
516-504-0387
fax: 516-504-0397
horsman@horsmanltd.com
www.horsmanltd.com

Kish & Company

Helen and Thomas Kish
1800 West 33rd Avenue
Denver, CO 80211
303-972-0053
fax: 303-932-2405
www.kishandcompany.com
collectors@kishandcompany.com
Kish Collectors Society
The Newsletter of the Kish Collectors Society

Käthe Kruse Puppen GmbH
Andrea-Kathrin Christenson, CEO
86609 Donauwörth
Alte Augsburger Str. 9, Germany
011-49-09-06-7-06-78-0
fax: 011-49-09-06-78-70
familie@kaethe-kruse.de
www.kaethekruse.com
Doll One
The Newsletter for the Käthe Kruse Family
Quarterly newsletter

The Lawton Doll Company
Wendy and Keith Lawton
1651 Lander Ave, Ste. 125
Turlock, CA 95380
209-632-3655
fax: 209-632-6788
info@lawtondolls.com
www.lawtondolls.com

Middleton Doll Company, Inc.
2400 Corporate Exchange Dr, #220
Columbus, OH 43231
800-242-3285
www.leemiddleton.com
www.mycollection.middleton-doll.com

Nancy Ann Storybook Dolls, Inc.
P O Box 5072
El Dorado Hills, CA 95762
Claudette Buehler and Delene Budd

916-961-1032
www.nancyannstorybookdolls.com

Terri Lee Associates
7600 El Camino Real #1-200
Atascadero, CA 93422
888-837-7450
info1@terrilee.com
www.terrilee.com

The Tonner Doll Company
Robert Tonner, CEO
459 Hurley Ave
Hurley, NY 12443
845-339-9537
fax: 845-339-1259
www.tonnerdoll.com
Tonner Doll Collectors Club
Quarterly newsletter

The Vogue Doll Company, Inc.
Linda Smith, President
P.O. Box 756
Oakdale, CA 95361-0756
209-848-0300
fax: 209-848-4423
www.voguedolls.com
The Ginny® Journal™
A Newsletter of the Ginny Doll Club
Quarterly

Internet

eBay auction site
www.ebay.com

Doll Collecting
Denise Van Patten
denise@dollymaker.com
www.collectdolls.about.com

Preservation

Light Impressions
P.O. Box 787
Brea, CA 92822-0787
(800) 828-6216
www.lightimpressionsdirect.com

Twin Pines of Maine, Inc.
Nicholas Hill
P O Box 1178
Scarborough, ME 04070-1178
800-770-DOLL (3655)
www.twinpines.com

Paper Doll Publications

Greetings
Louise Leek
10158 Land Catherine
Streetsboro, OH 44141

Now & Then
Arlene Del Fava
67-40 Yellowstone Blvd.
Forest Hills, NY 11375

Cornerstones
Deanna Williams
733 de la Fuente
Monterey Park, CA 91754

O.P.D.A.G.
Jenny Taliadoros
P. O. Box 14
Kingfield, ME 04947

Paper Doll Review
Jenny Taliadoros
P. O. Box 14
Kingfield, ME 04947

Paper Doll Pal
Jim Faraone

19109 Silcott Springs Road
Purcellville, VA 20132

Paklaeningsdukken
Lise Clasen
Stensbaekvej 53
Fjelso DK 9620
Denmark

The Paper Doll Circle
Lorna Currie Thomopolous
28 Ferndown Gardens
Cobham, KT11 2BH
Surrey, England

Publications

Antique Doll Collector
Keith Kaonis, Advertising & Creative Director
Donna Kaonis, Editor-in-Chief
Puffin Company, LLC
6 Woodside Avenue, Suite 300
Northport, NY 11768
631-261-4100
fax: 631-261-9684
AntiqueDollColl@optonline.net
www.antiquedollcollector.com
Monthly magazine

Collectors United
Gary Green, Publisher
711 S. 3rd Ave
Chatsworth, GA 30705
706-695-8242
fax: 706-695-0770
diang@collectorsunited.com
www.collectorsunited.com
Monthly newspaper

Contemporary Doll Collector
Ruth Keessen, Publisher and Editor
801 W. Norton Ave, Suite 200

Muskegon, MI 49441
231-733-9382
fax: 231-733-7635
www.scottpublications.com
www.contemporarydollcollector.com
Subscription information: 800-458-8237
Bi-monthly magazine

Doll Castle News

Barry Mueller, Publisher
Dorita M. Mortensen, Editor
37 Belvidere Ave, P O Box 247
Washington, NJ 07882
908-689-7042; 800-572-6607
fax: 908-689-6320
editor@dollcastlemagazine.com
www.dollcastlemagazine.com
Bi-monthly magazine

Doll Diary

Lauren Welker, Editor and Publisher
204 East Coover St
Mechanicsburg, PA 17055
dollsbylauren@paonline.com
www.laurenwelker.com
Quarterly publication

Doll News

UFDC Corporate Office
10900 N. Pomona Avenue
Kansas City, MO 64153
www.ufdc.org
Official publication of the United Federation
of Doll Clubs, Inc.
Quarterly magazine

Doll Reader

Susan Fitzgerald, Publisher
Jill Jackson, Editor
Madavor Media, LLC
420 Boylston Street, 5th Floor
Boston, MA 02116

617-536-0100
fax: 617-536-0102
Subscription information: 800-437-5828
www.dollreader.com
Nine times a year

Dolls

Joe Jones, Publisher
Nayda Rondon, Editor
Jones Publishing, Inc.
N7450 Aanstad Rd, P O Box 5000
Iola, WI 54945-5000
715-445-5000
JoeJones@jonespublishing.com
www.jonespublishing.com

Fashion Doll Quarterly

Pat Henry, Publisher
299 Eastern Parkway
Germantown, NY 12526
fdqmag@mac.com
www.fashiondollquarterly.com
Subscription information: 212-961-0662
Quarterly magazine

Haute Doll

Karen Caviale, Editor
5711 Eighth Ave
Kenosha, WI 53140
262-658-1004
fax: 262-658-0433
mcpub@hautedoll.com
www.hautedoll.com
Bi-monthly

Master Collector

Brian Savage, Publisher
Fun Publications, Inc.
225 Cattle Baron Parc Dr
Fort Worth, TX 76108
800-772-6673

Modern Doll Collectors Convention®

Modern Doll, Inc.
Patsy Moyer, President
P O Box 311
Deming, NM 88031-0311
moddoll@yahoo.com
moderndollcollectors.com
Yahoo group: http://groups.yahoo.com/
group/moderndollconvention/

Museums

Arizona
Arizona Doll and Toy Museum
602 E Adams Street
Phoenix, AZ
Hours: Tue – Sat 10 – 4; Sun: 12 – 4
www.artcom.com/museums/nv/
af/85004-23.htm

Colorado
Denver Museum of Miniatures, Dolls & Toys
1880 Gaylord St.
Denver, CO 80206
303-322-1053
Hours: Tues. – Sat. 10 – 4; Sun.: 12 – 4
Closed Mondays and holidays.
www.coloradokids.com/miniatures/

Louisiana
The Enchanted Mansion, A Doll Museum
190 Lee Drive
Baton Rouge, LA 70808
225-769-0005
Hours: Mon., Wed. – Sat. 10 – 5
Closed Sun. and Tues.

The Lois Luftin Doll Museum
120 South Washington Avenue
DeRidder, LA 70634
Hours: Tues. – Sat. 10 – 4

www.beau.lib.la.us/doll.html

New York
Museum of the City of New York
1220 Fifth Avenue @ 103rd St.
New York, NY 10029
212-534-1672
Hours: Open daily
www.mcny.org/toy.html

Margaret Woodbury Strong Museum
1 Manhattan Square
Rochester, NY 14607
716-263-2700

New Jersey
Princeton Doll and Toy Museum
8 Somerset St.
Hopewell, NJ 08525
609-333-8600
Hours: Mon., Fri. & Sat.10 – 5
www.princetondollandtoy.org

Ohio
Doll & Toy Museum
700 Winchester Pike
Canal Winchester, Ohio
Hours: Wed. – Sat. 11 – 5
April – mid Dec.
www.home.att.net/~dollmuseum
614-837-5573

The Children's Toy & Doll Museum
206 Gilman Street P.O. Box 4034
Marietta, OH 4575
740-373-5900
Hours: Sat. 1 – 4, May – Dec.
www.mariettaohio.org

Pennsylvania
The Philadelphia Doll Museum
2253 North Broad Street

Philadelphia, PA 19132
215-787-0220
bwhiteman@philadollmuseum.com

South Dakota
Enchanted World Doll Museum
615 North Main
Mitchell, SD 57301
606-996-9896
fax: 606-996-0210

Texas
Museum of American Architecture &
Decorative Arts
7502 Fronden Rd
Houston, TX 77074-3298
281-649-3811

Utah
McCurdy Historical Doll Museum
246 North 100 East
Provo, UT 84606
801-377-9935
Hours: Tues. – Sat., 12 – 6, winter: 1 – 5
www: myjoaquin.tripod.com/sites/
    dollmuseum.htm

Vermont
Shelburne Museum
U.S. Route 7, P.O. Box 10
Shelburne, Vermont 05482
802-985-3346
Hours: Summer: 10 – 5 daily
www.shelburnemuseum.org

Washington
Rosalie Whyel Museum of Doll Art
1116 108th Avenue N.E.
Bellevue, WA 98004
206-455-1116

fax: 206-455-4793
www.dollart.com

Wisconsin
La Crosse Doll Museum
1213 Caledonia Street
La Crosse, WI 54603
608-785-0020
www.dollmuseum.org
Hours: Mon. – Sat., 10 – 5, Sun. 11 – 4

The Fennimore Doll & Toy Museum and Gift
Shoppe
140 Lincoln Ave.
Fennimore, WI 53809
608-822-4100
www.fennimore.com/dolltoy
Hours: May 7 – Dec. 14, Mon. – Sat. 10 – 4

Doll Artists

NADDA
National Antique Doll Dealers Association
www.nadda.org

Raggedy Ann
Rags Newsletter
Barbara Barth, Editor
PO Box 823
Atlanta, GA 30301

Videos

Leonard A. Swann, Jr.
SIROCCO Productions, Inc.
5660 E. Virgina Beach Blvd., Suite 105
Norfolk, VA 23502
757-461-8987
iswann@specialtyproducts.net
www.siroccovideo.com

SYMBOL INDEX

LETTER INDEX

MOLD INDEX

MARKS INDEX

Alabama Baby

Alabama Indestructible Dolls Marks:
"MRS. S.S. SMITH//MANUFACTURER AND
DEALER IN// THE ALABAMA
INDESTRUCTIBLE DOLL// ROANOKE, ALA.//
PATENTED//SEPT. 26, 1905."

Henri Alexandre

Alt, Beck, & Gottschalck

Arranbee Doll Co.

ARRANBEE//DOLL
Co. or R & B

Max Oscar Arnold

Art Fabric Mills

Art Fabric Mills Marks:
"ART FABRIC MILLS, NY,
PAT. FEB. 13TH, 1900" on
shoe or bottom of foot.

Georgene Averill

Tag on original outfit reads:
"BONNIE BABE COPYRIGHTED
BY GEORGENE AVERILL MADE
BY K AND K TOY CO."

COPR GEORGENE AVERILL
1005/3652 GERMANY

Bähr & Pröschild

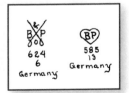

Barbie®

1959 – 1962
BARBIE™
PATS. PEND.
©MCMLVIII
BY//MATTEL, INC.
1963 – 1968
MIDGE™©1962
Barbie®/©1958
BY//MATTEL, INC.
1964 – 1966
©1958//MATTEL, IN.
U.S. PATENTED
U.S. PAT. PEND.
1966 – 1969
©1966//MATTEL, INC.
U.S. PATENTED//
U.S. PAT. PEND//
MADE IN JAPAN

E. Barrios

E 3 B
E. 8 DEPOSE B.

C.M. Bergmann

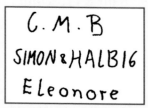

Bru

Fashion-Type Mark:
Marked "A" through "M," "11" to "28," indicating size numbers only

Bru Jne Marks:
"BRU JNE," with size number on head, kid over wood body marked with rectangular paper label.

Bru Jne R. Marks:
"BRU. JNE R." with size number on head, body stamped in red, "Bébé Bru," and size number.

Bébé Breveté Marks:
"Bébé Breveté"
Head marked with size number only; kid body may have paper Bébé Breveté label.

Bye-Lo Baby

© 1923 by
Grace S. Putnam
MADE IN GERMANY
7372/45

Catterfelder Puppenfabrik

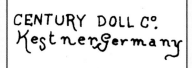

Century Doll Co.

CENTURY DOLL C°.
Kestner Germany

Chuckles mark on back:
"CHUCKLES//A
CENTURY DOLL"

Chase Doll Company

"CHASE STOCKINET DOLL"
on left leg or under left arm.
Paper label, if there, reads
"CHASE//HOSPITAL DOLL//
TRADE MARK// PAWTUCKET,
RI// MADE IN U.S.A."

Chase doll mark, 1889 – 1894.

Chase doll mark, 1908 – 1945.

Columbian

"COLUMBIAN DOLL,
EMMA E. ADAMS,
OSWEGO, NY"

Danel et Cie

E. (Size number) D. on head.
Eiffel Tower "PARIS BEBE"
on body; shoes with "PARIS
BEBE" in star.

Cuno & Otto Dressel

E.D.

EDEN BEBE
PARIS

Eegee

Trademark, EEGEE,
or circle with the words,
"TRADEMARK //EEGEE//
Dolls//MADE IN USA"
Later changed to just
initials, E.G.

Effanbee

Some marked on shoulder
plate, "EFFANBEE //BABY
DAINTY"
or "EFFANBEE //DOLLS//
WALK, TALK, SLEEP"
in oval

Fulper Pottery Co.

Gans & Seyfarth Puppenbabrik

Gladdie

Francois Gaultier

Wm. and F. & W. Goebel

Gesland

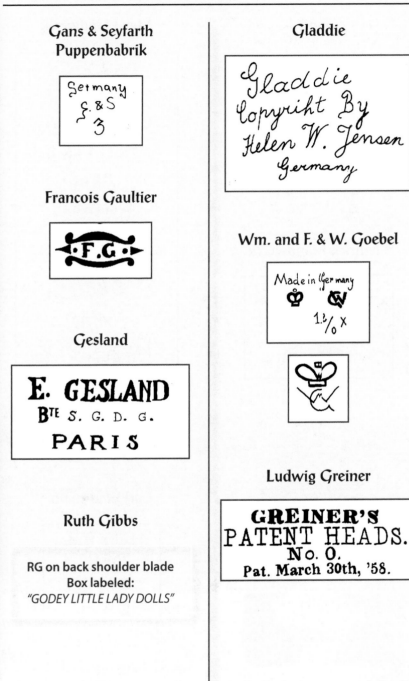

Ludwig Greiner

Ruth Gibbs

RG on back shoulder blade
Box labeled:
"GODEY LITTLE LADY DOLLS"

Gund

"A Gund Product, A Toy of Quality and Distinction." From World War II on: Stylized "G" with rabbit ears and whiskers. Mid 1960s – 1987: Bear's head above the letter "U." From 1987 on: "GUND."

Heinrich Handwerck

HANDWERCK
5
Germany

Max Handwerck

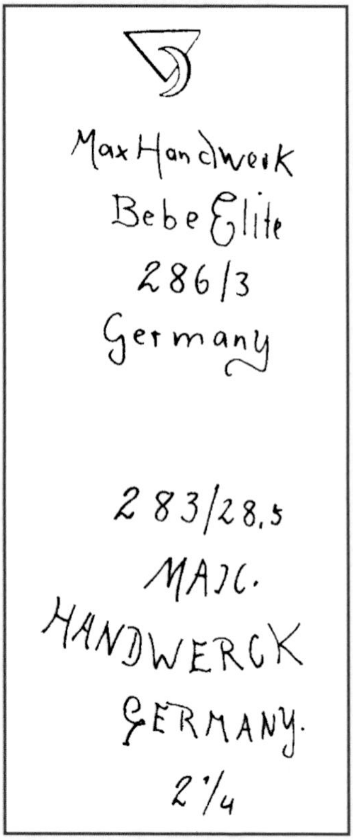

Max Handwerk
Bebe Elite
286/3
Germany

283/28.5
MAX.
HANDWERCK
GERMANY.
2 ¼

Carl Hartmann

Globe Baby
DEP
Germany
C 3 H

Karl Hartmann

Hasbro

1964 – 1965
Marked on right
lower back:
G.I. Joe TM//COPYRIGHT 1964//
BY HASBRO ®//PATENT PENDING//
MADE IN U.S.A.//GIJoe®

1967
Slight change in marking:
COPYRIGHT 1964//BY HASBRO
®//PATENT PENDING// MADE IN
U.S.A.// GIJoe®
This mark appears on all four
armed service branches, excluding
the black action figures.

Hertel Schwab & Co.

Ernst Heubach

Gebrüder Heubach

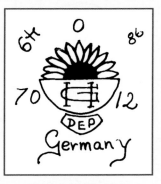

E.I. Horseman

"E.I. H.//CO."
and "CAN'T
BREAK 'EM"

Mary Hoyer Doll Mfg. Co.

"THE MARY HOYER DOLL" or "ORIGINAL MARY HOYER DOLL"

Adolph Hülss

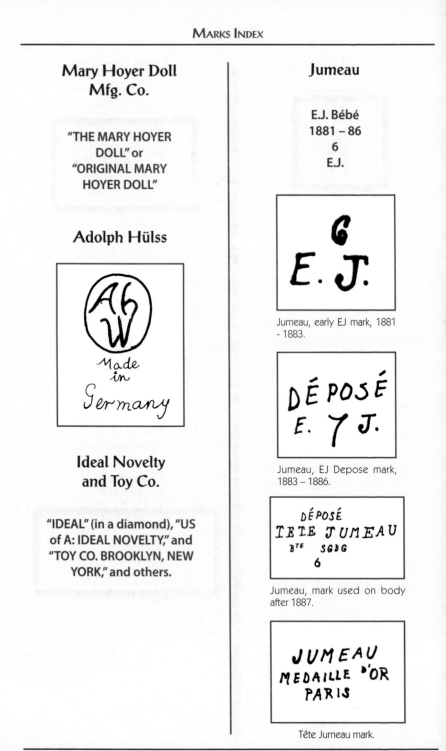

Ideal Novelty and Toy Co.

"IDEAL" (in a diamond), "US of A: IDEAL NOVELTY," and "TOY CO. BROOKLYN, NEW YORK," and others.

Jumeau

E.J. Bébé
1881 – 86
6
E.J.

Jumeau, early EJ mark, 1881 - 1883.

Jumeau, EJ Depose mark, 1883 – 1886.

Jumeau, mark used on body after 1887.

Tête Jumeau mark.

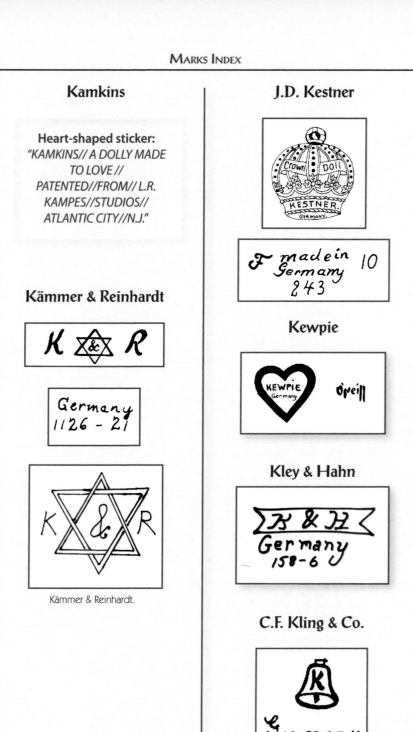

Kamkins

Heart-shaped sticker:
*"KAMKINS// A DOLLY MADE
TO LOVE //
PATENTED//FROM// L.R.
KAMPES//STUDIOS//
ATLANTIC CITY//N.J."*

Kämmer & Reinhardt

Kämmer & Reinhardt.

J.D. Kestner

Kewpie

Kley & Hahn

C.F. Kling & Co.

Gebruder Knoch

Konig & Wernicke

Richard Krueger

"KRUEGER NY//REG. U.S.
PAT. OFF/
/MADE IN U.S.A." on body
or clothing seam.

Käthe Kruse

Gebruder Kuhnlenz

Lanternier

Lanternier mark.

Lenci

A.G. Limbach

Armand Marseille

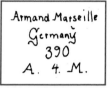

Armand Marseille
Germany
390
A. 4. M.

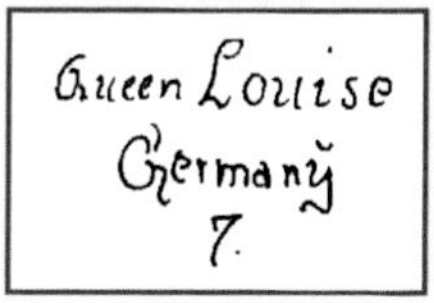

Queen Louise
Germany
7.

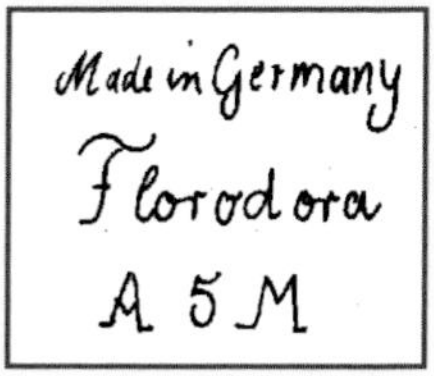

Made in Germany
Florodora
A 5 M

May Freres Cie

On head:
MASCOTTE
On body:
Bébé Mascotte Paris
Child marked:
Mascotte on head

Morimura Bothers

Mark for Morimura Brothers,
Japan 1915 on:

Gebruder Ohlhaver

.Revalo.
Germany

Petite et Dumontier

P 3 D

Rabery & Delphieu

Mark: R.3. D

Theodor Recknagel

Rohmer

Bruno Schmidt

Franz Schmidt

or
S & C
ANVIL MARK

Schmitt & Fils

Shield on head, "SCH" in
shield on bottom of
flat cut derriere.

Schoenau & Hoffmeister

A. Schoenhut & Co.

Schuetzmeister & Quendt

S.F.B.J.

Shirley Temple

Shirley Temple//
IDEAl Nov. & TOY on
back of head and
SHIRLEY TEMPLE on
body. Some marked
only on head and
with a size.

Simon & Halbig

Margarete Steiff

Button in ear

Hermann Steiner

Swaine & Co.

Louis Wolfe & Co.

A. Thuillier

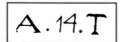

Unis France

Unis France mark.

Unis France diamond mark.

INDEX

INDEX

MAR 0 5 2009

Schroeder's
ANTIQUES
Price Guide

OUR **#1** BEST-SELLER!

FULL COLOR!

Schroeder's ANTIQUES Price Guide

OUR **#1** BEST-SELLER!

FULL COLOR!

Identification & Values of Over 50,000 Antiques & Collectibles

#1 BESTSELLING
ANTIQUES PRICE GUIDE

≈ Almost 40,000 listings in hundreds of categories
≈ Histories and background information
≈ Both common and rare antiques featured

only
$19.95
608 pages

COLLECTOR BOOKS

P.O. BOX 3009, Paducah KY, 42002-30

26.5420

orbooks.co